# THE PHILOSOPHY OF THOMAS REID

# PHILOSOPHICAL STUDIES SERIES

VOLUME 42

# THE PHILOSOPHY
# OF THOMAS REID

*Edited by*

MELVIN DALGARNO

and

ERIC MATTHEWS

*Department of Philosophy, University of Aberdeen*

**KLUWER ACADEMIC PUBLISHERS**

DORDRECHT / BOSTON / LONDON

Library of Congress Cataloging in Publication Data

The Philosophy of Thomas Reid / edited by Melvin Dalgarno and Eric
  Matthews.
      p.   cm. -- (Philosophical studies series ; v. 42)
    Bibliography: p.
    Includes index.
    ISBN 0-7923-0190-0
    1. Reid, Thomas, 1710-1796--Congresses.   I. Dalgarno, Melvin,
  1943-  .  II. Matthews, Eric, 1936-   .  III. Series.
  B1537.P49  1989
  192--dc19                                                 89-2297

ISBN 0-7923-0190-0

Published by Kluwer Academic Publishers,
P.O. Box 17, 3300 AA Dordrecht, The Netherlands.

Kluwer Academic Publishers incorporates
the publishing programmes of
D. Reidel, Martinus Nijhoff, Dr W. Junk and MTP Press.

Sold and distributed in the U.S.A. and Canada
by Kluwer Academic Publishers,
101 Philip Drive, Norwell, MA 02061, U.S.A.

In all other countries, sold and distributed
by Kluwer Academic Publishers Group,
P.O. Box 322, 3300 AH Dordrecht, The Netherlands.

*printed on acid free paper*

Printed in The Netherlands

# CONTENTS

Introduction                                                        1

Note on references to the works of Thomas Reid               5


**SECTION 1 — Perception**

Yves Michaud (University of Paris, France)                    9
    'Reid's Attack on the Theory of Ideas'

William P. Alston (Syracuse University, U.S.A.)              35
    'Reid on Perception and Conception'

Vere Chappell (University of Massachusetts, U.S.A.)          49
    'The Theory of Sensations'

Norton Nelkin (University of New Orleans, U.S.A.)            65
    'Reid's View of Sensations Vindicated'

A.E. Pitson (University of Stirling, Scotland)               79
    'Sensation, Perception and Reid's Realism'

Aaron Ben-Zeev (University of Haifa, Israel)                 91
    'Reid's Opposition to the Theory of Ideas'

Michel Malherbe (University of Nantes, France)              103
    'Thomas Reid on the Five Senses'

**SECTION 2 — Knowledge and Common Sense**

Keith Lehrer (University of Arizona, U.S.A.)                121
    'Reid on Evidence and Conception'

Dennis Charles Holt (Southeast Missouri State              145
    University, U.S.A.)
    'The Defence of Common Sense in Reid and Moore'

T.J. Sutton (University of Oxford, England)                 159
    'The Scottish Kant?'

Daniel Schulthess (University of Berne, Switzerland)        193
    'Did Reid Hold Coherentist Views?'

Claudine Engel-Tiercelin (University of Rouen, France)     205
    'Reid and Peirce on Belief'

C.A.J. Coady (University of Melbourne, Australia)     225
    'Reid on Testimony'

SECTION 3  —  Mind and Action

James Somerville (University of Hull, England)     249
    'Making Out the Signatures:  Reid's Account of
    the Knowledge of Other Minds'

R.F. Stalley (University of Glasgow, Scotland)     275
    'Causality and Agency in  the Philosophy of
    Thomas Reid'

John J. Haldane (University of St. Andrew's, Scotland)     285
    'Reid,  Scholasticism  and  Current
    Philosophy  of  Mind'

SECTION 4  —  Aesthetics, Moral and Political Philosophy

Peter Kivy (Rutgers University, U.S.A.)     307
    'Seeing (and  so forth) is  Believing
    (among  other things); on the Significance
    of Reid in the History of Aesthetics'

Henning Jensen (University of Arizona, U.S.A.)     329
    'Reid versus Hume: a Dilemma in the Theory
    of Moral Worth'

Peter J. Diamond (University of Utah, U.S.A.)     341
    'Reid and Active Virtue'

Kenneth Mackinnon (University of Aberdeen, Scotland)     355
    'Thomas Reid on Justice: A Rights-Based Theory'

Melvin T. Dalgarno (University of Aberdeen, Scotland)     369
    'Taking Upon Oneself a Character:
    Reid on Political Obligation'

SECTION 5  —  Historical Context and Influences

Charles  Stewart-Robertson  (University  of     389
    New   Brunswick,   Canada)
    'Thomas Reid and Pneumatology: the Text of
    the Old, the Tradition of the New'

Kathleen Holcomb (Angelo State University, U.S.A.)      413
    'Reid in the Philosophical Society'

Jack Fruchtman, Jr. (Towson State University, U.S.A.)   421
    'Common Sense and the Association of Ideas;
    the Reid-Priestley Controversy'

Paul Wood (University of Toronto, Canada)               433
    'Reid on Hypotheses and the Ether:
    a Reassessment'

David F. Channell (University of Texas, U.S.A.)         447
    'The Role of Thomas Reid's Philosophy in
    Science and Technology: the Case of
    W.J.M. Rankine'

Carolyn E. Channell (Southern Methodist University,     457
    U.S.A.)
    'George Jardine's Course in Logic and Rhetoric:
    an Application of Thomas Reid's
    Common Sense Philosophy'

Bibliography                                            467

Index of Names                                          483

Index of Subjects                                       487

# INTRODUCTION

In September, 1985, the Philosophy Department of the University of Aberdeen organized an International Conference to mark the two-hundredth anniversary of the first publication of Thomas Reid's Essays on the Intellectual Powers of Man. By the time these Essays were published in 1785, Reid had occupied the Chair of Moral Philosophy at Glasgow University for many years and had greatly increased his reputation. It was nevertheless appropriate that it should be Aberdeen which played host to this Bicentennial Conference, for in all the most important respects Reid was a philosopher of that region. He was so by birth and education: he was born in the village of Strachan, some twenty miles from the city of Aberdeen, and was a student (later librarian) at Aberdeen's Marischal College which was a separate University until it merged with King's College in 1860 to form the present University of Aberdeen. But more importantly, it was in Aberdeen that he formulated his central philosophical positions, during his years as a parish minister at Newmachar (1737-51), during his term as a Regent at King's College (1751-64), and in his discussions with his fellow-members of the Aberdeen Philosophical Society in which he played a leading part. Also it is in the University Library at Aberdeen that the most important Reid papers are preserved, with the Minute Book of the Philosophical Society in which the initial Minutes are in his hand. It was fitting, therefore, that it should be at Aberdeen where the publication of his major work was commemorated in this way.

The Conference attracted interest from scholars from all parts of the world, testifying to Reid's continuing worldwide influence and appeal. Altogether 79 delegates were present in Aberdeen, of whom the majority came from outside Britain – from the rest of Europe, from North America, Australia, Japan and South Africa. Four plenary sessions with invited speakers were arranged, although unfortunately one had to be cancelled because of the illness of a principal speaker, Keith Lehrer. (Professor Lehrer's paper is nevertheless included in the present volume). In addition, there were 42 contributed papers, presented at smaller gatherings. Both invited and contributed papers covered virtually the whole range of Reid studies, as had been intended, though naturally the bulk of them concerned Reid's theories of knowledge and perception. In addition to the serious proceedings, there

1

*M. Dalgarno and E. Matthews (eds.), The Philosophy of Thomas Reid, 1–3.*
© *1989 by Kluwer Academic Publishers.*

was a visit to Reid's birthplace at Strachan and a very enjoyable Bicentennial Dinner with appropriate musical entertainment. The University Library staged an exhibition on Reid and the Enlightenment to coincide with the Conference.

Some of the papers presented analyses of Reid's arguments, some comparisons of Reid with other philosophers, some explored the contemporary philosophical relevance of Reid's insights and some placed Reid in his historical, cultural and social context. Virtually all of the papers presented would have had some claim to be included in a volume of proceedings such as this. Unfortunately, for technical reasons it proved impossible to include them all. This made our task as editors extremely difficult: we had to make a balanced selection from the good and the very good. This is what we have attempted to do. We should like to express our gratitude to Reidel's reader and to the General Editor of the series, Keith Lehrer, for their invaluable assistance in this difficult task. In the end of the day, however, the responsibility for the selection rests with us, and we can only hope that readers will agree with us that this collection represents an important addition to published work on Reid.

The papers have been arranged in sections by subject-matter, though inevitably in some cases it was arbitrary to assign a particular paper to one section rather than to another. The volume thus begins with the largest group of papers, those on Reid's theory of perception. There then follows a section on his theory of knowledge more generally. The later sections deal with Reid's moral, political and legal philosophy; with his aesthetics; and with the history of ideas and the philosophy of science. The volume thus helps to make clear, as did the Conference itself, the range of Reid's philosophical and scientific interests and his continuing relevance to modern philosophy. It was striking how the Conference underlined so many themes in such modern thinkers as Wittgenstein, Austin, Searle and Davidson which had been anticipated by Reid.

We have tried to intervene editorially as little as possible in the content of the papers, believing that, whether or not we agree with them, the authors' views are valuable contributions to Reid scholarship and to philosophy. In some cases, we have sought to improve the style of an author's paper, especially where the author's native language is not English. We have standardized spelling on the British, rather than the American, model and have tried to adopt consistent spellings of words such as 'judgment' for which there are two equally legitimate spellings. We have adopted a uniform system for referring to passages in the works of Reid himself, explained on a later page, and have brought into line with this the very various methods of referring to Reid found in the original versions of the papers. We have also adopted a uniform method of referring to works by other writers: all references, other than those to Reid himself, can be traced by consulting the Bibliography at the end of the volume. Finally, we have provided an Index which we hope will make it easier to find discussions of particular topics within the volume.

In addition to those acknowledgements already made, we should like to express our thanks to a number of people and institutions. First, thanks are due to our fellow-members of the Conference organizing committee for their sterling work. We, and they, are grateful to the Royal Society of Edinburgh (of which Reid was an early member), the British Academy, the British Council, the Cultural Section of the French Embassy in London and the University of Aberdeen for financial and other support. Wendy de Veer of Reidel has been consistently encouraging and helpful. And last, but by no means least, we owe a considerable debt to our secretarial assistants: Mrs Mannell Parker, the Philosophy Department secretary who gave us unstinting help both during the Conference itself and subsequently in the preparation of some of the papers for publication and in correspondence with authors and publishers; and Mrs. Barbara Rae and Mrs. Kay Duggan who made an excellent job of preparing the remaining papers.

Melvin T. Dalgarno
Eric H. Matthews
Aberdeen, April, 1987.

# REFERENCES TO THE MAJOR WORKS OF THOMAS REID

A uniform system has been adopted throughout this volume for referring to passages in Reid's most often quoted works. The works themselves are indicated by the following abbreviations:

**AL**        A Brief Account of Aristotle's Logic

**AP**        Essays on the Active Powers

Corr       Correspondence

I           An Inquiry into the Human Mind

**IP**        Essays on the Intellectual Powers

Manuscripts held in University Libraries are referred to by the following abbreviations:

AUL       Aberdeen University Library
EUL       Edinburgh University Library
GUL       Glasgow University Library

Passages in **AP** and **IP** are indicated by Work (e.g. AP), Essay, Part (where appropriate), chapter and page: page references are to the 6th edition of Hamilton's edition of the Works of Thomas Reid, Edinburgh, 1863 (abbreviated to Works). Thus, 'IP, II, x (Works, p.285)' means 'Essays on the Intellectual Powers, Essay II, chapter x, p.285 in Hamilton's edition'. Similarly, passages in the Inquiry are referred to by Work, Chapter, section and page-number in Hamilton's edition: thus, 'I, VI, iii (Works, p.135)' means 'Inquiry, Chapter VI, section iii, p.135 in Hamilton's edition'. Passages in the correspondence are identified by the letter in which they appear.

Other works by Reid are listed in the general Bibliography, under 'Reid'. Modern editions of Reid's works are also listed in the general Bibliography.

# SECTION 1 – PERCEPTION

Yves Michaud


## REID'S ATTACK ON THE THEORY OF IDEAS:
from a reconsideration of Reid's arguments
to a reassessment of the theory of ideas


At the beginning of his book Why Does language Matter to
Philosophy, Ian Hacking writes: "it is not until the time of
John Stuart Mill's System of Logic (1844) that one regularly
began a philosophy book like this: 'Book One of Names and
Propositions; Chapter 1: of the necessity of commencing with
an analysis of language".(1)   Had he traced back the way of
words and meanings to Reid's Essay on the Intellectual Powers
of Man Hacking would have been nearer the truth. For Reid's
book begins thus: Essay I, Chapter I: Explications of words.
It also constitutes a general and sweeping criticism of the
way of ideas which prevailed in philosophy from Descartes to
Wolffius.

On the other hand, Hacking is quite perceptive when he
paradoxically opens his account of the relationships between
language and philosophy with four chapters on the heyday of
ideas.  For, whatever the favour and vogue enjoyed since then
by conceptual and linguistic approaches to philosophy and now
the discursive one, it really is a puzzling fact for the
philosopher, and especially for the historian of philosophy,
that from Descartes and Locke to Reid and Kant philosophy
followed the way of ideas.

This fact is puzzling for two reasons at least.  First,
because of Reid's criticisms and, more recently, those of the
philosophy of language, it is hardly intelligible to us that
philosophers as penetrating as Descartes, Locke or Hume were
obtuse enough to use the desperately confused and polysemic
concept of idea as the cornerstone of their philosophies and
to adopt the theory of ideas with all its flaws. Second, it
is almost as puzzling that the theory of ideas, which seemed
to be so strong and pervasive as not to be shaken off easily,
suddenly vanished from the philosophical scene by a sort of
historical miracle.

In this respect, Reid and Kant play a major part: they


9

*M. Dalgarno and E. Matthews (eds.), The Philosophy of Thomas Reid, 9–34.*
*© 1989 by Kluwer Academic Publishers.*

are both actors and symptoms of this philosophical turn.

As regards Kant, he broke with the theory of ideas without much ado. He simply restores to the word 'idea' its Platonist meaning, with its teleological and meta-empirical connotations. As is clear from his Logic or his Critique of Pure Reason, for the classical concept of idea he substitutes that of representation, which more adequately expresses the synthetic activity of the understanding. Thus, after detailing the various species which constitute the genus representation, he writes in the Critique of Pure Reason:

> A concept formed from notions and transcending the possibility of experience is an idea or concept of reason. Anyone who has familiarised himself with these distinctions must find it intolerable to hear the representation of the colour, red, called an idea. It ought not even to be called a concept of understanding, a notion.(2)

But for this critical remark, as far as I know, Kant never thought it necessary to attack the system of ideas. Things are very different indeed with Reid.

In this paper, which is a reconsideration of Reid's various and intricate charges against ideas, I wish to consider Reid's own position at this turning point in the history of philosophy. I also want to make a few suggestions concerning the historical fortune of the way of ideas, its advantages and weaknesses. Finally I will claim that Reid's philosophical enterprise, whatever its achievements and shortcomings, testifies to a new conception of the understanding. Reid's criticism of the theory of ideas is not only meant to do away with the dangers of scepticism or to establish a new science of the human mind: it is mainly a consideration of the understanding as an active faculty endowed with powers. The theory of ideas was to account for the nature of knowledge when knowledge was thought of as an accurate description of things as they are. The thorough criticism of this theory and the offering of an alternative conceptual way go hand in hand with a conception of the understanding as an active power and of science as an activity.

I

According to Reid's own declarations, his philosophy may be viewed in two lights.

From the standpoint of its historical development and major achievements, as they are emphasized in the well-known letter to Gregory quoted by Stewart,(3) Reid's philosophy calls into question the theory of ideas because of its sceptical consequences. From another point of view, which Reid insists upon as vigorously as upon the former, his philosophy is a decisive contribution to the science of the human mind on the same model as that of Newton's philosophy of nature. The notion of common sense is supposed to bridge the gap between these two versions: the calling into question of scepticism rests upon the strength of natural beliefs and the principles of common sense constitute the roots of the tree of knowledge. Be it in philosophy or in science – but in Reid they still remain indiscernible – common sense is the starting point.

The first version is well-known and I will not linger on it. It pervades the Inquiry. Facing Hume's scepticism concerning the external world and the existence of minds, Reid comes up with the hypothesis that the premise of the theory of ideas is responsible for this sceptical outcome. From the moment Descartes attempted to derive all certainty from consciousness alone, it was bound to happen that sooner or later philosophers would lose any certainty but that of the ideas in their minds. Malebranche, Locke, Berkeley, each in their manner, attempted to escape this sceptical predicament. Hume alone went the whole way. Reid's conviction is that in order to set aside scepticism, we must drop the ideal premise and instead examine the powers of the mind. Then common sense and natural beliefs will be restored. For the time being I only wish to underline that this criticism of scepticism leads Reid to reconstruct the history of the ideal system and results in an attack on the private and hidden mental world of ideas. In contradistinction to this world, Reid sets forth the public and practical certainty of linguistic uses and the conduct of everyday life. Seen in this light, Reid's enterprise looks rather contemporary and foreshadows analytical philosophy or pragmatism.

The second approach is less contemporary. It even has a definite eighteenth-century flavour: philosophy is not supposed to be specially interested in opposing the views of common sense to scepticism; it has to build up a science of intellectual reality on the same model as that of the philosophy of nature.

In spite of many exaggerations and simplifications, L.L. Laudan(4) was right to emphasize Reid's importance in the Newtonian turn of English methodological thought. He certainly overemphasizes both Reid's originality and faithfulness to Newton. In fact Hume did not confine himself to mere slogans of inductivism and experimentalism: there is good evidence in his works that he had grasped the main points of Newton's methodology and their special import for the science of man. Laudan is nevertheless right to stress that Reid, whose perusal of Newton's major works appears clearly in his letters to Lord Kames, and who used to lecture on Newton's natural philosophy, demonstrably handles Newton's method pretty well.

At any rate, he always introduces his books as contributions to the science of man after the same pattern as that of the science of material bodies.

Thus, the Inquiry claims to study the human mind through observations and experiences. It almost immediately adds that Newton's Regulae are maxims of common sense. Incidentally, Newton would not have agreed with him, for his Regulae are the conditions of, or the stipulations indispensable to, scientific investigation; they are, literally, rules for reasoning in philosophy, not principles. Be that as it may, Reid then points to the various obstacles which lie on the way to knowledge, especially those that pertain to the complexity of mental events. His study of visual perception proceeds through a careful examination of the mechanisms of vision which are supposed to convey the retinal images to the brain and the mind. He concludes that most of them are nothing but conjectures or, worse, hypotheses which have no more value than the elephant of that Indian philosopher who professed that the world rested on a tortoise and the tortoise on an elephant. The Indian philosopher's elephant was an hypothesis and conversely in philosophy hypotheses are elephants. Any philosophy built on hypotheses is itself an elephant.

To be serious, the Inquiry, in spite of its limitation to the study of perception and the investigation of the five senses, can be viewed as the first step in the development of Reid's programme. For he repeatedly says that perceptions constitute the first principles of knowledge, that "The more obvious conclusions drawn from our perceptions, by reason, make what we call common understanding... The more remote conclusions which are drawn from our perceptions, by reason, make what we commonly call science in the various parts of nature".(5) If we are to take these claims seriously, the Inquiry studies the roots of the tree of the science of nature, whose trunk is common understanding and whose branches are the sciences. Ironically enough, if we compare this Reidian tree of knowledge to Descartes' tree of philosophy in the Principles, we must conclude that Reid's absolute belief in perception is the very equivalent of the Cartesian doubt.

The Essay goes through with this programme. The first essay certainly does not shun methodological display. The explication of words in Chapter I is supposed to give the definitions or the special meanings the author gives to the main terms. Reid obviously remembers Newton's definitions at the beginning of the Principia. In Chapter II, the principles taken for granted are compared to Newton's axioms but Reid goes too far again and draws a parallel between these and the rules of reasoning in philosophy. Chapters III and IV warn against hypotheses and the dangers of analogical reasoning, while recommending patient and accurate observation. Now, for the second time, in the stand he takes on analogy, Reid proves less Newtonian than is usually thought. More of an Aristotelian than a Newtonian, he claims that each science has or must have its own explanatory principles and that analogical reasoning is dangerous though not always useless. Yet Newton's third rule asserts the analogy of nature. Newton himself does not seem to have been particularly afraid of a possibly unified materialistic account of phenomena by mechanical philosophy. Finally, Chapters V and VI sketch the proper method of observation in the intellectual domain and point to the possible traps. This method is mainly that of reflection; it results in an analysis of complex mental states. The philosopher may also proceed through the observation of linguistic uses, behaviour and conduct, since the universal features of languages, the characters of actions, the nature of intellectual productions (such as those of the history of philosophy for instance) are as many mirrors or, rather, expressions of the mind's powers.

Once this methodological preliminary is completed – I have tried to suggest on the way what is Newtonian and what is not – the Essay sets out to build the new science.

It starts from the first principles of perception (Essay II) and thence proceeds to the study of some other powers of the mind (memory, conception, judgment, reasoning, taste), that is, to the study of what the Inquiry called the common understanding. Basically the Inquiry confined itself to the roots of science; the Essay carries on the task.

Now I suggest that Reid's various arguments against ideas can be sorted out and set in order from the consideration of these two views of his philosophical enterprise.

I will consider first Reid's attack on ideas in the name of their sceptical consequences and then the arguments which depend on the project of a science of the human mind. I will assess the value of each set of arguments as I go along.

## II

The rejection of the so-called theory of ideas or ideal system because of its sceptical outcomes is the best known aspect of Reid's philosophy. In my opinion, it is also its weakest aspect and Reid himself did much to depreciate his philosophy by locating here the originality of his contribution. A passage from the Inquiry which states, as it were, the cannibal nature of ideas adequately summarizes his reasoning:

> Ideas seem to have something in their nature unfriendly to other existences. They were first introduced into philosophy, in the humble character of images or representatives of things; and in this character they seemed not only to be inoffensive, but to serve admirably well for explaining the operations of the human understanding. But, since men began to reason clearly and distinctly about them, they have by degrees supplanted their constituents, and undermined the existence of everything but themselves. First, they discarded all secondary qualities of bodies; and it was found out by their means, that fire is not hot, nor snow cold, nor honey sweet; and, in a word, that heat and cold, sound, colour, taste, and smell, are nothing but ideas or impressions. Bishop Berkeley advanced them a step higher, and found out, by just reasoning from the same principles, that extension, solidity, space, figure, and body, are ideas, and that there is nothing in nature but ideas and spirits. But the

> triumph of ideas was completed by the 'Treatise of
> Human Nature', which discards spirits also, and
> leaves ideas and impressions as the sole existences
> in the universe. What if, at last, having nothing
> else to contend with, they should fall foul of one
> another, and leave no existence in nature at all?
> This would surely bring philosophy into danger; for
> what should we have left to talk or to dispute
> about?(6)

From the moment one claims that we perceive things through
the medium of mental objects, the existence of the external
world is to be proven or guaranteed by God, or else the world
is sublimized into a Berkeleyan world of ideas 'in the mind'.
Moreover, the existence of other minds becomes in its turn
problematic and we end in solipsism or egoism. Finally, even
our own minds vanish and no reality subsists but that of
ideas. Such radically sceptical conclusions are obviously
contrary to the dictates of common sense. So, by a sort of
modus tollens, we have to drop the ideal premise of the
argument.

This reasoning itself is not safe from possible
criticisms:

1) To begin with, the theory of ideas is not the only
possible premise for sceptical conclusions. As is clear from
the history of scepticism, arguments taken from the
contradiction of opinions, from relativism, from the
possibility of universal and radical doubt, have certainly
been more frequent than the argument taken from ideas in the
mind. Berkeley did not think he was a sceptic: on the
contrary, he wanted to prevent the sceptical consequences of
Locke's representative theory of perception. As to Hume, his
scepticism is at least protean and multifarious, and the
outcomes of his analyses of the causal relation and of our
belief in the uniformity of nature are decisive. His
scepticism concerning reason is at least as important as his
scepticism concerning the senses.

2) Reid's use of arguments from common sense is still more
threatening. He keeps on saying that the ordinary man is not
a sceptic: he feels sure he perceives objects which exist, he
remembers events which once took place and he has not the
least idea of ideas in his mind. Well. But here Kant's rebuke
in the Prolegomena is relevant: there is no reason why the
ordinary man should be trusted rather than the sceptic —

unless we decide to settle philosophical controversies by a vote. Reid has some threatening remarks in this sense when he reckons among the principles he takes for granted "such facts as are attested to the conviction of all sober and reasonable men, either by our senses, by memory, or by human testimony".(7)  This should invite one to go back to the contrary assertions against maxims in the first book of Locke's Essay. In fact common sense itself has to be justified, though perhaps not by reasoning.

Reid characterizes the principles of common sense as contingent principles whose negation is nevertheless absurd, which "the constitution of our nature leads us to believe, and which we are under a necessity to take for granted in the common concerns of life, without being able to give a reason for them".(8) They are common to all men – except lunatics, which is no slight concession. Elsewhere, Reid says that they are judgments of nature, original principles of belief, that reason can neither give birth to them nor destroy them.  Thus he seems to stick to Hume's conception of natural beliefs. The trouble is that to the brute fact of the existence of such common sense beliefs, when the common gardener says: "It must be so, it cannot be otherwise. This expresses only a strong belief which is indeed the voice of nature and which therefore in vain we attempt to resist", the sceptic is as entitled to reply: "I can't help doubting, it can be otherwise". He also might add perfidiously that it is somewhat embarrassing that such strong and irresistible principles could ever be challenged, even by lunatics if not by sceptics. Reid himself, in the letter to Gregory already referred to, acknowledges that the theory of ideas is "founded on natural prejudices, and so universally received as to be interwoven with the structure of the language".(9) This is a devastating admission from one who believes in the philosophical signification of linguistic forms and confesses that the history of philosophy is "a map of the intellectual operations of men of genius".(10) Even if he calls the theory of ideas a metaphysical lunacy, metaphysical lunatics do exist.

Actually Hume's conception of natural beliefs may help to clarify the issue.  For Hume clearly saw that their irresistible strength is a remedy to sceptical doubts, but he hastened to underline that the philosophical disposition which brings out scepticism is as natural as natural beliefs are. Our minds follow alternate dispositions which neither refute nor even neutralize each other but simply alternate.

The sceptic doubts and the ordinary man believes but neither refutes the other. The case may even be that the former and the latter exist successively in the same person. Such is the claim presented by the conclusion of Book 1 of the <u>Treatise of Human Nature</u> in the shape of a literary drama.

We are left with only one way out which consists in viewing the principles of common sense as transcendental conditions of the possibility of experience. Reid hints at this solution but very confusedly. I will come back later to this point in my conclusion.

## III

I now come to grips with the other part of the story: with the cluster of arguments linked to Reid's efforts to develop a science of the mind. For the sake of simplicity I will list them under three headings:

a) The study of the mind's activities does not reveal any idea in the mind. Ideas are mere fictions, hypotheses of philosophers who tried to explain the functioning of the mind.

b) Ideas, supposing they exist, do not account for anything.

c) Ideas, again supposing they exist, prove inefficient for an adequate description of mental activity.

Of course, these three arguments are not unrelated. If Reid argues that ideas do not exist 'in the mind', we can yet think that they are either organic impressions or conjectural entities which help us to account for our intellectual operations. Then Reid will reply that these impressions explain nothing or that these conjectural entities are grossly inadequate and distort what they are supposed to explain. My opinion is that Reid shuttles back and forth between these strategies according to the facts he deals with.

## IV

A merely negative argument consists in saying that reflection and a careful observation of our mental activity uncover no ideas in the mind. Whenever we reflect on what goes on inside us when we perceive, feel, imagine or remember, we cannot discover the least mental object or image. We perceive objects, but not ideas of objects; we remember past events, but not ideas of past events; we conceive chimeras or centaurs, but not ideas of chimeras or centaurs. Those philosophers who stood up for the theory of ideas never actually had any clear idea of their nature.(11) To put it simply, to have an idea means to think and in this restricted sense only do we have ideas. In any case Reid cannot search very long for mental entities whose main characters are invisibility and privacy, and he is naturally led to consider them as ideal entities, explanatory conjectures.

Now how did it happen that philosophers imagined such strange entities? At least their illusion must be accounted for. Reid tackles this question in a methodological chapter of the first Essay and he takes it up once more in Essay VI, Chapter VIII on prejudices. In both cases, he blames man's fondness for hypotheses, analogies and simple explanations. Being used to seeing objects acting directly and immediately one upon another through impulses, philosophers try to understand the actions of the objects on our faculties in the same way. They regard as impossible any action from a distance and therefore they imagine ideas as the point of contact between objects and minds. Ideas are the device made up by philosophers in order to assign a place to contiguous action in perception. In the case of the ideas of memory or conception, Reid suggests a slightly different but consonant explanation: ideas are still fictions but the operations of the mind are conceived on the model of object making; the memory is viewed as a store for ideas and conception consists, as it were, in a manufacturing of mental objects.(12)

If ideas do not exist at all, Reid can confidently conclude that there is nothing to explain. We must go back to the principles of common sense which had been temporarily forgotten, or rather which we wrongly imagined we could overcome.

Finally, this negative criticism ends in two ways: either it turns into a gross search for caricatural entities or Reid has to reorientate his investigation and to consider what kind of explanation of mental life ideas allow. Priestley's and Brown's severe criticisms aim at the former possibility. Truly, neither Descartes nor Locke nor Berkeley nor Hume conceived ideas as reified and hidden entities in a reified mind and, as Brown put it, if Reid believes that, he impugns "a true relic of an obsolete theory of perception".(13)

Actually Reid did not believe that.

As a matter of fact, his position is more complex: he considers that the theory of ideas is a tentative explanation of our mental activity and his verdict comes down to a condemnation: the theory fails to account for the facts it is supposed to explain or it provides an inadequate and distorted account of them.

What about the verdict of total failure? Reid has to consider in each case two possible versions of the theory: one which places ideas among the elements of a neuro-physiological process, another which does not embark upon determining their physical or ontological nature but views them as explanatory devices.

As regards perception, our knowledge of the physiological phenomena which take place during the perceptual process is more precise than anywhere else. Reid attempts to show that to view ideas as the last step in a chain of contiguous physiological impressions does not solve the problem but postpones it. Even if we knew still more accurately than we do the physiological process, it would not explain perception, in what manner physiological impressions cause the perception of an object. Reid follows carefully the perceptual process through to the sensation.(14) In any case, we always reach a point where we are confronted with a gap in the process: mental events, sensations, never resemble their physiological causes (impressions on the sense organs, on the brain or on the sensorium). Of course, Reid does not deny that the physiological process is a necessary condition of perception. Perception requires various material conditions: a medium of communication of actions, a physical impression on the sense organ, a nervous transmission of this impression to the brain; but the resulting sensation and the ensuing perception are absolutely different from these phenomena. The effects might be connected with entirely different causes, and we must be content to say that the sensation suggests the perception as a sign suggests what it means. Ideas are ad hoc hypotheses to bridge the gap. Yet in spite of their hybrid nature qua sensory impressions and representations of objects, the gap is still wide open.(15)

Now, if we leave aside the physiological explanation and look on ideas as mere references to the objects, we still are in a predicament: either we perceive the image but not the object or we perceive the object but not the idea. Chapters

VII to XIII of Essay II study the ways in which philosophers wavered between the two horns of the dilemma. Descartes and Locke struggled with the nature of ideas to maintain some connection with reality, whereas Berkeley and Hume severed the ties and acknowledged that ideas are autonomous entities which have no reference to any external reality.

What is the value of these arguments? In my opinion they spring from Reid's assumption of a dualistic ontology. In the very preface of the Essay he talks of "two great kingdoms of nature",(16) the material world or the system of bodies and the intellectual world or the system of minds. Unlike Reid, we might adopt a materialistic view which would take ideas to be merely physiological events in the mind itself thought of as a material though subtle or ethereal substance. Strangely but significantly enough, Reid passes Hobbes over in his survey of the history of the ideal system. Priestley, who was a materialist too, would easily subscribe to such an explanation. Conversely, one might also adopt a phenomenalist or idealist point of view and undertake to account for the different sorts of things (be they people, dreams, ghosts or colours) from the different qualities of our perceptions only. Things would simply be constructions out of ideas or sensations. In his introduction to his edition of the Essay, A.D. Woozley touches on these points.(17)

As for memory, Reid proceeds in a similar manner, but the relative want of physiological evidence simplifies his task. If the ideas of memory are physiological impressions, we still face the same gap between the physiological impression and the particular feeling and reference of the memory itself. If by ideas of the memory we simply mean what we have in mind when we remember something, this is no explanation at all and we can do without ideas.(18)

Finally, to explain conceiving by the medium of ideas proves blatantly absurd, for conceiving through an idea something which does not exist brings up the question of the strange existence of this idea while the thing itself does not exist.(19) When conceiving a centaur, I do not perceive two objects, the centaur and its idea. Neither do I conceive the centaur as an image of itself. I merely conceive a centaur.

I have already raised several objections. Now I want to point out another defect of Reid's analyses: they often distort the positions they criticize. Reid sticks to his

claim that ideas are images without being fair to
philosophers' actual positions. I will briefly give three
examples.

First, Descartes. Descartes makes a point of saying that
ideas are not resemblances of things. Of course, he uses the
term 'image' but he makes clear that we must take them as
having a definite ratio of similarity to the things they are
the ideas of. They are not mental likenesses of things or
resembling images or reproductions: strictly speaking, they
are analogous to things, they have, as I said, a ratio of
similarity to things, in the mathematical sense. That is why
Descartes usually says that the mind sees, not the eye, for
the mind alone can see a ratio of similarity. In the
Dioptrique, Descartes goes so far as to say that the
relationship between the idea and the thing is closer to the
one which obtains between signs or words and thoughts than
the relationship between things and images. Ideas obey a
principle of non-resembling similarity, which is also the
principle of perspective representation in painting. I quote
from the Dioptrique:

> Often, in order to be more perfect images and better
> represent an object, copper plate engravings must be
> unlike it. We must think the same of the images in
> our brains and remark that the only question is to
> understand how they can give the soul the
> possibility of being aware of all the various
> qualities of objects to which they refer but not how
> they have in themselves their resemblance.(20)

I cannot reconcile Reid's criticisms with this text, for
Descartes' claims tie in with Reid's thesis of the
non-resemblance between the sensation and the perception of
the object.

Second, Locke. Reid always skips the fact that for Locke
ideas are signs. What Locke calls Semeiotike at the end of
the Essay(21) is intended to be a general theory of signs,
which bears on linguistic signs (words) but also and mainly
on those other signs of things, namely ideas. Of course, when
he deals with the ideas of primary qualities, Locke often
expresses himself as if they were likenesses of things or
even in the things, in just the way they are in the mind; yet
his view of the ideas of secondary qualities and mere powers
is not easy to distinguish from Reid's own version of
secondary qualities. No wonder, for Locke's distinction

between the ideas of primary and secondary qualities is meant
to make  room for  a distinction between  those qualities  of
things we have a clear conception of and those we are unaware
of. Is  it that  different  from the  similar distinction  in
Reid?

    Finally, Hume. Though his philosophy  stems from  Hume's
perplexities, Reid does not  do him justice. He  perceptively
remarks that Hume wanted to arrange our perceptions according
to a  scale of  vivacity,  to the  various degrees  of  which
various  beliefs  would   correspond.  Reid  ridicules   this
conception and in that  he is right,  but he fails to  notice
that Hume entertained  another view  of belief, less  passive
and definitely  non-atomistic:  beliefs  are  organized  into
systems, they  are  linked,  related,  associated,  and  they
buttress one another. Thus  Reid overlooks Hume's hints of  a
theory of  mental activity.  That is  why he  is mistaken  or
onesided in his  appraisal of  Hume's scepticism. For  Hume's
scepticism centres around  the value  and the reliability  of
these  associative  links  rather  than  on  the  problematic
reality of the external world. A version of Hume's philosophy
which would leave out the  theory of ideas would still be  as
dangerous for  common  sense as  before. Kant  realized  that
transcendental arguments alone could count as a reply to that
challenge.

                                V

I come now to the milder version of Reid's attack: the theory
of ideas distorts what it  is supposed to describe. It  fails
to account  adequately  for our  mental activity. The  ideal
system is not  a mere fiction  or a gross  illusion: it is  a
defective description.

    This last argument is both less radical and perhaps  more
promising than the preceding  ones. It does  not embark on  a
frustrating quest for non-existing entities, it asks  whether
or not ideas are powerful explanations of what we can do when
we think,  perceive, imagine  and remember. In  spite of  his
radical claims, Reid often  confines himself to that kind  of
questioning. In  this  case he  grants philosophers  under
examination a careful attention  and suggests on the way  his
own views of what  should count as  a correct description  of
the facts instead of rushing to the shelter of common sense.

    At bottom, the common  theory of ideas proves  inadequate
because it grossly  mishandles what we  say, do and  believe.

For Reid, language is "the express image and picture of human thoughts; and, from the picture, we may often draw very certain conclusions with regard to the original".(22) Like our intellectual productions it expresses our thoughts. In this respect, the theory of ideas is contrary to our most established ways of speaking. We do not have ideas, we don't get ideas from objects, we never conceive ideas: instead we perceive things, we feel sensations, we imagine. Before Reid, Hume remarked that Locke had perverted the sense of words when calling an idea "whatsoever is the object of the understanding when a man thinks" or "whatever it is the mind can be employed about in thinking", but Hume did the same when in his turn he called perceptions all the operations of the mind. Likewise, were we to follow Berkeley up, we should change almost all our ways of speaking of things and reality. Reading these remarks of Reid is sometimes like reading Ryle on Locke or Bennett on Hume or Berkeley.

Those deadly consequences of the theory of ideas are far reaching. Berkeley's theory of ideas rules out other minds:

> What I call a father, a brother, or a friend, is only a parcel of ideas in my own mind; and, being ideas in my mind, they cannot possibly have that relation to another mind which they have to mine, any more than the pain felt by me can be the individual pain felt by another.(23)

Hume's contribution is devastating: after him we cannot even talk of persons any more; the conscious self vanishes, being replaced by a cluster of discontinuous mental states. It becomes a fictitious entity consisting of loosely connected perceptions. Strictly speaking, we must say that one set of ideas addresses another, is under obligation of duty or gratitude to another. In this new world, "there may be treason without a traitor, and love without a lover, laws without a legislator, and punishment without a sufferer".(24) "One set of ideas makes a covenant, another breaks it, and a third is punished for it".(25)

Reid's claim is that, should we accept the theory of ideas, we should also reform our language from top to bottom. It would result in a kind of 'newspeak' not only absolutely contrary to our ordinary uses but totally ineffective for describing our ordinary conduct.

In a like manner, the theory of ideas accounts very

poorly for our beliefs, judgments and conceptions. For example, concerning belief, when we make use of the theory of ideas, we are under the necessity of beginning with elementary perceptions to which will be added degrees of belief or what the phenomenologists call an intentionality. But for Reid, perception is not an idea plus a strong belief: it is the immediate conviction that the object exists. Belief comes first.

In this respect Hume's conception of belief is especially weak and Reid is merciless. Hume's view of the ideas of memory as something in between ideas and impressions is untenable: shall we say that a man who "strikes his head smartly against the wall [has] an impression; now, he has a faculty by which he can repeat his impression with less force, so as not to hurt him: this, by Mr. Hume's account, must be memory. He has a faculty by which he can just touch the wall with his head, so that the impression entirely loses its vivacity. This surely must be imagination".(26) If, with Hume, we define the belief as a manner of conceiving an idea which bestows on it a greater vivacity, we can still easily comprehend that a strong belief and a weak belief differ only in degree, "but that belief and no belief should differ only in degree, no man can believe who understands what he speaks. For this is, in reality, to say that something and nothing differ only in degree; or, that nothing is a degree of something".(27)

The theory of ideas is not more successful when it deals with judgment. There are indeed judgments which connect ideas, that is general conceptions.(28) Then we use ideas in the Pythagorean or Platonist sense, which Reid admits only if we do not attribute to them an ideal existence. Those ideas are concepts, we make them, know them and they make possible a perfect and accurate demonstrative knowledge.(29) But there are other judgments dealing with existence and contingent truths, in which case the Lockean definition of knowledge as a relation of ideas which agree or disagree no longer obtains.

Finally, ideas do not provide a satisfactory account of conception either. Universals are not ideas. They are not acts of the mind since each act is a particular mental event. They are not general images of what is conceived. Even if we had such general images, they still would be individual since everything that exists is particular. Nevertheless acts of forming general conceptions exist. They consist in nothing

else than understanding the meaning of general words.
Universals have no real existence in the mind: they exist in
individual subjects, when we attribute them to these
subjects: their existence consists in being attributed to a
subject.(30)

These developments call for three remarks:

1) Reid triumphs easily over the theory of ideas when it is
sketchily stated. In a sense, he has his share in this
oversimplification of doctrines which actually are often more
sophisticated. But he must not be overblamed for that. In the
twentieth century many have joined him and done the same. One
may even regret that the lack of familiarity with his works
did not put an end to some poor imitations. Moreover, there
has never been an oversimplified Kantian doctrine: even if
the theory of ideas was not as bad as Reid pronounces it,
there is no smoke without fire. Any Locke scholar can confirm
it.

2) One may regret that Reid's hasty retreat on common sense
principles often prevents him from presenting his own
conceptions. As Brown noticed, in Reid's philosophy, common
sense and scepticism are on the same footing. Once ideas have
been defeated, we have no way out but to subscribe to common
sense: we must believe what we perceive, trust our memory, be
confident of being a subsisting self. But the strength of
common sense is also its weakness: it is as fragile as any
claim that things are so and cannot be otherwise. As Brown
astutely wrote:

> the sceptic and the orthodox philosopher of Dr.
> Reid's school thus come precisely to the same
> conclusion. The creed of each on this point is
> composed of two propositions and of the same two
> propositions; the first of which is that the
> existence of a system of things such as we
> understand when we speak of an external world,
> cannot be proved by argument; and the second that
> the belief of it is of a force which is paramount to
> that argument and absolutely irresistible.(31)

3) Many of Reid's criticisms depend on his project of
building a science of the human mind. I suggested that
nevertheless Reid does not always offer a very convincing
answer: afraid of possible scepticism he avoids deep
researches and withdraws prematurely to the principles of

common sense. This view was that of Dugald Stewart when he said that Reid's "views tend to damp the ardour of intellectual curiosity by stating as ultimate facts phenomena which may be resolved into principles more simple and general".

## VI

Nevertheless, Reid's attempt to demonstrate that the common theory of ideas mishandles the activity of the mind is the most perceptive and promising of his criticisms. It suggests that we are to invent a wholly new conceptual apparatus if we wish to account for the human mind as a collection of active powers. Even if we add force, vivacity and belief to ideas, even if we describe them as elements in systems in which they are enlivened and strengthened by associations and dispositions, it won't do. Thinking cannot be accounted for by enumerating the various patterns in which mental atoms are arranged, since the mind is basically active. As I underlined at the beginning of this paper, Kant for his part, though influenced by Wolffius whose psychology makes use of the ideal system, does not use the concept of ideas any more but talks instead of representation, for a representation in itself presupposes a synthesis. Now, let us return to the theory of ideas.

To put it straightforwardly, there are not many possible interpretations of the theory of ideas. I even think that we face a dilemma: either we take ideas to be physiological impressions caused by objects or we view them as concepts embodied in definite linguistic forms through the medium of which we describe what goes on (not necessarily in the mind) when we think. On the one hand, as Reid highlighted it, we go back to the ancient theory of perception, with all its effluvia, sensible species or phantasms. On the other, whatever the fuss about what goes on in the mind, we basically must deal with what we do when we think and what we say about it.

The first type of view was worked out in the materialistic theories. Hobbes adopted it. Likewise the French materialist thinkers of the eighteenth century, Helvetius, Diderot, La Mettrie held it. In England, Hartley perhaps and Priestley certainly did the same. Such a view fits in with the mechanistic account of the unity of nature. Nevertheless, the idea of idea proves here gradually superfluous: movements and sensations easily do for representations. Reid's criticism consists in replying that there will always remain a gap between the physiological processes and what we call thinking. Whatever the precision of physiological descriptions, they will never be descriptions of thinking.

The second type of view cannot be proved illusory simply by challenging the existence of mental entities. We will have a hard time proving the non-existence of something which does not exist. Reid is not always clear about that and too frequently he beats about the bush looking for mental images. Nevertheless he also realizes that the right challenge to the theory of ideas consists in aiming the criticism at the descriptive power of the language of ideas.

Now what does this language look like? As is evident from Descartes, Locke, Berkeley or Hume, the language of ideas identifies qualities, enumerates them, states their relationships, attributes them to things. It is the language of the analysis of things into simple elements, be they mental or physical, which are related in various ways and arranged into patterns.

To understand the fortunes of this language, we must trace this theory back to its epistemological models: the model of mathematical analysis, especially in Descartes, and that of Optics, without omitting the resolutive compositive method of the new mechanical philosophy. My opinion is that the power of these epistemological models and their scientific success are not alien to the attractiveness of the theory of ideas. The suggestions that follow might well be too general but I will take that chance.

In my opinion the theory of ideas proved attractive for at least two reasons:

First, ideas were thought of on the model of Optics. On the same model as that of the optical discoveries of Kepler and Descartes, the theory of ideas suggested a manner of conceiving the perception of truth as that of present evidence. The idea was viewed as a sign of the thing. To this thing it has a relation of non-resembling similarity, just as the optical image has a definite mathematical ratio of similarity to what it is the image of. As in the case of refraction, we even know the coefficient of distortion of the representation: we know whether an idea is an accurate, approximate or illusory sign of the thing. The benefit of

this theory is by no means small: instead of having faith in
authority, tradition, instead of repeating maxims, our only
duty is to trust what we see, the present evidence of the
senses in the light of reason. We have only to go back to
things. The laws of Optics, the mathematical principles of
perspective, are the models for this new attitude towards
knowledge. As I have already pointed out concerning
Descartes, ideas are like engravings: they are not engravings
in the mind, they are, like these, reliable signs of things.
Interestingly enough, engravings do not represent the
secondary qualities of things but some of their primary
qualities: their size, figure, distance. The accurate and
thorough knowledge of the optical process, of the path of the
rays of light, of their angles of incidence, etc., rules out
any surreptitious illusion and leaves no room for prejudice.
We must simply see with our eyes and confront present
evidence.

Another reason why ideas are so attractive is that they
seem to account for what thinking is: thinking is having
images and composing them into various arrangements. This
does not mean having actual images in the mind: thinking is
simply like drawing pictures or figures or diagrams: it is
something like picture-making. This conception of ideas as an
explanation of thought through picture-making lasted quite
long: it is still pervasive in Russell, for example in 'On
Propositions, What They Are, How They Mean'. Thus conceiving
boils down to imagining and we cannot figure what is
impossible or absurd. In this respect, Reid's rejection of
ideas goes hand in hand with his denunciation of the
absurdity of making our conception the criterion of the
possibility of things.

After the same model as that of Optics, our capacities of
knowing are equated with those of perceiving – and perception
is essentially visual perception. We should never overlook
the importance of Descartes' Dioptrique for his theory of
knowledge and we should also grasp the full significance of
the fact that the main part of Hobbes' De Homine bears on the
mechanism of vision and its laws.

One might object that this is not the whole story and
that the mechanical and corpuscularian conception of nature
was at least as important a model for seventeenth century
philosophers as the laws of Optics were. I do not disagree
but it does not undermine my claims. On the contrary, I would
even suggest that the corpuscularian philosophy strengthened

and confirmed this optical theory of ideas: it provided a mechanical model for the actions of things on us and, what's more, the all-important distinction between simple elements and complex arrangements. We usually focus our attacks on such easy targets as ideas, but in so doing we miss another target: the seemingly unquestionable distinction between simple and complex mental states. For what does the analysis reach? A clear and distinct idea or a simple perception, in a word, some simple elements which can be viewed alternatively as mental elements (ideas of qualities) or as qualities of things themselves.

At any rate, the conjunction of the optical model and of the mechanical philosophy of nature resulted in the common theory of ideas: born from Optics as a conception of truth and knowledge, it turned into an overall conception of the mind. The success of the mechanical philosophy which reaches its peak with Newton's system also prompted a similar attempt in the intellectual field. Hume avowedly sets out to be the Newton of the human mind.

It also seems to me that the advantages of the theory of ideas were attractive enough to make philosophers overlook its overwhelming defects: as we have all experienced in reading the philosophers of the ideal system, what on earth can be the idea of an emotion, that of a passion, that of a smell if we still conceive ideas as non-resembling similarities? What strange thing can be the idea of a power or that of a process if ideas are elements or atoms?

As a matter of fact, the philosophers of the way of ideas got all the profit they could out of the theory of ideas and passed over its worse outcomes. These benefits consisted in the possibility of accounting for knowledge as intuition, vision and accurate description of things. This fitted in both with the development of mathematics and with the Baconian enterprise of sorting out things into species and classes.

Yet, it required that we should not question the adequate relationship of our sorts to the natural ones, that we were confident of sorting out things in accordance with their natural kinds, that our ideas were really true representations of things. This confidence soon began to vanish. It began when Locke stressed the gap between real and nominal essences. I will not go into this view.

From now on,another point of view gradually appears: knowledge is not contemplation, it is not the perception of the agreement or disagreement of our ideas, it is an activity, it sorts out things according to their qualities and puts characters together so that they form new conceptions. Now the theory of ideas is virtually condemned. It had accounted for the conception of knowledge as something descriptive, figurative, as a mapping of the world. It will prove more and more inadequate to account for knowledge when the latter consists in comprehending a manifold of characters so as to make a concept. Hobbes and above all Locke sowed the seeds of this instrumental conception of science and both had to conclude to the hypothetical character of our knowledge of nature. Significantly, Hobbes forbids any mention of faculties of the mind and Locke gives a prominent place to the notion of power. Berkeley, while turning things into ideas, gets rid of those same ideas when he deals with the mind: he prefers to talk of our notions of the mind. It becomes more and more obvious that ideas are of no use for describing the mind as an active power. The mind has ideas, it is not an idea. Hume, who was the most tortuous of Reid's predecessors, was both a supporter of the theory of ideas and its deadly enemy: he manages to deny any identity to the self since we are mere bundles of perceptions, and yet he brings in a large supply of dispositions, propensities,beliefs and associations which are as many hints at a rhapsodic theory of mental activity.

Reid comes into the picture when the heyday of ideas is already fading away and his blows hasten its decline. He also plays the part of a sort of Hegelian consciousness of that epistemological change. What he says amounts to one thing: if we really decide to consider the powers and actions of the mind, we must sweep away the theory of ideas. The new science will have to start afresh, to start from scratch.

Though it gives us only a sidelight on his thought, I wish to underline that Reid's artistic model is no longer that of engraving but that of pictorial illusion, as found in Cozens or, soon, in Turner. The painter paints our sensations, whereas we jump over them to perceive objects. The art of the painter reveals that our sensations, though suggestive of objects, are nothing like them: "Perspective, shading, giving relief, and colouring, are nothing else bu copying the appearance which things make to the eye".(32) For Descartes, the engravings were representations of the real qualities of things, for Reid the paintings present the appearance of things but this appearance, which we ordinarily overlook, suggests the things, it is not a likeness of them. Besides the remark concerning the suggestion of objects through sensations, Reid thus claims that we do not need to represent things any more: we have to suggest them through artificial techniques which finally result in a better picture than a resembling image. Where there used to be an image, we need an artificial suggestion. Might I suggest that the epistemological counterpart of this statement is that instead of describing and representing things, we must know them by the medium of concepts and categories which are nothing like them – which are not ideas.

I have repeatedly blamed Reid for his shortcomings. In my opinion he remained too faithful to Hume though at the same time he never was faithful enough. In so saying I call into question his too frequent use of the natural beliefs argument. He uses it to defeat the theory of ideas and also to escape the consequences of the collapse of this very theory. Hume had made clear that natural beliefs are simply natural: there is no rational principle to the effect that they should prevail, – but they do prevail. Nevertheless for Hume, unlike for Malcolm Lowry, the fact that everything happens anyhow somehow is not a justification: it only reassures us.

Reid's mistake – but it is the mistake of any common sense philosophy – was to overlook the irresistible sceptical element which lies at the heart of natural beliefs themselves: they are merely natural.

On the contrary, Kant understood rather well that the answer to the sceptic, if any, should consist in a transcendental argument establishing that some definite principles must obtain if the experience is to be possible. For Kant, there is no other demonstration for a metaphysical dogma (See 'The discipline of pure reason in its dogmatic employment' in the Critique of Pure Reason). I must add that sometimes Reid is not very far from this interpretation.

Among other things he claims that without the principles of common sense we could neither think nor talk to others.(33) Elsewhere he remarks that we can't discover anything concerning memory from experience for the latter presupposes the former. Likewise he underlines that the identity of the self is a necessary condition for the exercise of reason.(34) In other words a synthesis is necessary. Kant was to call it the synthesis of apprehension in intuition and it is connected with the original synthetic unity of apperception.

As a matter of fact, Reid could not be quite the Scottish Kant because his conception of science and philosophy was still too Newtonian. To put it bluntly, many problems in Reid's philosophy stem from the fact that he reaches Kantian foundationalist insights while developing an empirical inquiry on the nature of the mind. Thus he replies to the sceptical challenge in the course of an attempt to build up an empirical science of the human mind. Instead of answering philosophical questions through a philosophical examination of our intellectual powers – a critique of our intellectual powers as it were – he presents us with an inductive and empirical review of our intellectual operations. Such an inductive and empirical task could be, and actually is, very promising, for it can result in a descriptive philosophical psychology. Many of the most remarkable views of Reid actually belong to such a psychology and Reid opened up the way. That is why it is so tempting (and after all legitimate) to read back into Reid later developments, such as those of the Brentanists or of Husserlian phenomenology. But now the irony of the situation is that Reid's foundationalist concerns damp the ardour of his psychological curiosity, just as his empirical concerns damped his philosophical ardour. Such is the pervasive ambiguity of his achievement.

Some philosophers, like Hacking, have shown in what manner the heyday of meaning succeeded to that of ideas. It would be historically more accurate to make a bit of room for the heyday of concepts: Reid and Kant belong here. In any case, it is to Reid's credit that he stood on the watershed between ideas and concepts and decisively contributed to the epistemological change from ideas to concepts. More than ever we are indebted to him for that.

## NOTES

1   Hacking (1975, p.15).

2   Kant (1929, A320/B377).

3   **Corr** (Works, p.88).

4   Laudan (1970, pp.103ff).

5   I, VI, xx (Works, p.185).

6   I, I, vi (Works, p.109).

7   **IP**, I, ii (Works, p.233).

8   I, II, vi (Works, p.108).

9   **Corr** (Works, p.88).

10  **IP**, I, v (Works, p.239).

11  **IP**, II, xiv (Works, p.305).

12  **IP**, IV, ii (Works, pp.369–370).

13  Brown (1851, p.156).

14  **IP**, II, i–iv; I, VI esp. x–xx.

15  I, IV, xxi (Works, pp.186–87).

16  **IP**, Preface (Works, p.216).

17  Reid (1941, p.xxii).

18  **IP**, IV, ii (Works, pp.369–74).

20  Descartes (1965, p.113).

21  Locke (1975, Book IV, ch.xxi).

22  **IP**, I, ii (Works, p.233).

23  **IP**, II, x (Works, p.285).

24  **I**, II, vi (<u>Works</u>, p.109).

25  <u>Ibid</u>.

26  **IP**, III, vii (<u>Works</u>, p.357).

27  **IP**, III, vii (<u>Works</u>, p.359).

28  **IP**, VI, iii (<u>Works</u>, p.427).

29  **IP**, VI, iii (<u>Works</u>, pp.428–9).

30  **IP**, V, vi (<u>Works</u>, p.407).

31  Brown (1851, p.177).

32  **I**, VI, iii (<u>Works</u>, p.135).

33  **I**, V, vii; **IP**, V, iv–vi.

34  **IP**, III, iv (<u>Works</u>, p.344).

William P Alston


## REID ON PERCEPTION AND CONCEPTION


In opposition to the reigning 'theory of ideas' Thomas Reid
sought to develop an account of sense perception according to
which we, in some sense, directly perceive independently
existing objects.(1) This paper is primarily concerned to
determine just what sense this is, just what sort of
directness Reid meant to be espousing.

I

Here is Reid's usual way of saying what perception is:

> If, therefore, we attend to that act of our mind
> which we call the perception of an external object
> of sense, we shall find in it these three things:-
> First, some conception or notion of the object
> perceived; Secondly, a strong and irresistible
> conviction and belief of its present existence; and,
> Thirdly, that this conviction and belief are
> immediate, and not the effect of reasoning.(2)

To perceive a tree is for a conception of the tree and a
belief in its present existence to occur in the mind without
having been arrived at inferentially. We find substantially
the same formulation in a number of other passages.(3) And
some variations pose no substantive problems. For example,
when Reid says that "Perception implies an immediate
conviction and belief of something external",(4) we may take
that to be an alternative locution for the above, rather than
supposing that this second version is intended to distinguish
perception from what it 'implies'. (Presumably Reid meant to
be speaking of what is implied by the word 'perceive', or by
a statement to the effect that someone is perceiving
something). There may seem to be a more significant
difference when Reid speaks of perception as "that act of my
mind, by which I have the conviction and belief of this
quality".(5) I am thinking here not of the omission of the
conception, which can be put down to the fact that it is the
belief that is explicitly under discussion in this passage,
but rather to the fact that Reid seems to be distinguishing

*M. Dalgarno and E. Matthews (eds.), The Philosophy of Thomas Reid, 35–47.*
*© 1989 by Kluwer Academic Publishers.*

an act of the mind from the belief it produces by that act,
and identifying perception with the former rather than with
the latter. However when we remember how resolute an act
psychologist Reid was, we will realize that no such
distinction was seriously intended. In many connections Reid
denies that there is anything 'in' the mind except its acts
and operations.(6) He took the main psychological mistake of
the 'theory of ideas' to be the supposition that cognitive
acts require an immediate object 'in the mind'.(7) In
opposition to all such views Reid insisted that to speak of
an 'idea of sensation', for example, was simply to use a less
than maximally felicitous term for an act of sensation,(8)
that a 'conception' is simply an act of conceiving,(9) and so
on. Thus Reid would be the last person to distinguish an act
of the mind from the conception and/or belief thereby
produced.

One serious issue we will have to leave aside in this
paper concerns the possibility of perception without an
actually existing external object, as in hallucinations. The
canonical account quoted above does not require an existing
object. It does make reference to an object, but Reid,
notoriously, insists that conception, though it always has an
object, need not always have an existing object.(10) As for
perception, Reid sometimes stipulates that there must be an
existing object(11) and sometimes explicitly allows
perception in the absence of any such object.(12) Since the
former view is prominent in the Inquiry, while the latter
surfaces in the Essays, there may be a development in Reid's
thought on this point, stimulated by the need to take account
of perceptual illusions. In any event, to avoid distraction
from the issues on which we are concentrating, we shall
restrict attention to those cases in which there is an
existing external object.

In what ways might our perception of physical objects be
direct? I will distinguish three:

1. Presentational directness. In perception an external
object is directly 'presented' to our awareness; it is
'given' to consciousness. We are immediately aware of it, as
contrasted with just thinking about it, forming a concept of
it, or believing something about it. Our awareness of it is
'intuitive' rather than 'discursive'. This is 'knowledge by
acquaintance' rather than 'knowledge by description'.

2. Doxastic directness. The belief involved arises

'spontaneously' rather than through inference or other intellectual processes.

3. Epistemological directness. The belief involved is justified, warranted, rationally acceptable, apart from any reasons the subject has for it. It is 'intrinsically credible', 'prima facie justified', just by being a perceptual belief.

Note that although only the second of these modes is labelled 'doxastic', both the second and third have to do with the belief component of perception; while the first has to do with a non-conceptual, non-propositional mode of awareness.

There is no doubt but that Reid takes the perception of external objects to be immediate in the second and third ways. We have seen that the spontaneity of perceptual beliefs is part of his basic account of the nature of perception. And he repeatedly avers that we are proceeding quite reasonably in forming those beliefs without any support from reasoning:

> ...we ask no argument for the existence of the object but that we perceive it; perception commands our belief upon its own authority, and disdains to rest its authority upon any reasoning whatsoever. (13)

> If the word axiom be put to signify every truth which is known immediately, without being deduced from any antecedent truth, then the existence of the objects of sense may be called an axiom.(14)

However there would appear to be no room for presentational directness. If perception wholly consists of a conception of an external object and a belief in its present existence, it does not involve any direct presentation of that object. In explaining the concepts of direct presentation and direct awareness we contrasted them with merely forming a concept of an object and merely believing something about it. On Reid's account, perception would seem to be purely a matter of believing (judging) about external objects. For the conception involved would appear to be simply a constituent of the belief. We cannot judge or believe, as Reid often insists, without conceiving that about which we are judging.(15) Therefore the conception requirement would seem to add nothing to the belief requirement, and we are left with perception as simply the formation of non-inferential beliefs about external objects. 'Seeing is believing' indeed. Reid would appear to be a proto-Armstrong.(16)

## II

Before continuing the discussion of perceptual directness in Reid, we must make explicit another aspect of Reid's understanding of perception. This can be approached by way of the following criticism. If perception according to Reid is solely a way of believing, then Reid has not only left no room for a direct perception of external objects; he has left perception out of account altogether. For perception is distinguished from thinking and believing precisely by incorporating an intuitive, sensory element. Perception essentially involves sensory awareness, awareness of sensory qualities; that is precisely what distinguishes seeing a tree from merely remembering it or thinking about it. So Reid has escaped a representational, ideational theory of perception only by talking about something else altogether.

Reid is not subject to this criticism in the way his twentieth-century successors are. Armstrong and Pitcher, in their portrayals of perception as a process of forming beliefs about the physical environment by means of the senses, are, inter alia, activated by a Wittgensteinian aim of avoiding any recognition of an irreducibly private, phenomenal aspect to perception, of anything that involves a qualitative distinctness to which the subject has a privileged epistemic and semantic access. Now Reid was mightily concerned to reject the ideationalist's account of this side of the matter, an account according to which it involves the immediate awareness of 'ideas' or 'impressions' that are 'in the mind'. Reid stoutly denied the existence of any such items. But he was far from denying any private phenomenal aspect to our perceptual commerce with the world. He located it within what he called sensation:

> Sensation is a name given by philosophers to an act of mind, which may be distinguished from all others by this, that it hath no object distinct from the act itself.(17)

This official definition might suggest something without the qualitative distinctiveness of our experience of colours, sounds, tastes, and the like. Nevertheless, Reid constantly speaks of these as sensations:

> When I smell a rose, there is in this operation both
> sensation and perception. The agreeable odour I
> feel, considered by itself, without relation to any
> external object, is merely a sensation ... This
> sensation can be nothing else than it is felt to be.
> Its very essence consists in being felt; and, when
> it is not felt, it is not.(18)

So which is it? Is a sensation an object of feeling or a
mental act without an object? Reid wants both. The act is
self-directed. It consists in an awareness of itself; and
somehow this act of self-awareness embodies all the felt
qualitative distinctiveness of pains, colours, tastes, etc.
Reid continues the last quotation as follows:

> There is no difference between the sensation and the
> feeling of it – they are one and the same thing. It
> is for this reason that we before observed that, in
> sensation, there is no object distinct from the act
> of the mind by which it is felt – and this holds
> true with regard to all sensations.

If someone finds the idea of phenomenally qualified mental
acts unintelligible, the twentieth-century 'adverbial'
account of sensory consciousness may help to elucidate Reid's
view of sensation.(19) According to this view, what we tend
to think of as our awareness of colours, odours, and so on
should really be construed as ways of being conscious. The
situation is most perspicuously represented by saying that
one senses bluely rather than that one is aware of blue. Thus
an act that has no object other than itself can be an
'awareness of blue', in that in being aware of itself it is
aware of a certain way of being conscious, viz., seeing
bluely, and in that way the phenomenal quality of blueness
gets into the picture.

To return to our main concerns, the present point is that
Reid gets the phenomenal element into the perceptual
situation by his account of the way sensation figures in the
genesis of perception. My conception of the object and my
belief in its present existence is 'suggested' by a
sensation, which is a 'natural sign' of the object.(20) My
hand comes in contact with a table. A physiological process
is generated, eventuating in a sensation in my mind, which,
by a law of my nature, gives rise to a perception of the
hardness of the table. The phenomenal 'feel' of hardness
resides in the sensation. Even though this 'feel' has no

place within what Reid is willing to count as perception, it
is most emphatically recognised in what we may call his
picture of the total perceptual situation.

One may well be struck by the fact that Reid does not
include the origin from sensation in his account of the
nature of perception, either by taking perception to include
the whole sequence from sensation to the resultant conception
and belief, or by making the sensational origin part of the
defining characteristic of perception. No doubt, one thing
that inhibited him from going down this route was his deep
conviction that his adversaries had darkened counsel by
taking perception to just be sensation, misrepresented
moreover as the awareness of 'ideas'. By way of reaction,
Reid was much concerned to stress the distinctness of the
two. A more theoretically respectable reason can be found in
Reid's views that the visual perception of extension takes
place without any sensation;(21) and he holds that this could
be the case with all perception.(22) It is only because of
our constitution that most perception requires a sensational
origin.

III

Let's return to the main thread of the discussion. Thus far
it looks as if Reid takes the perception of external objects
to be direct in the doxastic and epistemological ways, but
not in the presentational way. This has implications for his
epistemology of perceptual knowledge. Let us say that one
takes perceptual knowledge (of the external environment) to
be direct provided it doesn't require the knower to have
adequate reasons for the beliefs involved. I can know that
there is a tree in front of me whether or not I have any
reasons for supporting this, provided the belief originated
in the right way. But what is the right way? A more
traditional, 'intuitive', formulation is in terms of a direct
perception of the external object. Provided the tree is
presented to me and I 'read' the content of my belief off
that, put into the belief just what is given to my awareness,
my belief is justified and, if true, will count as knowledge.
This is to follow the neo-realists and the elusive 'man in
the street' in making non-inferential perceptual knowledge
(what we have called 'epistemological directness') depend on
presentational directness. But if one disavows presentational
directness, one can still espouse non-inferential perceptual
knowledge. One simply finds some other way of identifying
normal perceptual beliefs and then pronounces them to be

'intrinsically credible', justified just by virtue of being beliefs of that sort. This other mode of identifying may still be in terms of origin, provided no direct presentation of an external object is required. For example, we can refer to what physiological psychology tells us about the origin of normal perceptual beliefs, or we can require that the belief stem from 'being appeared to' in a certain way. This non-presentational version of direct perceptual knowledge is propounded in different forms by reliabilists like Armstrong, Goldman, and Dretske, by 'prima facie credibility' theorists like Moore, Price, and Chisholm, and, it would seem, by Reid himself. All forms of the view can take the non-inferential justification accruing to perceptual beliefs to be prima facie only, subject to being overridden by opposing considerations.

A clear picture of Reid's psychology and epistemology of perception has emerged from these considerations. But now the time has come to muddy these peaceful waters; we have arrived at the place where, as Austin once said, we take it all back. Thus far we have suppressed a prominent statement of Reid's that sorts ill with the interpretation we have been constructing. Reid chooses the first chapter of the Essays on the Intellectual Powers of Man, in which he is providing definitions of key terms, to say: "...perception is most properly applied to the evidence which we have of external objects by our senses".(23) We don't know how to take this, of course, until we find out how Reid is using 'evidence', but fortunately he has been fairly explicit about this in Chapter XX of Essay II, 'Of the Evidence of Sense, and of Belief in General'. From that chapter it is clear that he is not restricting 'evidence' to the most common contemporary sense of a body of facts or propositions that provide logical support for some hypothesis: "We give the name of evidence to whatever is a ground of belief".(24) The ground could be other beliefs from which the belief in question is inferred, but it could also be some experience. This formulation leaves us dangling between a psychologically descriptive and an epistemologically evaluative sense of 'ground'. Is a ground anything that gives rise to a belief; or must it give the belief some support, render it justified or rational in some degree? I think the answer must be: both. That it provides rational support is suggested by Reid's saying: "To believe without evidence is a weakness which every man is concerned to avoid".(25) And he is unambiguous in building the notion of a psychological basis into the concept. In speaking of the various kinds of evidence he says: "They seem to me to agree only in this, that they are all fitted by Nature to produce belief in the human mind".(26) It is the psychological aspect in which I am presently interested.

This account of perception as the evidence we have from our senses (for beliefs about external objects) makes trouble for our developing interpretation. According to that interpretation perception is simply belief about external objects that arises in a certain way. Conception was also specified as a component, but we have been taking it that this is just the conceptualisation that is required for the belief's propositional content. Without employing the concepts of a tree and of leaves I cannot form the belief that the tree has leaves. So there is nothing to perception, on this account, except a belief. But the evidence formulation represents perception as the ground of beliefs about external objects (presumably the same beliefs that constitute perception on the other account) that we have from the senses. On the one account perception is a belief of a certain sort; on the other it is the ground of beliefs of that sort. Could a discrepancy be more blatant?

It is tempting to dismiss the 'evidence' account as a careless way of speaking. But, although Reid does not, so far as I know, define perception in this way elsewhere, there are many formulations that treat perception as a ground of belief. For example:

That I now write upon a table covered with green cloth, is a contingent event, which I judge to be most undoubtedly true. My judgment is grounded upon my perception, and is a necessary concomitant or ingredient of my perception.(27)

This distinctly says that the perception of the table is a ground of the judgment. Nor should we seize on the point that Reid here writes 'judgment' rather than 'belief'. He generally uses the terms interchangeably; and if there is a difference in that judgment is episodic while belief is dispositional, it is the former that has the better claim to be identified with perception. The suggestion, at the end of this quotation, that judgment might be regarded either as a necessary concomitant or as an ingredient is flatly inconsistent with taking perception to consist solely of a judgment. So the discordant voices will not be stilled.

Now if Reid's account of perception allowed for a direct

awareness of external objects the apparent discrepancy could be reconciled. We could take the direct awareness of the tree to be the ground, the 'evidence', on which the belief about the tree is based. Our two accounts would differ only in stressing one or another of the two components of perception. But that way out seems to have been foreclosed.

But maybe not. Remember that in developing our pure belief interpretation we took the conception component to be merely the conceptual aspect of the belief. That is, we took it that in speaking of conception what Reid had in mind was the exercise of an ability to classify things, to range them under some general kind, category, or type, rather than something 'intuitive'. That is a natural reading for us post-Kantians, trained to distinguish between conception and intuition and to regard the former as essentially a matter of taking things to be of a certain sort. But Reid was not a post-Kantian, and to see how he understood 'conception' we had better take a look at his extended treatment of the subject in Essay IV. There we learn that conception is the most basic intentional act; it is what logicians call 'simple apprehension'. It is simply the directing of consciousness on to some object, without making any judgment about it or taking up any other attitude toward it.(28) The object can be of any sort whatever – simple or complex, particular or general, sensuous or abstract. Whenever we are aware of any sort of object in any way whatever we will be said to 'conceive' it.

It is clear just from this that Reid by no means confines conception to the use of 'general concepts', to the exercise of capacities for classification, or predication, to thinking of something as being of a certain sort. One unmistakable indication of this is Reid's insistence that "conception enters as an ingredient in every operation of the mind".(29) This even includes sensation. "We cannot feel pain without conceiving it, though we can conceive it without feeling it."(30) Unless Reid thinks that one cannot feel pain without thinking of it as an instance of a type, and I see no indication of this, it is clear that he takes conception to be present where no general concepts are being deployed. It is true that most of the discussion in Essay IV has to do with general concepts. But his most inclusive statements make it clear that he takes the general category to range more widely, and that general conceptions are distinguished from others by the fact that their object is a universal.

But then there would appear to be a way out of our dilemma. The conception of an external object that is involved in perception can be understood as a direct awareness of that object, rather than as the application to it of some general concept. At least there is nothing in Reid's account of conception to rule this out. Nor is there anything in these statements about perception themselves to inhibit such an interpretation.

But before we rush to construe Reid as a proto–neo–realist, there are other matters to be considered. Most crucially, if the conception involved in perception is the direct awareness of an external object, how is that object presented to that awareness? There would seem to be no alternative to holding that it is presented as exhibiting 'sensible' or 'phenomenal' qualities – colours, shapes, heat and cold, texture, timbres of sounds, odours, and so on. It certainly seems that in visual awareness we are presented with objects that are variously coloured and shaped and spread out in space. If visual awareness is an awareness of external objects, those objects appear to us as so qualified; there is no other candidate in sight. Again, if touch involves a direct awareness of external objects it is an awareness of them as disposed in space and exhibiting various textures, shapes, and degrees of warmth and cold. Similar statements can be made for the other sense modalities. But this construal is not open to Reid. For, as noted earlier, he places all the qualitative distinctiveness of perceptual consciousness (except for visual extension) in the sensations, which he takes to involve no awareness of any object other than itself. What it is natural to refer to as an awareness of colours, warmth, and odours (or of objects as coloured, warm, and odorous) Reid construes as modes of feeling (awareness), as ways of being aware, directed on to no object beyond themselves.(31) And these sensations are sharply distinguished by Reid from the conception and belief that constitute perception. The sensation 'suggests' the conception and belief. It is a 'natural sign' that evokes the conception and belief of the object. Even visual extension, which Reid does not treat as a type of sensation, is regarded by him as playing the same role in perception as sensations, being a sign of the external object, evoking a conception of and belief in the object, rather than constituting an object of the conception, or an aspect thereof. Thus since Reid has placed sensible qualities in a different aspect, indeed a different stage, of the perceptual transaction, he is debarred from taking them to be ways in which external objects appear to that 'conception' of those objects that is partly constitutive of our perceiving them. That is, he is debarred from this unless we are aware of a colour or a sound twice in one perceptual episode, once as a mode of sensing and once as the way a physical object presents itself to us. But this is clearly not the way perceptual consciousness is structured.

Hence I am forced to admit that the escape route we seemed to glimpse in Reid's account of conception is blocked after all. There would appear to be no alternative to taking Reid as a doxastic and epistemological direct realist only, not a presentational direct realist at all. And we are still without a satisfactory construal of the notion of perception as a kind of evidence. To be sure, as George Pappas has suggested to me, one might try to develop a modified Reidian view by softening the boundaries between sensation and perception, allowing the phenomenal character of sensation to appear simultaneously, and without apparent distinction, as features of the external object of direct awareness. This would be something like H.H.Price's suggestion that perception "is, as it were, a dreamy half-awake state, in which we are unaware of a difference between the sense-datum and the ostensible physical object".(32) And it is even more like Moreland Perkins' recent suggestion that phenomenal qualities are instantiated in our sensory consciousness but also function as the content of a 'sensuous attribution' to the physical object we perceive.(33) But, however promising these suggestions, they clearly go beyond anything that can be found in Reid's works, and so they leave that thinker without any resources for embracing presentational direct realism.

NOTES

(1) Reid was, of course, opposed to the theory of ideas not just with respect to sense perception, but across the board; the opposition extended to sensation, memory, and conception. But the application to sense perception was given a central place in Reid's writings.

(2) **IP**, II, v (Works, p.258).

(3) See, e.g., **IP**, II, xvii (Works, p.318); II, xviii (Works, p.319); II, xx (Works, pp.326–7,329); III, i (Works, p.340).

(4) **IP**, II, xvi (Works, p.312). Cf. I, VI, xx (Works, p.183).

(5) **IP**, II, xvi (Works, p.310).

(6) See, e.g., **IP**, II, ix (Works, p.277); II, xi (Works, p.292); II, xiv (Works, p.298).

(7) See esp. **IP**, II, vii & xiv; esp. xiv.

(8) See, e.g., **IP**, II, xi (Works, pp.290,292).

(9) See, e.g., **IP**, IV, ii (Works, p.373).

(10) **IP**, IV, i (Works, p.368).

(11) **IP**, I, i (Works, p.222); I, VI, xx (Works, pp.182–3).

(12) **IP**, II, xviii (Works, p.320).

(13) **IP**, II, v (Works, p.259).

(14) **IP**, II, xx (Works, p.329). See also **IP**, II, xx (Works, p.328).

(15) See, e.g., **IP**, VI, i (Works, p.414).

(16) Armstrong (1968, p.212) characterises perception as "the acquiring of true or false beliefs about the current state of our body and environment by means of the senses". See also Armstrong (1961), and George Pitcher (1971).

(17) **IP**, I, i (<u>Works</u>, p.229).

(18) **IP**, II, xvi (<u>Works</u>, p.310).

(19) See Ducasse (1951, ch.13); Chisholm (1957, ch.8.).

(20) **IP**, II, xix (<u>Works</u>, p.325); II, xxi (<u>Works</u>, p.332); VI, v (<u>Works</u>, p.450). I, II, ix; V, i–iii.

(21) **I**, VI, viii.

(22) **IP**, II, xx (<u>Works</u>, p.327).

(23) **IP**, I, i (<u>Works</u>, p.222).

(24) **IP**, II, xx (<u>Works</u>, p.328).

(25) **IP**, II, xx (<u>Works</u>, p.328).

(26) **IP**, II, xx (<u>Works</u>, p.328).

(27) **IP**, VI, i (<u>Works</u>, p.414).

(28) **IP**, IV, i (<u>Works</u>, pp.360–1).

(29) **IP**, IV, i (<u>Works</u>, p.300).

(30) **IP**, IV, i (<u>Works</u>, p.300).

(31) Reid does, of course, attribute colours, smells, textures, or the like to physical objects in some sense. He makes it quite explicit that in the belief component of perception we attribute to the object an unknown power to produce such sensations in us. But the phenomenal qualities that give these sensations their distinctive 'feel' are not attributed to the external object.

(32) Price (1950, p.168).

(33) Perkins (1983).

Vere Chappell

## THE THEORY OF SENSATIONS

To those who knew him personally, Thomas Reid was a man of "uncommon modesty and diffidence" – so says Dugald Stewart in his Memoir.(1)   But what mere reader of the Inquiry and Intellectual Powers would have imagined any such thing of their author?  On page after page of these works Reid insists that, in their efforts to understand the human mind, not just some but all of his philosophical predecessors (with the possible exception of Arnauld) were mistaken, and mistaken not just in detail but on a matter of basic importance.  The mistake was always the same; yet no philosopher had ever been able to detect it, much less avoid or correct it – no philosopher, that is, until Reid himself appeared on the scene.  The mistake consisted in holding some version of what Reid often called 'the theory of ideas'.  To be sure, the term 'idea' was only used in Reid's intended sense by modern philosophers, beginning with Descartes.  But the entity it was meant to refer to figured also, Reid claimed, in the thought of the ancients.  The central fault of the theory of ideas is the supposition that such beings as ideas exist, whatever they are called.  In Reid's view these ideas "are a mere fiction of philosophers"; there simply are no such things.

Reid's criticisms of the theory of ideas are well known, and I don't propose to spend much time going over them.  I want to concentrate rather on Reid's own positive account of sense perception, which is the best-developed part of his treatment of the human mind.  There are no ideas in sense perception, according to Reid, but there are other entities, which he calls sensations, whose nature and role he spends considerable time discussing.  It is these sensations that I want particularly to focus on.  I shall argue that the sensations which Reid favours are not all that different in conception and function from the ideas which he rejects; and that some of the very considerations with which he seeks to discredit the latter apply to the former as well.  My conclusion, however, is not that Reid's account of sense perception is devastated by this result.  On the contrary, I believe that it can get on quite well without sensations, and I shall end by suggesting how this is so.

49

*M. Dalgarno and E. Matthews (eds.), The Philosophy of Thomas Reid, 49–63.*
*© 1989 by Kluwer Academic Publishers.*

These ideas that Reid found so objectionable, how did their champions conceive of them? An idea, in the first place, is the object of a mental act or operation. It exists wholly within the mind of the agent or operator – thinker, perceiver, imaginer, or whatever – whose idea it is. It could not exist apart from or outside a mind, and it exists only while perceiving or thinking is actually occurring. Furthermore, the mind in which an idea exists is immediately acquainted with it: ideas are immediate objects of thought and perception, and there is no mistaking their existence or nature. Finally, every idea stands for or represents something distinct from itself, usually something external to the mind in which it occurs.

This suffices to specify what an idea is; what then is the theory of such entities that Reid objected to, the theory of ideas? Its central tenet, of course, is just the existence of such things as ideas, so specified. Some further existential claims are presupposed by 'this: that there are minds and mental operations, that mental acts have objects, that there are things outside minds, or at least outside any given mind, and so on. Besides all of these, Reid attributes three special propositions to the idea theorist: (1) that all mental operations have ideas for their objects; (2) that ideas are the only things that are immediately thought and perceived; and (3) that ideas resemble their representata.

The theory of ideas is a theory of mental functioning in general, and all of his predecessors, Reid claims, subscribed to it. But the nature of specific operations of the mind, such as memory and imagination and sense perception, is not fully determined by this common theory; many differences appeared in different thinkers' treatment of these operations. In the case of sense perception, what is dictated by the idea theory, and what everyone agreed on, is that perception either consists of or else essentially includes an event in which a mind apprehends or is aware of an idea. This event was held to be prompted by certain things or happenings outside the mind; and to include or produce a cognitive state relating somehow to the thing represented by the idea. It was in their theories respecting these occasioning factors, this cognitive state, and the representata of peceptual ideas, that different thinkers diverged from one another.

In place of all these theories of perception, Reid

proposed what he claimed was not another theory at all, but a simple description of what occurs when perception takes place – "a faithful delineation of what every man...may feel in himself".(2) What occurs, in his view, is the following. A physical object causes motions in the sense organs, nerves, and brain of a percipient being. These motions give rise to, though they do not really cause, a sensation in the mind of the perceiver. This sensation is an act of the mind in question; and it is something of which that mind is conscious, though it need not be noticed or attended to. Whether noticed or not, the sensation suggests to the perceiver's mind both a conception of some quality in the physical object, and a belief in the existence of this quality. Again, the sensation does not really cause the conception and belief: suggesting is not a species of causing. But nor is it a species of reasoning, by which the mind infers the quality from the sensation. The sensation functions rather as a sign of the quality, and indeed as a natural sign, the signification of which is not learned by experience. The end result of this process is thus a judgment, to the effect that a certain physical object has a certain quality. Perception is itself an act of the mind, though a complex one, consisting of a sensation, a conception of a quality corresponding to this sensation, and a belief in the existence of this quality. As with all acts of the mind, perception is attended with consciousness; the perceiver is conscious, while he is perceiving, of his perception. The object of perception, however, the quality conceived and believed to exist, is outside the mind, and as such is not an object of consciousness.

The difference between Reid's account of perception and the common portion of his predecessors' theories is thus that, for the latter, ideas and not sensations are involved in perception, whereas the opposite is true for the former. Of course there are other differences than this, those which follow from Reid's rejection of the idea theorists' three special propositions noted earlier. Not all of these propositions have implications for sense perception taken by itself; but some of them do, and Reid's rejection of them is based partly on grounds other than just that they presuppose ideas. My concern in this paper, however, is less with the finished analyses of perception put forward by Reid and his predecessors than with the central concepts about which these analyses turn, that of an idea in the one case, that of a sensation in the other.

What then is the difference between these two sorts of
entities, as conceived by their respective defenders? In
several respects the answer turns out to be: very little.
First of all, as we have seen, ideas are mental entities, and
they exist only while they are being entertained by the minds
in which they occur. Exactly the same is true of sensations.
"The sensations of touch, of seeing, and hearing," Reid
writes, "are all in the mind, and can have no existence but
when they are perceived".(3) Second, ideas are immediately
present to the minds wherein they exist, in such wise that
they can be neither overlooked nor misapprehended. So also
with sensations: "we are conscious of all our sensations, and
they can neither be any other in their nature, nor greater or
less in their degree than we feel them".(4) Finally, ideas
are representative beings; they stand for or represent things
distinct from themselves. The same again is the case with
sensations. It is true that Reid rarely uses the language of
representation in connection with sensations. What he says
rather is that sensations suggest things to the mind in which
they occur, that they are signs which 'carry the mind' to
that which they signify. But representation too is a species
of signification, as Reid acknowledges and as some at least
of his predecessors explicitly maintained.

So far considered, ideas and sensations appear to be
remarkably similar in nature. And so Reid himself must have
regarded them, at least on occasion, for he sometimes
interchanges the words 'idea' and 'sensation' in discussing
both his own and his opponents' positions. There are even
passages, especially in the Inquiry, in which he identifies
sensations with an opponent's ideas, and others in which the
identification is made the other way round. Thus in his
chapter on Seeing he says: "there is a certain apparition to
the eye, or to the mind, which we have called the appearance
of colour" [and later will call the sensation of colour] "Mr.
Locke calls it an idea; and, indeed, it may be called so with
the greatest propriety".(5) And in the chapter on Touch he
says that according to "the received hypothesis of ideas...,
external things must be perceived by means of images of them
in the mind;" [which is what the hypothesizer means by
'ideas'] "and what can those images...be, but the sensations
by which we perceive them?".(6)

On the other hand, Reid makes one point about sensations
that seems clearly to differentiate them from his opponents'
ideas. Ideas are supposed to be objects of mental operations
or acts. But sensations, Reid insists, are themselves mental

acts, and acts, furthermore, of a peculiar sort. For unlike most acts of the mind, sensations have no objects, or rather, as Reid most often puts it, no objects apart from themselves. Here are two characteristic passages from the Essays: "The ideas, of whose existence I require the proof, are not the operations of any mind, but supposed objects of those operations"; and "Sensation is a name given by philosophers to an act of the mind, which may be distinguished from all others by this, that it hath no object distinct from the act itself".(7)

There is less to this difference between ideas and sensations, however, than meets the eye. Sensations are acts and ideas are objects, but ideas are objects of mental acts, and they never exist separately therefrom. So it is not that perception excludes a mental act on the idea theorist's view, whereas on Reid's view it includes it. Nor is it the case that sensations are not themselves objects of mental acts. For we can't have a sensation, he says, without being conscious of it; and consciousness is as much an act of the mind as is perception, or the apprehension of an idea, or sensation itself. Furthermore, though Reid says that sensation is peculiar among mental acts in having no object distinct from itself, it is consistent with and perhaps is even suggested by this that it has itself for an object, and hence is the object of a mental act after all. But suppose Reid had said that a sensation has no object, period. He still would have had to allow that sensations have content or characteristics or features or natures; else how account for the obvious point, which he himself constantly takes for granted, that sensations differ from one another not just by occurring at different times or in different minds but also by answering to different descriptions? One sensation is of heat, of some particular degree of intensity. Another is a smell of a rose, which is more or less like the smell of some other flower. Reid can avoid saying that these sensations have (or are) different objects; but then he must allow some other way of expressing this obvious point. And the fact is that the language of different objects may be used just for this purpose. It is true that the term 'object' may suggest something detachable from a mental act, or at least from any one mental act: it is a major tenet of Reid's position that the objects of sense perception are so detachable. But the term need not be used with this implication; and it is not so used, as a matter of fact, by at least some of those who apply it to ideas – as Reid himself recognizes when, for example, he calls an idea the "inseparable concomitant" of the operation of thinking by which it is supposed to be present to the mind.(8)    It may well be the case that some idea theorists meant something more by calling an idea an object than merely that it had a specific content or nature; this is a question on which both followers and recent interpreters of Descartes and Locke have been divided.    But for all that Reid says about the 'system of ideas', I do not see that its proponents have to be taken as meaning more than this.   I also do not see that Reid's own sensations cannot be called objects in this minimum sense – and indeed cannot be called so "with the greatest propriety".

I conclude, therefore, that Reid's sensations are really quite similar in nature and function to the theorists' ideas, at least as these entities figure in sense perception.    I am not thereby claiming, be it noted, that Reid's account of perception is no different from that of his predecessors, and least of all that Reid himself was somehow a subscriber, in spite of himself, to the ideal system.    There is no doubt that Reid does, as I remarked earlier, reject the three special propositions that he attributes – and for the most part, in my view, justly attributes – to the idea theorist; and in fact many of his most vigorous arguments against his opponents are directed to these three propositions.  But Reid also disagrees with them simply on the issue of whether ideas exist.    The point I wish to make is that Reid's own sensations are very much of a piece with these ideas – so much so that the question of whether the case that Reid makes against the theory of ideas on this ground, that it supposes ideas to exist, does not apply also to his own position on the ground that it supposes sensations to exist.

. What are Reid's reasons for disbelieving the existence of ideas? These are really of two different sorts, depending on the basis on which he supposes the friends of ideas to be affirming their existence.    In some passages he seems to regard the idea theorist as making a straightforward empirical claim: that ideas are things that one observes or is conscious of in oneself – one simply finds them in one's experience.  To this claim Reid's response is one of flat denial: he finds no such things in his experience – nor, he adds, does anyone else who is not a philosopher.(9)    More often, however, Reid interprets his opponents as promoting ideas on theoretical grounds: such entities must exist in order to explain the workings of our minds.  Thus he speaks of them as having been "invented" with a view to making "the operations of the mind to be better understood";(10) and, even more pointedly, as having been "contrived to solve the phenomena of the human undestanding".(11) His rejoinder to this move is threefold. First, ideas "do not at all answer this end" of explanation: they do not serve to increase our grasp of things, and we are left with the same questions after introducing them that we had at the outset.(12) Second, ideas are not necessary to our understanding, since Reid's own positive (though merely descriptive) account of what actually passes in the mind suffices to account for whatever it is that needs or admits of explanation.(13) And third, ideas actually make matters worse, since their introduction "only serves to confound things that are different and to perplex and darken things that are clear".(14) (There is indeed a fourth point that Reid makes against the 'hypothesis of ideas', viz. that it is "the parent of those many paradoxes so shocking to common sense, and of that scepticism which disgrace our philosophy of the mind, and have brought upon it the ridicule and contempt of sensible men"(15) — the allusion is, of course, to the results of Berkeley and Hume. But since Reid shows these results to follow, not merely from the existence of ideas, but from one or the other of the idea-theorist's special propositions referred to earlier, I leave this point aside.)

Now let us see how Reid's sensations fare when confronted with objections similar to these. It might be thought, to begin with, that Reid's basis for believing in sensations is entirely empirical, that he regards them as items to be discovered in our experience rather than entities posited to serve a theoretical purpose. And yet, though it is true that Reid doesn't say that sensations are invented or contrived, there is no doubt that he assigns explanatory roles to them in his account of sense perception, and that he sometimes recommends them on the basis of their suitability for these roles. We can, therefore, make the same distinction with respect to sensations that we made above in considering ideas, between the question of the empirical evidence for their existence and that of their utility in theoretical terms.

What then is the empirical basis for sensations? Reid's official doctrine is that sensations are objects of consciousness: it is impossible to have a sensation without being conscious of it. But Reid also admits that most of our sensations are not noticed at the time of their occurrence. He has an explanation for this: sensations are fugitive, they come and go very quickly; and a perceiver's attention is

normally fixed on the external object of his perception, of
which the sensation is only a sign – just as a speaker,
having mastered a language, is so intent on "the sense of
what he would express" that he gives no heed to the words he
uses.(16) But even Reid is struck by how deeply entrenched
this "habit of inattention" is in the case of sensations, and
by the pervasiveness of our ignorance of them:

> It is indeed strange that a sensation which we have
> every time we feel a body hard...should yet be so
> much unknown as never to have been made an object
> of thought and reflection, nor to have been
> honoured with a name in any language; that
> philosophers, as well as the vulgar, should have
> entirely overlooked it.(17)

And consider the man who leans his head against a pillar:
"Undoubtedly," Reid says, "he hath...a sensation"; but it is
one "which nature intended only as a sign of something in the
stone; and, accordingly, he...cannot, without great
difficulty, attend so much to the sensation, as to be
persuaded that there is any such thing distinct from the
hardness it signifies".(18) How is such a man to be
distinguished from Reid's ally, the 'plain man' who cannot be
persuaded by the 'modern philosopher' that there are such
things as ideas in perception?(19) In fact, it is not at all
difficult for a speaker or hearer to attend to the words that
are used in a discourse; and every word in every language has
"been honoured with a name". Of course there are sensations
too that it is easy to name as well as to notice – the
sensation of pain, for example. The sensations whose
empirical status is in question – whose empirical credentials
Reid himself may have had doubts about – are those that are
alleged to occur in sense perception: sensations of smell,
taste, and hearing, of hardness, heat, and colour. At the
least we must grant that the empirical case for the existence
of such sensations is not decisive, and that the empirical
grounds for preferring sensations to ideas – if any – are
less than overwhelming.

Neither do sensations receive much support from
theoretical considerations – at least those used by Reid to
measure the success of his opponents' ideas. We have three
questions to consider. The first is whether sensations
suffice to explain the operations of the mind; the second is
whether sensations are needed to accomplish the explanatory
tasks assigned to them; and the third is whether sensations

themselves give rise to difficulties which would not have existed without them. The answer to the first question is that, although sensations do pull some explanatory weight — it is sensations that cause (or rather occasion) the mind to conceive and believe the existence of the external qualities which are the ultimate objects of perception – they certainly do not generate the kind of understanding that Reid criticizes ideas for failing to provide. The ideas which are supposed to account for mental operations themselves are known, Reid writes, "by a kind of feeling, or immediate perception". But he goes on:

> This feeling, or immediate perception, is as difficult to be comprehended as the things which we pretend to explain by it. [For] there must...be in the percipient a power to feel or to perceive. How this power is produced, and how it operates, is quite beyond the reach of our knowledge.(20)

But the same point holds, surely, for sensations. A sensation itself is an instance of "a kind of feeling, or immediate perception," and presupposes "a power to feel or to perceive" on the part of the sentient. But the source and nature of this power are quite as much "beyond the reach of our knowledge" on Reid's account as on that of the idea theorist.

Second, Reid concludes that ideas are theoretically dispensable on the basis that a doctrine other than the ideal system – namely, his own – provides an alternative way of explaining the things that can and need to be explained. In the case of sensations there is also an alternative to explaining things by their means, but it is Reid's doctrine itself that provides this alternative. The theoretical work that sensations are supposed to do on Reid's account is cause (or occasion) the conception of and belief in the objects of perception – in short, to suggest them. And this office they do perform, Reid says, with respect to every one of the five senses. Not with respect to every sensible quality, however, for he acknowledges that some visual qualities, figure and magnitude for instance, are perceived in bodies, and visually perceived, but have no sensations corresponding to them. How then do we come by the conception and belief of such qualities, which we must do in order to perceive them? By what means are they suggested to the mind? Reid's answer is that these qualities are suggested by something material, by impressions on the sense organs, of which, to be sure, we are

not conscious but which are nonetheless able to serve as
signs of qualities.(21)    Hence it is clear, by Reid's own
admission, that sensations are not needed to play the role
assigned to them.    And which normally they do play, with
respect to these sensible qualities. (Reid also says in one
passage that certain tangible qualities can be suggested by
material impressions, even though there are sensations which
normally perform this function.)    The trouble is that
material impressions similar to these exist in every instance
of sense perception according to Reid; in the normal
situation it is these impressions which serve as the
immediate occasions of sensations in the mind. But if such
impressions are capable of suggesting qualities directly,
without the intervention of sensations, in some cases, why
not in all?    If of course, there is another basis – an
empirical one, for example – for recognizing sensations, then
certainly there is reason to provide them with some useful
work to do, to give them some theoretical function.    But the
point is that theoretical need cannot by itself serve as a
reason for admitting them, any more than it can in the case
of ideas.

Finally, sensations do appear to generate some
difficulties of their own.   I shall mention two of these. The
first was pointed out by Timothy Duggan in the Introduction
to his edition of the Inquiry.(22)    There is an
inconsistency, Duggan claims, in Reid's conception of a
sensation.   On the one hand, since sensations are objects of
consciousness for Reid, it is not possible for a perceiver to
mistake his sensations.   This means not only that a sensation
cannot be felt (and so believed) to have any property it does
not have, but also that it cannot have any property it is not
felt and believed to have – including, so to speak, the
property of existing.  Duggan cites the following passage to
show that Reid did take this position: "when I smell it [sc.
the smell of a rose], I am necessarily determined to believe
that the sensation really exists.   This is common to all
sensations".(23)  On the other hand, it is also Reid's view
that it is possible for perceivers not to notice sensations
that exist in their minds.   Now surely, if I fail to take
note of a sensation I have, I fail to believe its existence
as well (which is different, as Duggan reminds us, from
believing its non-existence).   And this certainly does seem
to be a plain contradiction.

The second difficulty is this.   Reid holds that
sensations are only contingently related to the things that

precede and follow them in  the perceptual process.  It is  a
fact that, in the normal situation, a hard body gives rise to
certain impressions  in  the  perceiver's  sense  organs  and
brain; that these impressions give rise to certain sensations
in his mind; and that these sensations suggest the quality of
hardness to him, that is, prompt him both to conceive of this
quality and  believe that  it exists  in the  hard body  that
first started  the perceptual process,  which conception  and
belief constitute his perception of that quality.  But  there
is no necessity, Reid says, to any of these sequences.  It is
possible − at any rate  possible "for anything we know" −  to
have the perception without any sensations or any impressions
or both; it is possible  to have the impressions without  any
sensations or any perception or  both; and it is possible  to
have different  impressions  or  sensations  or  a  different
perception (the perception of a different quality) from those
we normally  have in  conjunction with the  other factors  in
that situation.(24)  Hence the following ought to be possible
on Reid's view: a man  holds a red billiard ball in his  hand
with his eyes  closed; he  has the impressions  in his  hand,
nerves, and brain that are normally consequent on touching  a
hard body;  these  impressions, however,  occasion  a  visual
sensation of  redness; and  yet this  sensation suggests  the
quality of hardness to him, so that the resulting  perception
is that  of  the billiard  ball's  hardness and  not  of  its
colour.  Such a case  ought, I say, to be possible for  Reid;
but there is reason to think that in fact it is not.

There are two  abnormalities in  the case as  described:
impressions of touch are followed not by a tangible but  by a
visual sensation;  and  a sensation  of colour  suggests  the
quality not of colour but  of hardness.  It is the second  of
these two conjunctions that is problematic for Reid, for  the
following reason.  A sensation,  as Reid conceives it, is  an
entity that  can  be  identified by  something  intrinsic  to
itself,  a distinctive characteristic or content which one is
acquainted with just  by having the  sensation.(25)  So  also
can material  impressions  be  identified, at  least  to  the
extent of  being tangible  or visible,  independently of  the
sensations  they  give  rise  to,  on  the  basis  of  their
aetiology, the sense organs in which or because of which they
occur.  But Reid's  doctrine provides no  means by which  the
quality that is suggested  by a sensation can be  identified,
apart from its relation to that very sensation.  The  quality
suggested by a sensation of $F$ can only be the  quality of $F$ −
which explains why it  is that, as  Reid contends, the  names
given to  many sensible  qualities  can be  applied to  their

corresponding sensations as well.   Hence it  is not just   an
empirical fact, it  is a necessary  truth that sensations  of
redness make  perceivers conceive and  believe the  existence
only of redness, never of  hardness.  Of course, it is not  a
necessary truth that the quality suggested by a sensation  of
redness is  identical  with the  quality that  initiates  the
process that eventuates in that sensation: it is just a  fact
that  the  quality that    produces  sensations of    redness
(normally) is redness and not hardness.  But there is nothing
that the quality suggested by the sensation of redness  <u>could</u>
be but redness.  That  this is indeed Reid's position can  be
argued from a point  that he himself  makes in the  following
passage:

> The     sensations      belonging    to      secondary
> qualities...are  not  only  signs  of  the    object
> perceived, but  they  bear a  capital part  in  the
> notion we form of it.  We conceive it only  as that
> which occasions  such  a sensation,  and  therefore
> cannot reflect  upon  it without  thinking of  the
> sensation which it occasions: we have no other mark
> whereby to  distinguish it.   The  thought of a
> secondary quality,  therefore,  always  carries  us
> back to the sensation  which it produces.  We  give
> the same name to both, and are apt to confound them
> together.(26)

What Reid  says in this  passage may  or may not  be true  of
secondary qualities considered as  the causes of  sensations;
but it certainly is true of such qualities conceived as their
<u>significata</u>,  and  it  applies  to  primary  as  well  as  to
secondary qualities so conceived.(27)

Both of these difficulties are, as best I can tell, deep
ones for Reid, and not  such that he can easily escape  them.
They constitute an objection, therefore, of a kind similar to
one that he himself makes to the theory of ideas,  to what (I
hope by now to have shown) may aptly be called  Reid's theory
of sensations.

This and the other  objections that I have been  urging,
however,  are   objections  to  Reid's  doctrine  of   sense
perception only to  the extent that  the latter includes  the
theory of sensations.   There is thus  an easy way to  render
Reid's doctrine immune  to these objections,  and that is  to
leave the sensations out of  it.  What would be the  negative
consequences of taking  this step?   None at  all that I  can

discover.  The theoretical function of sensations – to  cause
the mind to conceive and  believe in the external objects  of
perception –  could  be  taken over  completely by  material
impressions, which Reid  himself puts into  that role in  the
case of  some  sensible  qualities.  As  for  the  empirical
evidence  alleged  in  support  of  sensations,  this  is
inconclusive at best.  It is not clear that one is ever (much
less always) aware, in the course of perceiving, of some item
distinct  from  the  quality  that  one  perceives,  an  item
analogous  to  the  pain  that  one  feels  when  one  has  a
toothache, an  item existing  wholly within  one's own  mind.
Sense perception is certainly a conscious operation for Reid:
one is aware of something when one perceives.  But perception
on Reid's account includes  belief and conception as well  as
sensation.  These are mental operations as much as  sensation
is, and as such are things the mind not only  may but must be
conscious of  when  they  occur  in it.   Furthermore,  both
conceiving and believing have content for Reid; indeed he has
no reservation in  speaking of objects  of  conception  and
belief, as he does in the case of sensation.   Even if Reid's
doctrine  requires  particular  objects  of  consciousness  in
perception, there is no reason why conceptions or beliefs  or
their respective  objects might  not serve  in this  capacity
just as well as sensations.

My claim thus is not only that Reid's doctrine is better
off without sensations,  but that  it can be  purged of  them
without being weakened thereby.  I am not claiming,  however,
that the result is  an adequate or  an acceptable account  of
sense perception.  The big  question, I think, that needs  to
be settled  before that  claim can  be made,  is whether  any
account of  the  mind's operations  that  is founded  on  the
sharp, metaphysical  separation  of  mind  and body  can  be
defended.   For Reid,  though  he may  have  repudiated  the
Cartesian idea theory, was  never anything but the most  avid
proponent of Cartesian dualism.

## NOTES

(1)  Dugald Stewart in Reid (<u>Works</u>, p. 5).

(2)  **IP**, II, v (<u>Works</u>, p. 260).

(3)  I, VI, xii (<u>Works</u>, p. 159).

(4)  **IP**, II, xxii (<u>Works</u>, p. 335).

(5)  I, VI, iv (<u>Works</u>, p. 137).

(6)  I, V, viii (<u>Works</u>, p. 131).

(7)  **IP**, II, xiv (<u>Works</u>, p. 298) and I, i (<u>Works</u>, p. 229).

(8)  **IP**, II, ix (<u>Works</u>, p. 277).

(9)  Cf. **IP**, II, xiv (<u>Works</u>, pp. 289ff.).

(10) **IP**, II, xiv (<u>Works</u>, p. 305).

(11) I, II, iii (<u>Works</u>, p. 106).

(12) Cf. **IP**, II, xiv (<u>Works</u>, p. 305).

(13) Cf. **IP**, II, v (<u>Works</u>, p. 260).

(14) Cf. **IP**, II, xiv (<u>Works</u>, p. 305).

(15) I, II, iii (<u>Works</u>, p. 106).

(16) I, V, ii (<u>Works</u>, p. 120).

(17) <u>Ibid</u>.

(18) <u>Ibid</u>.

(19) Cf. **IP**, II, xiv (<u>Works</u>, p. 299).

(20) **IP**, II, xiv (<u>Works</u>, p. 305).

(21) Cf. I, VI, viii (<u>Works</u>, p. 146).

(22) Duggan (1970).

(23) **I, II, iii** (<u>Works</u>, p. 105).

(24) Cf. **I, VI, xxi** (<u>Works</u>, p. 187);  **IP, II, xx** (<u>Works</u>, p. 327).

(25) Cf. **I, III** (<u>Works</u>, p. 116).

(26) **IP, II, xvii** (<u>Works</u>, p. 315).

(27) It may not be true that the sensation of redness is of necessity caused by the quality of redness, as Reid suggests in this passage, because the intervening material impressions do give us a "mark whereby to distinguish" the quality: we might judge that the quality at the least is not redness on the grounds that none of the impressions occasioned by it are in the eye (assuming that redness is necessarily a visual quality). If what Reid says here is true, then I can't claim, as I did a moment ago, that it is just a fact that the sensation of redness is produced by the quality of redness. Even so, the corresponding claim for a primary quality such as hardness would hold, and that is all I need for the contrast I wanted to draw. In any case, my primary point is that the quality signified by the sensation of $F$ is of necessity the quality of $F$, for all qualities primary and secondary. This point is secure whatever the status of secondary qualities considered as causes.

Norton Nelkin


## REID'S VIEW OF SENSATIONS VINDICATED


To the second order question of where we should look if we
want answers to the questions about what exists in the world
and what those existents are like, Descartes gave a really
remarkable answer, one that would change the face of
philosophy for the next three hundred years.(*) It is such a
remarkable answer that it is hard to believe that it became
nearly universally accepted. And yet it did become so
universally accepted that very few philosophers since, even
in this century, have noticed just how remarkable the answer
is. Descartes said that if we want to know about the world,
we have to look inside ourselves. Becoming clear about one's
own conscious, introspectible experience is the key to
understanding the world.

The British Empiricist tradition, culminating in Hume,
bequeathed a still more remarkable addition to the Cartesian
answer; and this addendum, too, became almost as universally
accepted. Hume proposed that when one introspects one's
conscious experience all one discovers there are
sensations.(1) Thus, any knowledge of the world must begin
with knowledge of sensations, impressions and images. I will
call the tradition that accepted – and accepts – this
Cartesian-Empiricist answer as to where to begin our
research, the Traditional Position.

For the Traditional Position sensations do almost all the
work in our cognition of the external world. We distinguish
whether we are seeing the world or hearing it on the basis of
the different kinds of sensations we are having: visual
sensations just are different from auditory ones. It is
because blind people lack visual sensations that we say they
don't see. We learn our concepts by naming or describing our
sensations. For example, we have a certain kind of sensation,
which we call 'red', say, and then we ascribe that property
to items in the world. It is because red sensations are so
different from blue sensations that we discriminate one
colour from the other. Defenders of the Traditional Position
consider the cognitive element to be wholly dependent on the

*M. Dalgarno and E. Matthews (eds.), The Philosophy of Thomas Reid, 65–77.*
© *1989 by Kluwer Academic Publishers.*

sensory: in its most radical form the Traditional Position understands the cognitive element as just a level of strength of the sensation (Hume, for example) while in a less radical version the Traditional Position claims that we 'read off' from the sensations to the beliefs and concepts (Locke and Russell, as examples). Sensations are something like photographs, only not quite, since what they are photographs of might or might not exist. But, still, we are to think of sensations as representations only: in this upside-down world view, it is the representations we are first aware of, not the real things. Our concepts of the real properties of real things in some way have their origin in the 'mirror' of the properties of our sensations.

It is to Reid's credit that he rejected this Traditional Position. Reid's own belief is that it is the cognitive element that is crucial in perceptual experience, that there can be no 'reading off' from the sensation to the belief, nor can the belief be a mere level of strength of the sensation.(2) While Reid does not give us an account of how perceptual beliefs arise — nor does he think any such ultimate account is even possible(3) — he is convinced that sensations cannot play the role assigned to them in the Traditional Position. The belief cannot be identified with a strength-level of the sensory state because sometimes strong sensations accompany disbelief, while weak sensations accompany belief. For Reid, sensations generally accompany, perhaps even in some way cause, perceptual beliefs and thus their occurrence might serve as a sign for us to have the usual beliefs(4) but the belief is in no way identifiable with the sensations. Nor is there any way to 'read off' from the content of the sensation to the content of the belief. If sensations have content, it is not the right sort.(5) Sensations are not pictures of the objects which cause them. They share no properties in common with those objects, and so cannot lead to our beliefs about those properties (our perception of those properties) in any sense that might be thought of as 'reading off'. Reid believed sensations might serve as signs for our beliefs in the sense that usually when I have a certain sensation, call it 'R', it is reasonable to believe that there is a red object before me. That is because when I perceive red objects, I am in sensation state R as well. These two states, the perception and the sensation, are constantly conjoined. But there is no stronger internal relation than that. The 'red' sensation R is not itself red, and so one cannot 'read off' the properties of the world from the properties of sensations. For instance, smoke can be a sign that there is fire because the two are most often conjoined. But one can't 'read off' from the smoke to get one's concept of fire. The properties of the smoke are not adequate to our doing that. In the same way, Reid wants to argue that the properties of the sensations we get from the fire itself have no closer connection than those properties of the smoke have to the properties we conceive of as in, and perceive in, the fire. Again, there is no internal connection between these sets of properties. The sensations we get from the smell of the rose are not the properties of the smell of the rose, and the sensations we get when we feel hard things are not themselves hard. The sensations in each case borrow their names from the properties we ascribe to the things in the world.(6)

I say that rejecting the Traditional Position is to Reid's credit because he is basically correct. And in this paper I want to defend Reid's thesis that sensation plays, at best, a small, causal role in perception by discussing three sorts of actual laboratory and clinical cases. These cases will support Reid's belief that sensation is one mental state, perception another and that the former is not the source of our perceptual concepts. While all three types of case support Reid's general view, the latter two sorts call into question some other claims of Reid himself. I will say more about these latter claims, which I believe to be mistaken, at the time I discuss the cases themselves.

1. Most normal colour perceivers are trichromats. They are called 'trichromats' because they have three types of cone in their retina, each type dealing with the perception of complementary colours – red/green, blue/yellow, black/white – and from these three types we seem to produce all of our colour perception. The loss of any one pair causes a severe colour deficit. For instance, some people are born dichromats. Most dichromats lack the pair red/green. Such dichromats cannot distinguish red things from green things, nor can they distinguish either of these from blue or yellow things. They are what we call colour blind. While some people are born dichromats, others are changed into dichromats either through injury or disease. At least some of these latter dichromats (though none of the former) can be converted back into trichromats with specially fitted contact lenses which are tinted so as to act as artificial light filters and which then play much the same role as their red/green cones did. The persons for whom such lenses have proved successful have become able once more to make all the

colour distinctions they previously were capable of. However, some of these people complain that the colours no longer look the way they used to, and they miss their old 'look'.(7)

Such a case calls into question the idea that sensations are primary in perceptual experiences. These people now visually discriminate as red all the things they previously visually discriminated as red. They can tell them from green things and can tell both red and green things from blue and yellow things. But their sensations are different. Surely this is evidence that it is the visual discrimination that leads us to call the sensation 'red' and not the other way round. Consider two people, one of whom, when confronted with red things, has, and always has had, sensations just like the injured person before the injury; the other has, and always has had, sensations just like the injured person after the injury. Both would perceive red, but their sensations would be different. So what? Would this mean that one of them doesn't really see red? But why should we say that? Granted the sensation may play some kind of causal role in the discrimination, but such a case makes it doubtful that we first identify the sensations as red and then 'read off' from that sensation to identify the property of the object as also being red.

Let me just push a little harder. Suppose that each time, or just even sometimes, when you perceive a red thing your sensation isn't what it was on another occasion when you perceived that red thing under similar lighting conditions. Would it matter?  Wouldn't you still be perceiving red? Haven't you perceived red correctly many times in your life even if your sensations have been different each time? You might say you know they haven't been. Perhaps you do. But would having a faulty memory about your sensations matter? Surely it is not the sensation we are having that matters; rather it is the judgment we make, what we do, how we are affected that matters. In an important sense, the sensation itself is irrelevant.

Again, there are freshwater fish that seem to make all the sorts of colour discriminations that we make.(8) Yet their neurological visual systems are radically different from our own. Why should we think they have the same sensations?  That they make the same perceptual judgments is clear. That they have the same perceptual beliefs also makes some sense because it is easy to think of beliefs in functional terms, and correspondingly easy to think of the same function's being realized by different hardware. But it is very difficult to think of sensations as functional states. As Keith Gunderson says, sensations are programme resistant. It seems very natural to think that these fish see red, and very unnatural to think otherwise. Yet there is very good reason to think that their sensations must be very different from ours – given the radical difference in hardware, radically different. As the 'recovered trichromat' cases show, changes in neural structure seem to mean changes in sensation experience.(9) So how can it be the sensation that is most important in the perception of red? How can the perception called 'red' get its name from the sensation? How can the belief that an object is red be 'read off' the sensation? In each of these questions it makes much more sense to think of it the other way round. We call certain sensations 'red' because they are associated with certain perceptual beliefs. That your sensations might be different even when your belief is the same is irrelevant as far as the name of the sensation goes. All such sensations are legitimately called 'red'. That the sensations which accompany my seeing red might always be different from those that accompany yours is also irrelevant. We are both seeing red, both having red sensations. And that is why there seems something fishy with the inverted spectrum problem. How can I say that such different sensations as mine or yours, or mine and the fish's, or the born trichromat's and the recovered trichromat's can all legitimately be called 'red'? Because they can be and are. But how can one say they're different if they're both red? They just are. How does one recognize them as different? The people wearing the lenses just seem to be able to. Doesn't that show that we could give different sensations different names? Possibly so. But so far we have found no need to do so, and right now things work the other way round: our sensations get their names from the beliefs and not, as the Traditional Position would have it, vice versa. Our only means of describing our sensations, our only descriptive terms for sensations, arise from our perceptual processing, and from naming these perceptual processes prior to naming the associated sensations. Without such ready–at–hand names we have nothing to say about sensations. As a natural kind in themselves we are speechless about sensations.(10) Sensations, as Smart once said, really are raw feels;(11) or, at least, we have no non–parasitic vocabulary to name or describe them. As we divide things now, there is no reason to believe 'red' sensations form a natural kind. The sensations that for me are associated with (or perhaps play a causal role in) my discrimination of the property red may be ones that for the reader are associated with (or perhaps play a causal role in) her or his discrimination of cocoa flavour. If this possibility seems unlikely, given our closely similar neural structures, then one only has to think about those fish with their radically different visual systems. Their 'red' sensations are almost certainly not of the same type as ours. Yet whatever reasons we would have for thinking of our sensations as really red, an intelligent fish would have concerning that subset of its sensations.

Since 'red' sensations almost certainly do not form a natural kind, it is unlikely that one can 'read off' the sensation to form one's concept of the property or that the sensation is first named and then the property in the world. If 'red' sensations are tied to our discriminations of red, it is not by a conceptual, internal, link but at best by a causal link. But as the 'bad memory' case shows, causal links are quite different from conceptual ones. That sensations play a causal role in our discrimination of red, etc., is a very different claim from the much stronger, representational one that the Empiricist tradition wishes to maintain. In a later section of the paper I will present some cases that will raise the question of whether sensations are even causally necessary for visual discrimination and conception. And while I don't imagine that this colour case will convince everyone that sensations don't play the role envisioned for them by the Traditional Position, I hope the cumulative effect of all the arguments and examples I give in this paper will convince the reader.

2. To reinforce the colour case, let us consider one concerning pains. But when we consider this case, we part company to some degree with Reid; for Reid believed that pain states are primarily sensation states and nothing but that.(12) His thought was that holders of the Traditional Position were misled by considering pain states as a paradigm for perceptual states when pain states are not perceptual states at all. I, too, think that Traditional Position is mistaken – but not for the reasons that Reid does. I would agree with the Traditional Position that pain states are more like perceptual states than Reid believed, but I would disagree both with it and with Reid by denying that pain states are essentially sensation states. I think Reid's mistake arises from considering perceptual states too narrowly. Rather than there being two elements, cognition and sensation, in any perceptual experience, there are really

four, the other two being an <u>affective</u> state or states
(liking/disliking, among others) <u>and a behavioural</u> state or
states. For want of a better word, let me call the
combination of cognitive–affective–behavioural states an
<u>attitude</u>. I want to maintain that perceptual states are
<u>primarily</u> attitudinal states, not sensation states. I think
the previous sorts of examples support this view for vision,
and that the examples to come will support my view for pains.

Consider the case of patients in pain who are given
morphine or the case of some patients who are given
prefrontal lobotomies. Such patients fail to show the usual
behavioural and affective responses to pain. Lobotomy
patients fail to avoid painful situations and morphine
patients no longer writhe and groan. Yet both will report
that they have pains in this situation. However, most
remarkably, they say that these pains don't hurt.(13) Now we
have a lot of intuitions about pains. We believe we know
several necessary truths about pains; yet these intuitions
come into conflict in these cases. Among these are intuitions
such as that each person is in the best position to know if
he or she is in pain, that pains hurt, that one is in pain if
one has a pain sensation, that when one has pain – unless one
is being stoic – one behaves as if one is in pain, and so
forth. It seems impossible for all of these to be true in
these cases. How are we to understand such cases? Which
intuitions are we going to have to yield? The simplest
resolution of the dilemma, however surprising it may be, is
to maintain that the third intuition is wrong: one is not
necessarily in pain if one has the sensations one normally
has when one is in pain. Certainly that pains <u>hurt</u> is usually
considered the single most important fact about them. Much of
our morality hinges on that fact. And it is because of that
fact that we are inclined to say that the sensation is the
most important element in pain. Yet here are cases of people
who say they have the pain sensation but these sensations do
not hurt. What these cases illustrate is that the hurt of
pain is best taken, not as a sensory phenomenon but as an
affective one. Again, as with colour vision, it is the
attitude that is primary, not the sensation. These patients
call the sensations they are having 'pains' because they are
the kinds of sensations that either used to, or normally do,
accompany their pains. They have no other names for them.
These sensations got their names from the attitudes, not <u>vice
versa</u>. Thus, the corrected description of these patients <u>is
that</u> they have the sensations that normally accompany their
pains but do not have the pains. This is an unusual situation

for human beings, but its existence has much to say about the normal cases and how we name our perceptual experiences.

It has been found in laboratory experiments that different ethnic groups respond differently to different pain-inducing stimuli. Nordics, for example, will say they are in pain only at a higher level of stimulus than Mediterraneans. However, both groups have the same level of sensation awareness. That is, neither group feels any sensation until a certain level of stimulus is applied; and they both feel one at just that level. But they differ as to the level at which their experience is described as painful.(14) Given the neurological and (I would add, somewhat controversially) genetic similarity, and given the existence of the same sensation threshold, it is reasonable to infer that these people feel similar sensations throughout the experiment. It is just that for some of these people pain occurs only at a higher level of stimulation. But if so, it is not the sensation which constitutes the pain. For if I am right, these people have the same sensation when one of them is in pain and one is not.

Finally, consider the variety of sensations we do call painful. What do all of these share in common other than the attitudinal state? We tend to think of pain sensations as some monolithic kind of experience, but the only way it is the same is in the attitude, not in the sensations. Again, it is because we take certain attitudes that we call just these sensations 'pain sensations'. As the above cases show, we need not take those attitudes to these sensations. Sensations I associate as painful need not be ones which, if you had sensations just like them, you would find painful. Again, given that there seems to be, if current pain theorists like Melzack, Wall, and Sternbach are correct, a large neocortical input into human pain experience (and not just in the response to the pain already experienced, though that too),(15) and given that most non-primates have undeveloped neocortices, it is highly unlikely that the sensations of these animals are similar to our own. But surely they are in pain. And that is because they take certain attitudes, not because they have certain kinds of sensations. Our moral concern for these animals should not ride on the question of whether their sensations are really like ours. Their attitudes in the face of certain events are like ours, and that is all we need to know. Thus, even in that most paradigm of cases where sensations should matter most, we find that they do not matter most. Just as with 'red' sensations, there is no natural kind that can be labelled 'pain' sensations. Our concept of pain arises at a different level from that of the sensations associated with (or which cause) pains. Like Reid, I am unable to say how perceptions (our non-inferential perceptual beliefs) come about or to account for the concepts contained in them; but, like Reid once more, I am convinced that the Traditional Position cannot provide answers to such questions, and it is time we recognized it.

3. One final sort of case drives a deeper wedge between perceiving and sensing, and thus lends further support to Reid's general thesis that sensations are not the primary element in perceptual experience. At the same time, however, it calls into question Reid's weakly argued assertion that all perceptual experience, and therefore especially perceptual beliefs, must be conscious, or stronger, self-conscious. While he maintains that the perceptual processes that result in the belief are not introspectible, he believes that the belief itself is and must be.(16) I would agree with him that when perceptual beliefs are conscious we do not usually have access to the processes that brought about these beliefs, but I would deny his view that the perceptual beliefs must themselves be conscious; and the following sort of cases will support my denial.

We know that when split-brain subjects have pictures flashed to their left field of view, they deny seeing them; yet their left hand will immediately afterward reach out and grasp the pictured object. When asked why he or she picked up the object, the person will be perplexed as to his or her own motivations, shrugging the shoulders or inventing some reason. In more sophisticated cases the person is given the instruction to pick out a picture of an object only conceptually related to the object pictured in the tachistoscope. Thus, flashed a picture of a cherry, the person should pick up a picture of an apple, rather than one of a hat or a boat or a horse. For instance, Michael Gazzaniga reports a case of a patient who had a picture of a chicken flashed to his right field of view and one of a snowscene flashed to his left field of view. With his right hand he picked up a picture of a chicken coop and, when asked, said he had seen a picture of a chicken. Asked why he had a picture of a snow shovel in his left hand, he answered without hesitation, 'You need a shovel to shovel out the chicken coop'.(17) Despite the rational appeal of his reply, we are much more certain that he picked up that picture for another reason: although he did not realize it, he had seen a

picture of a snowscene. Here is a case of a person's seeing,
and there is absolutely no good evidence that the subject had
anything like the appropriate visual sensations, that his
right brain is even capable of bringing about, on its own,
such sensations. Some might say he must have had such
sensations if he saw anything, but the only reason I can see
for saying that is one's belief in what I called the
Traditional Position. Here is a case of seeing – fairly
sophisticated seeing – occurring despite the total absence of
anything like the appropriate sensations. If seeing can occur
without visual sensations, then why should we think that it
is the sensation kind which determines the perceptual kind?
Surely here is dramatic evidence that it is the other way
round.

Now one can question whether this is seeing at all. But
why would one raise such a question, other than one's
intuition that the Traditional Position is the correct view?
After all, if the patient's eyes were not open, if they
were not in good working condition, if the light were not on,
etc., this information would not have been received by the
subject. One can, of course, decide not to call this process
'seeing' – as long as one realizes it is a decision and not
an a priori truth. And however one decides, if that decision
is not to be merely arbitrary, one needs to provide reasons
for it.

Although allowing such cases to be instances of seeing,
one might claim that this is such an unusual case that it
cannot shed light on normal cases. But I think that claim is
mistaken for two reasons. First, given the sophisticated
visual processing the right brain is capable of and given the
very different eye–brain systems of non–primate animals, it
is conceivable that these animals receive information through
their eyes even though they have no visual sensations. Surely
we would not want to deny that animals see, even if it turned
out to be the case that they have no visual sensations. Of
course, whether animals have such sensations or not is a
factual, not an a priori matter. If we agree that animals see
and can conceive that nevertheless they do not have visual
sensations, then there are plenty of normal cases of seeing
that might not involve sensations and this possible fact
indicates that perceptual states cannot be essentially
sensation states nor take their names from them.

Though normal human perceptual states do involve
sensations, the unusual cases cited do shed light even on

these. In conjunction with the other anomalous cases of colour and pain perception, they suggest that perceptual states are not essentially sensation states, that different (or no) sensations can be involved in different perceptual states. And, suggesting this, they suggest that we were misled into thinking sensations had the essential role in perception by the fact that in normal human perception sensations seem to be there without fail (though even this claim is more suspect than one might think).(18) What these unusual cases suggest is that same–perceptual–state/different–sensation–states, same–sensation–state/different–perceptual–states, and perceptual states without sensation states at all, are all possible and do in fact occur. Whatever the role of sensations in perceptions, it is a much different and less central role than was thought by the Traditional Position. If one of our reasons for rejecting a Behaviouristic account of perceptual states is that the same behaviour is possible even though the perceptual state does not occur and the perceptual state can occur even though different behaviour occurs, then we have exactly that sort of reason for denying that perceptual states are essentially sensation states or even that sensation states are essential to perceptual states. Sensation states do not give their names to perceptual states but take their names from them. Sensation states are not the same as belief states, nor does one 'read off' from the former to achieve the latter. Those denials are the conclusions we should draw from these cases and from the many like them. Whatever errors of detail Reid made, and the second and third sorts of cases suggested that there are some, his general thesis is correct: sensations are not primary in perception. Sensations are neither beliefs themselves, nor can they account for the concepts and perceptions we have of the world.

NOTES

(*) I would like to thank Edward Johnson for helpful comments made on earlier drafts of this paper.

(1) And Berkeley comes close to this claim, but Berkeley also has 'notions'. It is not at all clear that Locke, who in some sense initiates Empiricism, would have agreed with Hume in any way on this issue.

(2) "That a strong belief and a weak belief differ only in degree, I can easily comprehend; but that belief and no belief should differ only in degree, no man can believe who understands what he speaks..." in **IP**, III, vii (<u>Works</u>, p. 359). Compare also <u>Works</u>, pp. 228, 291 and 357.

(3) "In what manner the notion of external objects, and the immediate belief of their existence, is produced by means of our senses, I am not able to shew, and I do not pretend to shew. If the power of perceiving external objects in certain circumstances, be a part of the original constitution of the human mind, all attempts to account for it will be vain." **IP**, II, v (<u>Works</u>, p. 260). Compare also <u>Works</u>, pp. 246, 248, 253–257, 309, 326, 327, 341 and 354.

(4) "In original perception, the signs are the various sensations which are produced by the impressions made upon our organs". **IP**, II, xxi (<u>Works</u>, p. 332). Also <u>Works</u>, pp. 310, 312, 331–2, 450 and 490.

(5) "...no sensation can give us the <u>conception</u> of material things, far less any argument to prove their existence." **IP**, II, xvi (<u>Works</u>, p. 313).

(6) See **IP**, II, xvi (<u>Works</u>, pp. 310–313, especially pp. 310–11).

(7) This example is from Hurvich (1981, pp. 256–257).

(8) <u>Ibid.</u>, p. 138.

(9) Reid recognizes this difference. See I, VI, xiv (<u>Works</u>, pp. 166–7).

(10) That Reid agrees that sensations take their names from

the perception rather than <u>vice</u> <u>versa</u> can be seen over and over again: "Almost all our perceptions have corresponding sensations which accompany them, and, on that account, are very apt to be confounded with them. Hence it happens, that a quality perceived, and the sensation corresponding to that perception, often go under the same name." **IP**, II, xvi (<u>Works</u>, p. 310). Compare also <u>Works</u>, pp. 229, 240, 265, 310–312 and 315.

(11) J.J.C. Smart, 'Sensations and Brain Processes', reprinted in V.C. Chappell, ed. (1962, p. 167).

(12) "Pain of every kind is an uneasy sensation." **IP**, I, i (<u>Works</u>, p. 229). Compare also <u>Works</u>, pp. 222, 280 and 310–311.

(13) See Ronald Melzack and Patrick D. Wall (1983, p. 168). Also in Ronald Melzack (1973, p. 95).

(14) Melzack, p.25; Melzack and Wall, pp. 30–31.

(15) Melzack, p.103; Melzack and Wall, pp.167–169; also see Richard Sternbach (1968). See especially Chapter 9.

(16) "...and to speak of a perception of which we are not conscious is to speak without any meaning." **IP**, II, xv (<u>Works</u>, p. 308). Compare also <u>Works</u>, pp. 223–4; 231; 242–3; 306 and 312.

(17) Gazzaniga (1977, p. 236).

(18) Gazzaniga argues for instance that even in normal people the corpus callosum is able to transfer only a small part of the information received by the right brain to the verbal, self-conscious left brain. Ibid., p.242.

A.E. Pitson


## SENSATION, PERCEPTION AND REID'S REALISM


In both An Inquiry into the Human Mind and also Essays on the
Intellectual Powers Reid provides accounts of the nature of
perception. There is a striking divergence of opinion amongst
commentators as to the way in which these accounts should be
understood.(1) I should like to consider some of the issues
of interpretation which arise here by reference to a recently
published article which claims that the Inquiry and
Intellectual Powers accounts of perception are interestingly
different.(2) In this article John Immerwahr tries to show
that while the direct realist interpretation of the
Intellectual Powers is correct, the theory of the Inquiry is
indirect realism. I shall argue, in opposition to this, that
there is a clear continuity between Reid's two accounts of
perception; and this will involve disputing, in particular,
what Immerwahr has to say about the Inquiry.

It seems possible that part of the explanation for the
differing interpretations of Reid lies with the unclarity of
the distinction between direct and indirect realism.
Consider, for example, the way in which Immerwahr formulates
this distinction:

> By direct realism I mean the theory that we are
> directly aware of external objects and that we know
> them without requiring an awareness of mental
> entities which act as cognitive links informing us
> of an external world. Indirect realism holds that we
> are directly aware only of certain mental entities
> (call them sensa) from which the mind makes some
> kind of inference or other mental transition to the
> existence of an external world.(3)

It becomes clear that the 'mental entities' to which
Immerwahr refers in his characterisation of both direct and
indirect realism are what Reid calls sensations. A problem
which then arises concerns the claim that Reid's theory in
the Intellectual Powers is direct realism. For, contrary to
Immerwahr, sensation remains there a causally necessary part

*M. Dalgarno and E. Matthews (eds.), The Philosophy of Thomas Reid, 79–90.*
© *1989 by Kluwer Academic Publishers.*

of perception, as we shall see. If direct realism denies that awareness of sensation plays any part in perceptual knowledge of the external world  then Reid can  never be credited  with such a  theory.  On  the  other hand,  the  indirect  realist interpretation of the Inquiry might also be questioned, in so far as it commits Reid  to the existence of sensa from  which the existence of an external world is meant to be inferred. I will begin, then,by considering what  Reid has to say in  the Inquiry about the relation between sensation and perception.

One of the matters to which Reid refers in the Inquiry is the nature of the perceptual state involved in, for  example, seeing or touching something. It seems clear that he  equates this state with the conception and belief of the existence of what is perceived.(4)  What part does  sensation play in  the acquisition of a state of this kind? The answer is  that, for Reid, sensation is one of the 'ingredients' which make up the causal process in  which the  perception of external  objects consists.(5)  The object makes some impression upon the organ of sense, either directly or via an appropriate medium  (such as rays of light, in the case of vision); this  impression,in turn, affects both the nerves and, ultimately, the brain; and the impression is followed by  a sensation which, in its  own turn,  is  followed  by  perception  of  the  object.  It  is important to recognise that  this account of perception  does not in itself support  Immerwahr's interpretation, for it  is consistent with  the  view that  in  perception one  is  made directly aware  of  physical objects  by  means  of  a  causal sequence of the kind described. What, then, is the basis  for this interpretation? It appears to lie in the claim that, for Reid, sensations  are  the  direct objects  of  awareness  in perception; while by comparison  the external world is  known only indirectly,  as that  which is  signified by  sensation. Surprisingly, Immerwahr says little, if anything, in  support of this  claim;  and, indeed,  there  seems good  reason  for rejecting it, as I will now try to show.

Consider, first, the claim that, for Reid, sensations are objects of direct awareness. Does this fairly represent  what Reid has to say  about sensation? It  is true that Reid  does sometimes  appear  to treat  sensations  as  objects  of (perceptual) awareness.(6)  But when he addresses himself directly to the  question of  the relation between sensation and perception, he explicitly  rejects the kind of view  that Immerwahr's interpretation requires.(7) If Reid is thought to be unclear on this point, it may be no more than a reflection of the  ambiguity  of the  notion  of sensation.  Reid's  own example of the case of smell illustrates this ambiguity. The sensation of smell might be taken to refer to what is experienced when one smells a rose or a lily; or it might be taken to refer to the experience itself. In either case, the sensation exists only as a feature of a mind or sentient being.(8) This ambiguity is perhaps an especially obvious feature of pain. For it seems evident that one may talk of pain either as <u>what</u> is felt or experienced, or as the feeling itself. What Immerwahr's interpretation apparently requires is that Reid should identify sensations, as they are involved in perception, with <u>objects</u> of experience to be distinguished from awareness of them. Reid's treatment of pain, as an instance of both sensation and perception, should therefore provide a test case for the correctness or otherwise of the indirect realist interpretation. What Reid has to say amounts to this:

> The same mode of expression is used to denote sensation and perception; and, therefore, we are apt to look upon them as things of the same nature. Thus, <u>I feel a pain; I see a tree</u>: the first denoteth a sensation, the last a perception. The grammatical analysis of both expressions is the same: for both consist of an active verb and an object. But, if we attend to the things signified by these expressions, we shall find that, in the first, the distinction between the act and the object is not real but grammatical; in the second, the distinction is not only grammatical but real.
>
> The form of the expression, <u>I feel pain</u>, might seem to imply that the feeling is something distinct from the pain felt; yet, in reality, there is no distinction. As <u>thinking a thought</u> is an expression which could signify no more than <u>thinking</u>, so <u>feeling a pain</u> signifies no more than <u>being pained</u>. What we have said of pain is applicable to every other mere sensation.(9)

Reid's considered view, then, is that we should not regard pain – or any other sensation – as the object of a mental act of sensation or perception. It might be argued that to say that there is no real distinction between act and object in this case leaves open the possibility that sensation has an object which is not, however, distinct from the sensation of which it is an object.(10) But Reid's equation between feeling a pain and being pained surely reflects an adverbial

account, in contrast to one which represents sensation as
comprising both act and object.(11) The example of pain
provides a model for Reid's account of the relation of
sensation to perception in general. For, according to Reid,
pain is a sensation which "by our constitution, gives a
perception of some particular part of the body, whose
disorder causes the uneasy sensation".(12) There is no
suggestion here that the experience of pain involves
awareness only of a 'mental entity' from which we arrive at
perception of its cause by some form of mental transition.

Immerwahr's interpretation of Reid's position in the
Inquiry emphasises the role of sensations as 'signs' by which
perception, in the form of conception and belief, is
'suggested'. Clearly we are meant to suppose that sign and
thing signified constitute, for Reid, different objects of
awareness. Now the question of how we should understand
Reid's theory of signs, and his use of the notion of
suggestion, is a topic worthy of detailed consideration in
its own right.(13) My own view is that when Reid says that
perception arises from sensation, and that the operation
involved is one of suggestion, he is referring to the fact
that there is a causal – as opposed, for example, to an
inferential – relation between the two. The point of speaking
of sensations as signs in this context is that perception is,
after all, a cognitive state of affairs: we are provided in
this way with information about the external world as the
object of which we are directly aware. It is, in any case,
sufficient for my purpose to establish that Reid's doctrine
of sensations as signs in the Inquiry does not have to be
understood in accordance with Immerwahr's interpretation. An
important context for Reid's doctrine is his discussion of
what we should now call perceptual constancy:

> The original appearance which the colour of an
> object makes to the eye, is a sensation for which we
> have no name, because it is used merely as a sign,
> and is never made an object of attention in common
> life: but this appearance, according to the
> different circumstances, signifies various things.
> If a piece of cloth, of one uniform colour, is laid
> so that part of it is in the sun, and part in the
> shade, the appearance of colour, in these different
> parts, is very different: yet we perceive the colour
> to be the same; we interpret the variety of
> appearance as a sign of light and shade, and not as
> a sign of real difference in colour. But if the eye

could be so far deceived as not to perceive the
difference of light in the two parts of the cloth,
we should, in that case, interpret the variety of
appearance to signify a variety of colour in the
parts of the cloth.(14)

What is the sensation, or 'original appearance', to which
Reid is referring here? It seems clear that he is talking
about the colour which an object looks or appears to have in
what may be described as the phenomenological sense of these
notions.(15) In other words, this is a matter of the
appearance(s) which the object presents as an item in one's
visual field rather than one's belief as to the actual colour
of the object. This latter belief is a product of the way in
which the object appears phenomenologically – in Reid's
terms, the colour of the object is signified by the sensation
of appearance. The point about perceptual constancy is that
there is a sense in which the object may genuinely be said to
appear the same colour (namely, in what has been described as
the epistemic sense)(16) even though there is variation in
the way it appears phenomenologically, to the extent, even,
where this variation may not be consciously noticed.

Now the kind of sensation or appearance to which Reid has
referred here as a sign is not, as Immerwahr's interpretation
demands, a mental entity with the status of a sensum. The
colour which an object appears phenomenologically to be is
something which is available to the experience of different
perceivers even if, as Reid notes, it is not normally made an
object of attention. Colour constancy is a feature of the way
in which this kind of appearance is interpreted. It is true
that Reid does sometimes talk of visual appearances in terms
which seem to suggest that they are a kind of private object:
as, for example, when he refers to their being
two-dimensional.(17) But consideration of the kind of example
Reid has in mind - namely, that of perspective - should help
to make his position clear. We are frequently reminded by
philosophers of perception that a circular object like a
plate will sometimes appear, in the phenomenological sense,
elliptical. But the elliptical appearance presented by a
plate when viewed from an angle is a perfectly objective
phenomenon which may be captured in a painting (or
photograph) and this is, I believe, the purport of Reid's
remark that "the visible figure of bodies is a real and
external object to the eye, as their tangible figure is to
the touch".(18) In fact, I think it is misleading to
interpret Reid as saying that visible figure is a kind of

object in its own right, as Duggan apparently does.(19)  When
we look at the  plate from an  angle, it appears  elliptical:
this is the appearance it presents phenomenologically or,  in
Reid's terms, its visible figure.  But it is not really  true
that we perceive  an object which  is elliptical; rather,  as
Reid himself says,  "a circle seen  obliquely will appear  an
ellipse".(20) In other words, while the elliptical appearance
presented by the plate  in these circumstances is, for  Reid,
an objective feature of  perception, it is not an  additional
object of perception.

     It is perhaps worth  adding that Cummins'  interpretation
of Reid  also  goes astray  on  this crucial  point.  Cummins
notes(21) that in taking account of perspective as a  feature
of visual perception, direct realism must make allowance  for
the different perceptual experiences  involved in viewing  an
object like  a coin  from  different positions.  But he  also
suggests  that  for  the  direct  realist  committed  to  the
existence  of  the  objects  of  perception  "the  difference
concerns the objects of perception", something circular  when
the coin appears circular,  and something elliptical when  it
appears elliptical.  This might  be  thought to  amount to  a
reductio ad absurdum of direct realism. But we should ask, in
any case, why the different  shapes presented by the coin  in
these circumstances must be represented as perceptual objects
in their own right, rather than merely different  appearances
of the  same object  (i.e. in the  phenomenological sense  of
'appearance'). Cummins' response to this approach seems to be
that it involves "a new and surprising category of property",
namely, the look of a thing. But there is nothing  mysterious
about this  notion so  long  as we  avoid the  temptation  to
assume, as Cummins appears to do, that the look or appearance
of a  thing  must be  regarded  as an  additional  object  of
perception.

     We saw  earlier that  sensation is  often represented  by
Reid  as  a  subjective  aspect  of  perception:  a  mental
'ingredient'  of  the  causal  process  which  is  ordinarily
involved in perception.  The notion  of appearance  is  also
sometimes used  by Reid  to  refer to  a  feature  of  the
perceiver's state of  mind: as, for  example, in his  comment
that "It is impossible to  know whether a scarlet colour  has
the same appearance to me which it hath to another man".(22)
We have seen already, however, that this does not, in itself,
justify the  claim that sensations,  or appearances in  the
'subjective'  sense,  form  the only  direct  objects  of
perception in the Inquiry. What Reid has said indicates  only

that sensation is necessary for a perceptual state like seeing, and this is true also, for example, of the material impressions involved. So while sensation may suggest (or signify) something external – a quality of the object perceived – to the extent that it is constantly conjoined with perception of that quality, this is not to say that the sensation is itself an object of perception. To repeat: the part played by sensation in the Inquiry is that of a condition which is causally necessary for the occurrence of a perceptual state in the form of conception and belief.

Immerwahr's claim about the development of Reid's realism depends crucially upon establishing not only that sensations function in the Inquiry as objects of direct awareness, but also that their role in the Intellectual Powers is "drastically altered".(23) Thus, he notes that Reid sometimes speaks in the Inquiry of sensation as being followed by perception, whereas in the Intellectual Powers he characterizes them in terms of the one being accompanied by the other.(24) This, Immerwahr suggests, reflects the shift from indirect realism to a form of direct realism. In fact, however, the language employed in these works, to characterize the relation between sensation and perception, does not involve any marked difference of expression. Reid makes it clear in the Inquiry that sensation gives rise to perception 'immediately'(25) and there are, after all, many contexts in which to say that A is accompanied by B is quite consistent with saying also that A is immediately followed by B. In addition, there are various passages in the Intellectual Powers which echo Reid's treatment in the Inquiry of the connection between sensation and perception, for example:

> We know that, when certain impressions are made upon our organs, nerves, and brain, certain corresponding sensations are felt, and certain objects are both conceived and believed to exist. But in this train of operations nature works in the dark.(26)

And, in regard to the perception of things by touch, Reid says later "By the constitution of my nature, the sensation carries along with it the conception and belief of a round hard body really existing in my hand".(27)

The important point is that Reid, in picking out the various items in the sequence which goes to make up the causal process of perception, is simply attempting to

identify the physical, physiological, and psychological
conditions which obtain when a person perceives something.
There is no doubt that for Reid perception is a mental – as
opposed to physical – state, in particular a cognitive one
involving conception and belief. But it is also a _sentient_
state, as the references to sensation and appearance are
meant to remind us. Hence the remark that "The external
senses have a double province – to make us feel, and to make
us perceive".(28) We are sentient beings who also have the
faculty of acquiring information about our environment by
means of our senses. For human beings, then, perception
always occurs in the form of a sentient state.(29) Thus
Immerwahr is simply mistaken when he says(30) that in the
_Intellectual Powers_ sensation is no longer a causally
necessary part of perception. There is, however, no logical
necessity about the connection between sensation and
perception:

> For anything we can discover, we might have been so
> framed as to have all the sensations we now have by
> our senses, without any impressions upon our organs,
> and without any conception of any external object.
> For anything we know, we might have been so made as
> to perceive external objects, without any
> impressions on bodily organs, and without any of
> those sensations which invariably accompany
> perception in our present frame.(31)

This explains why, in the _Intellectual Powers_, Reid defines
perception, as such, in terms of conception and belief. But
Reid's accounts of the relation between sensation and
perception in both the _Inquiry_ and the _Intellectual Powers_
serve to show that a state of sensory awareness ('sensation')
is causally necessary for perception.

While I have rejected Immerwahr's view of the relation
between the _Inquiry_ and _Intellectual Powers_ accounts of
perception, I would not want to claim that there is no
difference between them. It is clear, for example, that they
are directed towards different kinds of question about the
nature of perception. Thus, in the _Inquiry_ Reid is mainly
concerned with the nature of perception as a causal process;
while in the _Intellectual Powers_ he is concerned, rather,
with the analysis of the concept of a perceptual state like
seeing.(32) But when we consider these accounts from
Immerwahr's perspective – i.e. where what is in question is
Reid's view of the objects of direct awareness in perception

— it is difficult to find any justification for the claim that there is a radical difference between them. One may agree with Immerwahr that there is discernible development in Reid's philosophy, for the later of his major works reflects a closer concern with conceptual issues about perception. In the Intellectual Powers Reid confesses that on the question of how we perceive external objects he has no theory to offer.(33) What Immerwahr fails to establish, however, is that sensation ceases to play the same role that it did in the Inquiry and therefore that Reid has provided us with two different accounts of perception. As for the view that emerges from these accounts, it amounts to something like the following: when a person is correctly described as perceiving (seeing, hearing, etc.) there is an object involved;(34) the person's state is both sentient and cognitive, involving the presence of sensation (or appearance), conception and, normally, belief; and this complex state involves direct awareness of an external object or, more precisely, some quality of that object.(35) This view of perception constitutes, I believe, a significant contribution in its own right to the philosophy of perception, representing an attempt to combine a cognitive element, of the kind stressed in epistemic theories of perception,(36) with an adverbial analysis of the sensory aspect which is the predominant concern of the Empiricist theory of perception. I am inclined to think that this account, or something like it, is fundamentally correct; but that is another, and much longer, story.

## NOTES

1    Thus, A. Woozley (introduction to his edition of the
Intellectual Powers) sees Reid as an indirect realist; Duggan
(introduction to his edition of the Inquiry) interprets Reid
as being, in general, a direct realist; and Cummins (1974)
represents Reid as being a direct realist in the Intellectual
Powers but does not consider directly the relation of this
work to the earlier Inquiry.

2    J. Immerwahr (1978).

3    Immerwahr, op.cit., p. 247.

4    I, V, iii (Works, p. 122); I, VI, xx (Works, p. 183).

5    I, VI, xxi.

6.    I, II, i–iii, passim.

7    I, II, vi (Works, p. 108).

8    I, VI, xx.

9    I, VI, xx (Works, pp. 182–3).

10   Cf. R.C. Sleigh, in Barker and Beauchamp (eds.) (1976,
p. 80).

11   This terminology occurs in T. Nagel (1965). See also  G.
Pitcher (1969).

12   I, VI, xii (Works, p. 159).

13   See, for example, P. Winch (1953, p. 320). Cf R.E.
Beanblossom (1975).

14   I, VI, xxiii (Works, pp. 193–4).

15   This terminology derives originally from R. Chisholm
(1957, ch.4). See also C.W.K. Mundle (1971, Ch.1); and F.
Jackson (1977, Ch.1).

16   See Chisholm, op.cit., Mundle, op.cit., and Jackson,
op.cit.

17 ' I, VI, iii (Works, p. 136).

18  I, VI, viii (Works, p. 146); cf. IP, II, xiv (Works, pp. 304–5).

19  Duggan, op.cit, p.xiv.

20  I, VI, ii (Works, p. 134). (my italics).

21  Cummins, op.cit., pp. 331–332.

22  I, VI, ii (Works, p. 134).

23  Immerwahr, op.cit., p. 248.

24  Ibid., pp. 248–249.

25  I, V, viii (Works, p. 131).

26  IP, II, xx (Works, p. 327) (my italics).

27  IP, VI, v (Works, p. 450).

28  IP, II, xvii (Works, p. 318). See also IP, II, xxi (Works, p. 330).

29  IP, II, xvi (Works, pp. 311, 312); II, xvii (Works, p. 318).

30  Immerwahr, op.cit., p. 249.

31  IP, II, xx (Works, p. 327).

32  Cf. D. Tebaldi, in Barker and Beauchamp, op.cit., p. 28.

33  IP, II, xv (Works, p. 309).

34  In other words, Reid is apparently committed to denying the view that there is such a thing as 'intransitive' seeing where, for example, a person may be described simply as seeing, without seeing anything in particular. Cf. G. Warnock, in Swartz (ed.) (1965, pp. 66–67); and Sibley, in Sibley (ed.) (1971, p. 108).

35  On this last point see, for example, IP, II, xvii (Works, p. 313).

36   See, for   example,   D.M.   Armstrong   (1961,   Ch.9),   and
(1968, Ch.10); and G.Pitcher (1971).

Aaron Ben-Zeev


# REID'S OPPOSITION TO THE THEORY OF IDEAS


Reid directs his main criticism against what he terms the
'Theory of Ideas', i.e., an indirect, representational view
of the mind. I will examine whether Reid does indeed abandon
the basic assumptions underlying this theory: the
substantive nature of the mind, the causal theory of
perception, and the indirect nature of perception. After
showing that Reid does reject those general assumptions, I
shall explore Reid's alternative to them.


## I

Reid's criticism of the theory of ideas is directed against
the conception of the mind as a storage of internal entities
representing the external objects. According to Reid,(1) the
three basic contentions of the theory of ideas are: (a) the
soul has its seat in the brain, (b) there are images formed
in the brain of all the objects of sense and (c) the soul
does not immediately perceive external objects, except by
means of those images. Without examining the thoughts of the
historical figures regarded by Reid as having maintained the
theory, we can assert that these contentions are based upon
three general philosophical assumptions shared by many
philosophers: (a) the substantive nature of the mind, (b)
the causal theory of perception, and (c) the indirect nature
of perception. I shall now examine Reid's attitude toward
these assumptions.

The substantive nature of the mind is an important
constituent of the traditional theory of ideas. The theory
ascribes to the mind substantive features such as internal
entities and storage for them. This description is evident
in the following passage from Locke:

> the understanding is not much unlike a closet wholly
> shut from light, with only some little openings
> left, to let in external visible resemblances, or
> ideas of things without; would the picture coming
> into such a dark room but stay there, and lie so
> orderly as to be found upon occasion, it would very

91

M. Dalgarno and E. Matthews (eds.), The Philosophy of Thomas Reid, 91–101.
© 1989 by Kluwer Academic Publishers.

much resemble the understanding of a man.(2)

If the mind is an internal entity – or composed of such entities – it cannot be in direct contact with external objects; as Locke says, it can directly know only "visible resemblances or ideas of things". The mind is described in passive and mechanistic terms in such a substantive, or container view. The natural predicates for describing the mind in this view are essentially mechanical: the entities are stored, or lie orderly in the internal storage and then are moved to the centre (when we attend to them) or to the periphery (when not in use).

Reid, on the other hand, has a dynamic conception of the mind: the mind "is, from its very nature, a living and active being".(3) The mind consists of powers, i.e., faculties, capacities, habits and dispositions. Reid (4) claims that when the mind is thought to consist of impressions, as the theory of ideas assumes, it is very passive, whereas he is of the opinion that the mind consists of mental acts such as sensation, imagination, memory, and judgment, and therefore is very active.

Mental acts or powers are not internal parts of an organism, but properties of the whole organism. Consequently, Reid does not have to locate mental properties within the depths of the brain. He is even careful to point out that when we speak about things in the mind we refer to things of which the mind is the subject. The "distinction between things in the mind and things external, is not meant to signify the place of the things we speak of, but their subject".(5) Since mental properties are not internal entities, but properties of a whole organic system, the internal–external dichotomy, which is at the basis of the theory of ideas, does not arise.

The second important feature of the theory of ideas is the causal relation between physiological and mental entities and in particular the causal relation between physiological processes and mental percepts as assumed in the causal theory of perception. When the mind is an entity as the body is, it is natural to assume that the relation between them is causal. The internal location of the mental entity is also compatible with this causal relation. The mind is here like an internal part of the body and as such it interacts with other internal parts.

In his earlier work, Inquiry into the Human Mind, Reid did not as yet realize the close connection between the theory of ideas and the causal theory of perception. He thought that the relation between physiological and mental events is unknown, though a causal relation is not excluded by him:

> But how are the sensations of the mind produced by impressions upon the body? Of this we are absolutely ignorant, having no means of knowing how the body acts upon the mind, or the mind upon the body.(6)

Nevertheless, in a manner that recalls the language of the causal theory of perception, Reid remarks that:

> Our perception of objects is the result of a train of operations; some of which affect the body only, others affect the mind.(7)

Notwithstanding his claim that "we are absolutely ignorant" of the relation between physiological and mental events, Reid uses a causal terminology in this work.

In his mature work, Essays on the Intellectual Powers of Man, Reid accepts the physical part of the causal chain in perception and describes it as consisting of a physical object, a sense organ, a nerve, and the brain.(8) However, he seems to reject the causal theory of perception. Here also he does not know the relation between physiological and mental events, but he knows that it is certainly not a causal one. Thus he observes that "it is too absurd to admit ... that, in perception, an impression is made upon the mind as well as upon the organ, nerves, and brain" or "to think that the impressions of external objects upon the machine of our bodies can be the real efficient cause of thought and perception".(9) Reid agrees that the physical causal chain and perception conjoin, but denies that the former is the cause of the latter. Likewise, day and night "have been joined in a constant succession since the beginning of the world; but who is so foolish as to conclude from this that day is the cause of night, or night the cause of the following day?".(10) Reid maintains that an object, in being perceived, "does not act at all", and there is little reason to believe "that in perception the mind acts upon the object".(11)

Reid's opposition to the causal theory of perception, though not always very clear, is an important conceptual shift toward achieving his goal of refuting the theory of ideas. This opposition, however, is not accompanied by a positive account. Reid sees the difficulties in the causal theory of perception, but does not offer a real alternative to it. He concludes that we perceive "because God has given us the power of perceiving, and not because we have impressions from objects".(12) The causal theory and God are not the only shows in town.

II

In the preceding section I considered Reid's attitude toward two basic assumptions of the theory of ideas: the internal-storage view of the mind, and the causal theory of perception. In this section I shall examine Reid's attitude towards the third assumption of the theory of ideas: the indirect nature of the perceptual process. These three assumptions have direct implications for how we characterize the perceptual process. I shall therefore begin by considering these implications and then go on to examine whether they are present in Reid's own description of the perceptual process.

When the mind is assumed to be an internal entity, it cannot be in direct contact with external objects, and must only know them through internal mental entities representing them:

> Percepts are in our heads, for they come at the end of a causal chain of physical events leading, spatially, from the object to the brain of the percipient.(13)

Accordingly, there should be a perceptual stage which is the first mental stage on the physical-mental chain, and as such is the result of physiological, but not mental, causes. Hence, contributions which are due to typical mental characteristics of the agent - e.g., the agent's memory, motivation, emotions, and moods - are absent in this stage. Since these characteristics seem to exist in everyday perception, one has to assume the existence of two perceptual stages: sensation and perception. After the stage of sensation, the causal chain continues with inferential processes which interpret the sensory raw materials and which result in the stage of everyday perception. Perception, then, is indirect. This is indeed the prevailing formulation of the distinction between sensation and perception. (14)

Postulating a stage of pure sensation which precedes the perceptual stage is supposed to bridge the gap, created in the theory of ideas, between internal mental entities and external physical objects. Although sensations are determined by physical events, they already exhibit some primitive mental features. These features do not require the typical active and complex operations of the mind; hence they can be regarded as mediators between the physical and the mental realms. The role of sensation as an intermediate stage, or as a "boundary between the mental and the physical", is evident in Russell's (1921) position: "Sensations are what is common to the mental and physical worlds; they may be defined as the intersection of mind and matter".(15) And "those that have physical causes and mental effects we should define as 'sensations'".(16) The intermediate role of sensation is also connected with the causal theory of perception. An underlying principle in causal theories is that the effect cannot be greater than its cause. That is, there are no properties of the effect which were not, somehow, in the cause – since otherwise something would be produced out of nothing. This principle, as well as other considerations, raises the problem of how mental properties can be the effects of physical causes. Regardless of the solution to this problem, the difficulty is less severe when the effect is a very primitive mental stage – one which is devoid of complex, active mental contributions.

Although Reid is often regarded as the founder of the distinction between sensation and perception,(17) his opposition to the theory of ideas is not compatible with the traditional formulation of this distinction in which perception is indirect. In his earlier work, Reid's formulation of the sensation–perception distinction is still close to the traditional one. But in his mature work, Reid realizes the affinity between this formulation and the theory of ideas and revises the distinction in a way that is compatible with his criticism of that theory.

In order to make perception direct, the postulation of two perceptual stages – one of which (perception) deals with internal sense data (sensation) – has to be abolished. This is exactly what Reid does in his mature work. While in his earlier book, Inquiry into the Human Mind, Reid conceives of sensation and perception as separate stages – as posited in the traditional formulation - in his Essays on the Intellectual Powers of Man, sensation and perception are two aspects of the same experience. Thus, while in the Inquiry Reid says that "sensation is followed by the perception of the object",(18) in the Essays sensation and perception take place at the same time: "The perception and its corresponding sensation are produced at the same time".(19)

The same applies to the cognitive relation between sensation and perception. In the Inquiry this is the relation of suggestion which exists between two successive, separate stages: "a certain kind of sound suggests immediately to the mind, a coach passing in the street".(20) In the Essays sensation is not a separate stage preceding perception but a simultaneous aspect of it. It is the feeling dimension in the complex perceptual experience:

> The external senses have a double province - to make us feel, and to make us perceive. They furnish us with a variety of sensations, some pleasant, others painful, and others indifferent; at the same time, they give us a conception and an invincible belief of the existence of external objects.(21)

Similarly Reid writes:

> Our senses may be considered in two views: first, As they afford us agreeable sensations, or subject us to such as are disagreeable; and, secondly, As they give us information of things that concern us. (22)

It is not the case that we first have a stage of noninformative (meaningless) sensation after which, through a cognitive process such as reasoning, a stage of informative (meaningful) perception is reached. Rather, these are two simultaneous (but different) dimensions of the perceptual experience.

Reid's formulation of the sensation-perception distinction is different from the prevailing one. Reid has contributed more than anyone else to clarifying the importance of the distinction. But his own mature formulation - in accordance with his criticism of the theory of ideas - has not prevailed, since the representational view of the mind, of which the theory of ideas is a popular version, continues to prevail.(23)

In his mature view Reid correctly identifies the basic features of the theory of ideas and avoids them. Reid does not describe the mind as an internal entity, he rejects the causal theory of perception, and he does not assume the existence of mediating internal entities and processes such as sensations and reasoning processes.

So far I have pointed out that Reid does not incorporate into his own view the basic assumptions of the theory he criticizes. It remains to be seen whether he offers a real alternative to that theory.

## III

Does Reid have a positive alternative to the theory of ideas? It is clear that he has no detailed alternative to offer. He admits to not knowing an alternative to the causal theory of perception. But perhaps we can find a general outline for such an alternative in Reid's mature work.

In the substantive approach assumed by the theory of ideas, internal mental entities, such as ideas, have a central explanatory role. They explain the different contents at which mental acts are directed, the connection between mental acts and external objects, the storage of knowledge, the development of mental capacities, etc. Reid thinks that this use of 'idea' is "a mere fiction of philosophers".(24) The explanatory role of ideas should therefore be transferred to something else. I believe it is transferred to structural features, or, in Reid's terms, to features due to 'our constitution'.

When we consider the mind as a storage for internal entities, structural or relational features play a small role. This storage is usually indifferent to the internal entities stored within it; and these entities, which are by and large isolated things, are often indifferent to each other. Thus the addition of one idea or disappearance of another is a local event, usually affecting neither the structure of the mental storage nor the relations among the various ideas. The storage itself is not altered as a result of a change in the stored entities. All that happens is that the shelves in the storage are filled with more entities or emptied of some of them. A mental change here is not structural, but is a passive change in the quantity or content of the stored ideas.

In his manuscript 'Of Constitution' Reid argues:

> Everything that is made must have some  constitution
> ... from which all its qualities, appearances,
> powers and operations do result.(25)

The mental constitution  consists of  various powers such  as
reasoning, abstraction, memory,  the  senses,  taste,  moral
perception, the passions, and appetites.  It is

> A very important part  of our constitution that  all
> or most of these powers are capable of a high degree
> of improvement by being properly exercised.(26)

In this view, mental changes are structural since the  powers
which the  mental  system  consists  of  are  relational  and
dynamic properties  of  the whole  system.  A  change  in  a
certain power  of the  system  is expressed  in a  structural
change of the system's  behaviour.  It usually affects  other
powers as  well  as  the  structure  of  the  entire  system.
Powers, or  dispositions, are  not separate  things within  a
certain system;  they  are patterns  of behaviour.  One  does
not have a disposition in  the same sense that one has a  leg
or is  doing  something.   A mental  power,  like  a  mental
disposition, is a structural feature typical of a certain set
of one's behaviours.(27)

It seems, then, that in regard to the nature of the mind,
Reid indeed replaces the  substantive features of the  theory
of ideas with structural ones.  I shall now consider  whether
this is true in the case of the other two issues – namely the
causal theory  of  perception, and  the  sensation–perception
distinction.  I begin with the latter.

Reid's unique  formulation of  the  sensation–perception
distinction does  not  postulate  the  existence  of  internal
entities and  processes as does  the prevailing  formulation;
rather it is based upon structural features.  Thus, Reid says
that a perceptual belief is not based upon internal processes
such as reasoning  or association  from past experience,  but
"it is the result of our constitution, and of the  situations
in which  we  happen  to  be  placed".(28)   The  perceptual
judgment or belief,  "is not  got by comparing  ideas, it  is
included in the very nature of the perception".(29)  In  this
sense, perception is direct.(30)   Sensation is also  defined
by Reid as "an act of mind"(31) and not as an internal object
of a mental act.  As such it depends upon structural features

of the mental system. Consequently, sensation "is conjoined with perception", and with other acts of our minds, "by our constitution".(32)

Concerning the third issue, Reid does not have an alternative to the causal theory of perception, but we can suggest a structural account which is compatible with Reid's position concerning the other two issues: the paradigm of emergent properties.

The paradigm of emergent properties assumes that mental states emerge out of a certain complex organization of the physiological parts. The emergent properties are not separate in time or space from their underlying properties. In this sense the relation of emergence is different from causality: the cause is separate (often in both senses) from its effect. The emergent mental properties are properties of a structural whole. The part-whole relation is not a causal one, since something cannot be caused by one of its parts. A whole is not actually separated from its parts, as the causal relation requires; rather it belongs to a different level of description. Accordingly, there are no separate physiological and mental events: we can treat the same event as a physiological or a mental state. The paradigm of emergent properties is a structural one. It is the structure, the unique organization of the lower-level physical parts, which confers the new emergent mental properties.(33)

Combining the above three positions makes quite a plausible structural view of the mind. In this view the mind is an active system of various capacities. These are emergent properties of the whole organism and not internal parts of it. Accordingly, perception is not a contemplation of internal sensory data. Though this view in its entirety is not found in Reid's writings, it is compatible with his general approach. As such, Reid's approach is a very valuable step towards a real alternative to the theory of ideas and the Cartesian approach to the mind.

A. BEN-ZEEV

## NOTES

(1)  **IP**, II, iv (Works, p. 256).

(2)  Locke (1975, II, xi, 17).

(3)  **IP**, I, i (Works, p. 221).

(4)  I, II, x (Works, p. 115).

(5)  **IP**, I, i (Works, p. 221).

(6)  I, VI, xxi (Works, p. 187).

(7)  I, VI, xxi (Works, p. 186).

(8)  **IP**, II, ii (Works, p. 248).

(9)  **IP**, II, iv (Works, p. 253).

(10) Ibid.

(11) **IP**, II, xiv (Works, p. 301).

(12) **IP**, II, iv (Works, p. 257).

(13) Russell (1927, p. 320).

(14) Cf. Ben–Zeev and Strauss (1984); Ben–Zeev (1984).

(15) Russell (1921, p. 144).

(16) Russell (1921, p. 138).

(17) Cf. Herrnestein and Boring (1965, p. 172); Pastore (1971, p. 114).

(18) I, VI, xxi (Works, p. 186).

(19) **IP**, II, xvii (Works, p. 318).

(20) I, II, vii (Works, p. 111).

(21) **IP**, II, xvii (Works, p. 318).

(22) **IP**, II, xxi (Works, p. 330).

(23) Cf. Ben Zeev (1986a).

(24) **IP**, I, i (Works, p. 226).

(25) AUL MS 3061/8 'Of Constitution'.   I am   rateful to  A.
Sinclair of  the University  of Strathclyde  who provided  me
with a transcription of Reid's manuscript.

(26) Ibid.  Emphasis mine.

(27) Cf. Ryle (1949).

(28) **IP**, II, xxi (Works, p. 332).

(29) I, VII (Works, p. 209).

(30) Cf. Ben-Zeev (1988).

(31) **IP**, I, i (Works, p. 229).

(32) **IP**, II, xvi (Works, p. 310).

(33) Cf. Oatley (1978); Ben-Zeev (1986b).

Michel Malherbe

## THOMAS REID ON THE FIVE SENSES

Why the five senses? Like many other philosophers, Reid does not answer this question, because it is out of place: philosophy (which is the study of the human mind) has nothing to say about the senses, except that, as a matter of fact, they are five.

But a reader of Reid's work cannot dismiss the question, since the Inquiry follows the order of the five senses. And it is improbable that an author as aware as Reid would have chosen this plan, without any reason other than that of providing an easier introduction to his philosophy. At the very least, if he wants to account for the structure of the text, the commentator must try to clear up the part played by the senses, more especially as it disappears in The Essays on the Intellectual Powers of Man which follow the order of man's intellectual powers, the five senses being not, strictly speaking, one of these powers. And our claim is that the senses have a double office: at first, they serve, in Reid's strategy, as a critical means (which can easily be understood) against the theory of ideas; secondly, they play a more positive, but metaphysical, part, which is both indispensable and obscure to common sense philosophy.

I

The most immediate reason why Reid chose to take the senses as a guide is explainable by examining the first chapter of the Inquiry, where the theory of ideas and its sceptical consequences are exposed. The ideal system arose from the philosophy of Descartes who laid the foundations of the science of the human mind in the evidence of consciousness, and made ideas the only objects of this consciousness. Now, the clearness and distinctness of consciousness does not prove that it cannot be deceived; it is unable to warrant its ideas which, being mere representations, are creatures of the mind. Therefore, the only way to attain truth and to secure an inquiry into the human mind is common sense, so far as common sense proceeds from the determination of our consciousness by the constitution of our own nature. And, if

103

M. Dalgarno and E. Matthews (eds.), The Philosophy of Thomas Reid, 103–117.
© 1989 by Kluwer Academic Publishers.

the senses are not the noblest part of human nature, they are
doubtless the most natural part of it. Reid, then, by
following the order of the senses, maintains a clearly
critical view: the inquiry concerning the human mind must be
freed from the false pretences of the ideal system and rest
on principles and an order which nobody argues about, because
they belong to the original constitution of our nature.

The senses are not only the most natural, but also the
simplest principles of our constitution. Just as the
experimental knowledge of the body results from dissection,
so too philosophical knowledge must proceed through the
anatomy of the mind:

> All that we know of the body, is owing to anatomical
> dissection and observation, and it must be by an
> anatomy of the mind that we can discover its powers
> and principles.(1)

The experimental method requires an analysis which endeavours
to extract the simplest principles of the phenomena of the
mind, phenomena that philosophers restrict too quickly to
rational systems, without examining the most immediate facts
of our nature. And the senses are undoubtedly the most
primary and elementary principles:

> It is so difficult to unravel the operations of the
> human understanding, and to reduce them to their
> first principles, that we cannot expect to succeed
> in the attempt, but by beginning with the simplest,
> and proceeding by very cautious steps to the more
> complex. The five external senses may, for this
> reason, claim to be first considered in an analysis
> of the human faculties.(2)

Nevertheless, the senses are not the only original
principles, since the other faculties of the human mind show
the same simple and natural character. Reid's purpose is not,
as in Condillac's philosophy, to generate all the acts of the
understanding by composition and transformation of sensation:
even perception cannot be reduced to the process of the
senses. Therefore the prerogative of the senses does not
result from any elementary or atomic character, but from the
mode of evidence which belongs to them. Their evidence is
more immediate, more natural, than the evidence of other
faculties. By a pre-reflective knowledge, every man knows
that he has five senses and that these senses are the means

of his perception and his knowledge of the external world. The other powers of the mind are worked up by education and experience and too much involved in the action of knowledge for their operation to be grasped without the strain of reflection. And

> Reflection, the only instrument by which we can discern the powers of the mind, comes too late to observe the progress of nature, in raising them from their infancy to perfection.(3)

Therefore the evidence of the senses, of their number and their specific function, is pre-reflective and can be used as a thread for the analysis by which the human mind enters the understanding of itself. But the quality of this evidence is in itself a problem. For it succeeds in being free from obscurity and intrication of reflection, only because it is the evidence of the body to the mind. Its simplicity depends on the immediate certainty that we have about our own body. Thus, as clear as it may be, this evidence immediately gives rise to two languages: the sense will be considered now as the organ of the body, now as the operation of the mind (sensation). The specific function of hearing or sight will be ascribed here to the ear or the eye, there to sensations which are different in themselves.

The evidence of the senses, then, however original, rests on two distinct facts: the physical fact of our created nature; the subjective fact of sensible data (which Reid calls affection). And these two facts agree with two orders that should not be confused: not only there is no resemblance between organ and sensation, but we cannot even link them by causality, since the mental fact is as original as the sensorial fact; sensation, as such, showing itself as being "a simple and original affection or feeling of the mind, altogether inexplicable and unaccountable".(4) The original character of sensation for consciousness forbids us to consider the senses as more original principles which would explain sensation. Reid earnestly destroys one of the foundations of the idea-theory, the one which says that things could affect the mind by means of the senses and that there could be, due to the senses, a representation of things in the mind.

Now, the question being to inquire into the human mind and not into the physical and physiological processes, it is quite clear that, as soon as it is stated, the physical fact

is forgotten in favour of the mental fact, and the
distinction and order of the five senses is actually the
distinction and order of the five kinds of sensations. It
being agreed that sensations are not ideas, philosophy will
not speak of the senses, except by analysing sensations, that
is, the most original content of consciousness. Therefore,
the method will be as follows: it

> ought to determine us to make a choice even among
> the senses, and to give the precedence, not to the
> noblest or most useful, but to the simplest, and
> that whose objects are least in danger of being
> mistaken for other things.

> In this view, an analysis of our sensations may be
> carried on, perhaps with most ease and distinctness,
> by taking them in this order: Smelling, Tasting,
> Hearing, Touch, and last of all Seeing.(5)

One can conceive that Reid is satisfied with applying to
sensations the same synthetic proceeding of the experimental
method that Locke employed in the Essay in regard to simple
and complex ideas. And there is no doubt that the plan
followed by the Inquiry complies with the requirements of
such a scientific method. But why does the inquiry into the
human mind consist only of the study of the five kinds of
sensations (and not of the other powers of the mind)? To what
end is the progressive complexity of sensations displayed?

The first three sensations, smelling, tasting, and
hearing "are very simple and uniform, each of them exhibiting
only one kind of sensation and thereby indicating only one
quality of bodies".(6) Their simplicity is due to the
uniform character of the sense experience and to the
monovalent indication they give to the mind as to how to
distinguish a thing by a quality. More precisely, as is
underlined by an ambiguity of language which Reid points out
constantly, smell first signifies the sensation in the mind
and secondly informs us immediately that there is a virtue or
a quality in the thing which is connected with the present
sensation. "The rose is considered as a cause, occasion, or
antecedent of sensation".(7) The present sensation suggests
a present thing, according to such a quality. The difference
between the two is that, if the experienced subjective
content is entirely determined in its mode and degree, the
concomitant quality is not otherwise known. Sensation simply
signifies an unknown quality which is in the thing that

accompanies or produces the sensation. This indication does not give rise to knowledge, since I cannot say anything about the thing, and the determined content is on the side of the lived experience; but it is enough for me to discern this thing from another thing, by a mark the nature of which cannot be explained.(8)   Smell is in the sentient subject, but it is also attributed to the rose which is this way distinguished from lilac or from the sound of a trumpet.

Each of these three sensations is of a separate kind (sound is not identical with taste or smell) and includes a great variety of degrees, although we cannot distinguish in the experience of sensation a moment which would set forth the character proper to the generic unity and give the reason why, for all their variety, smells are joined with smells, tastes with tastes, sounds with sounds, and not one kind with another.(9) And if a justification for beginning with smell, before dealing with taste and then hearing, is needed, then it is achieved by evoking, not a difference of kind between these three sensations (they are equally uniform), nor a distinct way of indicating qualities (they equally designate secondary qualities), but only greater variety: hearing happens to show a wider range of sensations than smell, since we can discern a large number of tones and a great variety of aspects in the same tone.(10) There is more distinctiveness in sounds than in smells, even though there is the same clarity.

On the contrary, the nature of touch is far more complex, since the sensation signifies qualities of a very different order:(11) the same tactile sensation indicates secondary qualities (heat and cold) and primary qualities (hardness and softness, roughness and smoothness, figure, solidity, motion and extension), which are real qualities of bodies, determinable in a clear and distinct conception,(12) whereas the notion of secondary qualities remains obscure.(13) Thus touch gives greater information in two respects: at first, it is plurivalent, since it refers to several sorts of qualities of things (not only to several sorts of degrees); secondly, concerning primary qualities, it advises the mind of the very reality of things. While the sensible cause of hearing is an unknown quality of the thing, and the intelligible cause a certain property of the medium that is between thing and body, the figure or solidity are properties which belong to the nature of the external thing. Consequently, not only is sensation determined in its subjective reality, but also the thing itself in its objective reality.

Seeing is still more complicated. The given information is equally plurivalent (colour, extension, figure, motion) and indicates primary qualities (extension, figure, motion) as well as secondary qualities (colours). In one respect, it is not larger than the information of touch, even if sight can by a single intuition seize what touch must compose: a blind man may comprehend nearly everything that is acquired by sight.(14)    But, whereas, like other senses, touch requires the distinction between sensation (a subjective reality) and the secondary or primary quality which, determined or not, is taken as being real because it is felt, sight introduces a second structure of designation or signification, which is superimposed on the first, without being confused with it. Undoubtedly, sensation is the subjective sign of the quality of the thing; but this objective quality, such as it is offered, (for instance, the side of a cube which I look at) is itself the sign of the appearing thing (the cube with its six sides). The objective determination itself here includes the representation of the thing by its visible quality. And it must be concluded that:

There is certainly a resemblance, and a necessary connection, between the visible figure and magnitude of a body, and its real figure and magnitude.(15)

Thus a new relationship, by which the visible quality represents the thing that is seen (and its actual quality) is grafted on to the original relationship by which the sensation designates the thing without the mind. But the originally clear division between the subjective and the objective parts of sensible perception becomes uncertain. For what precise status must be given to this visible quality by which the thing seen is represented? What is a visible figure or size that can be distinctly determined in its relation with the real figure or size of the thing? On the one hand, like sensation, this quality signifies the thing itself, and therefore it has a transitory role. But, on the other hand, owing to its representative content, it is endowed with a qualitative reality: it is "a real and external object to the eye".(16)  As regards sight, the only sensible datum seems to be the felt sensation that corresponds with the colour (the secondary quality). But this sensation, beyond the fact that it indicates some unknown quality of the object, producing the red or the blue in the mind, "suggests likewise the individual direction and position of this cause with regard to the eye";(17) whereby the visible figure is apprehended as a relative object or the appearance of the real thing such as it is in itself.

> The position of the coloured thing is no  sensation;
> but it is by  the laws of my constitution  presented
> to  the   mind  along  with   colour,  without   any
> additional sensation.(18)

This remarkable reasoning is important, because it grafts  on
to the sensible relationship a properly notional relationship
(which by  return enables  a  blind man  to reconstitute  the
visible appearance itself, by argument).

> It is not therefore without reason that the  faculty
> of seeing  is looked  upon, not only  as more  noble
> than the other senses, but as having something in it
> of a nature superior to sensation.(19)

Being more  than  a simple  sensation,  seeing is  already  a
knowledge.

Thus  we  proceed  in  orderly  fashion  from  simple  to
complex, from  sensation  to  knowledge,  from  a  subjective
content of sensation indicating  some unknown quality of  the
thing to 'a  sensation losing  its subjective  presence,  but
gaining in  objective character,  in the  case of  touch,(20)
and, a fortiori, in the  case of seeing, where the  sensation
itself is not  reachable but  by complete concentration,  for
the benefit of a presence of the thing henceforth complex and
informed enough to enclose the relationship between appearing
and being.(21) Sensation is  truly of a different kind,  from
one sense to another or, more precisely, from the first three
senses  to  touch  and  from  touch  to  sight,  because  the
structure itself  of the relationship  between sensation  and
object changes  and  becomes  more intricate.  The  error  of
theorists of the idea was,  in this respect, to believe  that
sensation would  be uniform,  and this  despite its  variety,
from one sense to another,  and to comprehend all the  senses
on the same pattern  as sight. In  this way, they  introduced
representation into sensation and made sensation an idea; but
they corrupted  representation itself, because  they did  not
understand that seeing  is already a  conception. Thus,  the
order of the five senses or sensations in the Inquiry has in
itself the weight of a refutation.

But it also  plays a positive  part, because it  provides
Reid's philosophy with a substitute for the ideal theory. Let
us sum up the whole  argument. A common sense philosophy  can

destroy the theory of ideas, by studying the more original parts of our human constitution, that is, the five senses. Nothing can be said by philosophy about these five senses, as a fact of our natural constitution, except that they are the simplest way by which this natural constitution determines our mental consciousness. As there are naturally five distinct senses, so there are five distinct kinds of sensations in the mind. But, if we consider the order of the five sensations, we see that five senses in human nature mean in the human mind the order and the progress of the whole mental activity. And the study of the five sensations, tied down to the factual being of human nature, shows that we originally know the existence of the external world, and allows a new theory of conception that is free from representationalism.

II

There remains a question: how can we understand this tie by which sensation, that is, sensible consciousness, is fastened to the senses, that is, to our natural constitution? And an answer is needed, since common sense draws its strength from this relationship of consciousness with human nature.

In fact, the Essays, which have the more important ambition of giving a theory of the system of the intellectual powers of man, deepen the difficulty, by widening the gap keeping apart sensorial organ and sensation.

As organs of the body, the senses are not, strictly speaking, powers of the mind, but make up a link in the physiological chain: this impression is carried to the nerves and thence to the brain. This is a series of causes and effects that does not inform us about the nature of impression; in particular, we know nothing about cerebral impression, except that it is not mental(22) and that we can doubt its resemblance, which could be only physical, with things and their qualities.(23) The whole physico-physiological process has nothing to do with consciousness and cannot be perceived by the mind, when considering its own operations.(24) Reid enlarges this gap by using a mechanical metaphor: organs are instruments of parts of this wonderful machine of the human body.(25) And he spontaneously comes back to Descartes' metaphysical dualism: the body is a part of the material world and, as such, it belongs to what is causally explained; but the data of consciousness depend on common sense and can be apprehended as original evidence that does not belong to external experience.(26)

Nevertheless, even without the problem of knowing if the experience of our own senses is only external and material (does not Reid himself, when dealing with sight, consider the eye as a constitutive moment that makes sensible figures or sizes relative?), something, however brief, should be said about the relationship of organs to the mind:

It is a law of our nature, established by the will of the Supreme Being, that we perceive no external object but by means of the organs given us for that purpose.(27)

Let us assume that organs do not perceive by themselves and that we perceive because God has given us the power of perceiving. It remains that we perceive by means of the senses. What do we signify, when we say: by means of, since the severance of the mind from the body prohibits us from giving a causal explanation? Or what do we say exactly when we say that the five kinds of sensations correspond to the five senses?

The Essays take up again the traditional answer that the Inquiry was working out. Our perceiving by means of the senses depends on the will of God:

The intention of nature in the powers which we call the external senses, is evident. They are intended to give us that information of external objects which the Supreme Being saw to be proper for us in our present state.(28)

This appeal to God's wisdom is a metaphysical justification of a fact about which we cannot say anything except that it is. To call our constitution a natural law is only to say that it is for us a radical experience that cannot be explained by any reason. So we must accept it as the sign of our finiteness. Since they are the means imposed on our knowledge, the senses are our limits. And the sense experience is at the same time the experience of the mind's imperfection. Undoubtedly, our perception would be more perfect, if it was not mediatized by sensorial impressions: (29)

In the constitution of man, perception, by fixed laws of nature, is connected with those impressions;

but we can discover no necessary connection.(30)

Thus philosophers have been wrong to change the
connection between sense impressions and object perceptions
into a causal relationship, since it cannot be established
that material causes may generate intellectual effects. A
fortiori, a resemblance cannot be established between things
and perceptions or between sense impressions and these
perceptions; we cannot even suppose that objects would
produce an impression in the mind which would be concomitant
with that of sense organs. Nevertheless, even though we
would agree with Reid on those conclusions that he repeats
all the time, we should observe that he cannot wholly
neutralize the connection between sensorial impressions and
the perceptions of the mind, and reduce the mediating
function of the senses to the one fact of our limitation.
The appeal to God's wisdom is certainly more than the simple
metaphysical mark of a matter of fact. For, at the risk of
introducing a doubt about the truthfulness of our perceptions
and, more generally, the truth of our knowledge, we must
suppose that the connections between sense impressions and
the perceptions of the mind are constant, regular and
unvarying, and that there is a permanent correspondence, even
if we can assign no relationship of causation or likeness to
it. An assumption which widely surpasses the evidence that
common sense gives us, since it does not bear on a phenomenon
within the mind, but on the mind-body relationship. Hence
the metaphysical thesis of a 'bon genie' is required.

For Reid's analysis stumbles over a double anteriority:
the anteriority of the senses, depending on the limitations
of our nature, and the anteriority of consciousness, by which
the mind apprehends itself originally. The second is the
basis for the authority of common sense, whereas the first
one can be dealt with only by metaphysics. Now, how can we
combine metaphysics and common sense? Having forced back the
senses towards the body, so that the idea-philosophies could
be fought more easily, Reid has to secure common sense
metaphysically and justify the sense-perception
correspondence by a final argument. In more modern terms, he
is not far from taking up a phenomenological language; but,
because he does not take the step that would lead him to give
the evidence of common sense a founding role, as evidence of
the pure consciousness, and he has by assimilation to deal
with the intellectual powers of the human mind as
constitutive principles of our nature, he remains a prisoner
of a negative metaphysics that can say nothing (save God's

wisdom), but is needed to warrant the correspondence between
the senses.

Let us examine the relationship between sensation and
perception within consciousness. For, whatever the status of
the senses may be, they are present to the mind; and this is
sensation. And it would seem that this mental presence may
diminish our previous criticism. If the organic order was
quite different, it would not be relevant to consciousness.
Thus, the senses exist for the mind, in sensations. This
being so, could not we avoid the metaphysical problem of the
sense-mind correspondence and deal, within the mind, in the
evidence of common sense, with only the relationship between
perception and sensation, which both are operations of the
human mind?

Sensation is, indeed, an operation of the mind that is
remarkable, because, although it is present in many acts of
the mind, it is not itself, strictly speaking, one of these
acts. We cannot find in it the conception or notion of an
external object nor, with greater reason, the belief in the
existence of this object:

> Sensation, taken by itself, implies neither the
> conception nor belief of any external object. It
> supposes a sentient being, and a certain manner in
> which that being is affected; but it supposes no
> more.(31)

So the smell of a rose "affects the mind in a certain way;
and this affection of the mind may be conceived, without a
thought of the rose or of any other object".(32) Taken in
its original determination, sensation is purely subjective;
and it is so subjective that it is the subject itself, taken
as affection. In this way, we can understand what looks like
passivity in sensation (since it is not an act resulting in
the thought of the object nor the belief in its existence):
the subject has no other original mode of being than this
affective life that it finds in it. The Essays stress even
further this melting of subjectivity in affection. Whereas,
in the Inquiry, the suggestion theory kept sensation and
subject apart, by the distance of an immediate inference, the
Essays make stronger the division between sensation and
perception, subjective and objective operation:

> The external senses have a double province – to make
> us feel, and to make us perceive. They furnish us

> with a variety of sensations, some pleasant, others
> painful, and others indifferent; at the same time,
> they give us a conception and an invincible belief
> of the existence of external objects.(33)

So affection gradually becomes identical with affectivity:
sensation becomes an agreeable or disagreeable experience,
pleasure or pain, with Reid even creating an indifferent
sensibility, when the subject is less concerned by the
sensation of its own experience than by the perception of the
object (cf. I, Works, p 114). In short, sensation must not
be dealt with as the matter of perception or any other act of
the mind, but as the subjective sign, the conscious
apprehension of which is more or less lively, more or less
subjectively determined, and which indicates some quality of
the object, to which the mind turns its attention.

Thus by giving sensation only a subjective content
without any necessary internal link with the objective
reality that is thought or posited into existence (cf. I,
Works, p 310), Reid carries on his endeavour to make every
kind of representation disappear from the mind, as if what
has already been fought on the side of sensorial impression,
must be again hunted down in the sentient subject itself.
Neither as body nor as mind is the sensation idea. And the
same abstraction which characterizes the body-mind
correspondence prevails in the correspondence between
sensation and perception inside the mind.

But is such a neutralization of the relationship between
sensation and perception lawful, within the mind itself?

Let us come back to the problem of how we can distinguish
the five senses. The smell of a rose is pleasant; this
sensation is the sign of an unknown quality of the thing,
which is said to be the cause of sensation. But the colour
of the rose is also pleasant; this sensation equally
designates some quality in the thing, which is said to be its
colour. But in both cases the subject experiences a pleasant
sensation, whereas the rose is thought and posited through
two distinct qualities, its smell and its colour. If the
relationship between sensation and perception is truly a
relationship between a sign and its signified, and if,
consequently, we must distinguish a purely subjective
determination (the pleasant character, liable only to
degrees) and objective determinations (secondary properties,
in this example), without any necessary connection between

one and the other order, how can various degrees signify
various kinds? How are we able to discern five kinds of
objective qualities in accordance with the five senses? Of
course, Reid takes care to assert that there is "a great
variety of sensations, differing in kind, and almost in every
kind an endless variety of degrees",(34) so that sensations
"serve as signs to distinguish things that differ; and the
information we have concerning things external, comes by
their means".(35) But how can a subjective affection be a
principle for the distinction between different things and
different qualities? Either Reid infers the distinction of
the signified (the external things), but it is paradoxical;
or he comes back to the distinction of the five senses, which
does not belong to consciousness, but to human nature.

Thus, while speaking of the senses, the Inquiry was
speaking of sensation and was referring to the external
things and their qualities. But it made the five kinds of
sensation correspond to the five senses, without any
explanation. The Essays forbid any philosophical explanation
concerning the senses and, by not considering sensation as an
act of the mind, change it into an affection. But how can
affectivity be a sign for distinct things and qualities? So
there remains the information of the five senses. The senses
inform us: they are five for that purpose. But what do they
tell us? As a fact of our constitution, they inform us of
our natural imperfection; as the fact of sensation, they
inform us of our subjective existence; as a sign (through
sensation) of the external things, they indicate that
something exists and can be discerned according to distinct
qualities. But that information is metaphysical. The five
sense are metaphysics for the common sense philisophy.

NOTES

(1)   I, I, ii (Works, p. 98).

(2)   I, II, i (Works, p. 104).

(3)   I, I, ii (Works, p. 99).

(4)   I, II, ii (Works, p. 105).

(5)   I, II, i (Works, p. 104).

(6)   I, V, i (Works, p. 119).

(7)   I, II, viii (Works, p. 112).

(8)   cf. IP, II, xxi (Works, p. 331).

(9)   I, III, (Works, p. 116).

(10)  I, IV, i (Works, p. 117).

(11)  I, V, i (Works, p. 119).

(12)  I, V, iv (Works, p. 123).

(13)  cf. IP, II, xvii (Works, p. 313).

(14)  I, VI, ii (Works, p. 133).

(15)  I, VI, vii (Works, p. 142).

(16)  I, VI, viii (Works, p. 146).

(17)  I, VI, viii (Works, p. 145).

(18)  Ibid.

(19)  I, VI, i (Works, p. 133).

(20)  I, V, ii (Works, p. 120).

(21)  I, VI, iii (Works, p. 135).

(22)  IP, II, iv (Works, p. 257).

(23) **IP**, II, ii (<u>Works</u>, p. 248).

(24) **IP**, II, i (<u>Works</u>, p. 245).

(25) **IP**, II, i (<u>Works</u>, p. 247);  II, iv (<u>Works</u>, p. 257), etc.

(26) **IP**, II, v (<u>Works</u>, p. 258).

(27) **IP**, II, iv (<u>Works</u>, p. 257).

(28) **IP**, II, xx (<u>Works</u>, p. 326).

(29) **IP**, II, i (<u>Works</u>, p. 246).

(30) **IP**, II, ii (<u>Works</u>, p. 248).

(31) **IP**, II, xvi (<u>Works</u>, p. 312).

(32) **IP**, II, xvi (<u>Works</u>, p. 310).

(33) **IP**, II, xvii (<u>Works</u>, p. 318).

(34) **IP**, II, xvi (<u>Works</u>, P. 311).

(35) **IP**, II, xvi (<u>Works</u>, p. 312).

SECTION 2 – KNOWLEDGE AND COMMON SENSE

Keith Lehrer

## REID ON EVIDENCE AND CONCEPTION

It has become popular recently to attempt to reconnect
theories of conception with theories of evidence, the
psychology of cognition with epistemology. Reid developed a
theory of conception and evidence in the 18th century that
connected conception and belief, on the one hand, with
evidence and justification on the other. The theory is
simple to state. There, are, according to Reid, original
perceptions, which imply conception and belief, that are
evident or justified in themselves without the mediation of
reasoning or inference. Original perceptions are operations
of the mind wherein sensations give rise to conception and
belief as a result of innate principles of our mental
faculties. Reid gives us a number of marks for
distinguishing conceptions that are original, that is, the
result of such innate principles, from those that are not.
The most important of these are that the conceptions occur
too early to have been learned, that they are universal, as
evidenced, for example, by the facts of language, and that
they are irresistible.

The innate principles of conception are also first
principles of evidence. The conceptions and beliefs they
yield in response to sensation are evident and justified in
themselves. Reid admits he has no reply to a total sceptic
who denies that any belief is evident or justified. To a
sceptic affirming that only some of the conceptions resulting
from innate principles are justified, our conception of our
own mental operations, for example, while denying that other
such conceptions are justified, our conception of the
qualities of material objects, for example, Reid raises the
charge of inconsistency. All such conceptions must be
regarded as justified in themselves, at least until
experience teaches us otherwise, or none should be regarded
as justified. They are all equally the results of our
faculties, and we must trust all our faculties or none at
all. To attempt to prove that one of our faculties is
trustworthy and the others are not is already to assume the
trustworthiness of one faculty, that of reason. That
assumption is only warranted, however, if we assume that all
of our faculties, reason among them, are trustworthy and not

121

*M. Dalgarno and E. Matthews (eds.), The Philosophy of Thomas Reid, 121–144.*
© *1989 by Kluwer Academic Publishers.*

fallacious. It is, moreover, a first principle that our faculties are trustworthy and not fallacious. The child trusts his faculties without being taught to do so, and all men trust their faculties, says Reid, with the exception of lunatics and some philosophers.

It is clear, as I note below, that Reid's theory of conception and evidence is intended to avoid the scepticism of Hume as well as a theory of the mind, which Reid calls the Ideal Theory. That theory Reid traces from Descartes, through Locke and Berkeley, to Hume, while remarking that the theory has more ancient origins. The theory is that what is immediately before the mind·is always some mental entity, an idea. It is a consequence of the Ideal Theory that our conception of anything that is not an idea must be constructed from ideas, and, moreover, the justification we have for thinking anything exists must be based on reasoning from the existence of ideas. Reid has a complex argument against this theory which I shall not attempt to articulate in detail here.

Reid contends, however, that the Ideal Theory leads to scepticism and to a psychology inconsistent with the facts of human conception. He says that we need not despair of a better. He argues that we have an immediate conception of some things that are not mental, not ideas, primary qualities of material bodies, for example, and that we cannot obtain such conceptions by constructing them out of ideas. He concludes that they are the result of innate principles. Sensations give rise to these conceptions, but the conceptions are not conceptions of the sensations nor a construction based on conceptions of sensations. The conceptions, though occasioned by the sensations, are the products of innate principles of the mind. These principles, being innate psychological principles, provide us with an immediate conception of primary qualities, and, being epistemological first principles as well, provide us with an immediate justification for believing in the existence of such qualities.

The problem of this paper is to give an account of the conceptions that are the products of innate first principles. There is a problem in interpreting Reid in a consistent manner on this point because the account of the Inquiry appears to be inconsistent with the account of the Essays. There is, moreover, some problem of giving a consistent account within the Essays. The crux of the problem is that, in his early work, Reid gives us an account of the conception of primary qualities as an automatic response to sensation, while, in the later work, his account of conception is one involving abstraction based on the direction of attention and generalisation based on utility. These operations do not appear to be automatic but, instead, appear to be voluntary and reflective. The problem is deepened by Reid's contention that there are innate principles of moral conception combined with his claim that our moral conceptions depend on instruction and social intercourse. This raises the problem of nature versus nurture. I shall attempt to resolve this apparent inconsistency and to explain Reid's solution to the problem of nature versus nurture.

I

Conception in the Inquiry. Reid's theory of conception in the Inquiry suggests that some of our original perceptions, including the perceptions of primary qualities, arise as an automatic response to sensation. To understand this theory, it is important to notice that Reid distinguishes between physical impressions on the organs of sense, including stimulation of the nerves and brain, on the one hand, and sensations of the mind, on the other. This account was motivated by Reid's adamant dualism. Stimulation of the organs of sense and the nervous system, which he thought a mere extension of the organs of sense, were physical impressions. These physical impressions occasion sensations in the mind.

Here Reid is careful not to subscribe to the doctrine that the physical impressions cause the sensations. Reid thought that to do so would lead to adverse consequences. First, it would reduce causality to mere constant conjunction or occasioning, which he thought to be a mistake, and, secondly, he thought it would lead to materialism. Once one admitted that causality was no more that a nomological relationship, then there would be no objection to the idea that physical events could cause mental events. Given that, Reid thought the doctrine would soon follow that mental events really are physical events. It is interesting that, though it is obviously a logical fallacy to argue that because mental events are caused by physical events, they really are physical events, there was historical wisdom in Reid's contention. Once it was conceded that physical events caused mental events, philosophers were led to materialism. The development is puzzling, but Reid's explanation may be

correct. Once it is agreed that mental events are
sufficiently similar to physical events to be caused by them,
interest in parsimony may drive one to materialism.

There is a terminological problem here that bedevils any
attempt to make sense of Reid's theory of conception. He
argues that a cause, properly speaking, must be an agent, a
being having understanding and will. He concedes, however,
that in ordinary and even scientific discourse the term is
used in another way, namely, to indicate nomological
connection. Since Reid is loathe to counter ordinary usage,
he agrees that this is an acceptable way to speak. Moreover,
he speaks that way himself. He says, for example, that our
conception of a secondary quality is a conception of some
quality in the object that gives rise to or causes a certain
sensation in us, even though he obviously rejects the idea
that a quality can be a cause, properly speaking, that is, an
agent. It is, I believe, better to use the word 'cause' in
an ordinary way, as Reid, in fact, does, and to distinguish
between agent causality and causality simpliciter. Thus, I
shall speak of physical impressions causing sensations and
sensations causing or giving rise to conceptions, and shall
attribute this manner of expressing things to Reid. I
concede and, indeed, insist, however, that there is
ambivalence in Reid concerning this manner of speaking,
though he himself employs it as a matter of course.

Physical impressions on the organs of sense occasion in
some way, we know not how, sensations in the mind. These
sensations then occasion certain conceptions, those of
primary qualities, as a result of innate principles of the
mind. Reid calls these particular principles. He
distinguishes them from other principles of the mind, a
principle of induction, for example, which he calls general
principles. The hallmark of particular principles is that
they yield the same conceptual response to a particular
sensation, the conception of a primary quality, motion, for
example, as an innate response to a particular kind of
sensation. General principles, such as the principle of
induction, yield a conceptual response as well, but the
connection between what gives rise to the conception and the
thing conceived is determined by experience rather than
innately. General principles are innate principles
connecting things through experience. Particular principles
are innate principles connecting things innately.

The theory of innate principles may also be interpreted

as a theory of signs. The conception is a response to a sign
which signifies the thing conceived. Particular principles
effect a sign relation innately. A sensation signifies a
primary quality innately as a consequence of the principle.
General principles effect a sign relation experientially in
that the sign signifies something as a consequence of the
principle connecting things in experience. The theory
becomes immediately more complicated, however, because Reid
distinguishes not two but three kinds of signs.

There are, according to Reid, three kinds of signs. I
quote:

> The first class of natural signs comprehends those
> whose connection with the thing signified is
> established by nature, but discovered only by
> experience. The whole of genuine philosophy
> consists in discovering such connections, and
> reducing them to general rules.(1)

> A second class is that wherein the connection
> between the sign and thing signified, is not only
> established by nature, but discovered to us by a
> natural principle, without reasoning or experience.
> Of this kind are the natural signs of human
> thoughts, purposes, and desires, which have been
> already mentioned as the natural language of
> mankind.(2)

> A third class of natural signs comprehends those
> which, though we never before had any notion or
> conception of the thing signified, do suggest it,
> or conjure it up, as it were, by a natural kind of
> magic, and at once give us a conception and create
> a belief of it.(3)

This theory of signs clearly has an epistemological
implication. Justified hypotheses in philosophy and science
are the result of the discovery of the first sort of signs.
On his theory of the laws of nature, our knowledge of them is
the result of discovering the relation of such natural signs
to what.they signify. The second kind of signs are necessary
for our knowledge of the thoughts of others and are
presupposed for the learning of an artificial language,
English, for example. In order to form the agreements
necessary for an artificial language, one must know when
others agree, and, therefore, something of what they think

and intend.

The third class of signs is the most important for an understanding of the nature of primary qualities. The third kind of sign is necessary for our conception of bodies as well as of external qualities. Reid assumes that:

> we cannot, by reasoning from our sensations, collect the existence of bodies at all, far less any of their qualities. This hath been proved by unanswerable arguments by the Bishop of Cloynes, and by the author of the 'Treatise of Human Nature.' It appears as evident that this connection between our sensations and the conception and belief of external existences cannot be produced by habit, experience, education, or any principle of human nature that hath been admitted by philosophers.(4)

Reid concludes that the connection between sign and thing signified is "the effect of our constitution, and ought to be considered as an original principle of human nature."

Thus, the effect of nature in the first kind of signs is merely to establish the capacity to discover the relation between the sign and the thing signified, a relation also established by nature. The effect of nature in the second kind of sign is stronger, for here nature establishes also an understanding of the relation between the sign and the things signified. The effect of nature in the third kind of sign is yet stronger, for here nature not only establishes the relation and an understanding of the relation in us but also establishes an understanding of the thing signified.

Reid then proceeds to articulate the distinction between primary and secondary qualities in more detail. The crux is that our conception of primary qualities is clear and distinct in contrast to our conception of secondary qualities which is a relative conception of some quality in the object that gives rise to a sensation in us. Sensations give rise to both primary and secondary qualities, according to Reid, but the conception of secondary qualities incorporates a conception of the sensation as a conceptual or semantic component. We just conceive of a secondary quality, a smell, for example, as a quality in the object that gives rise to the sensation we experience. Our conception of secondary qualities is thus acquired, and the sign relation is the first kind.

By contrast, our conception of primary qualities, though signified by a sensation, that is, occasioned or caused by the sensation, does not incorporate a conception of the sensation into the conception of the quality. The sensations that give rise to our conception of primary qualities may themselves go unnoticed and are no part of our conception of the quality. I quote:

> Further, I observe that hardness is a quality, of which we have as clear and distinct a conception as of anything whatsoever. The cohesion of the parts of a body with more or less force, is perfectly understood, though its cause is not; we know what it is, as well as how it affects the touch. It is, therefore, a quality of a quite different order from those secondary qualities we have already taken notice of, whereof we know no more naturally than that they are adapted to raise certain sensations in us.(5)

Reid's conclusion concerning the distinction between primary and secondary qualities is that, although it was previously drawn in an erroneous manner which assumed a resemblance between sensations and qualities, "there appears to be a real foundation for it in the principles of our nature." The principles of our nature yield a clear and distinct conception of primary qualities in response to sensations which are the signs of those qualities. Those principles do not yield such a conception of secondary qualities. As a consequence, we must depend on scientific investigation for a clear and distinct conception of a secondary quality but not for such a conception of a primary quality. Our nature provides such a conception of primary qualities.

> If any man should say, that hardness in bodies is a certain vibration of their parts, or that it is certain effluvia emitted by them which affect our touch in the manner we feel -- such hypotheses would shock common sense; because we all know that, if the parts of a body adhere strongly, it is hard, although it should neither emit effluvia nor vibrate.(6)

This way of drawing the distinction may seem strange. One may be tempted to object that the definition of 'hardness' should be distinguished from a scientific account of hardness. One might continue by objecting that it does not follow from the fact that we have an adequate definition that no scientific account of the matter is possible. This is, of course, no objection to the distinction that Reid has drawn. It might well be true that our conception of primary qualities differs from that of secondary qualities in terms of our innate understanding of the qualities. Reid would reply that our conception of secondary qualities imposes no restriction on hypotheses about the nature of secondary qualities other than that they be the cause of certain sensations, but our conception of primary qualities imposes a definite restriction on any hypothesis about the nature of primary qualities in that it must be consistent with our original conception. When hypotheses conflict with common sense and the judgments resulting from innate principles, it is the hypotheses that must go to the wall.

The third kind of sign is, for our puposes, the most interesting. In this kind of sign, the sign gives rise to a conception that one did not previously have, as Reid says, as though by inspiration or a kind of natural magic. This kind of sign, which I shall call originative, originates the conception in us without our having acquired the concept previously. These concepts arise due to our natural constitution, that is, due to an innate principle to respond to certain signs with such conceptions. Our natural constitution, without the effects of custom or reason, gives rise to a conception of primary qualities, as well as to a conception of sensation and thought. It also gives rise to a conception of an object which has the qualities and a mind which has the thoughts.

The contrast between the second kind of signs, which I shall call communicative signs, and originative signs is important, even though the understanding of both is innate. In the case of communicative signs, the thing signified is a mental state, an intention, thought or feeling. Although the intentions, thoughts and feelings of others are, as Reid puts it, invisible to us, and such that we could not, therefore, learn by induction that there is any connection between the gestures, sounds, and countenances of others and their intentions, feelings, or thoughts, we do have immediate knowledge of intentions, thoughts and feelings in ourselves. Thus, communicative signs are innately understood, but the conception of what they signify is not originated by such signs. On the other hand, originative signs are both innately understood, that is, the connection between the sign and what it signifies is innately interpreted, and the conception of what is signified is originated by the sign.

The epistemological significance of the distinction between communicative and originative signs is that it shows that Reid noticed the distinction between the problem of other minds and the problem of the external world. He noticed that Hume's arguments left us with two distinct problems. As he conceived of the import of those arguments, they showed that one could not obtain the conception of an external object if the immediate object of thought were always some impression or idea. Neither could we know or be justified in believing that the object existed. Reid's solution was to argue that such conceptions, at least the most fundamental conceptions of objects and their primary qualities, arose from our natural constitution and that our belief in the existence of such qualities and objects was justified without the intervention of custom or reasoning.

The problem of our knowledge of the mental states of others was somewhat different. In this case, the problem of how we could have the mere conception of a mental state is easily solved, since we obtain the conception of mental states from our own consciousness. The conception of mental states gives rise to a conception of a mind that has them as a result of innate principles of our constitution. There remains, however, the problem of how we could ever know or be justified in thinking that others have mental states. Here the problem is that we have no consciousness of the mental states of others as we do of our own and, therefore, could not experience a constant conjunction between external bodily states of others and their internal mental states. Though we can conceive of the mental states of others because we can conceive of our own mental states, the external bodily states of others cannot be inductive signs of their internal mental states. Experience cannot provide the inductive connection. Where experience is wanting, the connection is supplied by our natural constitution. We do not require experience or reason to find the connection between behaviour of others and their thoughts. Certain external bodily states of others are innately understood signs of internal mental states. These conceptions and beliefs of the internal mental states of others are the result of innate principles of our constitution. They are immediate and are not the result of habit or reasoning. They are, therefore, evident and justified in themselves.

It is clear that Reid thought that no inductive argument for the mental states of others would suffice. It naturally occurs to one to ask why Reid did not consider that we might know of the mental states of another by analogy. He would, I think, allow that we could conceive of the mental states of others by analogy to our own mental states. Reid does discuss argument by analogy as a general form of argument, and he considers it a weak form of argumentation at best. Such argumentation would lead to a lower level of justification for beliefs about others than we sometimes have. We can be certain that a man injured in a certain manner is suffering pain, and to suppose it is less than certain, only probable say, is contrary to experience. The fundamental reason for Reid's neglect of the argument by analogy is, I believe, the empirical fact that people, children for example, have such knowledge before any such reasoning might occur to them. It would, therefore, be contrary to the facts to suppose the evidence of our beliefs about the mental states of others depends on an argument from analogy. We are certain that others feel and think before analogical reasoning enters our minds. One who never reflected on such analogical reasoning would know what others think and feel quite as well as those more given to ratiocination and analogical reasoning about such matters. Thus, the evidence of such beliefs is not that of reasoning. It is the justification that beliefs have as a result of first principles. Such beliefs constitute the premises of sound reasoning rather than the conclusion.

It is interesting to notice the extent to which this line of reasoning is indebted to Berkeley and Hume in spite of their being the target of his criticism. The importance of the sign relation is surely derived from Berkeley. Berkeley contended that visible ideas were signs of tangible ideas to come. Reid noticed that the relation between sign and thing signified was fundamental for Berkeley. Moreover, Berkeley, at least in his published work, says that we have a notion of mind — that which has the ideas. Hence, the ideas that we have give rise to the notion of a mind that has them. This was very problematic for Berkeley in that minds are not ideas, and Berkeley is committed to the thesis that what is before the mind is always some idea. The notion of a mind appears to be before the mind as well, though it is not an idea or collection of ideas. In Berkeley's notebooks, as Turbayne (7) has shown, it is clear that Berkeley contemplated a critique of mental substance exactly analogous to his critique of material substance. It is, nevertheless, a fact that Berkeley did commit himself to our having the notion of mind. Be that as it may, when we put together the thesis of signs and the thesis of our having a notion of something that is not a mental state, the natural result is to affirm that some mental states can be the sign of something that is not a mental state. If such mental states, sensations for example, can be the sign of the existence of something other than mental states, then why not the sign of external qualities, of objects that have those qualities, and of the thoughts and minds of others? A positive response was prompted by the sceptical arguments of Hume. For Reid took those arguments to show that if we did not suppose that mental states such as sensations might be the sign of such qualities and objects, we should be left with the conclusion that we can have no conception of such qualities or objects, of minds or the thoughts of others, let alone justified belief or knowledge of their existence.

In short, the argument that I believe generated Reid's theory was a combination of a positive suggestion in Berkeley and the negative arguments of Hume. The latter convinced Reid that we must give some account of how we obtain the conception of minds, qualities of objects, and the objects themselves that did not depend on the assumption of the ideal theory that all our conceptions are constructed from sensations. For, if we accept the latter assumption, Reid was convinced we would be led to the conclusion that we have no such conceptions, a conclusion that is contrary to common sense, the facts of introspection, and, therefore, absurd.

II

Conception in the Essays. This account of conception has been drawn from the Inquiry. The account of conception offered in the Essays may appear to be at variance with this model. The crux of the problem is that the account of the Inquiry gives a theory of conception, at least of primary qualities, as an automatic response to sensations, while his account in the Essays is more sophisticated. It affirms that conception of general qualities, which would seem to include primary qualities, is a two step process involving abstraction and generalization. Reid here supposes that one initially confronts experience as an undigested whole and that in order to obtain any conception of individual qualities one must focus attention on those qualities. This focusing of attention he calls abstraction, meaning that one

abstracts the particular quality from an undifferentiated
mass. This operation of the mind does not, by itself, yield
any general conception, the conception of motion or hardness
shared by different individuals, for example. The general
conception is obtained from a second operation,
generalization, whereby different objects are conceived to
agree in some common attribute.

This division of the operations of conception into
abstraction and generalization is not, in itself,
inconsistent with the notion that our conception of primary
qualities is an automatic response to sensation, the doctrine
of the Inquiry. It would be open to Reid to argue that these
two operations occur automatically in response to sensation
to generate our conception of primary qualities. The problem
is to reconcile the early account with Reid's further remarks
concerning generalization or the sorting of things into
kinds. He says that utility determines how we sort things
into kinds. Man and not nature sorts things into kinds
according to their common attributes for the sake of utility.
Reid acknowledges, moreover, that with respect to genera and
species, nature invites us to do this one way rather than
another.

He writes:

> It is utility, indeed, that leads us to give general
> names to the various species of natural substances;
> but, in combining the attributes which are included
> under the specific name, we are more aided and
> directed by nature than in forming other
> combinations of mixed modes and relations. In the
> last, the ingredients are brought together in the
> occurrences of life, or in the actions or thoughts
> of men. But, in the first, the ingredients are
> united by nature in many individual substances which
> God has made. We form a general notion of those
> attributes wherein many individuals agree. We give
> a specific name to this combination, which name is
> common to all substances having those attributes,
> which either do or may exist.(8)

This way of sorting things may, moreover, be essential for
our preservation. Reid writes:

> Without some general knowledge of the qualities of
> natural substances, human life could not be

preserved.  And there can be no general knowledge of
this kind  without reducing  them  to species  under
specific names.(9)

It remains Reid's doctrine,  however, that we generalize  one
way rather than another because of utility.  I quote  Reid at
length on the subject:

> Things are parcelled  into kinds  and sorts, not  by
> nature, but by  men.  The  individual things we  are
> connected with, are so  many, that to give a  proper
> name to every  individual would  be impossible.  We
> could never  attain the  knowledge of  them that  is
> necessary,  nor  converse  and  reason  about   them
> without sorting  them according  to their  different
> attributes.  Those that agree in certain  attributes
> are thrown into one parcel, and have a general  name
> given  to  them,  which belongs  equally  to  every
> individual in that  parcel.   This common name  must
> therefore signify those  attributes which have  been
> observed to be  common to  every individual in  that
> parcel, and nothing else.
>
> That such general words may answer their  intention,
> all that is  necessary is, that  those who use  them
> should affix  the same meaning  or notion––that  is,
> the same conception to them.  The common meaning  is
> the standard by which  such conceptions are  formed,
> and they are said to  be true or false according  as
> they agree or disagree with it.  Thus, my conception
> of felony is true and just, when it agrees with  the
> meaning of that word in the laws relating to it, and
> in authors who understand  the law.  The meaning  of
> the word is the  thing conceived;  and that  meaning
> is the conception  affixed to it  by those who  best
> understand the language.
>
> An individual is expressed  in language either by  a
> proper name,  or by  a general word  joined to  such
> circumstances as  distinguish that  individual  from
> all others;  if  it  is unknown,  it may,  when  an
> object of sense, and within reach, be pointed out to
> the senses;  when beyond the reach of the senses, it
> may be ascertained by  a description, which,  though
> very imperfect,  may  be  true,  and  sufficient  to
> distinguish it from every other individual.(10)

This is a splendid passage in many ways. It is a clear indication of the origin of the division of labour theory of meaning. Those who best understand the language provide a standard conception, and the conceptions of others are correct if they agree with the experts. The theory concerning our conception of individuals is equally modern. It is, however, difficult to reconcile all of this with Reid's account of our conception of primary qualities as an automatic response to sensation. Such conceptions appear to arise in order to serve the ends of general knowledge and common meaning. The way in which we generalize or sort things into kinds is a consequence of the usefulness of doing so rather than being a consequence of innate first principles.

There seem to me to be three lines of response to this apparent inconsistency between the earlier and later writings. One is to say that Reid simply changed his theory of conception concerning primary qualities. What he writes about primary qualities in the Essays indicates that Reid did not think he had changed his doctrine, however. That is not decisive, of course, he may have unknowingly changed his doctrine. Secondly, he may have thought some general conceptions, those of primary qualities, are such that their utility determines our general conception by nature rather than by reflecting on their utility. In short, it may be that, due to the utility of some conceptions in preserving our lives, we automatically generalize in response to sensation with an operation of an innate first principle. Though this is an attractive line of thought, I am convinced that Reid thought that generalization was voluntary, not automatic, and, therefore, that our general conception of primary qualities was not an automatic response to sensation.

The solution to the problem depends on recognizing the importance of Reid's distinction between general attributes, universals, and particular qualities. This distinction is critical for an understanding of his work. Reid says that there are attributes that are common to many individuals. He considers the objection "the whiteness of the sheet of paper upon which I write, cannot be the whiteness of another sheet", and replies:

> To this I answer, that the whiteness of this sheet is one thing, whiteness is another; the conceptions signified by these two forms of speech are as different as the expressions. The first signifies

an individual quality really existing, and is not a
general conception, though it be an abstract one:
the second signifies a general conception, which
implies no existence, but may be predicated of
everything that is white, and in the same sense. On
this account, if one should say that the whiteness
of this sheet is the whiteness of another sheet,
every man perceives this to be absurd; but when he
says both sheets are white, this is true and
perfectly understood. The conception of whiteness
implies no existence; it would remain the same
though everything in the universe that is white were
annihilated.(11)

Here, then, Reid distinguishes between the whiteness of this
sheet of paper, an individual quality that really exists in
the world, but is the quality of one individual only, and
whiteness, a general conception or universal which does not
exist at all, but is a quality of all white individuals. The
theory of general conceptions is metaphysically interesting.
General conceptions are our creations, the products of our
mind, and have no real existence. They are, however,
necessary for our knowledge of the world. That involves the
predication of universals or general conceptions of
individuals. Reid holds that only individuals and individual
qualities exist. This is a fascinating metaphysical theory,
but what is of central importance is that it permits us to
make consistent sense of his theory of conception in the
early and later works.

The task of reconciling the Inquiry with the Essays is
mirrored by the task of reconciling the Essays with
themselves. In the Essays, Reid notes that we first abstract
and then generalize. Abstraction is an operation of the mind
wherein the mind focuses on a single quality. Generalization
is an operation whereby the mind forms a general conception
of a universal. If abstraction were an operation which
focused attention on a universal, generalization would be
superfluous. Thus, the distinction between individual
qualities and universals is required to make consistent sense
of the doctrine of the Essays. Abstraction directs attention
to an individual quality and yields a conception of it.
Generalization is an operation that generalizes from these
conceptions of individual qualities and yields a conception
of a universal.

This leaves us with two problems of interpretation. The

first is to make some consistent sense of the idea articulated in the Inquiry that our conception of primary qualities arises automatically from sensation. The solution is to note that Reid allows that some development may be necessary before these operations of the mind take place. Once attention is directed to a sensation, the conceptual response occurs automatically. One may need to learn, however, to focus attention on the sensation. This does not imply that conscious reflection is involved in the direction of attention. One may direct the attention of a small child to some quality, some movement, for example, without the child reflecting on the matter. In short, the direction of attention may result unreflectively, but it is necessary for the sensation to give rise to conception. Once the mind is directed to a sensation, even if it does not reflect upon it, a conception automatically arises. What I propose is that Reid held that sensations give rise to conceptions of individual qualities once the mind is directed toward the sensation. The role of directing attention is given greater emphasis in the Essays, but Reid was also aware of the importance of it in the Inquiry. There he raised the question of whether the mind is active in sensation and came to the conclusion, somewhat tentatively, that the mind must always be active.

There remains a second problem. Reid says in the Inquiry that we have a clear and distinct conception of primary qualities, such as hardness, figure, motion and extension, though we have a relative conception of secondary qualities and, indeed, most other qualities. He reiterates this in the Essays. His discussion of hardness as a conception of a cohesion among the parts appears to be a general conception. He also says in the Essays that our conception of motion is undefinable and, therefore, simple. Yet if our original conception of hardness is a conception of a cohesion among the parts of an object, it would seem that our original conception of motion would be that of a change of place, and both such conceptions are surely complex.

The answer to this problem is, I believe, that Reid developed a somewhat more complicated theory of our conception of primary qualities than he articulated in the sections on those matters. The clue to what he thought is to be found in the section on the thousand sided polygon. This occurs in the opening section of the Active Powers. There he notes that we may have a conception from sight of a thousand sided polygon, one that we have perceived, and this

conception, though simple, is indistinct. The reason that it
is indistinct is that the conception we have from sight is
insufficient to distinguish it from other polygons, those of
a thousand and one sided polygon. It is, however, also
possible to have a relative conception, a mathematical
conception in which such polygons are related to others,
which is clear and precise and enables us to derive the
geometrical properties of the polygon. I quote:

> In like manner, I can form a direct notion of a
> polygon of a thousand equal sides and equal angles.
> This direct notion cannot be more distinct, when
> conceived in the mind, than that which I get by
> sights, when the object is before me; and I find it
> so indistinct, that it has the same appearance to my
> eye, or to my direct conception, as a polygon of a
> thousand and one, or of nine hundred and ninety-nine
> sides. But, when I form a relative conception of
> it, by attending to the relation it bears to
> polygons of a greater or less number of sides, my
> notion of it becomes distinct and scientific, and I
> can demonstrate the properties by which it is
> distinguished from all other polygons. From these
> instances, it appears that our relative conceptions
> of things are not always less distinct, nor less fit
> materials for accurate reasoning than those that are
> direct; and that the contrary may happen in a
> remarkable degree.(12)

Here Reid recognises that we may have an original conception
from perception that is simple, though not mathematically
articulate, and another conception that is complex but
mathematically articulate.

This distinction between two different conceptions of a
primary quality, the figure of a body, should, it seems to
me, have entered into Reid's theory of primary qualities
generally. He says in the Active Powers that our conception
of motion cannot be defined, that is, is simple, though it
seems obvious that we all have a relative and complex notion
of motion as change of place. It seems to me, therefore,
that he ought to have said something similar with respect to
hardness and the other primary qualities generally. What he
should have said is that we at first have a simple and
original conception by means of the senses and that we later
have a conception which is the result of generalization and
is complex and scientific. For it is very difficult to see

how one could reasonably hold that we have an original
conception of hardness as a cohesion among parts and not have
an original conception of motion as change of place.  I think
that it is, therefore, better to suppose that there is a line
of development in Reid that would have enabled him to combine
the theory of the Inquiry with that of the Essays in a
consistent manner.

The account would be as follows.  We have a simple
conception of primary qualities, while we have only a
relative conception of secondary qualities.  The simple
conception that we have of a primary quality is original  and
is the conception of an individual quality.  Such conception
occurs automatically  once attention is  directed toward  the
individual quality.  There is a further general  conception
that we  obtain as  a result  of generalizing  and forming  a
conception of  a  general  attribute  or  universal.   This
conception is  clear, distinct,  precise, and  mathematically
articulate.  This is the theory that he should have  held.  I
am not sure whether it  is his theory or not, however.  Reid
says that  we  obtain  a  clear and  distinct  conception  of
primary qualities by means of the senses.  He also  says that
such conceptions are original.  Now, strictly speaking,  this
is consistent with the account that I have just given, that I
have said he should  have held.  For the senses give us  the
original conception of individual  qualities.  The  further
step of  generalization  to  obtain  a  conception  of  the
universal, which is precise  and distinct, is the end  result
of an operation starting from sensation, from the senses.

My only doubt about  whether this is Reid's theory  stems
from his  obvious  motivation  for holding  the  doctrine  of
primary qualities he did.  His motivation  was to avoid  any
taint  of  the  Ideal  Theory  by  downgrading  the  role  of
sensation in our conception of the fundamental properties  of
the physical world.  Sensation merely occasions or gives rise
to those conceptions without  being a conceptual or  semantic
component of them.  These conceptions might have arisen in us
in some other manner  without the intervention of  sensations
at all.  The relation between sensation and conception is  an
arbitrary relation of signification, like that between a word
and its meaning, and any conception that we might have of the
sensations that  occasion  these fundamental  conceptions  of
primary qualities is conceptually and semantically irrelevant
to our conception of them.  Reid was, I conjecture,  so eager
to argue  that our  conception of primary  qualities did  not
involve any conception  of any sensation  that he picked  one

primary quality, hardness, and presented us with a conception that clearly did not involve any conception of a sensation, to wit, one of cohesion among the parts. Unfortunately, it is very implausible to suppose that upon merely pressing one's hand against a body one acquires a conception of cohesion and of parts of a whole.

How much more plausible it would have been to argue that we have a simple and unanalysable conception of an individual quality, a conception that one can only have by perceiving it, which then leads to a complex and mathematically general conception by the operation of generalization. Abstraction yields the conception of individual primary qualities which are simple and unanalysable. Generalization yields the general conception of primary qualities which are complex and analysable. When one asks what the various individual qualities of hardness have in common, in Reid's word, how they agree, one notes that they all have a certain cohesion of the parts. I do not insist that Reid clearly grasped this way of rendering his theory consistent. He was more preoccupied with avoiding the tenets of the Ideal Theory. It is clear, however, that a consistent rendition is suggested by his own ideas.

## III

Conclusion and Reflections on the Moral Sense. With these textual considerations before us, I offer an account of conception and evidence that seems to me the most consistent one that can be developed from the works of Reid. According to Reid, then, there are different faculties or original conceptual powers of the human mind. Each of these faculties has particular principles that determine operations of the mind that yield conceptions of individual primary qualities. A conception of these qualities and a belief in their existence is immediately occasioned once attention is directed toward the individual quality. This process is abstraction and need not involve generalization to a general conception. The theory of evidence that accompanies this theory of conception is that the conceptions of individual primary qualities are original, and, therefore, our irresistible conviction of the existence of these qualities and the objects that have them is evident without reasoning and justified in itself.

The most fundamental distinction for Reid is between those operations of the mind that yield conceptions and those that do not.  The faculties of mind are similar to what Fodor (13) called a module.  The particular principles of a faculty yield conceptual responses to states that signify the thing conceived.  These conceptual responses, accompanied by a belief in what is conceived, are automatic and are not influenced by reasoning or background information.  According to this theory of faculties, a sense is simply an original capacity of the mind to yield conceptual responses in response to the appropriate sign.  In the case of the physical senses, the conceptual response is a response to sensation.  A sense is an automatic conceptual response system.

The foregoing characterization of a faculty of sense may seem peculiar in that it renders the physical organ of sense, the eye for example, a mere instrument of the sense, vision for example.  In this, Reid both grasps the implication of traditional dualism and anticipates modern theory.  It is sensation that is an operation of the mind, not the physical impression on the organ of sense and the connected nerves.  A being endowed with the sensations and the particular principles yielding conceptual responses to those sensations possesses the mental faculty or sense whatever the state of the physical organs of sense.  Reid remarks that in a future state we might be able to see though we were disembodied.  A very similar modern point is that the sensations and particular principles of conceptual response might be realized by some creature who lacked the sort of body we possess.  A Martian, though made of different stuff, might see exactly the same thing that we see, even though he was made of something other than carbon, silicon, for example. What Reid noted is that the states and principles of the mind, including the senses, might be realized in a variety of different ways and are, in principle, independent of the specific physical structures with which they happen to be associated.

With this conception of a faculty or sense as an innate conceptual response system, it was open to Reid to argue that, in addition to the usual senses, we have a moral sense. This proposal was not without some complication, however. First of all, Reid was convinced that our moral sense yields moral conceptions and judgments in response to our contemplation of actions.  Thus, for Reid, there is an immediate disanalogy between the other senses that yield conceptual responses to sensations and the moral sense that yields conceptual responses to the contemplation of actions.

There is, as Reid insisted, a closer analogy in this respect between the moral faculty and the faculty of reason which yields conceptual responses to the contemplation of premises. This difference shows that there is a different role for learning in the case of morals, for one can surely learn to contemplate actions in one way rather than another, for example, one can compare a given action to one of great nobility. Reid acknowledges and, indeed, insists upon the importance of moral instruction. The question is how can moral instruction be essential if the moral sense automatically yields moral conceptions and judgments upon contemplation of actions?

The answer to this question is the key to understanding the role of nature versus nurture in innate responses of the faculties of the human mind. Reid often uses the example of walking as an analogy to an innate capacity like seeing or hearing, and, in analogy to the moral sense, he uses dancing. In both cases, the original capacity is innate. We shall, moreover, learn to walk unless hindered from doing so without instruction. We shall also learn to dance, at least in simple ways, but here we require intercourse with others who provide us with a model. Once we observe some simple dance, we are able to dance without further instruction, but without such examples we might never develop the capacity. The capacity is, in both cases, innate, but fulfilment in one case requires intercourse with others while in the other it does not. We need to contemplate the actions of others in order to develop the operation of the moral sense, while the operation of the other senses does not require the contemplation of the activities of others.

How are we to understand Reid's claim that the moral sense is a faculty, that is, something that automatically yields conceptual responses, indeed, moral judgment, to the contemplation of actions and, at the same time, requires intercourse with others, indeed moral instruction, in order to yield correct judgments? The answer is quite simple. The moral sense yields automatic responses to input, but we have considerable leeway as to what we supply as input. Different input will yield different conceptual output. Thus, if I contemplate an action as having features A and B, the moral sense yields the output that the action is wrong or unjust. A more considered contemplation of the action as having, not only features A and B, but also C, will yield the output that the action is right or just. Thus a very young child who contemplates an action of another as sticking a needle in his

arm may quite automatically judge the action to be unjust,
but the further reflection that the needle contains a
medicine that will cure his illness alters the way in which
the child contemplates the action, and, therefore produces a
different judgment. In one respect, therefore, the moral
sense is like the other senses. Given a specific input, the
conceptual response is irresistible. What is peculiar to the
moral sense, and what renders it analogous to the faculty of
reason, is that we are free to direct our attention to some
matters rather than others and, though the output is
determined once the input is supplied, it is in our power to
determine the input.

The fact that we are free to determine how we contemplate
actions and are influenced by instruction shows that the
epistemology of the moral sense is more complicated than the
epistemology of the other senses. The latter give rise to
irresistible belief in the existence of individual primary
qualities in response to sensations. Those beliefs are
evident and justified in themselves. They are the roots of
the tree of empirical knowledge. The moral sense gives rise
to beliefs concerning the rightness of actions in response to
the contemplation of actions, and, though these beliefs may
be irresistible responses to the way we contemplate the
actions, we cannot conclude that these beliefs are evident or
justified. The way in which the action is contemplated may
be partial and unenlightened. The belief, therefore, may be
unjustified.

How, then, can we arrive at moral knowledge? Reid
thought that some ways of contemplating actions yield beliefs
concerning the rightness of those actions that are evident
and justified in themselves. The way is to contemplate the
action impartially. I quote:

> In every case, we ought to act that part towards
> another, which we would judge to be right in him to
> act toward us, if we were in his circumstances and
> he in ours... If there be any such thing as right
> and wrong in the conduct of moral agents, it must be
> the same to all in the same circumstance. ... It
> is not want of judgments, but want of candour and
> impartiality, that hinders men from discerning what
> they owe to others. ... As the equity and
> obligation of this rule of conduct is self-evident
> to every man who hath a conscience; so it is, of
> all the rules of morality, the most comprehensive

... It comprehends every rule of justice without
exception.    ...    To sum up all, he who acts
invariably by this rule will never deviate from  the
path of  his duty,  but from an  error of  judgment.
And, as he feels the obligation that he and all  men
are under to use the best means in his power to have
his judgment well-informed in  matters of duty,  his
errors will only be such as are invincible.(14)

In conclusion, I leave it  to the reader to judge the  merits
of the proposal.  Reid held that the innate principles of the
human mind  yield  some  conceptions  and  beliefs  that  are
irresistible and, therefore, justified in themselves.   Those
beliefs are the roots of the tree of knowledge.   The rest of
growth results from  our nurturing.   When this nurturing  is
properly guided by  our nature, by  the innate principles  of
our constitution, what grows from custom and reason will also
be justified.  We are,  however, at liberty to nurture as  we
will, and, as a result,  we are liable to fall into the  pits
of error and scepticism when  we depart from the dictates  of
our nature and the principles of common sense.

## NOTES

*I gratefully acknowledge that research on this paper was supported by a grant from the National Science Foundation and a fellowship from the John Simon Guggenheim Foundation.

(1)  V, iii (Works, p. 121).

(2)  V, iii (Works, p. 122).

(3)  Ibid.

(4)  Ibid.

(5)  V, iv (Works, p. 123).

(6)  Ibid.

(7)  Turbayne (1959).

(8)  **IP**, V, iv (Works, p. 401).

(9)  Ibid.

(10) **IP**, IV, i (Works, p. 364).

(11) **IP**, V, iii (Works, p. 395).

(12) **AP**, I, i (Works, p. 514).

(13) Fodor (1983).

(14) **AP**, V, i (Works, p. 639).

Dennis Charles Holt


## THE DEFENCE OF COMMON SENSE IN REID AND MOORE


It is to be expected that two philosophers who set out
explicitly to defend common sense against idealism and
scepticism would proceed from common assumptions and employ
similar strategies of argumentation. This is, in fact, the
case with Reid and Moore. Neither Reid nor Moore are
prepared to accept philosophical positions, however acutely
argued, which deny outright realities that they take to be
constitutive of ordinary life – e.g., physical objects,
self-identity, other minds – or which deny the reasonableness
of our everyday beliefs concerning them. The beliefs of
common sense are defined in opposition to these denials; and
their philosophies, it is fair to say, are essentially
reactionary. If to the list of opponents (which for Reid
included the subjective idealism of Berkeley and the
phenomenalistic scepticism of Hume) Moore adds the absolute
idealism of Bradley, et al, this is merely the result of
historical circumstance. The essential spirit of their
argumentation is the same. One would expect Reid to have
been similarly disposed against the denial of the reality of
time or the assertion that only the Absolute is real.
Despite these similarities in predisposition, in basic
assumptions, and in strategies of argumentation (which have
been noted elsewhere by Keith Lehrer(1) and Edward Madden(2)
among others), there do exist interesting differences in the
development of their philosophies of common sense. Though
these disanalogies may indicate only a difference of
emphasis, it is hard not to think, once the question has been
examined, that the differences are more substantial. The
purpose of this paper, then, is (I) to review those elements
common to the defence of common sense in Reid and Moore, and
(II) to highlight points of significant difference.


I


Since Moore and Reid develop a self-conscious philosophy of
common sense, in opposition to idealistic and sceptical
philosophies, they must assume that a philosophy of sorts is
contained in the ordinary transactions of life, in the things
we ordinarily, unreflectively, do and say. This philosophy
is expressed in propositions of which we should not be aware

*M. Dalgarno and E. Matthews (eds.), The Philosophy of Thomas Reid, 145–157.*
© *1989 by Kluwer Academic Publishers.*

except for philosophical pronouncements to the contrary and
which is implied, because assumed in our everyday behaviour.
When in an ordinary circumstance the sales clerk exclaims to
his customer (who has just inquired about a sofa), 'Why, yes,
I am quite certain that that is the same sofa which was there
yesterday and which I told you about the day before, and, no,
the price is still the same as I quoted this morning when we
talked on the phone', he is making an assertion which
assumes, among other things, personal identity, the
continuity and existence of physical objects, the existence
of other minds, the legitimacy of claims to know, or to be
certain, etc., etc. And if it is not likely that the sales
clerk would independently formulate these general
assumptions, still they are operative in the things he does
and says. For to assert that the sofa is there, in the
display room, is to assert the existence of a physical
object; and to say that it is the sofa that I spoke to you
about (to claim this responsibility) is to assume an identity
of the present speaker with the individual who spoke earlier;
and to speak to the customer is to assume that he embodies a
consciousness which can hear and understand; and to claim
certainty (to proceed generally without doubt) is to assume
that certainty about sofas and persons and the past is
justified. Thus the defence of common sense insists that
philosophical positions must be measured against the things
we do and say in ordinary, philosophically unreflective life,
and the absurdity of certain philosophical pronouncements
arises because they seem to run contrary to ordinary life and
language.

Yet neither Reid nor Moore intend a wholesale defence of
the beliefs of the 'man on the street'. The beliefs to be
defended are only those which can claim to be foundational to
human knowledge. They are beliefs concerning the existence
of things falling within very general categories and the
possibility of holding rational beliefs about them,
including, for example, our knowledge of physical objects, of
past and future events, and of our own and of other selves.
But is there any way, other than ad hoc specification, to
identify these foundational beliefs, to separate the
authentic beliefs of common sense from those of mere
prejudice and custom?

Both Moore and Reid recognize how difficult it is to
separate the essential from the questionable beliefs of
common sense. How are mere dogmatisms to be distinguished
from legitimate propositions of common sense? As Moore

writes: "The phrases 'Common Sense view of the world' or 'Common Sense beliefs' (as used by philosophers) are, of course, extraordinarily vague; and, for all I know, there may be propositions which may be properly called features in 'the Common Sense view of the world' or 'Common Sense beliefs', which are not true, and which deserve to be mentioned with the contempt with which some philosophers speak of 'Common Sense beliefs'".(3)   And Reid admits, in his general discussion of common sense, that "what the precise limits are which divide common judgment from what is beyond it on one hand, and from what falls short of it on the other, may be difficult to determine".(4)   But both philosophers are in agreement that the beliefs of common sense by which they would stand are such that it would be absurd to deny them. Referring to the propositions enumerated at the beginning of his essay on certainty, Moore writes, "And I do not think that I can be justly accused of dogmatism or over-confidence for having asserted these things positively in the way that I did.   In the case of some kinds of assertions and under some circumstances a man can be justly accused of dogmatism for asserting something positively.    But in the case of assertions such as I made under the circumstances under which I made them, the charge would be absurd.  On the contrary, I should have been guilty of absurdity, if, under the circumstances, I had not spoken positively about these things".(5)   Likewise Reid, in what seems to be exact concurrence, states "that opinions which contradict first principles, are distinguished from other errors, by this: that they are not only false but absurd".(6)

These three assumptions – (i) that many of the conclusions of idealists and sceptics contradict propositions implicit in the conduct of ordinary life, which we may call 'propositions of common sense', (ii) that propositions of common sense are foundational to human knowledge, and (iii) that the denial of these propositions is not only false but absurd – naturally engender similar strategies of argumentation in Moore's and Reid's defences of common sense.

Because propositions of common sense are foundational, it is not possible to provide constructive, independent grounds for their acceptance.   The propositions of common sense constitute the final court of appeal; they cannot themselves be justified, at least in the manner appropriate to derivative propositions.  For that reason it must seem to the committed idealist or sceptic that the defender of common sense begs the question.  For if the common sense philosopher

can do no more than appeal to the evident absurdity of
contradicting a particular proposition, then he supports his
position by mere assertion to the contrary when what is
wanted are reasons and arguments. (Lehrer refers to this as
the "quandary of common sense").(7) Yet neither Reid nor
Moore are so naive as to be unaware of this problem. While
granting that in the end they cannot do much more than insist
upon the absurdity of the conclusions which they oppose, they
both justify in similar ways their failure to provide
constructive argumentation. And their first justification is
to remind us that this is to be expected of foundational
propositions: What more can we do but insist upon them?

Perhaps something more: It is a matter of some
significance to Reid and Moore that the troubling and
difficult pronouncements of the idealists and sceptics do not
occur to us except as a consequence of philosophical
argumentation. That one can do little more than assert the
propositions of common sense may seem, perhaps, a defect; but
if they are in fact foundational propositions, that is to be
expected. Though the presentation of arguments on behalf of
one's position is a philosophical virtue, it is also an
indication that one's position is a hypothesis. It is,
therefore, as vulnerable as the reasoning which led to it and
the assumptions upon which that reasoning is based. A
presumption is established in favour of the common sense
proposition, and scepticism about the arguments which lead to
the contradiction of common sense is surely as justified as
the rejection of common sense which these arguments seem to
imply. Thus there is, at the very least, a parity of
certainty (or uncertainty), since the sceptic and idealist
must themselves begin with unquestioned propositions. Even
more, there is a distinct advantage to the defender of common
sense precisely because he is not burdened with arguments
that might prove to be faulty. Thus Moore writes, concerning
Russell's scepticism: "What I want, however, finally to
emphasize is this: Russell's view that I do not know for
certain that this is a pencil or that you are conscious
rests, if I am right, on no less than four distinct
assumptions... And what I can't help asking myself is this:
Is it, in fact, as certain that all these four assumptions
are true, as that I do know that this is a pencil and that
you are conscious? I cannot help answering: It seems to me
more certain that I do know that this is a pencil and that
you are conscious than that any single one of these four
assumptions is true, let alone all four".(8) And Reid, for
his part, writes that if reasoning leads "to a conclusion

that contradicts the decisions of common sense", then "a man of common sense may fairly° reject the conclusion without being able to show the error of the reasoning that led to it".(9) Scepticism about the soundness of the sceptic's arguments is at least as justified as the scepticism which he urges upon us; rejection of the idealist's conclusions is at least as justified ·as the certainty with which he advances them.

Consistency between principle and practice is another consideration. For Moore and Reid both the sceptic and the idealist betray their positions in their conduct of ordinary life. Their philosophical principles conflict with their operative principles. Granted, the logician will remind us that the ad hominem charge of inconsistency is strictly fallacious. If a philosopher maintains two inconsistent propositions, it only follows that one of the propositions .that he maintains is false; but nothing is implied as to which of the propositions it is. On the other hand, consistency is a virtue, and Moore is clearly adducing considerations in favour of common sense when he writes: "...I am one of those philosophers who have held that the 'Common Sense view of the world' is, in certain fundamental features, wholly true. But it must be remembered that, according to me, all philosohers, without exception, have agreed with me in holding this: and that the real difference, which is commonly expressed in this way, is only a difference between those philosophèrs, who have also held views inconsistent with these features in 'the Common Sense view of the world', and those who have not".(10) And Reid himself explicitly asserts that "It is a good argument ad hominem, if it can be shewn that a first principle which a man rejects, stands upon the same footing with others which he admits: for, when this .is the case, he must be guilty of an inconsistency who holds the one and rejects the other".(11) These inconsistencies are implied by the sceptic's and idealist's use of our common language (even as they advance their theses) and by their conduct in ordinary life. Not mere inconsistency is at issue here, but inconsistency which is an inevitable consequence of inquiry, disputation, and human intercourse in general. The propositions of common sense are in a sense constitutive of rational life. To doubt (really, practically to doubt) that this is one hand or to reject the reality of the conscious subject, the objects of sense, etc., etc., is, unless one should choose insanity, impossible. This is, perhaps, what Wittgenstein meant when he characterized the propositions enumerated by Moore in

'Certainty' as 'hinge propositions'. It also perhaps characterizes the sort of absurdity which is involved in the denial of the propositions of common sense.

These three strategies together with the three assumptions described earlier provide a general characterization of common sense philosophy as it was advocated by Moore and Reid. It might seem that two philosophers could not be more alike in basic orientation, and indeed there is no denying that they are cut from the same cloth, but the cut of the cloth is also notably different.

## II

There are at least two enormous, and I think fundamental, differences in the approaches of Reid and Moore to the defence of common sense. First, Moore retains a representative theory of perception whereas Reid makes the refutation of such theories an essential part of his defence of common sense. And second, the epistemologically fundamental propositions of common sense enumerated by Reid, and their articulation within his philosophy of common sense, bear little resemblance to the comparable features of Moore's philosophy.

The first point has often been noted. For Moore it is undeniable that perception is mediated by sense-data. "I hold it to be quite certain", he writes, "that I do not directly perceive my hand; and that when I am said...to 'perceive' it, that I 'perceive' (in a different and more fundamental sense) something which is (in a suitable sense) representative of it".(12)   Directly opposed to this view – that we do not in the fundamental sense of the term perceive physical objects – is the following assertion of Reid: "All the arguments urged by Berkeley and Hume, against the existence of a material world, are grounded upon this principle – that we do not perceive external objects themselves, but certain images or ideas in our own minds. But this is no dictate of common sense, but directly contrary to the sense of all who have not been taught it by philosophy".(13) On Reid's view, if we concede this point the game is up; for the fault that leads us to the conclusions of Berkeley and Hume "is not in the reasoning, but in the principles, from which it is drawn".(14)   Moore will agree with Russell "that I don't know these things [e.g., that this is a pencil] immediately",(15) and yet sanguinely report his certainty concerning the truth of the proposition that this is a pencil. But for Reid we are never justifiably certain of propositions asserting the existence of physical objects unless we do sometimes perceive them immediately. In Reid's words: "if external objects be perceived immediately, we have the same reason to believe their existence as philosophers have to believe the existence of ideas, while they hold them to be the immediate objects of perception".(16)   Here, then, is a fundamental point of divergence. In their specification, use, and elaboration of the propositions of common sense this divergence widens.

Consider Moore's proof of the external world: "By holding up my two hands, and saying, as I make a certain gesture with the right hand, 'Here is one hand,' and adding, as I make a certain gesture with the left, 'and here is another'...I have proved ipso facto the existence of external things".(17)   Or consider the propositions enumerated at the beginning of his essay on certainty: "I am at present, as you can all see, in a room and not in the open air; I am standing up, and not either sitting or lying down; I have clothes on, and am not absolutely naked", etc., etc.(18)   The propositions which constitute the final court of appeal in Moore's defence of common sense are particular and situational. Propositions to the effect that physical objects, the past, other selves, etc., are real are, to be sure, propositions of common sense; but they are, or can be, supported by putting them to the test in a particular situation by appeal to a particular proposition which corresponds to them; they are generalizations from these.

The situational assertion of particulars in support of their general counterparts is, I think, the most striking feature of Moore's defence of common sense. It is a strategy which seems to have been anticipated, or recommended, by Reid when he wrote: "It is another property of this and of many first principles, that they force assent in particular instances, more powerfully than when they are turned into a general proposition...and it may be observed of those who have professed scepticism, that their scepticism lies in generals, while in particulars they are no less dogmatical than others".(19)   It is not to be inferred, however, that Reid's foundational propositions are of the kind to which Moore appeals. They are rather 'the first principles of contingent truths'. And the central principles among these are not to be construed as either existential or universal generalizations from particular propositions, but serve rather as procedural rules which 'validate' certain means of judging the truth of propositions together with assumptions necessary to inquiry and action. Reid does not require, as a first move, that we are able to make particular assertions which are beyond all doubt. The certainty of particular assertions is embedded in general assumptions about the grounds of legitimate doubt and justification. There is, consequently, a significant difference in emphasis between the epistemological theories of Moore and Reid. Reid offers a comprehensive, relatively systematic, common sense epistemology, which combines foundationalism and fallibilism and is rooted, through his attack upon the 'theory of ideas', in a rejection of the egocentric predicament. Though some of these elements may be present in Moore, their presence, if they are there, is considerably less pronounced.

The role of the 'first principles of contingent truths' in Reid's epistemology is best understood against the background of his fallibilism. Reid's defence of common sense does not rest upon the possibility of enumerating particular propositions whose truth can be known beyond all doubt (e.g. 'I exist', 'Here is one hand', 'There are many thinking, living human beings in this room' etc.). Though Reid, I imagine, would agree with Moore that we know such particulars with paradigmatic certainty, this certainty is to be understood in terms of a fallibilistic account of the powers, of faculties, whereby we judge the truth of these propositions. "That, in all our judgments", he writes, "we ought to be sensible of our fallibility, and ought to hold our opinions with that modesty that becomes fallible creatures...I think, nobody denies".(20) But what follows from this? "It is granted, then, that human judgments ought always to be formed with an humble sense of our fallibility in judging. This is all that can be inferred by the rules of logic from our being fallible".(21) Not, for instance, that we can never be certain of any judgment; not that certainty in judgment is never justified. Hume had argued that in the process of adjusting for possible error in judgment (which I must undertake upon recognition of my own fallibility) I must arrive at the conclusion that I have no evidence for any judgment whatsoever, no justified certainty. "'When I reflect on the natural fallibility of my judgment, I have less confidence in my opinions than when I only consider the objects concerning which I reason. And when I proceed still farther, to turn the scrutiny against every successive estimation I make of my faculties, all the rules of logic require a continual diminution and at last a total extinction of belief and evidence.'"(22)  The fallibility in our initial judgment is compounded by the fallibility of the faculty with which we would adjust for the initial fallibility; and if we attempt to adjust for the second uncertainty, a third is introduced, and so on until we find ourselves in a state of perfect pyrrhonian ataraxia. The fault in Hume's reasoning, according to Reid, does not lie in the initial assumption – that human judgment is fallible – but in its conception of 'the rules of logic', that is, in its conception of the procedural rules which govern doubt and justification.

Hume, Reid argues, "supposes, that a man, when he forms his first judgment, conceives himself to be infallible; that by a second and subsequent judgment, he discovers that he is not infallible; and that by a third judgment, subsequent to the second, he estimates his liableness to err in such a case as the present".(23)  But infallibility is not an assumption of our original certainty.  The reasonable person maintains an ongoing sense of his own fallibility and of the causes of error in judgment.  "He knows what are the cases in which he is most or least likely to err".(24)  Therefore, if reasons are brought forward to think that a judgment of vision, memory, hearing, reason, etc., has gone wrong, he may, through the use of the very faculty which led him astray in the first place, correct for the original error. He is not required to invoke the 'testimony' of an additional faculty in vain search for a power of judgment which is infallible in itself or in its application.  He may check his original judgment by repeating his original procedure, providing that he corrects for possible sources of error.  "If it be a matter of importance, I return to weigh the evidence of my first judgment. If it was precipitate before, it must now be deliberate in every point. If, at first, I was in passion, I must now be cool.  If I had an interest in the decision, I must place the interest on the other side".(25)  Here Reid is speaking of the power of reason, or adjudication, but the point also holds for sense-perception. If for some reason we have occasion to doubt our eyes we do not necessarily turn away to means of another kind, but look again, more carefully, under more favourable circumstances.  Adjustment for error is relative to the assumed cause of error.

But if it should be necessary to look for an independent judgment upon the reliability of the original faculty, "the first judgment may be compared to the testimony of a credible witness; the second, after a scrutiny into the character of the witness, wipes off every objection that can be made to it, and therefore surely must confirm and not weaken his testimony".(26) That there is an inherent fallibility in the process of confirmation does not compound the uncertainty. Quite the contrary, the reliability of one's original judgment is increased to the point of certainty. It is reliability, not fallibility, which compounds.

In any case (and this, I think, is the most important point) we are not required to undertake this series of checks and rechecks, estimations upon our original judgment, unless there is some good reason to do so. "I know no reason", Reid argues, "...that requires that such a series of estimations should follow every particular judgment".(27) Barring evidence of error, there is presumption favouring an original judgment made in normal circumstances. But what if someone should question the right of presumption?

To do so would be to assume that our natural faculties – consciousness, the senses, memory, reason – might be generally fallacious and not merely fallible. And to make this assumption is to contradict certain first principles of contingent truths: for example, the 7th, "That the natural faculties, by which we distinguish truth from error, are not fallacious", which Reid calls the "fundamental truth on which all others rest",(28) and the 5th, which states "That those things do really exist which we distinctly perceive by our senses, and are what we perceive them to be".(29) These are clearly principles the function of which is to establish the general admissibility of certain kinds of evidence and certain means of discerning truth and falsity. Even the 8th principle, which asserts the existence "of life and intelligence in our fellow-men with whom we converse"(30) is construed as a ground of the possibility of action and inquiry. They cannot of course be supported by evidence or demonstration, since they are the ground of all evidence and demonstration. But they do bear the marks of first principles in that they are implied in the normal conduct of life and even in the sceptic's attack upon them. They are constitutive of common sense, which Reid defines as that "degree of understanding which makes a man capable of action with common prudence in the conduct of life", and which "makes him capable of discovering what is true and what is false in matters that are self-evident and which he distinctly apprehends".(31) To defend common sense just is to insist upon these general principles. To reject these principles is to reject all regulative rules of evidence and prudential action.

Thus Reid's defence of  common sense  is systematic  and theoretical, whereas Moore's is comparatively restricted  and ad hoc.   It is  an interesting  question, if one  is in  the market for a  common sense  philosophy, which is  preferable. One ought to give the advantage to Reid for having recognized the extent to which  scepticism and idealism rests upon  'the theory of ideas'.  Whether  he gains an advantage for  having made the  issue  of  scepticism  turn on  the  acceptance  of general principles of evidence and prudence is more difficult to say.

## NOTES

(1)  Lehrer, in Barker and Beauchamp (1976).

(2)  Madden (1983).

(3)  Moore (1959, p. 45)

(4)  **IP**, VI, ii (<u>Works</u>, p. 423).

(5)  Moore (1959, p. 227).

(6)  **IP**, VI, iv (<u>Works</u>, p. 438).

(7)  Barker and Beauchamp (1976, p. 6).

(8)  Moore (1959, p. 226).

(9)  **IP**, VI, ii (<u>Works</u>, pp. 425–6).

(10) Moore (1959, p. 44).

(11) **IP**, VI, iv (<u>Works</u>, p. 439).

(12) Moore (1959, p. 55).

(13) **IP**, VI, v (<u>Works</u>, p. 446).

(14) <u>Ibid</u>.

(15) Moore (1959, p. 226).

(16) **IP**, VI, v (<u>Works</u>, p. 446).

(17) Moore (1959, p. 146).

(18) Moore (1959, p. 227).

(19) **IP**, VI, v (<u>Works</u>, p. 448).

(20) **IP**, VII, iv (<u>Works</u>, p. 485).

(21) <u>Ibid</u>.

(22) Quoted in **IP**, VII, iv (<u>Works</u>, p. 486).

(23) **IP**, VII, iv (<u>Works</u>, p. 488).

(24) Ibid.

(25) **IP**, VII, iv (Works, p. 487).

(26) Ibid.

(27) **IP**, VII, iv (Works, p. 488).

(28) **IP**, VI, v (Works, pp. 447–8).

(29) **IP** VI, v (Works, p. 445).

(30) **IP**, VI, v (Works, p. 448).

(31) **IP**, VI, ii (Works, p. 422).

T. J. Sutton

## THE SCOTTISH KANT?
## A Reassessment of Reid's epistemology

## Summary and Introduction

In this paper I examine the similarities between Reid's and
Kant's responses to scepticism.(1) While I find neither
wholly convincing, I suggest that Reid's appeal to common
sense can be interpreted as a form of transcendental argument
and that this justifies a more favourable assessment than has
hitherto been usual of his contribution to the theory of
knowledge.

The structure of the paper is as follows. Section 1
highlights some important differences between eighteenth and
twentieth century approaches to the theory of knowledge.
Section 2 describes the sceptical position against which Reid
and Kant were reacting. In section 3 I argue that both are
foundationalists and so share the same antisceptical
strategy. In sections 4 and 5 I consider in turn the
theories each formulates to show that knowledge is possible,
and assess the difficulties into which they run. Section 6
highlights the similarities between their theories; I argue
for a transcendental interpretation of Reid's first
principles and his appeal to common sense in their defence.
In section 7 I suggest that Kant's idealism – which finds no
parallel in Reid – fails to dispose of the sceptic. I
conclude by considering the implications of my analysis for
the comparison between Reid and Kant.

Apart from the closeness of the dates of publication of their
major works (Reid's Essays on the Intellectual Powers of Man,
published in 1785, comes between the first (1781) and second
(1787) editions of Kant's Critique of Pure Reason), some
superficial resemblances between Reid and Kant are obvious.
Both claim to have been awakened by Hume to the realisation
that philosophers hitherto had been fundamentally in error;
both wanted to prove that knowledge is possible; both
developed a complete philosophical system in order to do so;
and each was responsible for a school of thought which
occupies a distinct chapter in the history of ideas. The
chapter headed 'Transcendental Idealism' is usually longer

M. Dalgarno and E. Matthews (eds.), The Philosophy of Thomas Reid, 159–192.
© 1989 by Kluwer Academic Publishers.

than that headed 'Scottish School of Common Sense Philosophy', and this is not just because of the greater difficulty of Kant's thought. The majority view among those who have considered their respective merits as epistemologists can I think be summarized as follows: Kant's transcendental idealism penetrates to the heart of the sceptical challenge while Reid's common sense, however appealing to the plain man in all of us, just misses the point or begs the question. This paper explains why I consider such a view no less superficial than the biographical similarities just noted.(2)

While it is beyond the scope of this paper to offer a point by point historical or critical comparison, I hope that historians of ideas will be encouraged by what I say to reassess Reid's epistemology, and that those who find his chief claim to fame elsewhere will be prepared to accept, even if only argumentis causa, the validity of assuming in company with both Reid and Kant that the sceptic does have something important to say which is worth answering.

## 1. Preliminaries

Several differences between the epistemologist of the eighteenth century (or of the seventeenth, for that matter) and his modern successor are important for the arguments which follow.

First, epistemology was closely connected with metaphysics. Knowledge was regarded as a belief of whose truth one was certain, or whose truth was guaranteed, and the concern was often as much with what facts one knew to be true of the world — how the world was — as with whether and how one knew these facts. Secondly, knowledge was often not distinguished as sharply as we would nowadays find natural from rational or justified belief (contrast for example Locke's discussion of sensitive knowledge in Essay IV chapters 2 and 3 with Hume's more carefully-developed distinction between knowledge, proofs and probabilities in Treatise I iii 11). Consequently it is often unclear whether a philosopher of the period is defending our knowledge of a proposition, or only the rationality of our believing it even though it may subsequently turn out to be false. Two connected effects of this are particularly relevant. First, epistemology was frequently blended with psychology in accounting for our beliefs. Hume, Reid and even Kant all at times fail to make distinctions which are important to modern debate in this area, and can seem as concerned to give a causal explanation of how we come by the beliefs we regard as knowledge as to discuss whether we are right so to regard them. Secondly, there is a considerable ambiguity over the concept of certainty. A long line of philosophers and theologians were able – not always consciously, of course – to exploit this, for example by distinguishing moral certainty (which might be psychologically convincing even if not strictly demonstrable) from deductive certainty or proof. A further difference is that foundationalism was widely if not universally accepted without question. Foundationalism can be defined as the beliefs, first, that any ordinary proposition that we know is supported or justified by other propositions also known by us; and secondly that, since either an infinite regress or a circle would be unacceptable, there must be at least one proposition known without the benefit of other propositions supporting or justifying it. This may sound suspiciously modern, and it is true that not everyone was as careful as Reid to make these beliefs explicit. There is also, as we shall see, some difficulty with the notion that the foundations must be propositions; the definition as it stands is not adequate to the accounts of the foundations of our knowledge given by Reid or Kant. But it is this line of reasoning which leads Descartes in the Meditations to the cogito; and Hume reveals in the First Enquiry that he holds such a view:

> When it is asked, What is the nature of all our reasonings concerning matter of fact, the proper answer seems to be, that they are founded on the relation of cause and effect. When again it is asked, What is the foundation of all our reasonings and conclusions concerning that relation? it may be replied in one word, Experience. But if we still carry on our sifting humour, and ask, What is the foundation of all conclusions from experience? this implies a new question, which may be of a more difficult solution and explication.(3)

I discuss Reid's and Kant's foundationalism in section 3.

All these points – the concern with metaphysics as well as epistemology, foundationalism, and the failure always to distinguish sufficiently sharply between knowledge and rational belief and its consequences (the ambiguity of 'certainty' and the tendency to run together epistemological and psychological questions) – need to be borne in mind in considering both the sceptical challenge thrown down by Hume and the responses to it formulated by Reid and Kant.

## 2. The problem: scepticism

We cannot adequately understand or evaluate the responses unless we have defined the problem clearly. It is not enough to say that both philosophers were reacting against the scepticism of Hume, for scepticism like Anglicanism is a broad church embracing a wide variety of distinct doctrines. The classification of varieties of scepticism is not concerned with the facts of the matter — such facts as whether there are causal connections in the world, whether the sun will rise tomorrow or whether the table in my study exists — but only with whether such propositions count, or can count, as knowledge or rational belief. In the modern idiom, the focus of concern is the truth-conditions of 'p'. The truth of 'p' is of course one of the truth-conditions of 'S knows that p', but this tends to be ignored or taken for granted by the sceptic. As Hume says:

> tis iń vain to ask, Whether there be body or not? That is a point, which we must take for granted in all our reasonings.(4)

Now Hume himself cannot be pigeonholed so neatly. As well as making clear his concern with whether we can know or rationally believe such propositions as the examples just given, he also holds dogmatically that some of them are false, e.g. (at least in the Treatise) that bodies have continued and distinct existence and (in both the Treatise and the First Enquiry) that necessary causal connections are a feature of the external world. Reid, especially in his Inquiry, mercilessly pillories Hume for all such lapses into what he sees — rightly in my view — as a cruder form of scepticism. But I intend to leave the niceties of Humean analysis to one side and concentrate on the somewhat idealized character I shall call simply 'the sceptic'. This character represents the strands in Hume's thought (best exemplified in his discussion of induction) which most exercised Reid and Kant.

The sceptic's challenge turns on the notion of justification. Without an adequate justification, the argument runs, we have no right to claim knowledge or even to regard our belief as rational. Justification is a concept rooted deep in the sceptical tradition. However it has not

until more recent times received as much attention as it
deserves, and affords both Hume and his opponents ample scope
for the substitution of causal psychological explanations in
place of the sort of response which the sceptic should be
demanding. It is far from clear what precisely it is that
the sceptic feels is needed. Hume usually speaks of
justification in terms of a "reason", concluding in the
Treatise:

> After the most accurate and exact of my
> reasonings, I can give no reason why I shou'd
> assent to it.(5)

This does not seem to get us much further forward. Note
however that according to the sceptic the need for a
justification applies equally to knowledge and to rational
belief. This means that his challenge cannot simply be
evaded by arguing that a proposition under attack can be
justified as a rational belief even if we cannot guarantee
its status as knowledge. It is tempting to interpret some
seventeenth and eighteenth century discussions of scepticism
as making this move (Locke on "sensitive knowledge", for
example). But whether or not such an interpretation is valid
here (and Reid as well as Kant lays sufficient stress on our
knowledge of the propositions under sceptical attack for its
aptness to be doubtful), it misses the point. This is not to
deny that the justifications required for knowledge and for
rational belief are different; indeed, recognizing the
nature of the difference is a central contribution of
twentieth century epistemology. It is just that the
rationality of belief comes under the sceptic's critical
scrutiny just as much as does knowledge.

The problem of justifying our knowledge or the
rationality of our beliefs is especially acute for a
foundationalist. For the sceptic questions precisely those
propositions which the foundationalist regards as basic to
the whole edifice of human knowledge – general propositions
concerning induction, causation, the external world. If our
knowledge of these propositions is shaken, the whole
structure is liable to come crashing down about our ears.
The position is made worse because it is a corollary of the
foundationalist thesis as defined above that such
propositions cannot have the same sort of justification as
the rest; that is what is meant by their being foundations.
Thus the sceptical challenge to penetrate dogmatic slumbers
is the challenge to show that we have a justification for

claiming knowledge of fundamental propositions such as these, or equally for claiming that our belief in them is rationally based. A central element in the defence of such propositions against scepticism will therefore be to develop a special sense of 'justification' appropriate to their peculiar status as propositions which, as Reid puts it:

> support all that are built upon them, but are themselves supported by none.(6)

As we shall see, for both Reid and Kant this requires us in some measure to qualify the description of their foundations, in keeping with the definition of foundationalism above, as propositions.

Finally it is worth observing that the concept of justification itself is still inadequately defined. A natural reaction might therefore be to refuse to play the sceptic's game. However neither Reid nor Kant responds in this way. I suggest that this is because to do so could seem to leave open the possibility that the sceptic was right; since Reid and Kant have set themselves the task of proving that knowledge is possible, they see themselves as having no choice but to do battle with the sceptic on his ground.

## 3. Foundationalist strategies

Before considering the detail of Reid's and Kant's responses to the sceptical challenge, which at first sight at least are very different, the closeness of the similarity between their strategies should be noted. In the first place, both Reid and Kant were foundationalists and so faced the particular difficulty described in the preceding section.

Reid makes his foundationalism quite clear in Essay VI chapter iv:

> I hold it to be certain, and even demonstrable, that all knowledge got by reasoning must be built upon first principles.

> This is as certain as that every house must have a foundation.(7)

Although Reid's first principles are not always expressed in a consistent form, it is clear from this and numerous other passages and from the analogy he draws betweeen the roles of axioms in Euclidean geometry and first principles in philosophy(8) that first principles are the foundations in his theory of knowledge. Reid offers two lists of first principles in the Essays (in Essay I chapter ii and Essay VI chapters v and vi). In defining foundationalism earlier I referred to propositions not supported by others. A key problem of interpretation is that Reid's first principles are not universally couched in propositional form. The I ii list includes "things wherein we find an universal agreement" which "we ought likewise to take for granted, as first principles";(9) and "such facts as are attested ... either by our senses, by memory, or by human testimony"(10) (my italics in both cases) while the list in VI v begins with "I hold, as a first principle, the existence of every thing of which I am conscious",(11) and includes "our own personal identity and continued existence, as far back as we remember anything distinctly".(12) Part of the reason for this variation in Reid's way of expressing his first principles is, I am sure, that he is concerned with metaphysical as well as epistemological questions. However the two lists do not correspond exactly: both the principles from the VI v list just cited have a propositional formulation in the I ii list.(13) So we could just reformulate all Reid's principles as propositions. His first principles would then express those beliefs we have to hold, on his account, if we are to go on to construct any knowledge at all. Reid's inconsistency in his formulations of these principles, though irritating, is not therefore fatal. Rather than eliminating it in this way, however, I prefer to regard it as a pointer towards the Kantian interpretation I outline in section 6.

A further point to be noted about Reid's first principles is that the lists contain a number of pretty specific principles (for example, that facial expressions indicate states of mind(14)) as well as general propositions about causation, personal identity and the external world. It is in my view necessary in order to accommodate this feature of his account to divide Reid's principles into two sets, of which only the first meets all of the criteria he himself specifies.(15) Again, this complication, forced on us by Reid's own discussion of the characteristics of first principles, is not fatal but points towards the interpretation I discuss in section 6.

Kant's theory of knowledge also has its foundations, although there is real difficulty in describing any of them in the terms strictly required by my definition earlier as

'propositions known or believed'.  In Kant, knowledge comes
from the synthesis of understanding and sensibility, and the
categories and the forms of intuition are meant to serve as
the foundations for each side of the synthesis.  The
categories are closer to concepts than propositions;  more
accurately, since the categories in so far as they serve as
foundations precede the schematization that 'concept'
implies, they are laws or rules:  principles according to
which we formulate propositions.  As Kant expresses it, the
unschematized categories are 'forms of thought', 'functions
of judgment' or 'rules for the understanding'.(16)  Because
they are a precondition for the synthetic operation of the
mind which produces propositions, or judgments, as the
objects of knowledge or belief, it is strictly incorrect to
say that we know or even believe them.  Nonetheless,
according to Kant, they do have to be true, or perhaps one
should say to obtain, if there is to be any meaningful
experience of the world.  The metaphysics here is equally
important for Kant:  he sees himself as showing how the world
necessarily is.  The boundary between how the world has to be
and the necessary truth of the set of propositions that
dscribes how the world has to be is not, after all, very
wide, especially when the features of the world for whose
necessity one is arguing are regarded as part of our own
understanding, so that the metaphysics becomes
(transcendental) psychology.  This is the case for Kant, as I
explain in section 5.  Furthermore, as I shall argue in
section 6, the categories' role as the preconditions for the
synthesis from which our knowledge of the world results is,
despite appearances, closely analogous to that of at least
the most important of Reid's first principles.  In fact –
perhaps because of the metaphysics – one could hardly wish
for a more thorough analysis than this of the unique status
of the foundations in a theory of knowledge.

Thus, while the application of my definition of
foundationalism to Kant is not entirely straightforward, the
fact that Reid's first principles are also not always
expressed in propositional form also suggests that there is
more to be said than the definition implied.  Whether it is a
set of propositions which have to be true before we can
construct any framework of beliefs or knowledge (as usually
in Reid) or a set of preconditions which must obtain or rules
which we must follow if we are to formulate any proposition
and believe or know anything at all (as in Kant), this basic
similarity of approach in my view justifies describing both
philosophers as foundationalists notwithstanding the

apparently considerable differences between their accounts of the nature of those foundations.

If this is right we should expect both philosophers to follow a similar concern first to define the foundations and make clear their foundational role, and then to show that we are entitled to use them as foundations for the rest of our knowledge. As Kant puts it:

> If we can prove that by their (the categories') means alone an object can be thought, this will be a sufficient deduction of them, and will justify the objective validity.(17)

Reid similarly observes that:

> if in other branches of philosophy the first principles were laid down, as has been done in mathematics and natural philosophy, and the subsequent conclusions grounded upon them, this would make it much more easy to distinguish what is solid and well supported from the vain fictions of human fancy.(18)

He goes on to discuss in Essay VI chapter iv how first principles are characterized and how they support our reasoning. It is no coincidence, I think, that both philosophers use legal metaphors to express the concept of justification as it relates to the foundations of knowledge. Kant explains his use of the term "deduction" by reference to the lawyers' proof of a right or legal title to something.(19) Reid speaks in the Inquiry of the dictates of common sense (a common periphrasis for first principles) as declining the jurisdiction and disdaining the trial of reasoning,(20) and being older and of more authority,(21) and in the Essays frequently describes first principles as believed on their own authority.(22) If a metaphor is needed for the elusive concept of justification so crucial to the sceptic's case, the legal one seems particularly apt: but apt or not, it serves to underline the similarity between Reid's and Kant's approaches.

## 4. Reid's response: common sense

As commentators have noted,(23) Reid uses the term 'common sense' with more than one meaning. It can refer merely to the worldly wisdom of the man who, as we say, has his head

screwed on the right way round.(24)  But common sense is also
a technical term for Reid.  It can mean the universal
consensus of mankind on a particular point(25) or, more
generally, the set of first principles (often called
'dictates of common sense').(26)  In its most technical
sense, it refers to a distinct faculty of the human mind
whereby we have knowledge of first principles.  A detailed
comparison of all the references to common sense in the
Inquiry and the Essays on the Intellectual Powers might
indicate the extent to which Reid's use of the term in these
different senses mirrors developments in his philosophy,
although it is often difficult to say which if any particular
sense is uppermost.  But in the Essays it seems to be the
last sense in which Reid uses it most frequently and which
assumes the greatest importance, as a consideration of the
separate chapter devoted to it (Essay VI chapter ii)
indicates.

Reid's account of common sense shows signs both of the
ambiguity of 'justification' and of the tendency to run
together the epistemological and the psychological noted in
section 1.  Much of what he says concerns how common sense
operates, and seems not to address the sceptic's concern
about whether we are justified in accepting what common sense
prompts us to believe.  However, Reid says enough on the
epistemological role of the faculty of common sense in the
Essays to make clear two major claims:  that it is a defining
characteristic of human beings, distinct from our powers of
reasoning;  and that it functions analogously to what we
would nowadays call intuition.  The first of these claims
defines a status and role for common sense appropriate to the
defence of the foundations of our knowledge against the
sceptic;  the second concerns the way that role is carried
out.  Reid's account deals more adequately with the first
than with the second.

Reid's formal definition in Essay VI chapter ii is as
follows:

Common sense is that degree of judgment which is
common to men with whom we can converse or transact
business ... an inward light or sense ... given by
heaven to different persons in different degrees.
(27)

This definition reveals several features of Reid's common
sense:  it is universal, independent of any human means of

acquisition, and relevant to practical questions of conduct. The consequences of its universality are spelt out by Reid in uncompromising terms:

> ...in a matter of common sense, every man is no less a competent judge than a mathematician is in a mathematical demonstration.(28)

That common sense is not dependent on any contingency of human life is a corollary of its universality: it is the 'gift of heaven', Reid repeats:

> And where Heaven has not given it, no education can supply the want.(29)

The close connection between common sense and ethics ('transacting business' in the quotation above) is also evident in his warnings against the hypotheses of philosophers which:

> lead to conclusions which contradict the principles on which all men of common sense must act in common life.(30)

(though here the 'horse sense' meaning is equally strong, I feel). All these features lead up to the major claim that there is a basic degree of common sense which is a defining characteristic of a human being and as such "entitles them to the denomination of reasonable creatures".(31) This is an extremely strong claim which is crucial to the status Reid affords common sense in the Essays. It amounts to the assertion that the proposition 'human beings possess common sense' is analytic (after saving clauses for the mentally deficient, which Reid has duly elaborated in the paragraph immediately following the reference quoted above to those "with whom we can transact business"). There is no parallel for this claim in the Inquiry, although the universality of common sense is frequently cited in opposition to the eccentricities of philosophers; and although the theme of the first of a series of drafts on the topic of common sense preserved among Reid's manuscript remains in Aberdeen(32) is that common sense is what distinguishes mankind from the animal creation, there is no suggestion there of Reid's wishing to argue that it is an analytic truth that we are endowed with common sense.

This claim immediately prompts the question 'How is

common sense related to our reasoning powers?'. The evidence
of a change in Reid's views between the Inquiry and the
Essays which several commentators have noted (33) is in my
view particularly clear on this point, though I have not
space to elaborate on this here. Reid answers the question
unequivocally in Essay VI chapter ii. His answer has two
parts. Using the term 'reason' in its widest sense to refer
to the totality of human rational powers, he states that
common sense is as much a part of our human reason as our
powers of deductive or inferential reasoning:

> We ascribe to reason two offices, or two degrees.
> The first is to judge of things self-evident; the
> second to draw conclusions that are not self-evident
> from those that are. The first of these is the
> province, and the sole province, of common sense;
> and, therefore, it coincides with reason in its
> whole extent, and is only another name for one
> branch or one degree of reason.(34)

Reid also gives common sense the pride of place, calling it
"the first-born of reason":

> It is absurd to conceive that there can be any
> opposition between reason and common sense. It is
> indeed the first-born of reason, and as they are
> commonly joined together in speech and in writing,
> they are inseparable in their nature.(35)

These two points are central to Reid's response to the
sceptic. By insisting on common sense as a part of reason,
Reid is attacking the sceptical view that reason in the
narrow sense – our powers of reasoning – is all there is to
reason in the generic sense of human rationality. On that
view, whatever is not known by inferential or by deductive
reasoning, is not known. If this view is accepted, the
sceptic need only point to our inability to prove
demonstratively that, for example, there is an external
world, or to justify inductively, say, the principle of
induction without begging the question. His case would then
be complete, and the defence of such foundational
propositions (which by definition cannot be justified by
deductive or inferential reasoning from anterior premises)
would be impossible. It is this view to which Hume seems to
subscribe in concluding that he can "give no reason"(36) why
he should assent to the most accurate and exact of his
reasonings. Reid rejects this view and proposes common sense

as a third means to knowledge, appropriate to the special
case of first principles. Moreover he accommodates the
special role of those principles as the foundations of all
our knowledge by arguing for the primacy of common sense over
our reasoning powers. The foundations have to be in place
before the superstructure of knowledge can be erected, and
the faculty which is the source of our belief in those
foundations has a similar priority.

As to Reid's second major claim, concerning how the
faculty of common sense carries out the role he has assigned
it, his set-piece account of first principles in Essay VI
chapter iv indicates quite clearly that he sees it as
functioning in the manner of intuition:

> One of the most important distinctions of our
> judgments is, that some of them are intuitive,
> others grounded on argument ... But there are other
> propositions which are no sooner understood than
> they are believed. The judgment follows the
> apprehension of them necessarily, and both are
> equally the work of nature, and the result of our
> original powers. There is no searching for
> evidence, no weighing of arguments; the proposition
> is not deduced or inferred from another; it has the
> light of truth in itself, and has no occasion to
> borrow it from another.(37)

The passage just quoted is one of many implying that doubting
the deliverances of our faculty of common sense is impossible
("no sooner understood than believed"). In Essay VI chapter
i, when speaking of what he calls 'judgments of Nature' —
what our senses, consciousness or memory tell us — Reid makes
this very clear:

> And as we have this belief by the constitution of
> our nature, without any effort of our own, so no
> effort of ours can overturn it.(38)

He frequently observes that all men find themselves "under a
necessity of believing"(39) what common sense tells them.

Now drawing an analogy between common sense and intuition
may not seem a promising way for Reid to explain his response
to scepticism; after all, the objections to intuitionism are
familiar. Everything turns on the sense in which it is
'necessary' to believe the dictates of common sense. Feeling

sure is no guarantee that we are in fact right, as all of us
know from personal experience – if not in philosophy, then in
daily life. Whether or not twentieth century attempts (for
example by G. E. Moore (40)) to build an antisceptical case
on our feelings of certainty and a revision of our concept of
knowledge in terms of the comparative rationality of
competing beliefs can succeed is here beside the point. In
terms of the eighteenth century concept of knowledge which I
outlined earlier, if subjective certainty is no guarantee of
truth, it is no guarantee of knowledge. Even if,
anachronistically and with some violence to the text, we
interpret Reid as arguing only for the rationality of belief
and not for knowledge, the case looks weak: feelings of
certainty alone are not a strong pointer to the rationality
of the beliefs they accompany. Either way, if Reid is
referring merely to a psychological propensity to believe, he
does indeed seem to have missed the sceptic's point.

It has to be admitted that Reid does sometimes write in a
way which suggests very strongly that he has subjective
feelings in mind: he talks of the dictates of common sense
as 'irresistible'(41) or of our being 'forced'(42) to believe
them. But it would be wrong to jump to the conclusion that
Reid is doing no more than confuse psychology and
epistemology: particularly since we are speaking of basic
beliefs allegedly common to all men, there is no reason why
they should not both be vouchsafed by a faculty of common
sense and also be accompanied by psychologically reassuring
feelings of certainty. As far as the success of Reid's
appeal to common sense against the sceptic is concerned,
provided that an epistemologically proper justification
(whether of knowledge or of the rationality of belief) is on
offer, the epiphenomenon of epistemologically questionable
subjective conviction is surely harmless.

However it is one thing to argue that Reid's references
to psychological certainty do not necessarily mean that he
has simply missed the point. We still need more than a few
references to intuition as an account of why we are justified
in our acceptance of common sense beliefs if Reid's appeal to
common sense is to be substantiated. Granting that common
sense may be the degree of reason particularly appropriate to
provide us with beliefs in first principles, and that it
functions as a form of intuition giving us subjective
conviction about those beliefs, still the question remains
'Are the beliefs with which common sense furnishes us true?'
If not, then it fails to justify first principles as the

foundations of our knowledge. References such as those in the passages already quoted to 'the constitution of our nature' and 'our original powers', along with the strong claim that 'having common sense' is part of what is meant by 'being a human being' suggest to me that Reid's answer to this difficulty lies in features of his account which can appropriately be described as Kantian. I return to this after considering Kant's response to scepticism.

## 5. Kant's response: the transcendental deduction

Kant's proof that knowledge is possible rests on the transcendental deduction of the categories and his doctrine of transcendental idealism. Some commentators have been tempted to regard him as providing two distinct answers: Strawson has little time for the "imaginary subject of transcendental psychology"(43) and in his own writings has tried the strength of transcendental arguments on their own as an engine for metaphysical system–building. However, Kant himself evidently regarded transcendental idealism as vital to the success of the deduction, and in my view the two certainly stand or fall together. In this section I concentrate on the Deduction. I discuss his transcendental idealism in section 7.

The precise formulation of a transcendental argument remains a matter of debate.(44) The orthodox view is that a transcendental argument to prove that the world exhibits quality 'q' moves from a major premise that 'q' is necessary for there to be any meaningful experience of the world whatsoever, via the unquestioned minor premise that we do have meaningful experience of the world, to the conclusion that 'q' is indeed a necessary feature of the world. While this formulation accurately expresses the logical form of a transcendental argument, it seems to me that it directs attention away from the real problem, which is how to establish the major premise. Kant concentrates on this problem in the Deduction almost to the exclusion of the remaining steps of the argument–schema. The "features of the world" for whose necessary presence he is arguing are the categories (or for that matter the forms of intuition, though my analysis here concentrates on the categories) which serve as the necessary preconditions for all rational activity. His first move is to state, as an assumption which needs no justification, the unity of the knowing subject (the "transcendental unity of apperception"(45)), which he describes as "the ground of the possibility of all

knowledge",(46) or "the pure form of all possible
knowledge".(47) Kant next argues for the presence in the
understanding of the categories, "the pure concepts of
understanding"(48) or "forms of thought",(49) and goes on —
this is the crucial step — to assert that their presence is
necessary because the categories are "grounds of the
recognition of the manifold":(50)

> This relation of appearances to possible experience
> is indeed necessary for otherwise they would yield
> no knowledge and would not in any way concern
> us.(51)

The thought is that because we can only make sense of
experience by applying the categories to it, without the
categories there would be no experience as far as we are
concerned. It is quite hard to do better in explaining this
argument than to quote Kant's own words. He sums up the
Deduction by remarking that pure understanding in the
categories "makes experience, as regards its form,
possible",(52) and that this establishes "the objective
validity of the pure a priori concepts".(53) Or, as he puts
it in the second edition:

> the categories are conditions of the possibility of
> experience and are therefore valid a priori for all
> objects of experience.(54)

The validity of the link between these two propositions — the
'therefore' of the last quotation — effectively determines
the success of Kant's response to the sceptic.

Kant's argument has some affinity with the standard
anti-sceptical argument that runs 'because you have to assume
the truth of 'p' to argue that 'p' is false, your argument is
self-defeating', but Kant is doing much more than highlight
the paradoxical nature of some sorts of sceptical questions.
This is because the categories are foundations in Kant's
theory of knowledge in the special sense of being
preconditions for all meaningful experience: having such
experience analytically involves bringing an appearance under
a concept ('analytically' because that is what it is for an
experience to be meaningful). Kant goes to some lengths to
make this clear. He repeats that:

> The categories ... have no kind of application, save
> only in regard to things which may be objects of

possible experience;(55)

while appearances, if they are to be possible experiences:

> lie a priori in the understanding, and receive from
> it their formal possibility, just as, in so far as
> they are mere intuitions, they lie in the
> sensibility and are, as regards their form, only
> possible through it.(56)

In this way Kant reverses the order of logical dependence, and thus of proof or justification, from that presupposed by what I described at the beginning of this section as the problem of establishing the major premise of the transcendental argument. It is no longer a matter of justifying the claim that the categories are the foundations of all our experience. The concepts of justification, knowledge, belief and experience itself in any intelligible form are brought within the scope of the categories and so cannot simply be applied to them as if the categories were within their logical scope. Because the categories and forms of intuition are the rules by which we classify and describe all our experience, Kant can even draw from his Deduction the striking conclusion that:

> the order and regularity in the appearances, which
> we entitle nature, we ourselves introduce.(57)

However the last quotation highlights a problem with this way of turning the tables to justify the major premise of Kant's transcendental argument. The problem can be expressed in two ways. First, Kant seems to make the foundations of knowledge contingent on the nature of our human faculties: this is how experience has to be if we are to find it meaningful, but a sceptic might ask 'What about beings with a different view of the world?' Kant admits the oddity of his position when stated in this way, but insists that this is what he means:

> However exaggerated and absurd it may sound, to say
> that the understanding is itself the source of the
> laws of nature, and so of its formal unity, such an
> assertion is nonetheless correct.(58)

Part of the difficulty here is that Kant also means literally the reference in this quotation to our understanding as the source. The view that the categories are part of the structure of our minds is the part of his theory which

Strawson labels 'transcendental psychology'. Its presence
indicates that, as I noted in section 1, even though Kant is
concerned to distinguish his transcendental psychology from
the empirical psychology engaged in by his predecessors,he
does not manage entirely to escape from the eighteenth
century concern with the origin of our beliefs. And if
Kant's argument amounts only to a statement of the
universality and inevitability of particular basic features
of our view of the world, he will not satisfy the sceptic any
more than did Reid with his statements of basic assumptions
that we cannot escape taking for granted.

The alternative way of expressing the problem with Kant's
argument sidesteps the psychological dimension and brings out
more sharply the limitations of the transcendental deduction
as an answer to scepticism. Kant's argument seems to leave
room for the question whether things really are as he says
that the structure of our knowledge assumes: it is not clear
whether the actual presence of causal regularity,
spatio-temporality, or whatever, is proved, or merely that it
is necessary for us to interpret the world as if it exhibited
these features. If this objection is sustained, it is
devastating. Granted that the categories determine how we
must interpret our experience and structure what we regard as
our knowledge, everything still turns on whether the fact
that the categories must apply also guarantees that they
describe reality truly and so provide a proper foundation for
knowledge. Of course, this objection does not bite in quite
the same way on a transcendental argument designed merely to
prove the rationality of our beliefs – though it does have
some force, unless a necessary belief is eo ipso rational.
But Kant leaves us no room to doubt that he was concerned to
justify knowledge and not just rational belief and so, as
with Reid's appeal to common sense, even ignoring the
historical and textual evidence and reworking the argument as
a defence of the rationality of belief will not turn it into
a satisfactory answer to scepticism.

## 6.  The similarities: Reid's transcendentalism

Kant finds an answer to this problem in his transcendental
idealism; but before discussing that I want to draw attention
to the close parallel which, as I indicated initially, I see
between Kant's transcendental deduction and Reid's appeal to
common sense against scepticism. In section 4 I showed how
Reid's argument ran into a difficulty which is precisely
similar to that now confronting Kant's Deduction. Is belief

in the dictates of common sense a mere psychological impulse
– 'custom or habit' as Hume would put it(59) –, or is it
necessary in a sense which provides a guarantee of the truth
of what is believed?  Only the latter will guarantee the
status as knowledge of what common sense prompts us to
believe and secure the rest of our knowledge against
scepticism.  The question, 'Does Reid's defence of first
principles as acquired through our faculty of common sense
provide the guarantee that what common sense tells us is
true?' is on all fours with the question, 'Does Kant's
transcendental deduction guarantee that the categories we
necessarily have to apply describe reality truly?'

As I hinted in sections 3 and 4, the parallel between
Reid and Kant extends to the nature of Reid's first
principles and to Reid's account of the faculty of common
sense.  I begin with first principles.  I noted in section 3
that Reid is not consistent in the way in which he expresses
his first principles.  The internal inconsistencies between
the two lists underline the point that too much weight should
not be put on whether or not Reid expresses his principles in
propositional form.  In my view, a better key to
understanding his view of them is his claim in Essay I
chapter ii that they are "the foundation of all
reasoning".(60)  This could just mean that they are the first
premises in individual specimens of reasoning, whether
deductive or inductive: but this would either be false (the
same dozen or so premises for all specimens of human
reasoning?) or it would lead to such a multiplicity of first
principles as would embarrass even Reid.  'Such facts as are
attested to by our senses etc.' (the formulation adopted in
the Essay I list for the principle that is meant to guarantee
the existence of the external world(61)) could be taken to
point to just such a multiplicity of principles.  On this
reading all our basic judgements of sense-perception could be
taken as first principles.  While this interpretation is
possible, I prefer to interpret 'the foundation of all
reasoning' in the light of the distinguishing characteristics
of first principles Reid enumerates in Essay VI chapter iv.
He argues there for their universal acceptance by mankind,
their self-evidence, the absurdity of denying them or of
proving them directly, their being believed from our earliest
infancy and their necessity to daily life.(62)  I take all
these characteristics as intended to support their necessity
for any process of reasoning which is the first claim he
makes for first principles in his formal account of them in
this chapter(63) and equates to the 'foundation of reasoning'

claim of Essay I chapter ii. Reid says in effect that first principles provide a framework of basic assumptions (explicit or implicit) without which no rational activity at all could take place:

> it appears to be demonstrable that, without first principles, analytical reasoning could have no end, and synthetical reasoning could have no beginning; and that every conclusion got by reasoning must rest with its whole weight upon first principles, as the building does upon its foundation.(64)

This interpretation requires Reid to claim logical and not just temporal priority for his first principles. It also helps to account for his concern with metaphysics which is apparent in such passages; when he argues for the necessity of first principles, he is arguing as much for them as necessary features of the world as for their necessarily being true propositions or beliefs and so genuinely known. In this respect too he resembles Kant, whose similar concerns I noted earlier. The case for this interpretation is helped by restricting it to the first few principles in each of Reid's lists, which provide for personal identity and our mental states known through consciousness, the existence of the external world known through perception and the reality of the past known through memory (and probably other minds known by analogy, though Reid's account here is less straightforward); and by distinguishing these principles from the others he cites,not all of which in any case match up to all the characteristics of first principles he notes in Essay VI chapter iv. It must also be acknowledged that the logical priority even of these first principles over all rational activity is not as clear in Reid as in Kant. It is obscured by his preoccupation with developmental psychology (which leads him to stress temporal as well as logical priority) and by his tendency also to regard first principles as beliefs (which I think accounts for his expressing them, usually, in propositional form although their priority over all rational activity could, strictly speaking, make this difficult). Nonetheless, he is fond of saying that first principles must be taken for granted and cannot be proved, and that we have no choice but to believe them: anyone who denies his own consciousness, for example:

> must be left to himself, as a man that denies first principles, without which there can be no reasoning.(65)

It is also surely significant that Reid so often speaks of first principles as 'principles of our constitution'.(66)  In assessing the significance of these passages we must  broaden our  focus  to  include   common  sense  as  well  as   first principles.   There  is  psychology  here  (as  with  Kant's reference,  already  quoted,  to  our  understanding  as  the 'source' of the categories(67)), and there is also  theology: in arguing for the primacy of these principles Reid  stresses that they are implanted in us by the Creator.  So too was the faculty of common sense,  which as we  saw in section 4  Reid describes as 'the gift of Heaven',(68) and I have noted  that Reid sometimes  uses  the term  'common  sense'  to  mean  the corpus of  common  sense beliefs.  But  the  epistemological point which Reid is also making in these and similar passages applies equally to belief  in the principles of common  sense and to the faculty: both are essential elements of our  human nature and in  virtue of  this prior to  the exercise of  our reasoning faculties.(69)  The  priority here is temporal  and psychological, but I am  sure that Reid  is also thinking  in terms of  logical  priority.   He  carefully  explains  that, though first principles come  to be articulated and  reasoned about only later in life, belief in them is present  from the start of our lives.(70)  To my mind, this argument  would not be necessary  if  he were  arguing  simply for  the  temporal priority of such principles over beliefs got by reasoning; he could make do with less implausible and more easily  verified claims about  our  psychological  development.   But  it  is necessary if  he is  arguing  for their  being part  of  'the constitution of our nature'(71)  from the start of our  lives as a mark  of their  logical  priority.   In other words,  the psychological claim about  their priority in  time has to  be maintained in this way, despite its apparent  implausibility, because it corresponds to the epistemological claim that they are logically prior to all the knowledge we get by  using our reasoning faculties  and .make up,  or stem  from  (depending which sense of 'common  sense' is uppermost) a faculty  which is an  essential  part  of  our  human  nature.  We  may  not entirely agree  with  Reid's  confusing  psychology  and epistemology in this way; but it is at least clear that he is making more than psychological claims.

Accordingly I think that Reid does give us grounds to say that he claims at least  for the most important of his  first principles logical  and not just  temporal priority,  arguing that they  are the  'foundation of reasoning'  in the  strong sense that they are preconditions for knowledge (or  rational belief for that matter).  As preconditions, they can be taken

as facts about the world which have to be true – principles
for beliefs rather than principles which are beliefs, if we
are to be strict – and so as evidence of Reid's concern with
metaphysics as well as epistemology; or they can be taken as
propositions expressing those truths, which (when we think
about it) we have to believe; or they can be taken as those
beliefs themselves. All three senses figure in Reid's
understanding of the matter, and, as with the term 'common
sense', which sense is intended in a given passage varies.
But the parallel with Kant's 'forms of thought'(72) is clear
enough, particularly given the first two senses, if we look
behind the eighteenth century psychology in both their
accounts and concentrate on the logical priority of first
principles over the knowledge we build on them as the
foundations.

Of course, Reid does not develop a full-scale
transcendental deduction, or discuss systematically what it
is for experience to be meaningful. He does however make one
claim for the faculty of common sense which points very
firmly towards a Kantian interpretation. This is the claim
discussed in section 4 that to have common sense is part of
what it means to be a rational human being. The reason why
we must believe according to common sense would on this
reading be that to do so is an essential feature of our human
nature. From this it follows that we cannot conceive of a
human being who denies common sense, any more than according
to Kant we can conceive of a world not structured according
to the categories. This would reinforce the argument for the
logical priority of first principles in relation to our
reasoning powers, which are not necessary in this way to our
being human beings. In support of this reading, it is
relevant that Reid notes that we have to learn to use our
reasoning powers and that some human beings never do so but
have to be content with common sense.(73)

To sum up, it is tempting to regard Reid's insistence on
the necessity of belief according to common sense as a form
of transcendental argument, defending a set of preconditions
or foundations not on the ground that without them there
could be no meaningful experience, but on the ground that
without them there could be no knowledge or rational
activity. Although this argument is not the same as Kant's,
it is similar; knowledge and rational activity are an
important subset of our meaningful experiences. I have
argued in the preceding paragraphs that Reid's view of the
nature of the necessity of believing what common sense tells

us is to be explained as much by his understanding of the
foundational nature of first principles as by his analysis of
the faculty through which we apprehend them. In Reid's
transcendental argument the major premise is 'first
principles are the foundation of all reasoning', the minor
premise is 'we do engage in rational activity' – even, he
would presumably say, in arguing with the sceptic – and the
conclusion is 'first principles can therefore be taken for
granted as true foundations for knowledge'. I have also
argued that there is a parallel between the seemingly
different analyses the two philosophers offer of the nature
of the foundations of our knowledge: at least the first few
of Reid's first principles are closer to Kant's categories
and forms of intuition than at first sight appears; and that
Reid's stress on first principles as 'principles of our
constitution'(74) and on common sense as a "degree of reason"
the possession of which "entitles [us] to the denomination of
reasonable creatures"(75) both resemble Kant's Deduction in
the blending of psychological, epistemological and
metaphysical considerations as well as in being arguments for
a necessity which is transcendental.

But this does not mean that Reid's response disposes of
the sceptic: Reid's insistence that we must believe in the
principles of common sense may be a transcendental 'must' but
its success is not guaranteed thereby. So long as we are
interested in knowledge, as I maintain Reid and Kant are, and
not just rational belief, the problem is, what guarantee do
we have that things are as we must believe they are? Reid
does not, I think, fully see the force of this objection: he
is perhaps too ready to reply that first principles are
implanted by God and that is an end of it. Such an answer is
unlikely to find universal favour, for all that it also
satisfied that tireless questioner, Descartes. But before we
conclude that faith is the only solution other than Hume's
recipe of 'carelessness and inattention',(76) we must return
to Kant for the next stage in his argument, which has no
parallel in Reid.

## 7. The difference: Kant's idealism

It might be argued on Kant's behalf that the question whether
the categories really apply is simply not meaningful. Since
the categories determine the range of meaningful experience
and not <u>vice versa</u>, an experience that did not fit the
categories would not be meaningful or intelligible to us and
the sceptic's question is, literally, non-sense. This is an

attractive defence of Kant's transcendental argument against
a persistent sceptic.   It would also underline a  difference
between Reid  and Kant  which the previous  section could  be
felt to have ignored  in claiming that  for a human being  to
deny common sense was  inconceivable in the  same sense as  a
world not structured according  to the categories: for  Kant,
it would just  not be  possible for the  sceptic to  question
whether the categories apply  because the words and  concepts
needed  to describe  or  imagine  a  world  not  structured
according to the categories  are simply not available;  while
Reid makes do with saying  that the sceptic who doubts  first
principles is talking nonesense  in the sense that he  cannot
be reasoned with.   That these  are different positions,  and
that Kant's would be the stronger, is clear if we  ask 'Could
either understand a  sceptical being who  tried to tell  them
that he did not accept their foundations?'  Reid's account of
how  to  deal  with  the  man  who  does  not  accept  first
principles(77) indicates  that  he could  (he  implies  quite
clearly, I think, that you don't know how to reason with him,
though you do understand what  he is saying to you − that  is
why you know to respond with ridicule rather than reason, for
example); while the account of Kant which this defence offers
suggests that Kant would not be able to understand what  such
a sceptical being was trying to communicate to him.   So this
defence of Kant's position against the difficulty I discussed
in section 5 is attractive.   It also seems to arise  readily
enough from the Deduction itself.  Unfortunately, its aptness
as a statement of Kant's own position is called into question
by Kant himself.  Kant  makes it quite clear that he  regards
the question,  whether the  categories do in  fact apply,  as
perfectly meaningful so  long as  it remains unclear  whether
the categories are being applied to appearances or things  in
themselves.  As he puts it:

> If the objects with which our knowledge has to  deal
> were things in themselves, we could have no a priori
> concept of  them ...  things  in  themselves  would
> necessarily ... conform to laws of their own.(78)

Kant's guarantee that his categories apply is provided,not by
a Reidian argument that  to deny first  principles is to  put
oneself beyond the scope  of rational debate (though not,  as
just noted,beyond  the scope of  human intelligibility),  nor
yet by the argument that  the question whether they apply  is
meaningless given the nature and scope of the  categories,but
by his  transcendental  idealism which has  no  parallel  in
Reid's firmly empiricist thought.   The distinction between

the phenomenal, the world of appearances, and the noumenal, the thing in itself, underwrites Kant's insistence against the sceptic that the categories do really apply and so guarantee knowledge. There could only be the possibility of an epistemic gap between how we necessarily have to see things, and how things are, if the objects of our experience – the world – were 'things in themselves'. But in fact:

> Pure concepts of understanding ... in relation to experience are indeed necessary, and this for the reason that our knowledge has to deal solely with appearances.(79)

And appearances, since they are appearances to us, must be interpreted according to the categories if they are to have meaning at all. According to Kant, the guarantee that the categories apply to the sensible world is provided by its status as phenomenal, and this in turn requires the existence of the noumenal world behind (or beyond) Spatial metaphors are hard to avoid, though strictly inapposite) the world of appearances whose form and order depend on us as perceivers.

Kant's way of drawing the line between phenomena and noumena avoids the standard difficulty for three-term representational theories of perception. The sceptic's question 'Do the categories apply?' assumes the possibility of an epistemic gap between appearance and reality; but this presupposes that reality is, in principle, within our grasp. Kant's noumenal world is by definition outside the scope of even possible human experience. The distinctions between appearance and reality, true and false or correct and incorrect descriptions of our experience, all find their application exclusively within the world of appearances, to the transcendentally ideal, where Kant's transcendental argument ensures that the categories apply with the certainty he needs. So the sceptic can only raise meaningful questions in a context where the categories necessarily apply, he cannot start a sceptical doubt about the categories themselves. The foundations of knowledge are secure. The end–product is the same as the defence of Kant's position I stated at the beginning of this section; but it rests on the status of the appearances to which the categories apply and not on the nature of the categories.

It thus seems that Kant through his idealism does indeed get to grips with the sceptic in a way that eludes Reid. But in fairness to Reid, I want to stay with Kant just long

enough to suggest that (despite appearances, so to speak) he
has not necessarily got us that much further. The noumena
are essential to the success of Kant's transcendental
idealism. They are what we might call a necessary postulate
of pure reason. Without that postulate Kant would be guilty
of the same error for which he criticizes Berkeleian idealism
at the end of the Aesthetic. He there argues that his way of
distinguishing the object as appearance from the object in
itself does not mean that, for instance, "bodies merely seem
to be outside me".(80) It is only if we ascribe objective
reality to appearances that:

> it becomes impossible for us to prevent everything
> being thereby transformed into mere illusion.(81)

Unfortunately for Kant, the epistemic gap is not closed as
easily as he thinks. As I have indicated, his own theory
requires that we can know nothing of the noumenal world, not
even, strictly, that it exists (assuming that 'exists' is
taken in the normal sense (schematized) meaning 'exists
within space and time'). Kant is quite definite about this.
Discussing the application of the categories to "an object of
a non-sensible intuition", he says:

> But what has chiefly to be noted is this, that to
> such a something not a single one of all the
> categories could be applied. We could not, for
> instance, apply to it the concept of substance ...
> For save in so far as empirical intuition provides
> the instance to which to apply it, I do not know
> whether there can be anything that corresponds to
> such a form of thought.(82) (my italics)

Given that even basic metaphysical sortal concepts cannot
apply to noumena, it seems that a persistent sceptic can
legitimately ask whether Kant's use of transcendental
idealism to underpin his transcendental deduction requires
that there by noumena (in some appropriate sense of 'be') or
just that we must believe that there are, so that the
phenomena can stand to them in the relation of appearance to
reality and be governed objectively and necessarily by the
principles our minds impose. Now transcendental idealism was
intended to block the question 'do the categories really
apply to all experience or is it just that we have to think
in a way that presupposes that they do?' which arose at the
previous state in my analysis of Kant's argument. The
question here is to my mind very similar: there remains a

doubt whether things are as Kant's theory would have us believe they are. Underpinning the transcendental deduction by transcendental idealism has clearly failed if transcendental idealism itself leaves room for this question.

Nor is the question idle. If it can indeed still be asked despite transcendental idealism, the sceptic can also ask Kant how he knows that the world of appearances is only phenomenal. We might have to do with 'things in themselves' after all, in which case according to Kant's own analysis we would certainly be confronted with the epistemic gap and unable to convince the sceptic that things must be as we see them:

> Things in themselves would necessarily ... conform
> to laws of their own.(83)

which might or might not coincide with the laws according to which we interpret them. That may not matter so much if our concern is only with the rationality of belief (though the point is arguable); but it is surely fatal to a Kantian justification of knowledge.

## Conclusion

It seems in view of the analysis in the last section that the defence of Kant's position I stated at the beginning of that section, although it is not Kant's own, is not only attractive but much to be preferred, and that whatever the independent attractions of Kant's idealism it fails in its purpose of guaranteeing the transcendental deduction against further sceptical questions. In that case, it is legitimate to conclude that although Reid and Kant part company when Kant introduces his idealism, Reid goes just as far as Kant safely does in answering the sceptic. I conclude also that neither succeeds finally in silencing the sceptic so long as there remains the possibility that he can sensibly ask whether things necessarily are as Kant's or Reid's theory states we know or must believe they are. A verdict of 'not proven' is quite enough to let the sceptic go free (this is, of course, one of the reasons why he is so hard to defeat).

I have suggested further parallels: that we can see them as following a closely similar foundationalist strategy; that, despite the differences of detail in their accounts of the foundations of their theories of knowledge, Reid also argues for the logical priority of those foundations; and that this points us towards a transcendental interpretation of his first principles and his justification of them by an appeal to our faculty of common sense. Finally I should add that both Reid and Kant apply their theories to other areas of philosophy, notably ethics, in pursuit of the goal of developing a complete philosophical system.

There is much more to be said about the similarities between the two thinkers, but my argument here should already have sufficed to call in question the superficial view of their epistemologies that Kant's Deduction, supported by his idealism, succeeds as obviously as Reid's common sense fails. If labels have any significance, of course Reid was an empiricist while Kant was an idealist; but there is room for debate whether they are always speaking such different philosophical languages. I have sought to show that in response to the sceptic Reid sometimes at least speaks the same transcendental language as Kant, albeit inevitably in a different dialect. If I am right, to describe Reid as the Scottish Kant would be no mere hyperbole.

## NOTES

(1)  I am  grateful to  Dr John Kenyon,  St Peter's  College, Oxford, who commented on an  earlier draft, and to those  who organized and participated in  the Reid Conference for  their constructive criticisms.  If I  have wrongly  ignored any  in revising the paper, the fault is mine.

(2)  'Majority view'  because  not all  have joined  in  this hasty dismissal of Reid. A notable exception is Victor Cousin who in his  (1857) considers the  parallels between Reid  and Kant at length.  While I  would not accept  the whole of  his analysis, I cannot fault his conclusion that:

> Reid est incontestablement...avec  Kant le  premier metaphysicien du  dix-huitieme  siecle.'  (op.cit., Introduction p. ix).

(3)  Hume (1975, iv 2 para. 28).

(4)  Hume (1978, I iv 2).

(5)  Hume (1978, I iv 7).

(6)  **IP**, VI iv (Works, p. 435).

(7)  Ibid. The metaphor of a building recurs frequently, e.g. I ii (Works, pp. 230–1); I vi (Works, p. 241);  VI, i (Works, p. 416).

(8)  **IP**, I  ii (Works,  pp.  230–1); cf.  VI iv  (Works,  pp. 436–7).

(9)  **IP**, I ii (Works, p. 233).

(10) **IP**, I ii (Works, p. 233).

(11) **IP**, VI v (Works, p. 442).

(12) **IP**, VI v (Works, p. 445).

(13) "that I really perform  all those operations of mind  of which I am conscious" (**IP**, I ii Works, p. 231;  "that all the thoughts I am conscious  of ... are  the thoughts of one  and the same thinking principle" (Works, p. 232). The latter  is

followed a few lines later by the non-propositional
formulation "believing his own identity and continued
existence".

(14) The full text is:

That certain features of the countenance, sounds of
the voice, and gestures of the body, indicate
certain thoughts and dispositions of mind. (**IP**, VI
v Works, p. 449).

(15) In **IP**, VI iv.

(16) Kant (1929) B150 p. 164, B143 p. 160 cf. B146 p. 161,
B145 p. 161 cf. A113 p. 140, A126-7 pp. 147-8.

(17) Kant (1929) A97 p. 130.

(18) **IP**, Vi iv (Works, p. 437).

(19) Kant (1929) A84; B116 p. 120.

(20) I, I iv (Works, p.101); cf "declines the tribunal of
reason" I, V, vii (Works, p. 127).

(21) I, I, v (Works, p. 102) (the formula is repeated at V,
vii (Works, p. 127); cf. **IP**, VI ii, (Works, p. 425).

(22) **IP**, VI v (Works, p. 442, p. 444); cf. II, xiv (Works,
pp. 302-3), where the same is said of "common sense and my
external senses".

(23) Eg. Stewart (1816), I iii, pp. 91-2 (cf. his Account of
the Life and Writings of Thomas Reid, D.D., F.R.S.E.,
prefixed to Sir William Hamilton's edition of Reid's works
(Works, pp. 27, 28), where however he is more guarded in
accusing Reid of using the phrase ambiguously); Sir Wm.
Hamilton in his edition (Works, p. 758); A.D. Woozley in the
Introduction to his abridged edition of the Essays (1941), p.
xxxii; S.A. Grave (1960), pp. 84, 114; R.E. Beanblossom in
his Introduction to the abridged edition of Reid's works by
him and K. Lehrer (1983), pp. xxvi-xxvii.

(24) Eg. **IP**, II xviii (Works, p. 321):

Thus we say that a ship sails, when every man of
common sense knows that she has no inherent power

of motion, and is only driven by wind and tide.

Cf. **IP**, II, xiv (Works, p. 304); **IP**, I, i (Works, p. 228);
vii (Works, p.210):

I appeal to any man of common sense...

cf. V, viii (Works, p. 132).

(25) Eg. **IP**, VI, iii (Works, p. 432):

This [Locke's claim that we know external objects
only by sensation] is perfectly agreeable to the
common sense of mankind.

Cf. **IP**, III, v (Works, p. 348); IV i (Works, p. 363).

(26) Eg. **IP**, VIII, i (Works, p. 492):

Philosophers should be very cautious in opposing
the common sense of mankind

(Cf. VI, ii (Works, p. 422); I, vii (Works, p. 209):

Such opinions and natural judgments ... make up
what is called the common sense of mankind.

(27) **IP**, VI, ii (Works, pp. 421, 422).

(28) **IP**, VI, iv (Works, p. 440).

(29) **IP**, VI, ii (Works, p. 425).

(30) **IP**, II, xii (Works, p. 293).

(31) **IP**, VI, ii (Works, p. 425).

(32) AUL MS 2131/2/III/7. The dating of this ms. — almost
certainly prior to 1769 — is discussed in D. Fate Norton,
'Thomas Reid's Cura Prima on Common Sense', published as an
appendix to Marcil-Lacoste (1982).

(33) Both Stewart (op.cit., I iii, footnote on p. 92) and
Hamilton (op.cit., footnotes at pp. 100b, 101a) note the
contrast between Reid's view expressed in the passages from
**IP** quoted here and the opposition between common sense and
philosophy based upon reason in I eg. at I, iii (Works, p.

100) and I, iv (Works, p. 101). The contrast Reid draws in I
between common sense and reason is especially clear in such
passages as:

> if she [Reason] will not be the servant of Common
> Sense, she must be her slave. (I, V, vii Works, p.
> 127; cf. II, v Works, p. 108).

Stewart suggests (op.cit., I iii, p. 85) that Reid's
"considerably more guarded and consistent" treatment of
common sense in IP owes something to Buffier's Traite des
premieres verites et de la source de nos jugements (Paris,
Veuve Monge, 1724). The parallels between Reid and Buffier
have been reconsidered by Marcil–Lacoste (op.cit.), who
concludes that they have quite different views on the nature
of an appeal to common sense.

(34) IP, VI ii (Works, p. 425).

(35) Ibid.

(36) Cf. n. 5 above.

(37) IP, VI, iv (Works, p. 434).

(38) IP, VI, i (Works, p. 416).

(39) Eg. IP, I, ii (Works, p. 232); cf. VI, v (Works, p. 443).

(40) See 'Four Forms of Scepticism' in Moore (1959, pp. 196–226, especially p. 226), 'Certainty', ibid., pp. 227–251, especially pp. 243–4, and part I of 'A Defence of Common Sense', ibid., pp. 32–45.

(41) IP, VI, v (Works, p. 442); II, i (Works, p. 247).

(42) IP, II, xxii (Works, p. 339); cf VI, v (Works, p. 448).

(43) Strawson (1966), p. 32.

(44) Stroud (1968), provides a good summary of the issues.

(45) Kant (1929) A108 p. 136; cf B135 p. 154.

(46) Kant (1929) A118 p. 143; cf B150 p. 164, B167 p. 174.

(47) Ibid.

(48) Kant (1929) A88; B120  p. 122, A119  p. 143; cf B168  p. 175.

(49) Kant (1929) B150 p. 164; cf A93; B126 p. 126.

(50) Kant (1929) A125 p. 147; cf B143 p. 160.

(51) Kant (1929) A119 p. 143; cf B148 p. 163.

(52) Kant (1929) A128 p. 149.

(53) Ibid.

(54) Kant (1929) B161 p. 171.

(55) Kant (1929) A147-8 p. 162; cf B166 p. 174.

(56) Kant (1929) A127 p. 148.

(57) Kant (1929) A125 p. 147; cf B163-4 p. 172.

(58) Kant (1929) A127 p. 148; cf A114 p. 140, B159-60 p. 170, B163-4 p. 172.

(59) Hume (1975 v, 1 para. 36).

(60) IP, I, ii (Works, p. 230).

(61) IP, I, ii (Works, p. 233).

(62) IP, VI, iv (Works, pp. 438-441).

(63) IP, VI, iv (Works, p. 435).

(64) Ibid.

(65) IP, I, ii (Works, p. 231). A very similar  reference to one who denies that qualities require a subject occurs on the next page:

> I leave  him to  enjoy  his opinion  as a  man  who denies first  principles,  and  is not  fit  to  be reasoned with.(I, ii Works, p. 232).

(66) IP, II, xxi (Works,  p. 333); VI,  v (Works, p.452);  cf

VI, iv (Works, P. 438).

(67) **IP**, II, xxi (Works, p.  333); VI, v (Works, p. 452);   cf
VI, iv (Works, P. 438).

(67) Cf p. 16 above and n. 58.

(68) Cf p. 10 above and n. 29.

(69) The passages quoted  on pp. 11  and 12 above  emphasised
this: common  sense "the  first-born of reason"  (**IP**, VI,  ii
Works, p.  425);  belief in  first  principles "the  work  of
nature and the  result of  our original powers"  (**IP**, VI,  iv
Works, p. 434).

(70) **IP**, VI, iv (Works, p. 441); cf II, xxi (Works,  p. 332),
where however  'reason'  is used  in  the narrower  sense  of
'reasoning' and not the wider sense of 'human rationality' as
in the key passage from VI, ii (see p. 9 above and n. 34).

(71) Cf n. 38.

(72) Kant (1929) B150 p. 164; cf n. 49.

(73) **IP**, II, xxi (Works, pp. 332-3).

(74) Cf n. 66.

(75) Cf n. 31.

(76) Hume (1978, I, iv 4).

(77) Cf p. 18 above and n. 65.

(78) Kant (1929) A128 p.149, B 164 pp. 172-3; cf A119 p. 143,
A 129 p.149.

(79) Kant (1929) A130 p. 150; cf A147-8 p. 162, B166 p. 174.

(80) Kant (1929) B69 pp. 88-9.

(81) Kant (1929) B70 p. 89.

(82) Kant (1929) B149 pp. 163-4.

(83) Kant (1929) A128 p. 149, B164 pp. 172-3; cf n. 78.

Daniel Schulthess


## DID REID HOLD COHERENTIST VIEWS?


In a recent paper, Keith Lehrer and John-Christian Smith show that Thomas Reid, while being mainly foundationalist and reliabilist in his conception of knowledge, also pays attention to the dimension of coherence within our system of beliefs.(1) They describe thus a hitherto not much discussed and very interesting feature of Reid's philosophy. As they give simultaneously a fallibilist interpretation of the knowledge claims we may derive — according to Reid — from the exertion of our faculties, the consideration of coherence gains in importance: the less we derive completely certain knowledge directly from the exertion of our faculties, the more coherence among our beliefs could become relevant for the justification of knowledge claims. I shall not discuss the question of Reid's fallibilism here, but restrict my discussion to the possible role of coherence among our beliefs in Reid's philosophy and give some development to Lehrer and Smith's argument.

The evidence which Lehrer and Smith bring in support of their argument concerning the idea of coherence in Reid consists mainly in the following passages.(2) In I, Reid states:

> The credit we give to [the testimony of nature and the testimony of men] is at first the effect of instinct only. When we grow up, and begin to reason about them, the credit given to human testimony is restrained and weakened, by the experience we have of deceit. But the credit given to the testimony of our senses, is established and confirmed by the uniformity and constancy of the laws of nature.(3)

This passage is indeed interesting. On the one side, Reid states that one of our first principles, the 'principle of credulity', undergoes a process of correction. It ceases to be compelling. This change is an answer to the lack of influence of the 'principle of veracity' on the actual human testimony. On the other side, we learn that another

*M. Dalgarno and E. Matthews (eds.), The Philosophy of Thomas Reid, 193–203.*
© *1989 by Kluwer Academic Publishers.*

principle, concerning the reliability of the senses, receives
some confirmation from experience. The framework of our
constitutive principles shows thus a kind of flexibility, at
least in certain respects. The idea of coherence among our
beliefs must play some role here.

A second passage serves as an argument for views about
coherence in Reid:

There must, therefore, be some order and consistency
in the human faculties.(4)

Here, however, Reid describes the necessary consistency
between reason – rightly understood – and common sense, as
due to their common Maker. The passage on this reading is
not really concerned with coherence among common sense
beliefs as such.

In the third of the cited passages, Reid comments on
establishing first principles. He does not hold that these
have to be proven – we would then be in need of other
principles as premises, which we should prove again, etc. –
but he maintains that they may be confirmed in various
ways.(5) One of the possible confirmations is the ad
absurdum proof. Reid argues that if you try to deny a first
principle, you will be led to absurd consequences:

There is hardly any proposition, especially in those
that may claim the character of first principles,
that stands alone and unconnected. It draws many
others along with it in a chain that cannot be
broken. He that takes it up must bear the burden of
all its consequences; and, if that is too heavy for
him to bear, he must not pretend to take it up.(6)

This passage sounds strange, coming just after Reid's remark
that he can offer no proof of first principles. The analogy
with mathematics is possibly misleading. In a mathematical
proof, to draw absurd consequences from a premise is to prove
the truth of the proposition contradictory to this premise.
But the notion of absurdity Reid wants to introduce here
cannot be the logical one (the derivation of a definite
contradiction). He would then be able to prove the first
principle. It is not easy to know what this absurdity is.
Elsewhere, Reid defines absurdity as something we detect by
means of a 'particular emotion' we have when common sense is
contradicted. But he would then be arguing in a kind of

circle.(7)  Thus, what Reid aims at in this passage  does not seem clear enough to  me to attribute  a large importance  to it.

Consequently, I hold the first of these three  quotations to be the most interesting in respect to our problem.  Now we are to ask  what the sense  is of Reid's  remarks about an  a posteriori confirmation of  principles first instantiated  on an instinctive basis.   The case of  human testimony I  shall discuss later.

In  order  to  answer  this  question  –  in  a  somewhat hypothetical manner,  as  Reid himself  did not  explain  the 'how' of  this  confirmation  –  let us  first  consider  the formulation Reid  has  given to  some  of his  principles  of contingent truths.  Let us take first the one Reid  evokes in the first quotation  above, and which  Lehrer and Smith  call the 'principle of perceptual reality':(8)

Those things  do really  exist  which we  distinctly perceive by  our senses,  and are  what we  perceive them to be.(9)

And second  let  us take  this similar  principle  concerning memory:

Those things did really happen which I distinctly remember.(10)

I am inclined to say that Reid exhibits here a correspondence theory of  truth, although neither  correspondence nor  truth are explicitly mentioned in the  quoted phrases.  But we  may say that  they  imply that  the  judgment  involved in  the operation of  perception (or  of  memory)  is true  when perception (or  memory)  is distinct.   Here,  distinct perception (or  memory) guarantees  the  relation of  the judgment with  the  object perceived  (or  remembered). Moreover, the  core  of  the doctrine  of  correspondence  is simply the view that a true judgment has this property by its relation to a fact.

What  is  now  the  importance  of  coherence  among  our beliefs, for  someone  holding  a  correspondence  theory  of truth, while seeking to find a codification of our principles of truth?  In order to explain this role, I shall construct a possible line of argument.

We must observe that, if we have stated the right principles of knowledge - the ones guaranteeing the correspondence of our judgments with the facts - we shall also have some order among our judgments, e.g. those made on the basis of distinct perception and of distinct memory. We can express this in the following way:

R: We have the right principles.
(In Reid's view, the principles govern the activities of our faculties. In that sense, belief acquisition always depends on principles.)

C: The system of our beliefs - our 'doxastic system'(11) - presents some order.

W: The world is made in such a way that true judgments about it do not lead to contradictions.

W is a very general metaphysical assumption which Reid would certainly admit. He even states a much stronger assumption since among his principles of contingent truths, he maintains "Nature is governed by fixed laws".(12)

We can now observe that the conjunction of W and R implies C:

$$[ \underline{W} \& \underline{R} ] - \underline{C}$$

In other terms, the ordered character of our doxastic system is implied by the conjunction of the right codification of our principles and of the ordered character of the world. Let us write the truth table of this implication:

|    | [W | & | R] | − | C |
|----|----|---|----|---|---|
| 1. | 1  | 1 | 1  | 1 | 1 |
| 2. | 1  | 1 | 1  | 0 | 0 |
| 3. | 1  | 0 | 0  | 1 | 1 |
| 4. | 1  | 0 | 0  | 1 | 0 |
| 5. | 0  | 0 | 1  | 1 | 1 |
| 6. | 0  | 0 | 1  | 1 | 0 |
| 7. | 0  | 0 | 0  | 1 | 1 |
| 8. | 0  | 0 | 0  | 1 | 0 |

Lines 1 and 3 to 8 - in which we take W, R and C as statements of possible 'facts' - characterize logically possible universes.   Let  me   comment briefly  on  the   whole series:

1.   The universe which Reid believes he lives in.

2.   This universe is logically ruled out.   It cannot be the case that we   have an   ordered world, correct   principles and yet no order among our beliefs.

3.   We have bad principles, but they happen to produce only beliefs showing some order.

4.   Bad principles and no order among our beliefs.

5.   The world is not ordered, but we have right principles which happen to give us an ordered set of beliefs.

6.   No ordered world and no order among our beliefs.

7.   Bad principles and a world without order happen to give us an ordered doxastic system.

8.   Complete confusion.

Provided that we encounter occasions of belief acquisition in respect to  a wide   range of  facts and  order our  knowledge claims under  a  variety of  principles,  we can  assume  the following statement:  If we have an ordered doxastic  system, it is plausible that $\underline{W}$ and $\underline{R}$ are true, because  the universes 3, 5 and 7,  though logically possible, suppose very  strange contexts.  A  sufficient   exertion of  our  faculties  makes universe 3 implausible, unless we admit some 'good spirit', a being having  the opposite  properties  of Descartes's  'evil spirit', cutting  out all   occasions of acquiring beliefs   not fitting in with our doxastic system though subsumed under our bad principles.  A  similar   remark applies  to universe  5. Here, the 'good spirit'  is to cut  out all the facts of  the unordered world we could encounter, preserving thus the order of  the   doxastic  system.    Universe  7   is  even   more extraordinary.   Our beliefs, subsumed  under bad  principles and concerning (more or less) a world in disorder, keep  some order.  This means almost double work for the 'good spirit'.

As a consequence of the implausibility of universes 3,   5 and 7, universe 1 is made plausible if our doxastic system is an  ordered one.   That  means  that  the  codification  of principles to  which our beliefs  correspond is  'established

and confirmed'.(13)        We  may  observe that  besides  $\underline{R}$,  $\underline{W}$
receives indirect confirmation in another context:

> Indeed, if we believe that there is a wise and  good
> Author of nature, we  may see a  good reason why  he
> should continue  the same  laws of  nature, and  the
> same  connections  of  things,  for  a  long  time:
> because, if he did otherwise, we could learn nothing
> from what is past,  and all our experience would  be
> of no use  to us.  But, though this  consideration,
> when we come to the  use of reason, may confirm  our
> belief of the continuance  of the present course  of
> nature, it is certain that  it did not give rise  to
> this belief.(14)

Thus, metaphysical  or  religious views  may  allow  rational
support of the 'inductive principle', and of $\underline{W}$ as well.

The account I  have given of  confirmation, based on  the
idea of coherence, of  our codification of principles,  shows
that this consideration can have another sense than it has in
contemporary theories of  belief justification  through  the
evaluation of coherence within a doxastic system.  In  Reid's
stated views,  coherence  is  no way  of  justifying current
beliefs at the level of common sense. We may ask if we could
ascribe a kind of  'rule coherentism', combining coherence  –
for  philosophical  discussion  of  the  principles,  with
foundations  –  for  particular  beliefs.(15)   What  speaks
against this line of interpretation is that it implies a kind
of freedom in matters of first principles.  Coherence as such
leaves a multiplicity of decisions concerning the  principles
possible.  But, in Reid's view, there  is no such choice  in
matters of principles, because  they express the  necessities
of our nature.   The consideration of  coherence can be  only
one  secondary  point  of  view  among  several  'reasonings'
concerning the first principles.  As is indicated by the term
'instinct' which Reid uses  sometimes, and  by the  argument
about  the  temporal  priority  of  beliefs  corresponding
intimately to  first  principles  in  respect to  other  later
beliefs,  we  simply  admit  them.(16)   Then,  if  we  are
philosophers, we can  test them in  various ways and  observe
that their adoption  leads to the  coherence of our  doxastic
system. We can make  it plausible that the coherence  occurs
as  a  consequence  of  the  appropriate  codification  of
principles we  have  succeeded in  giving.   Thus,  coherence
seems to play only a  fringe role in Reid's philosophy.

However, coherence, or at least consistency, plays a very important role in the case of human testimony. Here, lack of consistency proves to be the reason to defeat a first principle, or at least its most rigid interpretation. Thus, are we not to think that the notion of coherence in Reid's philosophy is of central importance? A possible move would be to divide first principles into a group of non-defeasible ones, like the 'principle of perceptual reality', and a group of 'second class', defeasible principles like the 'principle of credulity'. Reid goes so far in that direction, in respect to the latter principle, that he even treats it as a kind of prejudice, an idola tribus in the sense of Francis Bacon. In other words, a principle of contingent truths appears here as a possible source of errors.(17) Reid would probably not admit this of all his principles. However, we may observe that other principles may present a kind of defeasibility. I give some examples without commenting on them at length:

> There is life and intelligence in our fellow-men with whom we converse.(18)

> Certain features of the countenance, sounds of the voice, and gestures of the body, indicate certain thoughts and dispositions of mind.(19)

In connection with this latter principle, the possibility of escaping from the strict and natural correspondence of the external features with the inner dispositions is explicitly discussed by Reid in I, in terms reminiscent of Jean-Jacques Rousseau's critique of culture and education.(20)

Further:

> We have some degree of power over our actions, and the determinations of our will.(21)

> There are many events depending upon the will of man, in which there is a self-evident probability, greater or less, according to circumstances.(22)

In the two latter cases, the defeasibility is almost built-in to the formulation of the principles, as is shown by the expressions 'some' and 'greater or less'. This is even more striking in the 'principle of credulity' as stated in IP:

> There is a certain regard due to human testimony in

matters of fact, and even to human authority in
matters of opinion.(23)

Elsewhere, Reid also remarks that we should adopt a different
tactic towards the 'inductive principle' than towards the
'principle of credulity'.(24) The inequality of treatment
here is clear. The inductive principle holds stronger than
the instances, leading possibly to its rejection or to its
restrained interpretation. It is the contrary move which we
should make concerning the principle of credulity.

On the whole, the principles of contingent truths which
we may state in respect to our knowledge of other minds seem
particularly liable to be defeated – though not abandoned.
As a result, we would thus have, within our doxastic system,
a sub-system A including the beliefs corresponding to the
'hard' principles, and another sub-system B containing
beliefs corresponding to the 'soft', defeasible principles.
The beliefs belonging to sub-system B would have undergone a
critical control of their consistency with the first
sub-system, A. Before, and even after this control, they
would only be admitted conditionally in the doxastic system.
Nevertheless, the 'soft' sub-system B depends still on its
own first principles, which remain basic and irreducible to
other principles. The knowledge we get by the means they
describe is not to be drawn from other sources.

Mutatis mutandis, the situation here resembles universe 5
above. We are facing an unordered part of the world, partly
of a verbal nature. In certain cases (e.g. lies),
contradiction is already present as such (in contrast to what
is stated in assumption W) in that part of the world. But
this time, in order to preserve our doxastic system from
incoherence, we are to do the critical work of the 'good
spirit' ourselves.

All of this shows that the consideration of coherence is
not without interest, even if one is basically, like Reid, a
correspondence theorist in respect to truth and a
foundationalist in respect to the justification of our
beliefs. In that sense, Lehrer and Smith's attempt to make
sense of some hitherto almost unnoticed phrases in Reid's
writings presents much interest. However, I would maintain
that Reid is no 'coherentist' in the modern, strong sense.
The modern coherentist epistemology is based on the view that
we have no incorrigible beliefs about facts (e.g. about
immediate perceptual experience) and that the justified

acceptance of a belief depends on its coherence with our doxastic system or some alternative to it. If we have 'hard' principles as Reid maintains we do, for instance in relation to original perceptions and to consciousness, we have also incorrigible beliefs, including beliefs about material bodies and their basic properties and beliefs about our mind and its operations. On another level, Reid's praise of the inductive method and his rejection of the method of hypotheses suggests that the purely theoretical views cannot belong to the process of the acquisition of scientific knowledge. This means that, according to him, theories should not be introduced as evidence for our beliefs. In my view, these elements are sufficient to rebut the characterization of Reid's epistemology as 'coherentist'.

## NOTES

(1)  Lehrer and Smith (1985, MS version p.  26).  I wish  to express my gratitude to the authors for providing me with the manuscript version of their article and for their very valuable commentaries on the present paper.  I  am  also grateful to Timothy Oakley for very useful advice.  This research has  been supported  by the  Swiss National  Science Foundation.

(2)  Lehrer and Smith (1985, MS version pp. 7 and 23).

(3)  I VI, xx (Works, p. 184).

(4)  I V, vii (Works, p. 127).

(5)  IP VI, iv (Works, p. 438).

(6)  IP VI, iv (Works, p. 439).

(7)  IP VI, iv (Works, p.  438).  See also Schulthess  (1983, pp. 88–90).

(8)  Lehrer and Smith (1985, MS version p. 12).

(9)  IP VI, v (Works, p. 445).

(10) IP VI, v (Works, p. 444).

(11) Cf. Lehrer (1974, pp. 189ff.).

(12) IP VI, v (Works, p. 451).

(13) A reflection of this nature became a leading thought  in William Whewell's philosophy of  science:  "A coincidence  of untried facts with speculative assertions cannot be the  work of chance, but implies  some large portions  of truth in  the principles on which the  reasoning is  founded."   Whewell (1840, Vol. II, p. 229).

(14) I VI, xxiv (Works, p. 198).

(15) See Lehrer (1983, p. 182).

(16) IP VI, iv (Works, p. 441).

(17) **IP** VI, vii (Works, p. 469).

(18) **IP** VI, v (Works, p. 448).

(19) **IP** VI, v (Works, p. 449).

(20) **I** IV, ii (Works, pp. 117–9).

(21) **IP** VI, v (Works, p. 446).

(22) **IP** VI, v (Works, p. 451).

(23) **IP** VI, v (Works, p. 450).

(24) **I** VI, xxiv (Works, p. 199).

Claudine Engel-Tiercelin

## REID AND PEIRCE ON BELIEF

The influence Thomas Reid exerted on C.S. Peirce is well known.(1) The American founder of pragmatism more than once recognized his debt to the Scottish philosopher.(2)  Reid's theory of immediate perception, his sophisticated realism, and many aspects of his Common Sense approach are almost entirely adopted by Peirce,(3) who also stresses the acuteness and precision of Reid's analyses in psychology,(4) while he blames Hamilton for his frequent errors of interpretation.(5)

In this paper, I would like to indicate some elements of Peirce's debt, especially with regard to the concept of belief – a key-concept of Peirce's pragmatism and one which plays a crucial role in Reid's thought. I will try to show not only parallels but a real affiliation between Reid and Peirce. My intention is not to call Reid a pragmatist 'avant l'heure', but rather to underline the originality of his theory and the unjustified character of many attacks directed against the indubitable beliefs of his Common Sense philosophy.(6)

I

Belief is a pervasive concept throughout Reid's philosophy, and not surprisingly, since it is an essential ingredient of all mental, intellectual as well as active, operations:

> There are many operations of mind in which, when we analyze them as far as we are able, we find belief to be an essential ingredient. A man cannot be conscious of his own thoughts without believing. that he thinks. He cannot perceive an object of sense, without believing that it exists. He cannot distinctly remember a past event, without believing that it did exist. Belief therefore is an ingredient in consciousness, in perception, and in remembrance.

> Not only in most of our intellectual operations, but in many of the active principles of the human

*M. Dalgarno and E. Matthews (eds.), The Philosophy of Thomas Reid, 205–224.*
*© 1989 by Kluwer Academic Publishers.*

> mind, belief enters as an ingredient... In every
> action that is done for an end, there must be a
> belief of its tendency to that end. So large a
> share has belief in our intellectual operations, in
> our active principles, and in our actions
> themselves, that as faith in things divine is
> represented as the main spring in the life of a
> Christian, so belief in general is the main spring
> in the life of man.(7)

While belief is thus allowed a crucial role in all mental
operations, it is none the less one of those concepts, like
sensation or consciousness, which do not "admit of logical
definition, because the operation of mind signified by them
is perfectly simple, and of its own kind. Nor do they need
to be defined, because they are common words, and well
understood".(8) We are given some characteristics of belief,
such as: it has nothing to owe to reason or experience,(9) it
is a principle of our constitution, connected with
instinct,(10) it necessarily has an object,(11) involves some
kind of conception(12) and assent.(13) In fact, to get the
exact meaning of Reid's concept of belief, one should
describe and explain how it functions in the various mental
operations in which it is involved. This is beyond the scope
of this paper. But I think that Peirce's own theory of
belief may offer some help in the reconstruction of Reid's
multitudinous and often scattered insights on belief, in so
far as Peirce is not only one of the most acute analysts of
the concept of belief and of its relations with doubt,
knowledge and action, but as his own analysis presents
striking family resemblances with Reid's

Briefly, for Peirce (1931-58; II, 643), a belief is a
habit, namely "a rule active in us",(14) or "a general
principle working in man's nature to determine how he will
act"(II, 170), or "a tendency actually to behave in a similar
way under similar circumstances in the future"(V, 487). So
we may say generally that "the feeling of believing is a more
or less sure indication of there being established in our
nature some habit which will determine our actions"(V, 371),
or that a belief "is something on which a man is prepared to
act and is therefore, in a general sense, a habit".(15) More
specifically, a belief is "an intelligent habit upon which we
shall act when occasion presents itself"(II, 435); therefore
it is a habit which is deliberate or self-controlled (V,
480), which may be conscious in that respect (V, 242), but
does not imply consciousness;(16) it is propositional(17) in

so far as it involves "a word or phrase which will call up in the memory or imagination of the interpreter images of things such as he has seen  or imagined and may see again"(V,   542). That is to say, beliefs involve memorial and imaginary associations, which whenever  they become conscious,  involve representations functioning  as  signs.(18)    Though  Peirce distinguishes between theoretical and practical  beliefs,(19) he also insists that the distinction should not be too sharp, for "if an opinion can eventually go to the determination  of a practical belief, it, in so far, becomes itself a practical belief; and every proposition  that is not pure  metaphysical jargon and  chatter  must  have some  possible  bearing  upon practice"(V, 539). What  is also distinctive of  theoretical beliefs is that  they almost  always involve expectation  (V, 542), i.e.,  reference to  the  future,(20) as  well as  "the stamp of approval"(V, 540).   Yet, the unexpected, as  occurs in perceptual  beliefs as  Reid describes  them,(21) is  also part of  the belief,  in  so far  as in  order for  it to  be justified  and  real,  i.e. "enough  to  be  recognized  as external"(V,   540),   it   must   involve   some   kind   of unexpectedness.

Now, it  is quite  true  that Reid  does not  explicitly connect belief  with  habit, but  rather  with  instinct.(22) Moreover, he clearly says  that, for that reason, belief  has no connection with experience; and he opposes instinct (which is possessed by all animals)  to habit (which is the mark  of humanity as it implies  progress through experience) on  that ground.(23)  But on the other hand, instinct and habit are on the  same  level,  as  far  as  the  classification  of  the principles of action is  concerned: they both are classed  as mechanical principles of action, in contrast with the   animal and rational  principles,(24)  requiring "no  attention,  no deliberation".(25)   Now, if  we look more  carefully at  the various descriptions Reid gives  of the concept of habit,  he most often defines  it not  as "a facility  of doing a  thing acquired by  having done  it frequently", but  rather as  "an inclination or impulse to do the action";(26) in that respect habit differs from instinct,  not in its  nature, but in  its origin, the latter being natural, the former acquired;(27) so that "when  to that  instinctive  imitation ... we join  the force of  habit, it  is easy  to see,  that these  mechanical principles have  no small  share in forming  the manners  and character of  most men".(28)   In other  words, "as,  without instinct, the  infant could  not live  to become  a man,  so, without habit, man would  remain an infant through life,  and would be as helpless, as unhandy, as speechless, and as  much

a child in understanding at threescore as at three".(29)
The importance of habits is underlined in the moral domain
and particularly in the description of moral virtue:

> We consider the moral virtues as inherent in the
> mind of a good man, even when there is no
> opportunity of exercising them. And what is it in
> the mind which we call the virtue of justice when
> it is not exercised? It can be nothing but a fixed
> purpose, or determination, to act according to the
> rules of justice, when there is opportunity.(30)

Now, these rules are acquired by the conjunction of both will
and habits; will, since any moral act proceeds from some
"fixed purpose or resolution", which is mostly general, i.e.
"intended for some general end, or regulated by some general
rule", and habits, since the exercise of those rules
contributes to change "natural constitution or habit" into
"fixed principles of belief":(31)

> We may observe, that men who have exercised their
> rational powers, are generally governed in their
> opinions by fixed principles of belief; and men who
> have made the greatest advance in self-government,
> are governed, in their practice, by general fixed
> purposes. Without the former, there would be no
> steadiness and consistence in our belief; nor
> without the latter, in our conduct.(32)

Thus, "the judgment of most men who judge for themselves is
governed by fixed principles" and "they get a habit of
believing them, which is strengthened by repeated acts, and
remains immoveable, even when the evidence upon which their
belief was at first grounded, is forgot":

> A fixed resolution retains its influence upon the
> conduct, even when the motives to it are not in
> view, in the same manner as a fixed principle
> retains its influence upon the belief, when the
> evidence of it is forgot. The former may be called
> a habit of the <u>will</u>, the latter a habit of the
> <u>understanding</u>. By such habits chiefly, men are
> governed in their opinions and in their
> practice.(33)

In this passage, Reid clearly presents two possible
definitions of a habit: first, as a propensity or as a

natural or instinctive constitution; and second, as a general
deliberate and purposive rule governing action and fixing
principles of belief. If my account is correct, we are very
near Peirce's own concept of instinctive habit, for he
defines instinct as "an inherited habit, or in more accurate
language, an inherited disposition"(II, 170); while at the
same time he defines habit as a general rule active in us;
and belief as an intelligent, deliberate and purposive habit.
We have seen how the second definition could apply to Reid's
description, but the first seems adequate as well: indeed,
while distinguishing between faculties, which are "applied to
those powers of the mind which are original and natural and
which make a part of the constitution of the mind", and
powers, which "are acquired by use, exercise or study, and
are not called faculties, but habits", Reid also adds that
habits are not only due to the fact of experience, but that
"there must be something in the constitution of the mind
necessary to our being able to acquire habits – and this is
commonly called capacity".(34)

## II

To my reconstruction of Reid's concept of belief, it might be
objected that my examples are taken from the domain of active
power, and that it is not surprising that we should find Reid
there connecting belief with habit and action, just as Peirce
does in his pragmatical definition of belief. But what about
intellectual power? Although Reid explicitly maintains a
difference between speculation and action, it seems to me
that the rather more important distinction he makes is one
between faculties and powers. What I would like to argue as
characteristic of Reid's analyses concerning the mental is
his insistence on the dynamic character of mind. Mind has
not properties like bodies, but operations. Mind is active
in thinking and not passive, and the direct consequence is:

> Every operation supposes a power in the being that
> operates; for to suppose anything to operate, which
> has no power to operate, is manifestly absurd.
> But, on the other hand, there is no absurdity in
> supposing a being to have power to operate, when it
> does not operate. Thus I may have power to walk
> when I sit; or to speak, when I am silent. Every
> operation, therefore, implies power; but the power
> does not imply the operation.(35)

In other words, to get a clear meaning of what a power is, we

do not have to refer to our consciousness nor to  our senses,
but to infer it from its operations or effects:

> Power is not an object of any of our external
> senses, nor even an object of consciousness...
> Power is not an operation of the mind, and
> therefore no object of consciousness.  Indeed,
> every operation of the mind is the exertion of some
> power of the mind; but we are conscious of the
> operation only – the power lies behind the  scene;
> and, though we may justly infer the power from  the
> operation, it must be remembered, that inferring is
> not the province of consciousness, but of reason...
> I am conscious that I have a conception or idea  of
> power; but, strictly speaking, I am not  conscious
> that I have power.(36)

How do we get the conception of power?  This  is only "by the
effect which it is  able to produce"(37) for "our  conception
of power is relative  to its exertions or effects",(38)  even
if it is not reducible to its effects:

> Power is one thing; its exertion is another  thing.
> It is true, there can be no exertion without power;
> but there may be power that is not exerted...  But,
> though it be one  thing to speak,  and another  to
> have the power of speaking, I apprehend we conceive
> the power as something which has a certain relation
> to the  effect.  And of  every power we form  our
> notion by the  effect which  it is able  to
> produce.(39)

Finally, while Reid distinguishes  speculation and action  in
so far as there are  active and reflexive powers, he  notices
that "to constitute the relation between me and my action, my
conception of the action  and will to  do it, are  essential.
For what I never conceived nor willed, I never did":

> It seems, therefore, to me most probable that  such
> beings only  as have some  degree of  understanding
> and will, can possess active power ... active power
> cannot be  exerted  without  will  and
> intelligence.(40)

In that respect, this points  to the conclusion that the  way
belief functions in intellectual operations is not profoundly
different in  nature  from the  way  it functions  in active

operations: the difference lies rather in the objects of belief.

## II

At any rate, if our interpretation is right, we may understand Peirce's fascination for Reid's analyses, and why he took him as an illustrator of how belief operates in perceptual judgments.(41)  Anyone who is familiar with pragmatism will have recognized more than resemblances between the way Reid presents the mental and Peirce's own account. I need only mention formulation of the pragmatic maxim, enunciated by Peirce in his famous 1878 article How to make our ideas clear:

> Consider what effects, which might conceivably have practical bearings, we conceive the object of our conception to have. Then, our conception of these effects is the whole of our conception of the object.(42)

And Peirce adds:

> To develop its meaning, we have, therefore, simply to determine what habits it produces, for what a thing means is simply what habits it involves. Now the identity of a habit depends on how it might lead us to act, not merely under such circumstances as are likely to arise, but under such as might possibly occur, no matter how improbable they may be. What the habit is depends on when and how it causes us to act. As for the when, every stimulus to action is derived from perception; as for the how, every purpose of action is to produce some sensible result. Thus we come down to what is tangible and practical, as the root of every real distinction of thought, no matter how subtile it may be; and there is no distinction of meaning so fine as to consist in anything but a possible difference in practice.(43)

This does not mean, as we have already noticed, that Peirce reduces our conceptions to their effects, or theory to practice, but that it should always be possible to translate the concept we have into a set of conditionals (the habits involved), having for antecedents a statement of the conditions of perception and for consequents the phenomenal

quality observed. When applied to the mental, the maxim
signifies that in order to get a clear meaning of it, we
should rather be interested in the outward phenomena, or
signs, and the operations by which it manifests itself,
rather than in the deceitful testimonies of an hypothetical
self. It also means that we must not reduce the mental to
any present or actual consciousness or operation, but relate
it to its virtual or habitual effects: thus we cannot say
that to know a language (VII, 342), or to possess certain
mental powers (VII, 344), or to know of some body that it is
heavy (VII, 341), is to be able to talk actually, or to have
certain ideas present to the mind, or to refer to some actual
experiment testifying of the weight of the body; on the
contrary it is to know that, in each case, whether the
occasion presents itself or not, these powers are really and
continually there.(44)

We may now understand Peirce's judgment concerning
Reid's analyses. In a letter to William James, he qualifies
himself on the side of Reid among others, in that he adopts
the doctrine of immediate perception. He writes:

> I have myself preached immediate perception as you
> know; — and you can't find a place where I
> distinguish the objective and subjective side of
> things.

Here Peirce quotes an article he had previously written in
reviewing Karl Pearson's 'Grammar of Science':

> He tells that each of us is like the operator at a
> central telephone office ... Not at all! ... When
> we first wake up to the fact that we are thinking
> beings ... we have to set out upon our intellectual
> travels from the home where we already find
> ourselves. Now this home is the parish of
> Percepts. It is not inside our skulls but out in
> the open. It is the external world that we
> directly observe ... The inkstand is a real thing.
> Of course, in being real and external, it does not
> in the least cease to be a purely psychical
> product, a generalized percept. If I had had the
> least idea that I was uttering anything newer than
> the doctrine of immediate perception, I should have
> argued the matter more closely. Of course, this
> doctrine of immediate perception is a corollary
> from the corollary of pragmaticism that the object

perceived is the immediate object of the destined
ultimate opinion, ... I am quite sure that lots of
others have held the same view, some of them
pragmatists and some not. (I hope the word
'pragmatism' may be accepted, as I suggest, as the
term expressive of these things – perhaps we cannot
be sure just what they are – in which the group of
us is in agreement, as to the interpretation of
thought.(45)

We may understand why Peirce felt so near Reid, as far as the
realism involved in the theory of immediate perception is
concerned: it is also because he regarded the functioning of
belief in the perceptual judgment in an almost similar way.
As we have seen, Peirce explains that the judgment involved
in some of our beliefs calls up some representations which
function as signs, and he has a very specific account of the
way such signs as the icon, the index and the symbol
operate.(46) As has been underlined,(47) the language of
sensation and perception is also part and parcel of Reid's
analysis of the way our perceptual judgments are framed but
also of the way our beliefs immediately accompany them. And
part of the explanation of our belief in the external world
proceeds from the fact we immediately read, from the sign,
the thing signified,(48) while at the same time the
unexpected and inexplicable character of our sensations
places us under the necessity of believing in the existence
of our sensations.(49) The unexpected, unanalysable
character of our sensation is what is also called by Peirce
the "brute, reactive force of existence",(50) and we have
seen it to be part of the reality of our beliefs. It is "the
stamp of approval" or what Reid calls the 'assent' by which
we distinguish our beliefs from pure fancy, and by which
also we may be sure that our beliefs are not, as Locke would
say, a mere agreement or disagreement between ideas,(51) or
as Hume would argue, a simple change in vividness in our
ideas.(52)

Such a determining role played by belief in the
philosophies of Reid and Peirce also explains the
similarities which we may find in their respective treatments
of the relation of belief to doubt as well as their admitting
basically common sense beliefs.

Peirce insists, as does Reid, that beliefs are first,
i.e. they come before any knowledge, and are therefore not
only indispensable tools for developing rationality, but also

very hard, if not impossible, to discard. This is why, to a certain extent, we have to trust the testimony of others following what Reid called our principle of credulity,(53) or in Peirce's terms, follow the methods of tenacity, then of authority, which are the inevitable primitive methods of fixing belief.(54) The vital role of belief and its anteriority to reason and experience justifies the indubitable character of precritical belief, while it at the same time renders most kinds of doubts ineffective or simply irrelevant. Here again, Peirce's criticism of what he calls 'paper doubt' or 'Cartesian doubt', (as if "doubting were as easy as lying")(55) is on most points the replica of Reid's attacks against 'chamber doubt'.(56) And here, I would like to emphasize my opposition to a suggestion which seems to me to proceed from an incorrect interpretation of Reid's thought. It has been argued (57) that when Reid attacks idealism and scepticism, on the ground that the sceptic's doubts would be inaccurate, since the sceptic would never dream of behaving in practice as he would resolve to do in theory, his line of argument is naive and ill-founded. I hope to have shown that it is not at all the case, so long as we keep in mind that Reid's point is, if not pragmatical, at least theoretical, and not only moral or merely factual. What he rather means is that if any concept or any theory should <u>mean</u> anything, then we ought to be able to see at least some of its effects; and, if such is not the case, then it amounts to mere metaphysical jargon. His insistence on the necessity of being extremely cautious in not mistaking a pure distinction in thought or in our language for a distinction in reality,(58) or conversely in confusing things that are in fact separate, because of the ambiguities of our language,(59) goes in the same direction.

## IV

Still, it would be quite inaccurate to say that Peirce entirely adopts Reid's insights on belief or that he has no reservations about Reid's Common Sensism. What Peirce finds defective in Reid's analysis is, basically, the ambiguity which hovers around the concept itself: is it equivalent to an internal phenomenon or not? In other words, is it a mental state or the sign of some outward power, be it instinctive or dispositional? I must say that the ambiguity seems to be a real one. At times, Reid clearly adopts the latter view, which is the one I have tried to stress, but at others he simply equates belief with mere psychological states such as credulity, faith, or persuasion. The difficulty is exacerbated by the fact already mentioned that Reid does not see the need of a logical definition of the concept. Now such waverings around the concept explain why Peirce's judgment is both enthusiastic and reserved.

First, he refuses to accept the indubitability of Reid's beliefs if they are to function as first principles of knowledge. In his three articles published in 1868,(60) Peirce denounces what he calls the nominalistic tendency of trying to find some foundational principles, whether we call them Aristotelian first principles, Cartesian intuition, or Humean sense-data. The aim of the papers is to show the dispensability of such principles and to argue that all that is cognizable is in signs and inferential. One of the Questions is directly aimed at the empiricists and all those who, Reid included, believe in the existence of an internal world and of its method of analysis: introspection.(61) Peirce's claim is that although we have to admit the fact of consciousness which is embodied both by feeling (or firstness) and a sense of reaction (secondness), we are not entitled to give it a cognitive status, and even less a privileged one. And while he admires Reid for being one of the rare philosophers to have seen the importance of all three categories (thirdness being the quality of representation), he also blames him for having overlooked the different parts they play in our logical or phenomenological approach to reality.(62)

Second, and it is almost a consequence of what has been said, while, in the last period of his work, Peirce adopts the principles of Common Sensism, he explains why he departs from the Scottish School and particularly from Reid. He presents himself as an advocate of Critical Commonsensism: these two terms, seeming at first glance, as he himself admits, to present "two irreconcilable views"(V, 505). The first mark of distinction lies in the fact that Peirce only admits as indubitable those beliefs that are irreducibly vague.(63) Among them are all the beliefs that belong to a precritical domain (such as perceptual judgments, or the unconscious processes of instinct): they are indubitable, in Peirce's sense, for such beliefs are not 'accepted':

> What happens is that one comes to recognize that one has had the belief-habit as long as one can remember; and to say that no doubt of it has never arisen is only another way of saying the same thing.(64)

Although it may happen that some beliefs so held are true ones and some are false, the propositions contained in belief are not accepted uncritically:

> No man accepts any belief on the ground that it has not been criticized ... to criticize is to doubt, and ... criticism can only attack a proposition after it has given it some precise sense in which it is impossible entirely to remove the doubt.

Another mark of separation from the 'old school' is the evolutionary character of our instinctive beliefs, i.e. the fact that they must have grown up:

> [The Critical Common Sensist] opines that the indubitable beliefs refer to a somewhat primitive mode of life, and that, while they never become dubitable in so far as our mode of life remains that of somewhat primitive man, yet, as we develop degrees of self-control, unknown to that man, occasions of action arise in relation to which the original beliefs, if stretched to cover them, have no sufficient authority. In other words, we outgrow the applicability of instinct — not altogether, by any manner of means, but in our highest activities. The famous Scotch philosophers lived and died out before this could be duly appreciated.(65)

The third mark of distinction lies in the Common Sensist's "high esteem for doubt" (V, 514), in other words, Peirce's fallibilism, which makes him think that wht has been held indubitable one day may be proved on the morrow to be false.(66) Therefore, the Critical Common Sensist is also even more critical than a proponent of the Critical philosophy of Kant in so far as "he criticizes the critical method, follows his footsteps, tracks it to its lair"(V, 523). Following Reid in his charge against proponents of the theory of ideas, Peirce insists "it is difficult to find a Criticist who does not hold to more fundamental beliefs than any Critical Common Sensist does"(V, 523). Here again, Peirce insists that the most serious danger does not lie in believing too little, but in believing too much (V, 514).

V

Yet, I would like to conclude that there are more points of

agreement between the two philosophers than Peirce himself
would admit. I will briefly indicate some of these. It is
true that Reid thinks of a somewhat fixed list of indubitable
beliefs, which does not seem to allow many changes or
revolutions,(67) yet it more than once happens that he
envisages the possibility of some new principles or of some
more general law under which our beliefs would have to
bend.(68) What he retains from the Newtonian frame of mind
is less its dogmaticism than its scientific spirit, and the
modesty of the scientist constantly prevails when he talks of
the difficulties we encounter in the study of the mental or
when he carefully draws the list of the criteria that will
help us not to mistake genuine beliefs for mere prejudices or
superstitions.(69) But most of all, what seems to me
symptomatic of the scientific spirit which animates his
investigations, and here again he is very close to Peirce, is
the somewhat confused conviction that the methods of science
must, some time or other, meet real laws and the agreement of
the community in order to convey any truth at all. In that
respect, a study of the relations between belief and realism
in Reid's philosophy remains to be done. But it seems
obvious enough that such a study would at once prove that
Reid's concepts of belief, realism and Common Sensism, far
from being naive, are extremely subtle and profound.

## NOTES

(1) See, for example, Feibleman (1944, pp. 113–20) and Flower (1980, pp. 94–103). Reid, with Berkeley, Kant and Bain, was a favourite author for discussion among the group including Green, James and Peirce which was to found the 'Metaphysical Club' from which pragmatism arose. Peirce himself admitted that pragmatism was but a 'corollary' of Bain's definition of belief. See Fisch (1954, pp. 413–44).

(2) See, for example, Peirce (1931–1958; I, 19, 38, 240; V, 56, 444, 523, 539, 608; VII, 580n; VIII, 123n, 261). References are given by volume and paragraph number.

(3) Peirce (1931–1958; V, 444, 523; VI, 95; VIII, 261).

(4) For example, Peirce (1931–1958; V, 444) describes Reid as "a subtle but well-balanced intellect", and (VIII, 123n) as "a singularly accurate observer, whose lessons have not yet been thoroughly learned by psychologists". Further, (ibid.) Peirce cites Reid as having been the first "distinctly to recognise that we have something like a direct perception of duration, or at least, of motion" and to "draw the needful distinction between the lapse of time during the act of perception and the lapse of time represented in the percept".

(5) For example, Peirce (1931–1958; I, 38) writes how "Hamilton stupidly objects to Reid's phrase 'immediate memory'". Peirce's criticism merits recognition, since he anticipated the view which was later to emerge of Hamilton's responsibility for errors of interpretation and the relative disaffection Reid's philosophy was to undergo. See Greenberg (1976) or Brody (1971).

(6) See, for example, some judgments by Grave (1960) or Griffen-Collard (1979).

(7) IP, II, xx (Works, pp. 327–8).

(8) IP, II, xx (Works, p. 327). See also I, II, v (Works, p. 107).

(9) IP, II, xxi (Works, p. 332); Cf. I, VI, xxiv (Works, p. 196).

(10) I, VI, xx (Works, pp. 545–9).

(11) **IP**, II, xx (Works, p. 327).

(12) **IP**, IV, i (Works, p. 360).

(13) **I**, II, v (Works, p. 107).

(14) Peirce (1931–58; V, 487) explains its psychological meaning thus: "Multiple reiterated behaviour of the same kind, under similar combinations of percepts and fancies, produces a tendency – the habit – actually to behave in a similar way under similar circumstances in the future". Physiologically speaking, habits are general ways of behaviour which are associated with the removal of stimuli (VI, 264); as such, they may be found in all actual things, in rivers as well as in animals, in plants as well as in crystalline substances (VI, 260).

(15) This is scarcely different from Bain's definition of belief as preparedness to act.

(16) In that respect, Peirce's definition of belief seems perfectly compatible with the attribution of beliefs to animals. See the analysis of Engel (1984, p. 408): "Ce concept de croyance semble, dans la mesure ou l'assertion d'une proposition n'est pas necessaire a son attribution, parfaitement compatible avec l'attribution de croyances dispositionnelles a des animaux. Ainsi, l'assertion d'une proposition, un sentiment de conviction peuvent faire partie de cette conception dispositionnelle. Mais ils n'en sont ni la condition necessaire ni la condition suffisante". Compare Peirce (1931–58; II, 148): "A belief need not be conscious. When it is recognized, the act of recognition is called by logicians a judgment, although this is properly a term of psychology".

(17) "Every belief is belief in a proposition. Indeed, every proposition has its predicate which expresses what is believed and its subjects which express of what it is believed" (Peirce, 1931–58; V, 542). Compare Reid (**IP**, II, xx, Works, p. 327): "Belief is always expressed in language by a proposition, wherein something is affirmed or denied. This is the form of speech which in all languages is appropriated to that purpose, and without belief there could be neither affirmation nor denial, nor should we have any form of words to express either".

(18) Cf. Peirce (1931–58; II, 148): "What particularly

distinguishes a general belief, or opinion, such as is an inferential conclusion, from other habits, is that it is active in the imagination. If I have a habit of putting my left leg into my trouser before the right, when I imagine that I put on my trousers, I shall probably not definitely think of putting the left leg on first. But if I believe that fire is dangerous, and I imagine a fire bursting out close beside me, I shall also imagine that I jump back". In such a case belief involves judgment: "we virtually resolve, upon a certain occasion to act as if certain imagined circumstances were perceived"(II, 435). Thus beliefs construct imaginary conditions which "determine schemata or imaginary skeleton diagrams"(II, 148). This act "which amounts to such a resolve, is a peculiar act of the will whereby we cause an image, or icon, to be associated in a particularly strenuous way, with an object represented to us by an index. This act itself is represented in the proposition by a symbol, and the consciousness of it fulfils the function of a symbol in the judgment. Suppose, for example, I detect a person with whom I have to deal in an act of dishonesty, I have in mind something like a 'composite photograph' of all the persons that I have known and read of that have had that character, and at the instant I make the discovery, concerning that person, who is distinguished from others for me by certain indications, upon that index, at that moment down goes the stamp of RASCAL, to remain indefinitely".

(19) "It does not follow that because every theoretical belief is, at least indirectly, a practical belief, this is the whole meaning of the theoretical belief" (V, 538).

(20) "A belief is an intelligent habit upon which we shall act when occasion presents itself" (V, 398). Cf. V, 545; V, 542.

(21) Peirce explicitly cites Reid as illustrating the part of the unexpected necessary in accounting for the reality of our beliefs. Cf. Peirce (1931-58; V, 542).

(22) Cf. note 10 supra.

(23) AP, III, I, ii (Works, p. 545-6).

(24) AP, III, I, i (Works, p. 545).

(25) Ibid.

(26) **AP**, III, II, iii (<u>Works</u>, p. 550).

(27) <u>Ibid</u>.

(28) <u>Ibid</u>.

(29) **AP**, III, I, iii (<u>Works</u>, pp. 550-1).

(30) **AP**, II, iii (<u>Works</u>, p. 540).

(31) **AP**, II, iii (<u>Works</u>, pp. 539 & 541).

(32) **AP**, II, iii (<u>Works</u>, p. 540).

(33) **AP**, II, iii (<u>Works</u>, p. 541).

(34) **IP**, I, i (<u>Works</u>, p. 221).

(35) <u>Ibid</u>.

(36) **AP**, I, i (<u>Works</u>, pp. 512-3).

(37) **AP**, I, i (<u>Works</u>, p. 514).

(38) <u>Ibid</u>.

(39) <u>Ibid</u>.

(40) **AP**, I, v (<u>Works</u>, p. 525).

(41) Peirce (1931-58; V, 542).

(42) Peirce (1931-58; V, 402).

(43) Peirce (1931-58; V, 400).

(44) Such a conception has of course enormous consequences for the versions of Realism the two philosophers maintain. Thus Peirce holds: "To assert that a law positively exists is to assert that it will operate, and therefore to refer to the future, even though conditionally. But to say that a body is hard, or red, or heavy, or of a given weight, or has any other property, is to say that it is subject to law and therefore, is a statement referring to the future"(V, 545). So if I assert 'This wafer looks red', it can only mean that "so far as the character of the percept can ever be ascertained, it will be ascertained that the wafer looked

red"(V, 542); and to believe that a sulphur is yellow is to
say that "it would be perfectly meaningless to say that
sulphur had the singular property of turning pink when nobody
was looking at it"(V, 545). Compare this with the following
claim by Reid: "When the parts of a body adhere so firmly
that it cannot easily be made to change its figure, we call
it hard; when its parts are easily displaced, we call it
soft. This is the notion which all mankind have of hardness
and softness; they are neither sensations, nor like any
sensation; they were real qualities before they were
perceived by touch, and continue to be so when they are not
perceived; for if any man will affirm that diamonds were not
hard till they were handled, who would reason with him?"(I,
V, ii, Works, p. 120).

(45) Peirce (1931–58; VIII, 261).

(46) Cf. note 18 supra.

(47) See, for example, Grave (1960, ch.5) and Rollin (1978,
pp. 257–70).

(48) I, VI, xxi, (Works, p. 188); I, VI, xxiv (Works, pp.
194, 196, 199).

(49) I, VI, xx (Works, pp. 183, 209); IP, I, ii (Works, p.
231); II, v (Works, pp. 258–60); VI, v (Works, p. 445).

(50) This is what Peirce calls the category of secondness.
Cf. Peirce (1931–58; VII, 643; VII, 635, VII, 619; IV, 57;
III, 361 et al.).

(51) I, II, v (Works, p. 107); IP, VI, vi (Works, pp. 454–5).

(52) I, VI, xxiv (Works, p. 198); IP, VI, v (Works, p. 443).

(53) I, VI, xxiv (Works, pp. 196–7); IP, VI, iv (Works, p.
438); VI, v (Works, p. 450).

(54) See 'The Fixation of Belief'(1878) in Peirce (1931–58;
V, 358–87) and especially 377–81. To these methods, Peirce
opposes the only method which may now apply to the state of
knowledge, the Scientific Method.

(55) This is a very important theme in Peirce's philosophy.
Cf. Peirce (1931–58; V, 265, 319; VIII, 16 et al.).

(56) I, II, vii (Works, p. 110); VI, xx (Works, p. 184).

(57) Cf. note 6 supra. See also Griffin–Collard (1976, pp. 126–42).

(58) This lies at the core of Reid's discussion of universals, and especially on qualities. Are they in the mind, or in the body? Does a common name signify one or two things?

(59) Consider, for example, the errors of interpretation we make about the natural language of signs, and confusions arising from a single name meaning different things.

(60) 'Questions concerning certain faculties claimed for man', 'Some consequences of four incapacities', and 'Grounds of validity of the Laws of Logic' in Peirce (1931–58; V, 213–357).

(61) Peirce (1931–58; V, 244–9). For a more extensive analysis of this theme, see Engel–Tiercelin (1982).

(62) Peirce (1931–58; I, 19; V, 77n).

(63) Cf. Peirce (1931–58; V, 508).

(64) Peirce (1931–58; V, 523).

(65) Peirce (1931–58; V, 511) alludes to the Darwinian themes which exercised a deep influence on him.

(66) Fallibilism is a very important element in Peirce's philosophy of science, as in his metaphysics. It is the doctrine that there always remains indeterminacy and vagueness, so that we can never be cocksure that today's truth may not be falsified.

(67) Griffin–Collard (1976, p. 141) concludes that Reid develops a 'static' theory of knowledge.

(68) See, for example, I, V, iii (Works, p. 122); or IP, I, ii (Works, p. 234); or his discussion of analogy I, iv (Works, pp. 236–8); or his admission that Newton's principle of gravitation may be wrong in so far as "it is not a necessary truth, whose contrary is impossible" (IP, VI, iv Works, p. 436).

(69) **IP**, I, ii (<u>Works</u>, p. 233) and VI, viii (<u>Works</u>, pp. 468–75).

C.A.J. Coady

## REID ON TESTIMONY

Thomas Reid is one of the very few important philosophers in the European tradition to have recognised the epistemological significance of our reliance upon the word of others. Our dependence upon testimony is ignored by Aristotle and treated dismissively by Plato. Amongst the ancients only Augustine seems aware of the extent to which any given individual's belief structure is underpinned by his trust in what he is told;(1) amongst the moderns, Hume shows cognizance of the extent but not of the depth of this reliance. Locke and Berkeley are oblivious to the epistemological issues raised by this trust though they have some interest in related methodological problems. The Rationalist tradition is quite silent on the matter but Reid not only realizes the importance of the epistemological role of testimony, he says some very interesting things about what testimony is, he makes some bold speculations about its relation to perception and he tries to vindicate our reliance upon it.

## A    What is Testimony?

This question is not as easy to answer as it might at first seem but Reid's approach is, characteristically, suggestive and original. One might begin to tackle the question by looking to the law courts and the formal act of testifying but clearly we rely upon the information others provide in much less formal settings than that. We need a wide enough concept to incorporate relatively casual exchanges of information, historical records, documents etc. (which are frequently referred to as 'testimony' amongst historians and laymen) and the more ritualistic contexts of the courtroom. Reid adverts indeed to the giving of evidence in law courts but his more general categorization of testimony places it amongst what he calls "the social operations of mind".(2) These operations he charges other philosophers with neglecting. They are operations which presuppose understanding and will but also "intercourse with some other intelligent being". Reid cites the exchange of testimony, the giving and receiving of commands, promising, contracting, and asking questions as amongst these operations.(3)

*M. Dalgarno and E. Matthews (eds.), The Philosophy of Thomas Reid, 225–246.*
© *1989 by Kluwer Academic Publishers.*

Reid's discussion of the social operations, though tantalizingly brief, is penetrating and original. He contrasts them with the 'solitary' operations and insists that they are not reducible to the 'solitary' operations, being "original parts of our constitution". He sees attempts to reduce or analyse them "under the common philosophical divisions" as like the equally unsuccessful attempts "to reduce all our social affections to certain modifications of self-love".(4) Reid complains not only of reductionism but also of a widespread philosophical neglect of these social-intellectual phenomena. He ties them closely to the existence of language, claiming that the primary orientation of language is towards expressing these social operations.(5) In a passage which remarkably foreshadows the sort of concerns with language characteristic of some contemporary speech act theorists, Reid complains that although every language has the resources to express questions, commands and promises, as well as judgments, there has been no analysis of what is involved in the expression of the former in striking contrast to the "voluminous tracts" devoted to analysing the expression of judgment, namely, the proposition. Reid comments that, with regard to questions, commands and promises, the expression of them has not even been given "a name different from the operations they express".(6)

Reid's thought here is a little opaque. One thing he may mean, and it connects with modern issues in the philosophy of language, is that, just as the range of speech acts we call assertions can be said to express a thought that we call a proposition, so there is similarly something intellectual expressed by the utterances we call questions, commands and promises — something (or things) which we have no term for and have paid scant attention to. If this is what Reid means then it can no longer be said that the topic is neglected. Modern discussion of it takes J.L. Austin's distinction between illocutionary and locutionary acts as its starting point, though there are also pertinent contributions from the tradition stemming from the work of the later Wittgenstein. We shall not enter into that debate here except to signal support for P.F. Strawson's proposed schematism of the relationship between the meaning of what a speaker says and the force his saying has. On Strawson's proposal there will be certain basic categories of 'sayings', corresponding to basic types of locutionary act, and ranges of full blooded illocutionary forces appropriate to each category. Strawson distinguishes two such basic categories — propositions (having the form, that S is P) and imperatives (having the form that a person z is to do some act y) – but leaves it open that there may be more, as would be the case, for instance, if the range of speech acts associated with questioning could not be accommodated by the imperative grouping but required a basic category of interrogatives.(7)

Reid would no doubt be delighted at the shift of interest from constatives (or propositions, in one sense of the term) to imperatives or directives and an associated interest in satisfaction conditions rather than truth conditions, but the contrast between propositions and other basic categories of sayings is not strictly parallel to Reid's contrast between the solitary and social operations of mind.

The most significant difference, for our purposes, is that many of the social operations will express propositions rather than imperatives or something else. Certainly requests, commands and entreaties are social operations and do not express propositions but such social operations as accusations, warnings and reports just as certainly do. What each of those latter says is capable of being true or false. Requests, commands, entreaties, on the contrary, do not give expression to how the speaker thinks the world is but to how he wants it to be. This simple point not only invalidates the opposition of the social operations to the expression of propositions but also a good deal of what Reid wants to say in this connection about the nature of testimony. His classification of judgment as one of the solitary operations and of the proposition as what is peculiarly involved in the expression of judgment may have led him to think that testimony did not express propositions. He does not explicitly say this (which is just as well since it is palpably false) but he does strongly oppose judgment and testimony in ways which at least make it unclear what view he held of testimony and propositions.(8)

In his full discussion of judgment,(9) Reid rightly says that testimony is essentially social while judgment is not but then makes two highly dubious claims about the relation between the two. The first claim is that testimony does not express judgment; the second is that the public expression of an opinion in a matter of science or criticism is not testimony but (the expression of) judgment. I want to contest both these claims but it is difficult to know where to begin because Reid provides little in the way of argument for them. The distinction between social and solitary acts of mind (to which Reid adverts in the next paragraph after making the two contested claims) is, as we have seen, unable to support so strong a claim as the first nor does it seem to bear particularly upon the second. Reid does produce what may be intended as an argument for the first soon after when he says:

> In testimony a man pledges his veracity for what he affirms; so that a false testimony is a lie: but a wrong judgment is not a lie; it is only an error.(10)

It must be conceded that there is a tendency in ordinary speech to reserve the expression 'false testimony' for what is produced by deceitful witnesses but this seems to have resulted from the influence of that family of uses of the term 'false' which expresses our interest in treacherous, disloyal or dishonest behaviour. So we have 'false friend', 'false promise', 'played me false', 'false subject' etc. Nonetheless it is surely clear that the testimony a witness gives may be perfectly sincere and yet false (in the sense of not-true). It also seems clear that, in this sense, false (i.e. mistaken) testimony will sometimes (at least) express judgment, namely false judgment. Indeed so much seems required by Reid's own view of judgment which comes a little later in the chapter:

> I give the name of judgment to every determination of the mind concerning what is true or what is false.(11)

Reid may have felt that truthful witnesses normally get their testimony right so that our primary interest is in whether they are honest whereas the judgments we make on the basis of their reports are primarily open to the criticism of error rather than dishonesty. There is something in this although much depends on the interpretation of 'normally' but, in any case, the view will not support a position as strong as that Reid adopts. Moreover, modern experience of the workings of the law and extensive psychological research on the reliability of perception, memory, and the giving of reports tend to indicate that there is a good deal of room for mistake and error and certainly undermines any idea that a witness merely records or registers neutral facts.

In the quoted passages there is, however, another interesting point which needs attention. Reid appears to think it obvious that when a man publicly offers "his opinion

in a matter of science or of criticism" this is not
testimony; this obviousness can then support the view that
testimony and judgment are mutually exclusive since this view
explains why the "opinion in a matter of science or
criticism" is not testimony, namely, because it is the
expression of judgment. We have seen good reason to reject
the general view that an expression of judgment can never be
testimony and hence an argument of this type carries little
conviction. The premise it relies upon, however, cannot
simply be dismissed since it raises important questions about
the nature of testimony. Is it true that those expressions of
judgment that are opinions "in a matter of science or
criticism" cannot be testimony?

Reid's contrast is with the case in which a witness
speaks to what he has seen or heard or, presumably, observed
via one of the other senses. Perhaps his point is that, in
the matter of testimony, a sharp distinction must be drawn
between the sensory and the intellectual, between what is
observed and what is thought or opined. So, someone may
testify to a painting's being of a soldier dressed in a red
uniform but only express a judgment as to the beauty of the
painting or its market value or its date of composition or
the type of paint that has been used in it. There is
certainly something plausible about this sort of demarcation
but it is not without difficulties. If we think in terms of
formal testimony then something like the distinction Reid is
making is marked in English law and allied traditions by the
contrast between fact and opinion and the related  contrast
between fact and inference. A witness may testify to what he
has perceived but his opinions drawn inferentially from his
observations are, as a general rule, not admissible evidence.
Part of the legal justification for this certainly resides in
the idea that the point of the whole judicial apparatus is to
provide as its output (by way of the jury's verdict or the
judge's findings) precisely such conclusions or opinions, and
hence it is a sort of absurdity, a denial of the point of the
proceedings, for the witness who is there to provide the raw
material for the judge or jury's thinking to produce his own
opinions and conclusions.

On the other hand, the legal exclusion of opinion is by
no means absolute, nor could it be. To begin with, expert
testimony is plainly opinion and has long been allowed in
English law although sometimes with certain misgivings and
hedged about by restrictions. In line, for instance, with the
justification mentioned above for excluding opinion, the

general practice of judges is to prevent even an expert
witness stating his opinion on an ultimate issue such as the
reasonableness of a covenant in restraint of trade, the
validity of a patent, or the construction to be put upon a
document.(12) Nonetheless, in a complex civilisation like
ours expert testimony has come to assume a significant role
in legal proceedings. It is, moreover, particularly
interesting in the present connection, that an expert is
allowed to adopt statements made in scientific works as part
of his testimony although this is not only hearsay but often
hearsay to opinion.(13) Secondly, non-expert witnesses may
give testimony to matters of opinion where the factual and
inferential elements in a belief are so bound together as to
be practically inseparable. As one American judge has put it,
a witness may give his opinion or impression when:

> the facts from which a witness received an
> impression were too evanescent in their nature to be
> recollected or too complicated to be separately and
> distinctly narrated.(14)

Typical cases listed by Cross are claims about age, speed,
weather, handwriting and identity in general.(15)

   It will be clear to the philosophical reader that the
legal discussion of these matters has points of contact with
complex debates within philosophy about the degree to which
any viable distinction can ultimately be made between fact
and theory, observation and inference, the sensory and the
judgmental or intellectual. It may be that what a person can
observe, no matter how 'brute' he may suppose the observation
to be, is always a function of some beliefs he has, so that
his observation can be represented as an outcome of an
inference involving those beliefs and hence an 'opinion'. To
revert to my earlier example of the painting of a soldier in
a red uniform, it could be argued that an eye-witness report
of this would only be possible for someone who had the
relevant concepts and the understanding that goes with them.
By a familiar move such understanding is then equated with
theoretical thinking which is inferential and so our witness
is giving an opinion as may be seen by contrasting his
verdict with that of someone from a very different cultural
background faced with the same painting but unable to make
the 'inferential' move from, say, 'man in curious red
clothing carrying an implement' to 'soldier in red uniform'.
I cite this philosophical manoeuvre without intending to
endorse it, for I do not find its argument wholly persuasive,

but merely to emphasize the difficulties of sustaining too
sharp a distinction between fact and opinion. Nonetheless I
think a rough but workable contrast of the kind the law
envisages can be made by learning from the philosophical
debate without prejudging its eventual outcome.

One thing the philosophical discussion may be taken to
show, at the very least, is that whether someone is offering
a judgment or giving his opinion in a sense which would
contrast with merely recording a fact must be heavily
dependent upon context. (The strong philosophical claim can
then be seen as the claim that this context dependency is
strong enough to entirely eliminate the notion of 'recording
a fact' as a theoretically fundamental idea — but it may
nonetheless have a practical validity in context.) This
context–dependency is of two kinds. In the first place, and
most importantly, there is the context of expertise and
competence. To take the painting example again: let's suppose
that it is by Sir Joshua Reynolds. Most of us would merely be
offering an opinion, though not necessarily just guessing, if
we were to say when the work had been painted (particularly
if aiming at an order of precision like a decade). On the
other hand, an expert on 18th Century painting might be able
to say authoritatively at once that it was painted in 1782
and, at current prices, was worth $500,000. He might, or
might not, be able to decompose his judgment into the
elements of fact and inference that, in some sense, make it
up but, even where he can go beyond something like 'It has
that late Reynolds look about it', his facts and inferences
may be so loaded with expertise themselves as to put a lay
audience in no better position to judge his conclusion. In
these circumstances, the art expert can testify where the
layman can only given an opinion. At the other end of the
spectrum any native speaker is an expert (up to a point) on
the meanings of utterances in his native tongue but most
would be hard to put to provide the 'facts' about those
utterances upon which their semantic interpretations are
based.

In the second place, there is the context of inquiry. As
we have seen in the legal situation, the opinion of an
acknowledged expert may be inadmissible where it concerns the
ultimate issue which the tribunal itself has to decide upon;
the law is particularly anxious that the witness should not
usurp the function and responsibility of the tribunal itself
and this anxiety is acute where the expert's opinion
encompasses disputed questions for the resolution of which

the tribunal has been created.(16) The point can however be generalised in a way that returns us to Reid's position and the concern that underlies it because an expert's view on some matter within his competence may be disregardable as evidence whenever his audience is, or ought to be, or is presumed to be or is aiming to be, equally competent to have an independent view of the matter themselves. Hence the opprobrium attaching to 'the argument from authority'. Against Reid we should conclude that many statements on matters of 'science or criticism' can figure as testimony, depending on the speaker's status and the context of the communicative exchange. We may acknowledge, nonetheless, that Reid is right to attempt some distinction between testifying and merely opining.

## B    Testimony and Perception

Reid's account of perception has probably been as closely scrutinized by philosophers as any part of his positive philosophical contributions but the analogy he draws between testimony and perception has been somewhat neglected.(19) Reid mentions the analogy in the Essay, but principally to note a disanalogy, and his most extensive treatment is in the Inquiry (Ch. VI, Section xxiv). Reid thinks that in perception we have both original and acquired perceptions and he compares this distinction with that between natural language and artificial language. The basic point of the analogy between perception and testimony is that both involve the operation of signs and that the signs operate in each case in similar ways. In original perception Nature speaks directly to us through the signs of sensation affixing to particular sensation types particular property types and a tendency to believe in their present instantiation. We do not infer the nature and existence of the property instances from the nature of the sensation since there is no resemblance between the one and the other. We rather pass from the sensation to the perceptual judgment by the operation of a "particular principle of our constitution".(18) An example (given by Reid) would be a certain sensation of touch signifying hardness in the body handled. Reid sees this paralleled in the case of communication by those "signs in the natural language of the human countenance and behaviour"(19) which signify thoughts and dispositions of the mind and which constitute a natural language without which, he thinks, artificial languages, such as English, could never have arisen. Again, we do not infer to the relevant states of mind from threatening or welcoming or alarmed behaviour nor do we somehow gather the connection from experience since "previous to experience, the sign suggests the things signified, and creates the belief of it".(20) This link is due, once more, to a particular principle of the human constitution.

Though Reid thinks the analogy is greatest in the above comparison, there is also an analogy between acquired perceptions and communication in artificial languages. Acquired perceptions are indeed signs but their import is discovered by experience, though once discovered the sign operates like those of original perception and "always suggests the things signified, and creates the belief of it".(21) Again there is no inference, except in the initial stages, and the mind acts under the influence of general principles of the human constitution.

By artificial languages Reid simply means those that rely upon the will of human beings for the connection between sign and signified. This connection is discovered by experience with the aid of natural language and the progressive development of the artificial language itself and is dependent once more upon general principles of the human constitution. Once the connection is uncovered the mind passes naturally from the sign to the suggested reality and acquires the associated belief.

The language side of the analogy is clear enough in both its aspects, though more needs to be said about the general principles involved, but the perceptual side has a certain air of obscurity about its details. In some respects, Reid's distinction between original and acquired perceptions echoes the distinctions between direct and indirect, immediate and mediate objects of perception, but he would be hostile to any of the usual sense data or 'ideal theory' implications carried by such talk. Nonetheless his theory clearly arises from the great 17th and 18th century debates about perception and part of its very considerable interest lies in Reid's attempt to combine a realist hostility to the theory of (sensory) ideas with an acceptance of the reality of sensations and of the insights of such predecessors as Berkeley. Reid does not, however, make it clear just what category of objects or properties original perceptions disclose. Lehrer and Smith hold that the category is that of the primary qualities but it seems more plausible to hold with Timothy Duggan that the original perceptions are of what Aristotle calls the proper sensibles with the common sensibles treated as proper to more than one sense.(22) The Lehrer/Smith analysis seems directly to conflict with at least one explicit claim of Reid's, namely, "By this sense (sight) we perceive originally the visible figure and colour of bodies only, and their visible place...".(23) Our topic here is not Reid's philosophy of perception so I shall leave the interpretive issue about original perceptions noting only that Reid's text is not entirely conclusive.

Our acquired perceptions are the result of experience and develop in accordance with a general inductive principle provided by our nature. Acquired perceptions range from such cases as the visual perception of depth to an expert's visual perception of weight difference in ships. Reid thinks, for instance, with Berkeley and Locke that our visual perception of depth and distance is not direct (or, in his terms, original) but acquired as a result of correlating visual appearances with the results of tactile investigations. More clearly, the jeweller who perceives the difference between a true diamond and a counterfeit does so by relying upon the past conjunction of certain perceived properties (both original and acquired) and upon an inductive principle to do with the regularity of the course of nature.(24) So much for the perceptual side of the analogy, what about testimony?

If Reid is right about the analogy then a common picture of testimony and its epistemological status is quite wrong. This picture has it that all knowledge by testimony is indirect or inferential. We know that p when reliably told that p because we make some inference about the reliability and sincerity of the witness. Reid thinks that this is the wrong way about. Normally we accept what we are told as reliable just as we accept 'the testimony of our senses' or 'the testimony of our memory'. The young child begins with a basic attitude of trust in its senses and in those who communicate with it and this is a condition of its learning (artificial) language and of progressing in understanding. It acquires information from natural language by relying unconsciously upon the particular principles which associate certain bodily behaviours with certain mental states. By this and other means it comes to understand the ways in which others use the artificial signs of a vernacular language. In doing so it relies to some extent on the inductive principle but more pertinently upon two general principles which Reid calls the principle of credulity and the principle of veracity. These seem to be merely the two faces of the one reality or as Reid calls them 'counterparts'.(25) The

combined effect of these principles is like the effect of the
inductive principle in that it provides 'a kind of
prescience', in this case of human actions rather than
natural events. It guarantees a consistency of meaning in the
use of language and a certain truthfulness in communicating.
Reid claims that the principle of veracity, or "the
propensity to speak truth" is very powerful ("the natural
issue of the mind") and operates even in the greatest liars
"for where they lie once, they speak truth a hundred
times".(26) The tendency to believe what one is told
(principle of credulity) is strongest in the young child and
is gradually tempered and qualified by the experience of
dishonesty. Reid thinks that if nature had left the matter of
the reliability of testimony an open question to be decided
by experience alone then children would begin with
incredulity and grow with wisdom and experience to be more
trusting but "the most superficial view of human life"(27)
shows the process of growth to be quite contrary to this.

What Reid presents us with in pressing the analogy
between testimony and perception is a picture of
testimony-based knowledge which is, in some ways, similar to
the treatment of mind, perception and language found in some
modern proponents of 'cognitive science'.(28) Reid has the
same emphasis upon the innate contribution of the organism,
though his appeal to the contribution of the 'human
constitution' is not as extravagant as some. Nonetheless, his
account enables us to see the implausibility of treating all
cases of testimonial knowledge as inferential or indirect. If
we can have cases of direct knowledge in perception (as when
I see a red apple close at hand in full daylight) then surely
we can have cases of direct knowledge in testimony as when I
am told by a normally sighted, disinterested and
non-malevolent friend that there is a red apple on the table
in the next room. It is no objection to this to cite the fact
that I would not know unless the witness were visually
competent, disinterested and non-malevolent since it is
equally true that I would not know by my own perception
unless similar conditions, such as normal lighting and
properly functioning eyes, were fulfilled. In the perception
case, it is enough (in conjunction perhaps with the
satisfaction of a confidence condition) for my direct
knowledge that the sensory information mechanism is
functioning properly and the contextual circumstances are
normal; I do not need to determine in advance that this is so
and argue from it to my perceptual conclusion. Similarly, we
might conclude, from a perspective like Reid's, that it is

enough if the communicative mechanism is functioning
standardly and contextual circumstances are normal (no
particular reason for lying etc.) for us to know directly
that there is a red apple in the room next door.

It may of course be possible to offer inferential support
for a non-inferentially acquired belief. This is as true of
testimony as it is of perception and memory. In some cases,
indeed, such support may strengthen the belief, in the sense
of increasing one's confidence in the proposition involved.
Here the extra support may make the difference between a case
of belief and a case of knowledge. Reid is aware of this as
the following remarks show:

> And as, in many instances, Reason, even in her
> maturity, borrows aid from testimony, so in others
> she mutually gives aid to it, and strengthens its
> authority. For, as we find good reason to reject
> testimony in some cases, so in others we find good
> reason to rely upon it with perfect security, in our
> most important concerns. The character, the number,
> and the disinterestedness of witnesses, the
> impossibility of collusion, and the incredibility of
> their concurring in their testimony without
> collusion, may give an irresistible strength to
> testimony, compared to which its native and
> intrinsic authority is very inconsiderable.(29)

## C  The Epistemological Vindication.

Yet a nagging doubt surely remains. Let us suppose that Reid
has demonstrated his case for the analogy to the hilt. Does
it really have the epistemological consequences claimed for
it? It is one thing to show that we act as though we know
without inference all sorts of things on the basis of what we
are told and even that we do so in accord with an innate
principle of credulity. It is another thing to show that we
are rationally entitled so to behave. Reid's psychological
theory, it might be said, has some interesting and surprising
things to tell us about how we think and communicate, even
about how our make-up constrains us to behave, but it is
psychology not epistemology. Hume, by contrast, is surely
right to insist that an individual's trust in testimony is
only worthy of the name knowledge where it rests upon the
individual's perceptual experience of its reliability. We may
not, as a matter of fact, proceed in this way but knowledge
is normative and this is how we should proceed if we seek

knowledge as a goal.

This style of objection rests upon the idea that the role of epistemology is to bring our most cherished beliefs before the bar of Reason to see whether they are justified or not. Such justificationist enterprises look to some conception of Reason or Justification which is itself supposed to be independent of the beliefs, belief structures and practices being arraigned before it. Contemporary philosophers are much less confident that any such trial is even theoretically possible than were their predecessors, so the accusation of replacing epistemology with psychology is likely to be treated rather more lightly now than in the 18th or 19th centuries (witness Quine's project of 'naturalized epistemology').(30) Reid does not in any case merely produce a genetic or psychological account of our reliance on testimony and leave it at that. He fits the account of how this reliance arises from our constitution into a general epistemological framework of first principles which constitutes the positive side of his 'common sense' reaction against the scepticism he thought inherent in Hume and classical British empiricism. It is an assumption of this framework that if we construe the term reason as narrowly as Hume, for instance, does and as it is, in some respects, natural to do, then it is not possible to vindicate our most central knowledge claims before such a tribunal. Where reason is construed as reasoning, i.e., moving from old beliefs to new beliefs, attempting to support some beliefs by calling upon others or drawing out the consequences of holding certain beliefs, then Reid thinks this is quite clear since such reasoning cannot supply its own premises.(31) Reid is moreover hostile to the idea that, even if we give reason a wider meaning, there is one pre-eminent form of it to which all reason–giving must reduce or conform. Here, as elsewhere, the tendency of his thought is firmly anti–reductionist as can be seen clearly in his discussion of evidence in the chapter on the evidence of sense:

> Philosophers have endeavoured, by analysing the different sorts of evidence, to find out some common nature wherein they all agree, and thereby to reduce them all to one... I confess that although I have, as I think, a distinct notion of the different kinds of evidence... yet I am not able to find any common nature to which they may all be reduced. They seem to me to agree only in this, that they are all fitted by Nature to produce belief in the human

mind, some of them in the highest degree, which we
call certainty, others in various degrees according
to circumstances.(32)

The description of how our human constitution or natural
faculties operate (the 'psychology') is made normative by
Reid's invocation of the ideas of first principles,
self-evidence and human nature. The self-evident first
principles are very varied (consistent with his
anti-reductionism) but our knowledge and reasoning depend
upon them. They articulate as truths what might otherwise
merely be descriptions of how we are prone to behave. One
such principle, for example, is the perceptual one: "That
those things do really exist which we distinctly perceive by
our senses, and are what we perceive them to be".(33) Another
corresponds to the principle of credulity: "That there is a
certain regard due to human testimony in matters of fact, and
even to human authority in matters of opinion".(34) Reid
thinks that the first principles are incapable of direct
proof (they would not be first principles if they followed
from more fundamental premises), though in a broader sense of
reason than that considered above they are deliverances of
Reason, namely that branch of reason traditionally called
Common Sense.(35) The first principles do not, however,
concern only necessary truth, nor does the acknowledgment of
and reliance upon them deliver infallible certainties in
particular cases as the principle about testimony makes very
plain. Moreover, their truth is susceptible to certain
indirect proofs such as ad hominem and ad absurdum, those
from the consent of the generality of mankind, the structure
of language, the origin of the beliefs in our constitution
and the impracticality of denying them in real life. I cannot
here enter in detail into these indirect arguments for the
first principles except to note that they tend to rest upon
two basic ideas: the absurdity of doubting beliefs that in
practice you have no option but to act upon and the absurdity
of denying one first principle but accepting others. This
second point, which is somewhat undeveloped in Reid, stems
from his belief in the coherence of the faculties of
mind.(36)

In the case of testimony Reid could point to the futility
and folly of abandoning our trust in communication. Most of
the arguments for being suspicious of testimony, for
instance, depend upon accepting its general reliability
although this commonly goes unnoticed. Psychological evidence
in our day designed to prove 'the unreliability of testimony'

makes extensive covert use of the very 'faculty' supposedly
undermined by the experiments. "Eye witness testimony is
unreliable"(37), announces one psychologist as he reports to
us on experiments not all of which he has done himself. "As
long ago as 1895" he tells us, such experiments were
done.(38) All this would be laughable if it were not so
common. Of course, these experiments show something about our
dependence upon testimony but, more to the point here, their
inconsistencies illustrate both the unsuspected pervasiveness
of our reliance upon testimony in practice and also one way
in which the denial of one first principle runs foul of the
operation of others. Our psychologist thought he could deny
the general reliability of testimony in the name of something
more solid – scientific observations. But these observations
were only available, collatable and presentable by reliance
on testimony. The very word 'observation' is most commonly
employed in the sense of communal observation; most of what
we regard as matters of observation are so only by proxy.  I
shall not dwell further on this because I have written
elsewhere on the subject. It can also be shown, I believe,
that the very existence of language and hence of reports
entails the extensive reliability of testimony but again I
have argued this elsewhere(39) and will not press the matter
here except to note that although Reid does not argue thus it
would be consistent with his programme to do so.

I want to turn again now to Reid's comparisons between
perception and testimony. Although it is clear that Reid
thinks of our reliance upon both perception and testimony as
epistemologically primitive, as mediated by signs and as
governed by formally similar principles, he does highlight
certain disanalogies.  The most striking is that the
reliability of testimony depends upon the will of man and is
subject to the defect of deception, a flaw which perception
does not have. Indeed, as we saw earlier, Reid, most
implausibly, treats testimony as if it could only fail
through dishonesty. This is demonstrably false since a great
deal of testimony consists of passing on perceptual
information and, where it is mistaken, the mistake will, in
all honesty, usually be transmitted. Nonetheless there is the
possibility (frequently enough realized) of deception, and
Reid insists that perception has no analogy to it. As he puts
'it:

Men sometimes lead us into mistakes, when we
perfectly understand their language, by speaking
lies. But nature never misleads us in this way: her

language is always true; and it is only by
misinterpreting it that we fall into error.(40)

It is for this reason that Reid stresses that the principle
of credulity is strongest in children but less forceful
(though still considerable) in adults whose mature reason
"learns to suspect testimony in some cases, and to disbelieve
it in others; and sets bounds to that authority to which she
was at first entirely subject".(41)  By contrast, he allows
no such diminution in the strength of our trust in
perception. He is, of course, aware that we are prone to a
variety of what would commonly be called perceptual mistakes
and indeed that we speak of the senses 'deceiving' us. Reid
is, however, unsympathetic to this way of putting the matter
and shows a strong tendency to minimize the errors due to
perception. In his chapter on 'The Fallacy of the
Senses',(42) he equivocates between arguing that the senses
are not in general fallacious and that, strictly speaking,
the senses are infallible but we make mistakes by incautious
or short-term use of them.   This second position (which
echoes Descartes' theory of error) is supported in part by
treating perception proper as original perception.   Such
errors as mistaking a painting for the reality it represents
or the size and distance of the heavenly bodies are put down
to the operation of acquired perception. This is highly
unsatisfactory since Reid now splits his unified theory of
perception (and shows a certain amount of discomfort in doing
so) and only succeeds in keeping the purity of one natural
faculty by shifting the cause of error to another (that
operating by the inductive principle). Since, on Reid's view,
very few of our perceptions are original and the analogy with
testimony (in 'artificial' languages) is with acquired
perceptions, these errors should be attributed to perception
when pursuing the extent of the analogy. In any case, at the
end of the chapter on fallacy of sense, Reid admits a
category of strictly perceptual error which does deserve the
title of deception, namely, errors occasioned by sensory
disorder such as jaundice. It is also hard to see how certain
illusions to do with original perception could be handled by
the manoeuvres Reid adopts - the Muller-Lyer illusion, for
instance, does not seem to result from false inference, or
some form of association culled from touch, or disordered
eyesight.

We may safely proceed then by comparing the fallible
reliabilities of perception and testimony without much
concern for Reid's attempts to minimize the degree to which

the former is prone to error. In fact the admission of
fallibilities in perception should reinforce Reid's view that
individual perception is generally more reliable than
testimony since the transmission of information via testimony
usually involves perception twice over (in the witness and in
the recipient). Not only can the witness misperceive but his
audience can mishear or misread the message. Add to this the
possibilities of deception and misremembering and the
individual's perceptions appear much less risky
epistemologically. There is certainly some force in these
points but against them it should be said that the picture
they present ignores certain features of our cognitive
interactions with the world. It is a common modern criticism
of 18th century thought that it treats the subject as too
much a passive recipient and recorder of data. Reid is less
vulnerable to this criticism than many others but in the
comparison of perception and testimony it is easy to lose
sight of the fact that witness and audience are active
explorers of a common world. This means that habits,
expectations and skills can not only produce error but can
guard against it. Consequently, it may be more rational to
rely upon the testimony of another than upon one's own
perceptions in many common situations. The other may, for
example, have better eyesight, better recognitional
capacities for the subject matter of the observation, be
better placed and less emotionally involved. There may also
be more of him. Reid himself cites the way a mathematician,
who has made a discovery in his science and carefully
confirmed it for himself, will still be anxious about its
validity until he has had his judgment confirmed by the
calculations of his mathematical peers. If they disagree with
him he will return to a rigorous reexamination of his
proofs.(43) The same sort of thing can happen in perceptual
matters though we are often in no position to make a second
perceptual examination and can only consult our memory. Even
where we can look again it cannot be decided a priori that we
should trust our senses against the testimony of others. This
is so because agreement with the perceptions of others is a
prime test of the publicity of what is apparently perceived.
Such an agreement can often be evidenced only by testimony
(though it can sometimes be behaviourally indicated by
'natural language' or by other actions). The picture is thus
very complex and can be complicated further if we hold that
many (some would say, all) of the concepts in terms of which
we make perceptual judgments are socially provided. If the
notion of testimony covers such provisions then any claim
about greater reliability would have to take account of a

close mesh between perception and testimony at the level of thought itself. At the brink of such an issue we must, for now, halt our steps.

# NOTES

(1) Augustine's awareness of the problem's depth led him over the years to very different positions on the question of whether testimony can provide us with knowledge or merely useful belief. His strongest commitment to testimony as a crucial source of knowledge comes in De Trinitate, XV, 12:21. For an earlier view, see De Magistro, 39. For Plato's dismissive moves see Theaetetus, 201 and Meno, 97a–b.

(2) Reid discusses 'the social operations' both in Essays on the Intellectual Powers, I, viii and Essays on the Active Powers, V, vi.

(3) IP, I, viii (Works, p. 244).

(4) Ibid.

(5) IP, I, viii (Works, p. 245).

(6) The passage is worth quoting in full:

> In every language, a question, a command, a promise, which are social acts, can be expressed as easily and as properly as judgment, which is a solitary act. The expression of the last has been honoured with a particular name; it is called a proposition; it has been an object of great attention to philosophers; it has been analysed into its very elements of subject, predicate, and copula. All the various modifications of these, and of propositions which are compounded of them, have been anxiously examined in many voluminous tracts. The expression of a question, of a command, or of a promise, is as capable of being analysed as a proposition is; but we do not find that this has been attempted; we have not so much as given them a name different from the operations which they express. (IP, I, viii (Works, p. 245)).

(7) P.F. Strawson, 'Austin and 'Locutionary Meaning'', in Berlin and others (1973), p.60.

(8)  **IP**, VI, i.

(9)  Ibid.

(10) **IP**, VI, i (Works, p. 413).

(11) **IP**, VI, i (Works, p. 415).

(12) See Cross (1967), p.361. As Cross notes, the law is particularly concerned that the admission of expert opinion should not "shift responsibility from the bench or the jury to the witness box". Even here, however, there are exceptions to the general practice cited in the text; see Eggleston (1978) p. 124.

(13) See Cross (1967) p. 365 and also Eggleston (1978) p. 124.

(14) Justice Gibson cited in Wigmore (1940) p. 12.

(15) Cross (1967) p. 368.

(16) See Eggleston (1978) p. 124 for cases where an expert opinion may harmlessly be allowed on ultimate issues and for a slightly different account of the basis of the law's anxiety.

(17) Recently Gareth Evans drew attention to it in his (1982) p. 236, and Keith Lehrer and John Smith discuss it in their paper 'Reid on Testimony and Perception', Canadian Journal of Philosophy (forthcoming).

(18) I, VI, xxiv (Works, p. 195).

(19) Ibid.

(20) Ibid.

(21) Ibid.

(22) See his introduction to his edition of Reid's Inquiry (1970), especially pp. xvi–xix.

(23) I, VI, xx (Works, p. 185).

(24) For the way visual perception of depth is acquired see especially I, VI, xxii. Other cases of acquired perception

are discussed in I, VI, xxiv and elsewhere.

(25) I, VI, xxiv (Works, p. 196).

(26) Ibid.

(27) I, VI, xxiv (Works, p. 197).

(28) This is noted by Lehrer and Smith, op.cit.

(29) I, VI, xxiv (Works, p. 197).

(30) It is also none too clear what the successful completion of such a 'rational reconstruction' (supposing it to be possible) would show. That only those who have done (can do?) the reconstruction really know? Or perhaps others know vicariously if some philosophers can do it for them?

(31) His appeal to the impossibility of an infinite regress of reason—giving premises occurs at IP, VI, iv (Works, p. 435).

(32) IP, II, xx (Works, p. 328).

(33) IP, VI, v (Works, p. 445). Perhaps this principle should be added to the inductive principle (another first principle) in the discussion of the analogy of acquired perception and testimony. Lehrer and Smith do as much, though Reid doesn't do so explicitly, and they call it 'the principle of perceptual reality'.

(34) IP, VI, v (Works. p. 450).

(35) We ascribe to reason two offices, or two degrees. The first is to judge of things self—evident; the second to draw conclusions that are not self-evident from those that are. The first of these is the province, and the sole province, of common sense. (IP, VI, ii Works, p. 425).

(36) See IP, VI, iv (Works, p. 439). The point is rightly stressed by Lehrer and Smith, but we cannot pursue it further here.

(37) Buckland (1974) p. 23.

(38) Op.cit. p. 24.

(39) This and the previous "elsewhere" refer to my (1973). Some of the considerations in that paper are taken further in my (1975) and (1981).

(40) I, VI, xxiv (Works, p. 199). Perhaps Reid's view of the infallibility of the language of nature stems from his piety towards its Speaker, God.

(41) I, VI, xxiv (Works, p. 197). We can see this in the contrasting formulations of the first principles of perception and of testimony:

> 'That those things do really exist which we distinctly perceive by our senses, and are what we perceive them to be', as compared with, 'That there is a certain regard due to human testimony in matters of fact, and even to human authority in matters of opinion'. (IP, VI, v, Works, pp. 445 and 450).

In the Inquiry, after speaking of the way the experience of deceit modifies the strength of our reliance on testimony, Reid adds:

> But the credit given to the testimony of our senses, is established and confirmed by the uniformity and constancy of the laws of nature. (I, VI, xx, Works, p. 184).

(42) IP, II, xxii.

(43) IP, VI, iv (Works p.440).

SECTION 3 – MIND AND ACTION

James Somerville


## MAKING OUT THE SIGNATURES: REID'S ACCOUNT OF THE KNOWLEDGE OF OTHER MINDS


Reid's conception of his predecessors as belonging to "the Cartesian system"(1) gives him an up-to-date ring. He means not just Descartes' immediate disciples but all adherents to the theory of ideas, including Locke, Berkeley and Hume.(2) What unites them to Descartes is more fundamental than what divides them from him. This cuts across the ingrained division of nineteenth-century German historians of philosophy into rationalists and empiricists. Reid's account of his predecessors' treatment of the problem of other minds, however, comes across as more traditional, for the traditional problem virtually begins with him.(3) The very words 'other minds' first occur extensively in his pages. It is surprising how little his predecessors – Locke(4) for instance – have to say on the subject. It is absent even in Kant. True, Descartes concludes in the haunting words of the Third Meditation that he is 'not alone in the world' but he is referring to God, and as an external cause not as a person.(5) Not that Reid thinks there is any problem about other minds; it is a problem, he argues, only for holders of the theory of ideas. His account of Descartes, Berkeley and Hume has been so assimilated into the subsequent history of philosophy that it is forgotten that none of the three argues that knowledge of other minds is unattainable. Neither Descartes nor Hume raise the issue. Berkeley does, and clearly Reid is indebted to his approach to this and related topics. But Berkeley appears unaware what the problem is. He thinks nobody could seriously doubt the existence of others. He holds God's existence is as certain as, indeed more certain than, that of other finite spirits.(6) Reid concurs,(7) gleefully repeating Berkeley's argumentum ad hominem against atheists.(8) Where they differ is that Reid argues that the theory of ideas Berkeley holds leads to scepticism about other minds, so his system is inconsistent.

Reid's account of the relation of Hume to Berkeley is familiar because he has made it so. As Berkeley has "proved, beyond the possibility of reply, that we cannot by

*M. Dalgarno and E. Matthews (eds.), The Philosophy of Thomas Reid, 249–273.*
© *1989 by Kluwer Academic Publishers.*

reasoning infer the existence of matter from our sensations",
so Hume has "proved no less clearly, that we cannot by
reasoning infer the existence of our own or other minds from
our sensations".(9)  Hume says nothing expressly about other
minds.(10) It is questionable if Hume is a sceptic about them
for precisely the reason Reid cites: Hume, he complains,
promises

> a complete system of the sciences, upon a foundation
> entirely new – to wit, that of human nature – when
> [his intention] is to shew, that there is neither
> human nature nor science in the world.(11)

Nevertheless, it is arguable that on his principles Hume has
a problem about other minds. When Reid says he holds there is
'nothing in nature but ideas and impressions'(12), it is all
Hume is entitled to –– the logical outcome of the Cartesian
system, Reid argues. In

> admitting no other first principle with regard to
> the existence of things but their own existence, and
> the existence of those operations of mind of which
> they are conscious, and requiring that the existence
> of a material world, and the existence of other men
> and things, should be proved by argument(13)

followers of Descartes' method "have escaped the abyss of
scepticism by the help of weak reasoning and strong
faith".(14) Berkeley seeks to evade this outcome by denying
we have ideas of spirits, an unargued deviation from the
Cartesian system "occasioned by the terror of
scepticism".(15) An expedient, Reid objects, for if we can
think of spirits without ideas of them, what is to prevent us
from thinking of matter without ideas, as indeed Hylas
objects in the Third Dialogue.(16) Berkeley's system is a
half-way house to Hume's, the ultimate destination of the
theory of ideas, on Reid's reading of them.(17)

The germs of this commonplace of the history of
philosophy are already in Kames. Hume, Kames writes,
"observing Berkeley's reason for denying the existence of
matter to be equally conclusive against the existence of
mind, has with great intrepidity discarded both".(18)  The
point, though, betrays some misunderstanding of Berkeley's
position. Reid speculates why Berkeley denies we have ideas
of spirits:

Perhaps he saw that, if we perceive only the ideas of spirits, we shall find the same difficulty in inferring their real existence from the existence of their ideas, as we find in inferring the existence of matter from the idea of it.(19)

He ignores the reason Berkeley gives why specifically there can be no ideas of spirit as distinct from why there can't be ideas of matter.(20)   And Berkeley sees no difficulty in inferring spirits from ideas. This is his doctrine. The ideas, of course, aren't <u>of</u> spirits but "the ideas by them excited in us". Philonous answers the objection that matter is as conceivable as spirit:

My own mind and my own ideas I have an immediate knowledge of; and by the help of these, do mediately apprehend the possibility of the existence of other spirits and ideas.

But matter can't be similarly inferred from my ideas:

For you neither perceive matter objectively, as you do an inactive being or idea, nor know it, as you do your self, by a reflex act, neither do you immediately apprehend it by similitude of the one or the other.(21)

Reid protests, "I do perceive matter objectively — that is, something which is ... the immediate object of my touch and sight".(22)   He misses the point. Anticipating charges of inconsistency like Reid's (23) Berkeley puts additional words into Philonous' mouth in the 1734 edition:

I have no reason for believing the existence of matter. I have no immediate intuition thereof ... . Whereas the being of my self, that is, my own soul, mind or thinking principle, I evidently know by reflexion.

Hence, "there is a probability for" "the existence of other finite spirits", but material substances "can be inferred by no argument ... . There is therefore upon the whole no parity of case between spirit and matter".(24)   This version of the argument from analogy may not bear scrutiny, but Reid doesn't even consider what Berkeley has to say — which is odd since at times his own position turns out not too far removed from Berkeley's. His complaint,

> I can find no principle in Berkeley's system, which
> affords me even probable ground to conclude that
> there are other intelligent beings, like myself(25)

reveals an uncharacteristic lapse from his usually careful
examinations of other philosophers' doctrines.

Reid, then, says Berkeley's system has

> one uncomfortable consequence .... that, although it
> leaves us sufficient evidence of a supreme
> intelligent mind, it seems to take away all the
> evidence we have of other intelligent beings like
> ourselves.(25)

The basis of this criticism might simply be that Berkeley is
an utter, albeit inconsistent, sceptic. Kames misreads
Berkeley in the way made familiar by Kant:

> If I can only be conscious of what passes in my own
> mind, and if I cannot trust my senses when they give
> me notice of external and independent existences, it
> follows, that I am the only being in the world.(26)

Reid sometimes slips into this popular misrepresentation of
Berkeley:

> But the Bishop shews me, that this is all a dream;
> that I see not a human face; that all the objects I
> see, and hear, and handle, are only the ideas of my
> own mind; ideas are my only companions.(27)

Berkeley doesn't deny the testimony of the senses, as Reid
well knows: he notes that Berkeley doesn't deny our
sensations are real.(28) When more careful, Reid argues
instead that it is Berkeley's denial of the material world
which undermines the knowledge of others:

> Bishop Berkeley surely did not duly consider that it
> is by means of the material world that we have any
> correspondence with thinking beings, or any
> knowledge of their existence; and that, by depriving
> us of the material world, he deprived us, at the
> same time, of family, friends, country, and every
> human creature.(29)

This throws light on Reid's own account of the knowledge of

others. But, first, why does Berkeley have a difficulty about
other minds? Reid's answer is that if another

> is only a parcel of ideas in my own mind [then]
> being ideas in my mind, they cannot possibly have
> that relation to another mind which they have to
> mine, any more than the pain felt by me can be the
> individual pain felt by another.(30)

The bit about pain relates to a previously implied criticism
that Berkeley fails to answer satisfactorily another
objection of Hylas's, namely, that on his system "no two can
see the same thing".(31) A plausible interpretation of Reid's
criticism is that if ideas of sense are sensations like pains
they can't be perceivable by sense: there being "no
difference between the sensation and the feeling of it",(32)
sensations aren't objects; still less, then, can ideas of
sense be perceived by more than one person. This is an
overall objection to Berkeley – that sense-perception
requires publicly observable objects – not a specific one
about other minds. It seems Reid has run this together with
another more relevant objection. Granted that somehow
Berkeley can overcome the difficulty about the shareability
of ideas, the other mind which crucially for Berkeley must
share my ideas of sense is God's. It is not from piety that
Reid concedes that Berkeley's system "leaves us sufficient
evidence of a supreme intelligent mind".(33) Berkeley may
have placed the "evidence of an all-governing mind ... in a
more striking light"(34) but he has taken "away all the
evidence we have of other intelligent beings like ourselves".
For they, unlike God – or at least God the Father and God the
Holy Ghost – are embodied. The relation my ideas have to my
mind can't be the same as another's body has to his or her
mind, for the latter relation is that of being animated by
whereas the former on Berkeley's system is merely that of
being perceived by; therefore, another's body can't comprise
ideas of sense even if these were shareable. Though his words
bear this interpretation I'm not confident that Reid saw the
point clearly.

Reid's own account of the knowledge of others is twofold.
First, he annunciates two, supposedly first, principles –– of
contingent truths: "That there is life and intelligence in
our fellow-men with whom we converse";(35) and "That certain
features of the countenance, sounds of the voice, and
gestures of the body, indicate certain thoughts and
dispositions of mind".(36) As the "thoughts and dispositions

of mind" indicated are not mine but another's the latter
presupposes the former principle. The existence of another,
or of a certain thought in another's mind, is a contingent
fact. So Reid says "the evidence we have of the existence of
other men, is not demonstrative".(37) Neither does he think
it is a matter of probable conjecture. It is a first
principle, not a conclusion from any reasoning at all.
Philonous argues, "we have neither an immediate evidence nor
a demonstrative knowledge of the existence of other finite
spirits" only "a probability for" it.(38) It would seem that
Reid must hold the third possibility: in some sense there is
an immediate evidence for others' existence. Before going on
to this, the second part of Reid's account derives from the
metaphysical principle, <u>That design and intelligence in the
cause may be inferred, with certainty, from marks or signs of
it in the effect.</u>(39) It is said to be a necessary truth,
not a contingent one.(40) He must mean the principle of the
inference, not any particular conclusion inferred; for he
also says another "kind of probable evidence ... is that by
which we collect men's characters and designs from their
actions, speech, and other external signs".(41) 'Probable'
here means not that it is merely probable that, but inductive
evidence as distinct from demonstration.(42) And "the field
of probable reasoning is contingent truth".(43)

These two accounts should not be seen as rivalling but as
complementing one another. To a limited extent knowledge of
physical things is also twofold: it is based partly on
observations of sensible qualities, and partly on inductive
inferences drawn from such observations. By drawing
inferences from the past behaviour of things certain "secret
powers", in Hume's words,(44) besides sensible qualities are
attributed to them. The knowledge of others is based partly
on observations of "countenance, voice, and gesture",(45) but
to a far greater extent on inductive inferences drawn from
past bodily behaviour — or, as these other bodies are not
inanimate, not mere behaviour but <u>conduct</u>. Included are
others' words and deeds but also their works, what they
produce by their skill or effort. Reid is too eager to argue
that God's existence is on the same footing as that of other
human beings to appreciate Hume's objections to the argument
from design. All its persuasiveness comes from its comparison
of the world with products of human skill and effort. "A man
finding a watch or any other machine in a desert island,
would conclude that there had once been men in that island",
Hume allows.(46) Reid averts to Hume's difficulties in
accounting for human agency on his theory of causation, but

the nub of Hume's criticism is that the universe is not
sufficiently like a human artefact. He rejects the minor
premise, "That there are in fact the clearest marks of design
and wisdom in the works of nature", not the major one – the
principle itself – as Reid says.(47)   Much about others'
mental and emotional state can be discovered simply by
observing their posture, facial expression and tone of voice,
even if they are total strangers. But by far the greatest
knowledge of others is obtained from inferences from their
conduct or performance. By reading the writings of a
philosopher or examining the work of a designer I can infer
much about their characters, mental abilities and emotional
dispositions though I've never met them. It is an
exaggeration to say:

> we judge of men's talents with as little doubt or
> hesitation as we judge of the immediate objects of
> sense. ... We can as little avoid them as we can
> avoid seeing what is before our eyes.

But Reid strikes a Rylean note when he says:

> a man comes to know his own mental abilities, just
> as he knows another man's, by the effects they
> produce, when there is occasion to put them to
> exercise.(48)

But his twofold account is queered by theistic zeal:

> Setting aside this natural conviction [of the
> existence of others] the best reason we can give, to
> prove that other men are living and intelligent, is,
> that their words and actions indicate like powers of
> understanding as we are conscious of in ourselves.
> The very same argument applied to the works of
> nature, leads us to conclude that there is an
> intelligent Author of nature, and appears equally
> strong and obvious in the last case as in the
> first.(49)

This recalls Berkeley's argument from analogy which Reid
seems curiously ignorant of. But he is just argued that
belief in others' existence "stands upon another foundation
than that of reasoning"; it cannot be proved as he says
Cartesians require. He himself sees that "the best reason"
isn't good enough:

No man thinks of asking himself what reason he has
to believe that his neighbour is a living creature.
He ... perhaps could not give any reason which would
not equally prove a watch or a puppet to be a living
creature.

It is significant that Reid does not hold that belief in
God's existence is a first principle: it, unlike that of
other human beings, has to be proved. Berkeley can hold that
God's existence is known as certainly as that of other human
beings without inconsistency because the knowledge of both
for him depends on some inference. But not Reid. What is
proved from other men's words and actions is not that they
are living and have like powers of understanding as
ourselves: this is presupposed in regarding something as
another's words or action. As Reid recognizes elsewhere,(50)
this is not demonstrable. What we discover by inferences
from others' words and actions is not their very existence,
which is already presupposed, but what sort of people they
are. In reverting to the argument from analogy for the very
existence of other human beings, Reid runs together the two
ways of knowing others he elsewhere distinguishes -- his
contingent first principle and his necessary one. In a rather
different way he confuses them when he argues:

> that the man who maintains there is no force in the
> argument from final causes, must, if he will be
> consistent, see no evidence of the existence of any
> intelligent being but himself.(51)

Inferences from the effects of human actions, or
artefacts, may provide some evidence of others' existence, as
in Hume's desert island case; but it is not the sole
evidence. In reading others' facial features I thereby
believe in their existence; but my belief isn't based on any
inference at all. I must first have the belief that there are
others before I can draw inferences from what I take to be
their actions or works. On Reid's considered view there is no
argument for others' existence, so the argument from design
has no relevance to it.

These are minor distractions from the dominant account.
The criticism of Berkeley might be understood as objecting
that since matter is perceived immediately(52)
sense-perception is non-inferential, as indeed Berkeley
saw,(53) but that he failed to see that knowledge of others'
existence is too. But in a passage quoted above, Reid says

that "it is by means of the material world that we have ...
any knowledge of their existence".(54)    In his clearest
statement on the subject he writes: "Other minds we perceive
only through the medium of material objects, on which their
signatures are impressed".(55)     Is he using 'perceive'
literally? Reid has the distinction of being the first to
confine the term to sense-perception, the standard use of
philosophers and psychologists today. Though he states, "we
can have no communication ... with any created being, but by
means of our senses",(56) he also insists that other minds
are not actually perceived by sense: "life and intelligence
are not objects of the external senses";(57) "neither mind,
nor any of its qualities or powers, is an immediate object of
perception to man".(58)     The point is specifically made
against Berkeley: "But, my Lord Bishop", he asks
rhetorically, "are there no minds left in the universe but my
own?" To which Berkeley is imagined to reply, "Yes, indeed;
it is only the material world that is annihilated; everything
else remains as it was". To which Reid objects, "But do I see
those minds? No. Do I see their ideas? No. Nor do they see me
or my ideas".(59)   It is hard to see what to make of this. If
Reid is maintaining that other minds are mediately perceived,
isn't this open to the same criticism which Reid himself,
following Berkeley, brings against Locke? He complains that
philosophers, with the exception of Berkeley and Hume, don't
explain what they mean by a mediate object of perception: do

> they mean ... that we perceive external objects in
> that figurative sense in which we say that we
> perceive an absent friend when we look on his
> picture; or ... that, really, and without a figure,
> we perceive both the external object and its idea in
> the mind?(60)

This is like what Philonous says against Hylas' example of
the picture of Julius Caesar in the First Dialogue.(61)   The
questions Reid poses can equally be pressed against his own
talk of perceiving other minds through the medium of material
objects.

The notion of mediate perception has a use even in
Berkeley. Philonous grants that

> we may in one acceptation be said to perceive
> sensible things mediately by sense: ... For
> instance, when I hear a coach drive along the
> streets, immediately I perceive only the sound; but
> from the experience I have had that such a sound is

connected with a coach, I am said to hear the coach.
It is nevertheless evident, that in truth and
strictness, nothing can be heard but sound: and the
coach is not then properly perceived by sense, but
suggested from experience.(62)

In his Theory of Vision Vindicated Berkeley distinguishes
suggestion from inference:

To perceive is one thing; to judge is another. So
likewise, to be suggested is one thing, and to be
inferred another. Things are suggested and perceived
by sense. We make judgments and inferences by the
understanding.

He uses the phrase "suggested or perceived by mediation". The
coach in a sense is heard. It is a secondary object of
perception.(63) It is not merely inferred, as Sherlock Holmes
might infer that it has passed by the mud on the road. For
someone experienced, hearing a coach is psychologically
non-inferential: no conscious inference is drawn; the
inference justifying the belief that there is a coach is
disguised. But logically, the transition from the sound to
the coach, the tangible object, constitutes an inductive
inference, as Berkeley sees:

two things, by their mere coexistence, or two ideas,
merely by being perceived together, may suggest or
signify one the other, their connexion being all the
while arbitrary; for it is the connexion only, as
such, that causeth this effect.(64)

He tries to assimilate reading facial expressions to the
coach example. Speaking about seeing "shame or anger in the
looks of a man" in his New Theory of Vision, he remarks:

Those passions are themselves invisible, they are
nevertheless let in by the eye along with colours
and alterations of countenance, which are the
immediate object of vision: And which signify them
for no other reason than barely because they have
been observed to accompany them.(65)

But if the former are invisible how can the latter have been
observed to accompany them?

It is easy to see how Reid, struck by this objection to

Berkeley's application of the notion of suggestion to expressive features, was led to extend it to a non-inductive sort. Thus, he argues that there is a "natural language of mankind" whose elements are "signs ... naturally expressive of our thoughts", namely, "modulations of the voice, gestures, and features",(66) "so that, previous to experience, the signs suggest the thing signified, and create the belief of it".(67)  He goes on to give an example and draw an analogy:

> A man in company ... may behave himself gracefully, civilly, politely; ... We see the dispositions of his mind by their natural signs in his countenance and behaviour, in the same manner as we perceive the figure and other qualities of bodies by the sensations which nature hath connected with them.

So there is a third sort of suggestion, whereby sensations suggest or conjure up "as it were, by a natural kind of magic"(68) qualities of bodies. Here at last his charge of inconsistency against Berkeley gets to grips: if seeing shame or anger in a man's face is a case of mediate perception why can't matter be perceived through the medium of ideas? Philonous remarks sarcastically, "real things in themselves imperceivable, are perceived by sense";(69) but the same can be said of shame and anger. Reid's extension of Berkeley's term blurs several issues. His doctrine that sensations suggest qualities in bodies has had commentators ever since divided as to whether he holds a direct or indirect theory of perception. With other minds, the issue isn't, as Broad points out, whether knowledge of their existence is <u>reached</u>, but whether it can be <u>justified</u>, by inference.(70) Psychologically, the conviction of others' existence may be non-inferential but this has no bearing on its justification. That Reid's notion of suggestion is mainly psychological is seen by his talk of 'immediately suggests'.(71)  By 'immediately' he means 'at once', hence his use of words like 'instantaneously',(72) 'with ease',(73) and 'rapidly'.(74) He seems unaware that 'immediately' is a technical term for Berkeley, meaning 'not based on any inference'.(75)  Through ignoring Berkeley's distinction between suggestion and inference his language becomes lax. Talk of making or drawing inferences(76) or concluding(77) 'without reasoning' seems contradictory until it is realised that 'inference' and 'conclude' are to be taken in the psychological sense of the mind's passing from one thing, the sign (in some cases the effect) to the conception of another, the signified (or the

cause).(78)    So he can write, "I conclude immediately,
without reasoning, that a coach passes by".(79)    More
importantly, he means not merely that, psychologically,
there is no inference, but that, logically, none is required,
either a priori or inductively.(80)

In preferring the term 'suggested' to Berkeley's
alternative, 'perceived by mediation', Reid conceals the
difficulty confronting any mind-body dualist about how
knowledge of others is possible. For all his talk of the
Cartesian system, Reid's quarrel is with its theory of ideas,
not its logical separation of mind and body. He commends
Descartes for being "the first that pointed out the road we
ought to take in those dark regions"(81) in that he "must be
allowed the honour of being the first who drew a distinct
line between the material and intellectual world" and so
"laid the foundation" of "that part of philosophy which
relates to the mind".(82)  Natural philosophy, the philosophy
of body, is "its elder sister".(83)  Like Hume, he reassures
us that "it need not appear surprising, if the philosophy of
the human mind should be a century or two later in being
brought to maturity".(84)  But "an error in the foundation"
has "led men rather to scepticism than to knowledge" (ibid.).
He means the "analogical way of reasoning concerning the
powers of the mind from the properties of body, which is the
source of almost all the errors on this subject".(85)    He
concedes that the Cartesian system is less analogical than
the Peripatetic one,(86) but the theory of ideas it
hypothesizes, that when we perceive, remember, imagine or
think of things, ideas or images of them are in our minds, is
based on a false analogy.(87)  It assumes that as bodies are
put in motion by contiguous bodies, so ideas must at least be
contiguous to the mind since things themselves can't be.(88)
He contrasts "the way of analogy" with "the way of
reflection", "the only way" to study mind.(89)  "One obvious
consequence" of the distinction between mind and body, he
remarks, "was, that accurate reflection on the operations of
our own mind is the only way to make any progress in the
knowledge of it".(90)  Reflection is said to be "the only
instrument by which we can discern the powers of the
mind".(91)  In one place he speaks of reflection as "a kind
of intuition" which "gives a like conviction with regard to
internal objects, or things in the mind, as the faculty of
seeing gives with regard to objects of sight".(92)  Elsewhere
he seems to reject Locke's notion of reflection as an
internal sense. Though he agrees that "Mr Locke very properly
calls consciousness an internal sense",(93) he complains that

Locke "has restricted the word reflection to that which is employed about the operations of our minds ... For, surely, I may reflect upon what I have seen or heard, as well as upon what I have thought".(94) The word 'reflection', he says, "is applied to many operations of the mind, with more propriety than to that of consciousness".(95) What he calls 'attentive reflection'(96) would seem to be a prerequisite for all enquiry, not just philosophy of mind. It is reflection on consciousness he really means; consciousness alone is not enough.(97) Locke's bogus notion of an internal sense is thus retained in Reid. He stresses the difficulty of reflection,(98) but this confuses the issue. The difficulty of reflection need not be confined to reflection on consciousness, it can arise also with reflection on objects of sense: the physicist may not appreciate the significance of what is before his eyes. While he confidently proclaims that "we have sufficient evidence of" a thinking principle "in other men",(99) Reid remains unembarrassed by his acknowledgement that for "the anatomist of the mind" it is "his own mind only that he can examine ... This is the only subject he can look into". He may "from outward signs, collect the operations of other minds; but these ... must be interpreted by what he perceives within himself".(100) Despite his stress on expressive bodily features, Reid seems ultimately to deny that any non-inferential knowledge of others is possible. His notion of suggestion obscures his considered view that reading expressions is only psychologically non-inferential. "Intelligence, design and skill" are occult causes: "the effects are perceived by our senses; but the causes are behind the scene".(101) A man's work "may be an immediate object of perception" but "the design and purpose of the author cannot be";(102) "the thoughts and passions of the mind, as well as the mind itself, are invisible".(103)

Cannot Reid, as indeed he does, just appeal to an original principle? Sweeping aside what he takes to be Berkeley's and Hume's arguments he asks, "are we to admit nothing but what can be proved by reasoning?".(104) A proof that others exist would be even more absurd than a proof of the material world.(105) But by putting mental qualities 'behind the scene' he unwittingly lends credence to scepticism about other minds, the same charge he levels against Berkeley. There is a way, however, of taking mediate perception not open to Berkeleyan and Reidian objections. The supposition is that when Reid says we perceive other minds through the medium of material objects he has in mind a kind of perception similar to perception of aesthetic qualities. He thinks beauty is literally perceived in objects, though by an internal, not an external, sense.(106)   Further, he distinguishes between original and acquired perception, hearing Berkeley's coach being an instance of the latter.(107)   Here Reid does make some allowance for Berkeley's distinction between suggestion and inference, for he states that perception "whether original or acquired, implies no exercise of reason"; it is distinct from even the "more obvious conclusions drawn from our perceptions".(108) Original perception would appear to be of the proper objects of the senses − colours and visual extension, figure and magnitude; smells; tastes; sounds; and hardness or softness and tangible extension, etc.(109)   But there's a hint that original, like acquired, perception may rise above the purely sensory: "Our original or natural perceptions are analogous to the natural language of man to man".(110)   This analogy is pursued when he argues that we understand the meaning of expressive features "by a kind of natural perception similar to the perceptions of sense".(111)   Just as,

> When I grasp an ivory ball ... I feel a certain sensation of touch. ... But, by the constitution of my nature, the sensation carries along with it the conception and belief of a round hard body really existing ..., [so] In like manner, when I see the features of an expressive face, ... by the constitution of my nature, the visible object brings along with it the conception and belief of a certain passion or sentiment in the mind of the person.(112)

As Reid speaks of only an analogy between the two, it might seem that all he is saying is that it is as if mental and emotional qualities were literally, that is immediately, perceived. But to say their perception is mediate need not mean that logically they are inferred from the perception of bodily features. Reid recognizes that the perception of one sort of quality may depend, in a certain sort of sense, on the perception of another. Following Hutcheson, he holds that the perception of beauty and other aesthetic qualities by an internal sense differs from the perception by the external senses in that it depends upon some "antecedent perception".(113)   To hear the harmony of the music I must at least hear the sounds. In this way the perception of mental and emotional qualities can be original while going beyond the perception of purely sensory qualities. Acquired perception is dependent too, but causally, the effect of custom; it becomes a second nature.(114)  There might appear to be a difficulty in that Reid goes on to deny that objects of sense are literally beautiful; they can only be called such in an analogical or figurative sense: "all the beauty of the objects of sense is borrowed, and derived from the beauties of mind which it expresses or suggests to the imagination".(115)  He gives an example:

> The beauty of good breeding ... is not originally in the external behaviour in which it consists, but is derived from the qualities of mind which it expresses.(116)

But this only means that beauty is a quality of a quality of mind; it does not prevent mental and emotional qualities being likewise dependent – that is, supervenient – on some 'antecedent' perception. His juxtaposition of the terms 'express' and 'suggest' hints that his view is that the analogy between ordinary perception and reading expressive features is close, even though he regards the latter as understanding a natural language, not a form of perception. There are also hints in him of the closeness of taste and physiognomic perception. As taste may be instinctive in that we–know–not–what occult qualities please or displease us, or enlightened and rational in that we can give some reason for our judgment,(117) so the 'language' of features is natural in that it is universally understood(118) – there can be excellent practical physiognomists who know nothing of the proportions of a face – or it can be made into an art by those who use it.(119)  Dumb and deaf(120) people are such experts. Physiognomic perception is supervenient too: "we are often unable to say by what minute difference the distinction is made" when we distinguish between people's faces, voices or handwriting.(121)

Apart from this somewhat speculative interpretation, Reid has a more secure basis for the knowledge of others' existence than his far from up–to–date Cartesian orthodoxy permits. It is an argument from language. Distinguishing between the social and solitary operations of the mind, he comments: "It may indeed be affirmed, that, to express the former, is the primary and direct intention of language".(122)  These social operations, he says on the preceding page, "suppose a conviction of the existence of other intelligent beings". The use of the second person in language expressly refers to others. Berkeley also sees that language testifies to others' existence, hence his strange

doctrine that God speaks to us in a visual, natural
language.(123)   Unfortunately, it is one we can only
understand, not use. Reid's 'natural language' is more truly
language in that those with no common (artificial) language
"can communicate their thoughts in some tolerable
manner".(124)   But he goes too far in identifying expressive
features with language. They may be natural signs but this
doesn't make them language.(125)   For there to be language it
must be possible to use signs besides understand them.
Admittedly, they are not the sort of natural signs simply
"discovered only by experience" but are understood to a
greater or lesser extent by all, by "a natural
knowledge".(126)    But as a man's complexion may betray to
Conan Doyle's archetype of Sherlock Holmes that he has just
returned from Afghanistan, so his face may betray some
emotion he is striving to conceal. Reid seems unaware of the
ambiguity of the word 'express'. Bodily features may express
in the sense of being expressive of certain emotions or
moods, but this need not be because the person has expressed
them in the sense of intentionally articulating and
communicating them to others. A gesture, as distinct from
"the motion and attitude of the body",(ibid.) if
conventional, may well be an element in a non-verbal
language. A smile may be expressive, or indicative, of the
thought of some amusing incident, or, as with Hamlet's
villain, constitute a non-verbal lie. Reid is led to draw an
analogy between perception and language because he takes the
perception of expressive features to be the understanding of
a natural language. His dualism scarcely allows him to take
physiognomic perception as constituting perception at all.
Had it done so, he might have seen that 'body language' is
language only in an analogical sense. But there is nothing
analogous between ordinary perception and language: "the
testimony of nature given by our senses"(127) is a misleading
metaphor.(128)   Neither nature nor God - at least Reid reins
in his theistic zeal here - speaks to us through the
senses.(129)

Moore argues that to deny the knowledge that other human
beings exist is self-contradictory.(130)   What Reid shows is
that to try to argue for their existence must fail.(131)
It is scarcely possible to debate whether others exist
without ludicrously begging the question.(132)   Reid implies
it is not something that can be coherently questioned. The
questionings of a solitary Cartesian meditator presuppose the
sort of questioning which, being a social operation, in turn
presupposes others' existence. Such insight and subtlety

springs from Reid's pages that pervasive old-fashioned dualistic and theistic themes can be filtered out of any view of him which philosophy today can profit from.

NOTES

(1)    I, VII (<u>Works</u>, p. 204).

(2)    IP, VI, vii (<u>Works</u>, p. 468).

(3)    He himself acknowledges Buffier's recognition of the issue when he cites one of Buffier's principles of common sense,namely, "That there are other beings and other men in the universe, besides myself". IP, VI, vii (<u>Works</u>, p. 467).

(4)    T.E. Jessop cites the <u>Essay</u> (IV xi 12) – see Luce and Jessop (1949), II, p. 107n.. As Locke does not qualify, 'finite Spirits' by 'other' it seems he is talking about angels.  The absurdity of saying 'we' don't know of their existence if they were part of us would have struck even Locke. <u>Cf</u>. Hutcheson's reference to 'Other minds', (1973), IV, I.

(5)    Paragraph 16. There are some other hints.  At the beginning of the Second Meditation he says he has convinced himself "that nothing exists in the world, no sky, no earth, no minds,no bodies" (para. 3). More suggestive is the example further on of judging he sees men when all he sees are hats and coats which may cover automata (para. 13), and his discussion in part V of the <u>Discourse</u> of the difference between men and machines (para. 10).

(6)    Luce and Jessop (1949), II, p. 108 and III, Fourth Dialogue, 5, 6, 12.

(7)    IP, VI, v (<u>Works</u>, pp. 448–9).

(8)    IP, VI, vi (<u>Works</u>, p. 461).

(9)    I, V, vii (<u>Works</u>, p. 129). Moore evidently had this passage in mind in his first reference to Reid in his 1905 paper, 'The Nature and Reality of Objects of Perception' — reprinted in G.E. Moore, (1922), pp. 57–8.

(10) Again, there are some hints; see Hume (1888), I iv 7, paragraphs 2, 8, 10. Hume isn't denying the self exists, as Reid says IP, II, xii (<u>Works</u>, p. 293), only the self conceived as a Cartesian substance distinct from any impressions and ideas.

(11)  **I**, I, v (Works, p. 102).

(12)  **IP**, I, vi (Works, p. 242); Cf. **I**, VII (Works, p. 207).

(13)  **IP**, VI, vii (Works, p. 468).

(14)  Ibid. (Works, p. 465).

(15)  **I**, VII (Works, p. 207); Cf. **IP**, V, iii (Works, p. 432).

(16)  **IP**, II, xi (Works, p. 288); Cf. **I**, VII (Works, p. 208).
Cf. also Berkeley (1949), II, p. 231.

(17)  Cf. **I**, I, v (Works, pp. 101–2); **I**, V, vii (Works, p.
129); **I**, VII (Works, p. 207); **IP**, I, vi (Works, p. 242); **IP**,
II, xii (Works, p. 293); **IP**, II, xiv (Works, p. 299).

(18)  Kames (1779), p. 270.

(19)  **IP**, II, xii (Works, p. 293).

(20)  See Berkeley (1949), II, pp. 44, 51f, 52f, 80.

(21)  Quoted in **IP**, II, xi (Works, p. 288).

(22)  Ibid. (Works, p. 289).

(23)  Cf. Berkeley (1949), II, pp. 233–4.

(25)  **IP**, II, x (Works, p. 285)

(26)  Kames (1779), p. 252.

(27)  **IP**, VI, v (Works, p. 446).

(28)  **IP**, II, x (Works, pp. 283–5).

(29)  **IP**, VI, v (Works, p. 445).

(30)  **IP**, II, x (Works, p. 285).

(31)  Berkeley (1940), II, p. 247; Cf. **IP**, II, x (Works, pp.
284–5).

(32)  **IP**, II, xvi (Works, p. 310).

(33)  Unlike Kames, Reid does not tar Berkeley with atheism.

Berkeley's doctrine, Kames charges, "if it should not lead to universal scepticism, affords at least a shrewd argument in favour of Atheism" (1779, p. 252).

(34)   **IP**, II, x (Works, p. 285).

(35)   **IP**, VI, v (Works, p. 448).

(36)   Ibid. (Works, p. 449).

(37)   **IP**, VII, ii (Works, p. 479).

(38)   Berkeley (1949), II, p. 233.

(39)   **IP**, VI, vi (Works, p. 457).

(40)   Ibid. (Works, p. 459).

(41)   **IP**, VII, iii (Works, p. 483).

(42)   Ibid. (Works, p. 482).

(43)   Ibid. (Works, p. 481).

(44)   Hume (1975), IV ii, section 29.

(45)   **IP**, VI, v (Works, p. 449).

(46)   Hume (1975), IV i, section 22.

(47)   **IP**, VI, vi (Works, pp. 460–1).

(48)   Ibid. (Works, p. 458); Cf. **IP**, I, v (Works, p. 239).

(49)   **IP**, VI, v (Works, pp. 448–9).

(50)   **IP**, VI, ii (Works, p. 479).

(51)   **IP**, VI, vi (Works, p. 461).

(52)   **IP**, II, xi (Works, p. 289).

(53) Cf. the First Dialogue: "the senses perceive nothing which they do not perceive immediately: for they make no inferences" (Berkeley (1949), II, pp. 174–5). See also I, VI, xx (Works, pp. 183, 185–6); **IP**, II, v (Works, pp. 259–60); **IP**, II, xiv (Works, p. 303); **IP**, IV, xx (Works, p. 328).

(54)  **IP**, VI, v (<u>Works</u>, p. 445).

(55)  **IP**, VIII, iv (<u>Works</u>, p. 503).

(56)  **IP**, VI, v (<u>Works</u>, p. 445).

(57)  <u>Ibid</u>. (<u>Works</u>, p. 448).

(58)  **IP**, VIII, iv (<u>Works</u>, p. 503).

(59)  **IP**, VI, v (<u>Works</u>, p. 446).

(60)  **IP**, II, vii (<u>Works</u>, p. 263).

(61)  Berkeley (1949), II, pp. 203–4.

(62)  <u>Ibid</u>., p. 204.

(63)  Berkeley (1949), I, pp. 265–6.

(64)  Berkeley (1949), I, p. 264.

(65)  Berkeley (1949), I, p. 273.

(66)  I, IV, ii (<u>Works</u>, p. 118).

(67)  I, VI, xxiv (<u>Works</u>, p. 195).

(68)  I, V, iii (<u>Works</u>, p. 122).

(69)  Berkeley (1949), II, p. 203.

(70)  Broad (1925), p. 324.

(71)  I, II, vii (<u>Works</u>, p. 111); I, V, v (<u>Works</u>, p. 123); I, VI, xxii (<u>Works</u>, p. 191).

(72)  I, V, ii (<u>Works</u>, p. 120); **IP**, II, xix (<u>Works</u>, p. 325).

(73)  I, VI, vii (<u>Works</u>, p. 147).

(74)  I, VI, xix (<u>Works</u>, p. 182); <u>cf</u>. **IP**, II, xxi (<u>Works</u>, p. 331).

(75)  Though Berkeley himself slips into the ordinary sense of 'immediately' – see Berkeley (1949), I, p. 174; p. 191 does not have this sense.

(76)  **I**, II, vii (Works, p. 110); **I**, V, v (Works, p. 124); **I**, VI, xxiii (Works, p. 193); **IP**, VI, vi (Works, p. 460).

(77)  **I**, V, v (Works, p. 125); **AP**, V, vi (Works, p. 665).

(78)  **I**, V, v (Works, p. 120); **I**, VI, viii (Works, p. 147); **I**, VI, xix (Works, p. 182); **I**, VI, xxi (Works, p. 188); **I**, VI, xxii (Works, p. 192); **IP**, II, xix (Works, p. 325); **IP**, II, xxi (Works, p. 331).

(79)  **I**, IV, i (Works, p. 117).

(80)  As with Hume it is often unclear whether 'reasoning' includes inductive reasoning. At times Reid seems to mean a priori, demonstrative reasoning, sometimes expressly (Works, pp. 110, 122, 124, 332, 458, 460), sometimes implicitly (Works, pp. 117, 121, 125, 448–9, 450, 665), opposed to 'experience'. At other times he seems to include inductive reasoning within 'reasoning' (Works, pp. 188, 193, 199, 244, 481–2). Hume, when he is careful, rejects the contrast between 'reason' and 'experience' as 'superficial' – Hume (1975), V i note.

(81)  **IP**, Preface (Works, p. 217).

(82)  **IP**, II, viii (Works, p. 270).

(83)  **IP**, Preface (Works, p. 217).

(84)  **IP**, I, vi (Works, p. 241); cf. Hume (1978), Introduction, p. xvi.

(85)  **IP**, II, viii (Works, p. 270).

(86)  **I**, VII (Works, pp. 204–5).

(87)  Ibid. (Works, pp. 209–10).

(88)  **IP**, VI, viii (Works, p. 470); cf. **IP**, II, xiv (Works, pp. 301–2).

(89)  **I**, VII (Works, p. 201).

(90)  **IP**, II, vii (Works, p. 270).

(91)  **I**, I, ii (Works, p. 99).

(92) **IP**, I, ii (Works, p. 232). By 'things in the mind' he means the operations of the mind; the theory of ideas isn't making a stealthy comeback here.

(93) **IP**, VI, i (Works, p. 419).

(94) Ibid. (Works, p. 420); cf. **IP**, I, v (Works, p. 239), **IP**, VI, v (Works, p. 443).

(95) **IP**, III, v (Works, p. 347).

(96) **IP**, I, ii (Works, p. 232); I, v (Works, p. 239); VI, v (Works, p. 443).

(97) **IP**, II, v (Works, p. 258); VI, v (Works, p. 443).

(98) I, I, ii (Works, p. 99); VII (Works, p. 201); **IP**, I, vi (Works, p. 240); VI, v (Works, p. 443).

(99) **IP**, Preface (Works, p. 217).

(100) I, I, ii (Works, p. 98). In his index Hamilton, referring to Works, pp. 97 and 98, states that mind can only be studied in one way, by observation and experiment (Works, p. 1005). Reid in fact says "nature's works" (Works, p. 97); but contrast I, V, iii (Works, p. 122) on the method of "our philosophy concerning the human mind".

(101) **IP**, VI, vi (Works, p. 458).

(102) Ibid. (Works, p. 460).

(103) **IP**, VI, v (Works, p. 450).

(104) I, V, vii (Works, p. 129). Cf. Moore: "I can know things, which I cannot prove", 'Proof of an External World' in (1959), p. 150.

(105) Cf. Reid on the absurdity of Descartes' attempt to prove the existence of the material world, **IP**, I, vi (Works, pp. 241–2).

(106) **IP**, VIII, i (Works, p. 491).

(107) I, VI, xx (Works, p. 184).

(108) Ibid. (Works, p. 185). Cf. Gilbert Ryle, 'Sensation' in

(1971), II, pp. 343–5.  Ryle's example is similar to one of Reid's (loc.cit.).

(109) I, VI, xx (Works, pp. 184–5); IP, II, xxi (Works, p. 331).

(110) I, VI, xx (Works, p. 185).

(111) IP, VI, v (Works, p. 449).

(112) Ibid. (Works, p. 450); cf. IP, II, xxi (Works, p. 332).

(113) IP, VIII, i (Works, p. 492), cf. Hutcheson (1973), I VII, II.

(114) IP, II, xxi (Works, p. 331).

(115) IP, VIII, iv (Works, p. 507).

(116) Ibid. (Works, p. 502).

(117) IP, VIII, i (Works, pp. 490–1); IP, VIII, v (Works, p. 501).

(118) I, VI, viii (Works, p. 146); I, VI, xxiv (Works, p. 195), IP, VI, v (Works, p. 450); AP, V, vi (Works, p. 665).

(119) I, VI, viii (Works, p. 147); IP, VI, v (Works, p. 450); AP, V, vi (Works, p. 665).

(120) Dumb people: I, IV, ii (Works, p. 118); AP, V, vi (Works, p. 664). Deaf people: IP, II, xxi (Works, p. 333).

(121) IP, II, xxii (Works, p. 338); cf. I, VI, xx (Works, p. 185).

(122) IP, I, viii (Works, p. 245).

(123) Berkeley (1949), III, Fourth Dialogue, 6, 7.

(124) I, IV, ii (Works, p. 118); cf. IP VI, v (Works, p. 450).

(125) Cf. Austin's charge that Berkeley confused 'sign of' and 'sign for' – Austin (1970), p. 126.

(126) I, V, iii (Works, p. 121).

(127) **I**, VI, xx (<u>Works</u>, p. 184).

(128) Kames closes his essay, 'Veracity of the External Senses' with "a comparison between the evidence of our senses and that of human testimony" (1779 p. 261).

(129) <u>Cf</u>. Austin, (1962), p. 11; and (1970), p. 48 and p. 97.

(130) 'A Defence of Common Sense', in (1959), pp. 42–3; but contrast 'Hume's Philosophy', in (1922), pp. 158–9.

(131) **IP**, VI, v (<u>Works</u>, p. 448).

(132) <u>Cf</u>. Moore, 'The Nature and Reality of Objects of Perception', in (1922), p. 42.

R.F. Stalley


# CAUSALITY AND AGENCY IN THE PHILOSOPHY OF THOMAS REID


I shall be concerned here with two doctrines which are essential to Reid's account of agency and of causation. The first, expounded at some length in **AP** I, v, is that, so far as we can tell, only beings with will and understanding can exercise active power. The second, avowed at many points in Reid's writings, is that there must be an efficient cause for everything that comes into existence. Since Reid believes that only a being that exercises active power can truly be called a cause, these doctrines taken together have far reaching consequences in metaphysics, in the philosophy of science and in the philosophy of religion, as well as in the theory of action. They imply that material things cannot be genuinely active and thus cannot be regarded as causes in the truest sense of the word. Conversely only spiritual beings can be efficient causes and everything which happens must result ultimately from the agency of God, of man or of some other such being.

Reid's denial that material bodies can be active has led one recent critic to claim that he contradicts his own principles. Edward Madden has pointed out that according to Reid's account "one cannot say that any particular in the physical world is active as opposed to other ones that are passive"; but, complains Madden, we do say such things; therefore Reid's theory of agency conflicts with his own theory of common sense.(1)

This criticism, as it stands, would appear to rest on a misunderstanding of Reid's concept of common sense. He is not committed to accepting as true everything that the man in the street would say but only those principles which appear self-evident to a reasonable person who considers them with sufficient care.(2) He does in fact argue at length that the ordinary language in which we speak of material beings as acting is a misleading relic of a primitive anthropomorphism.(3) Thus the fact that Reid's account of agency conflicts with what people ordinarily say does not, in itself, show that it is inconsistent with the doctrine of common sense.

*M. Dalgarno and E. Matthews (eds.), The Philosophy of Thomas Reid, 275–283.*
© *1989 by Kluwer Academic Publishers.*

In considering these points it is important to bear in mind the historical background which lies behind Reid's theory of active power. At least since the time of Newton, a controversy had raged between those, on the one hand, who argued that matter is in itself inactive, having only the bare capacity to react to forces exerted on it from without, and those, on the other, who held that matter must itself be endowed with active principles. As Yolton has recently shown, this controversy soon became bound up with the question of the immateriality of the soul since, if matter is inert, there must be something non-material within human beings by virtue of which they can be active.(4)   Of course, those who believed in the inertness of matter did not deny that ordinary people often talk as though matter could be active — they merely claimed that such talk was, on metaphysical grounds, misleading.   Reid clearly means to commit himself to this party. He wishes to show that matter cannot be active and he does this by developing his own distinctive theory of agency.   The fact that this theory treats matter as inactive is no objection to it because that is precisely one of the things Reid seeks to prove.

Although Reid's theory of agency cannot simply be dismissed as manifestly contrary to common sense, it is certainly not without its problems. A major source of difficulty is that Reid does not offer very much by way of explicit argument in support of the two key doctrines which I mentioned at the beginning of this paper. Consider first his doctrine that, so far as we can know, only beings with will and understanding can exercise active power. Reid's exposition of this point starts from a consideration of Locke's argument that the observation of external bodies gives us no real idea of active power.(5) Locke takes this to imply that we acquire our only clear idea of active power from our awareness of our own agency, and he goes on, in a rather tentative way, to suggest that inanimate bodies may be altogether lacking in active power. Reid puts the point with much more assurance. He argues that the only exercise of active power of which we can form any conception presupposes will and understanding and that it is therefore probable that only beings with such attributes can possess active power. Admittedly his language is, to begin with, fairly hesitant, but by the beginning of the next chapter he treats the point as firmly established.

It is difficult to see how Reid could really justify his position here. If anything the thesis that active power

presupposes will and understanding might seem better  adapted
to Locke's philosophy than to his own.  Locke holds  that all
our ideas are derived  from sensation or  reflection.  If  we
are directly conscious of active power only when we ourselves
engage in action he can  argue quite reasonably that we  have
no idea of any kind of power apart from that which we possess
ourselves.  Reid, on the other hand, allows that we  can form
a conception of things of which we have no direct awareness –
active power is itself a  case in point.(6)  It is  difficult
to see therefore why he should think that we cannot  conceive
of any kind of power which could subsist in inanimate bodies.

There is a similar  deficiency in the arguments, such  as
they are, with which Reid supports his claim that there  must
be  an  efficient  cause  of  everything  that  comes  into
existence.  But before  considering these we must recall  how
Reid uses the term 'efficient cause'.

The concepts of cause and of active power are inseparably
linked in Reid's thought.  Active power is an attribute  that
can exist only in  a subject; and  a subject which  exercises
active power is  a cause.(7)  If only  agents with will  and
understanding can possess active power, it follows that  such
agents are the only true causes.  This, of course, raises the
question what we  are to  make of talk  of causes in  natural
science.  At **AP**  I, vi Reid  claims that even the  Newtonians
acknowledge  that  they  are  ignorant  of  the  true  (i.e.
efficient) causes of natural phenomena and content themselves
with  discovering  the  laws  by  which  the  unknown  causes
operate.  This ignorance is not as damaging as it might seem,
since for  practical purposes  we  do not  need to  know  the
causes of  events in  the  natural world.  We  need only  to
predict them, and for that a knowledge of the laws  of nature
suffices.  It is  only in the  case of human acts, which  are
liable to praise or blame, that we need to identify the agent
or efficient cause, and on this, Reid considers, "nature  has
given us all the light that is necessary for our conduct".(8)

The same view is to  be found elsewhere in Active  Powers
and in earlier writings.  In the  Inquiry, Reid argues  that
only in a popular sense can a rose be called the cause of its
smell: "having found the smell thus constantly conjoined with
the rose, the mind is at rest, without inquiring whether this
conjunction is owing to a  real efficiency or not".(9)  In  a
letter written in 1780 to  Kames, Reid dwells at some  length
on different  uses of  the  word 'cause'.(10)  In natural
philosophy the cause of a body's fall is said to  be gravity.

But gravity is not an efficient cause; it is rather a general law of which the body's fall is a particular instance. Reid goes on to expound what he takes to be the Newtonian view of natural science as a matter of discovering general laws by induction. It cannot discover efficient causes but rather "exhibits to our view the grand machine of the material world". It is the task of natural theology or metaphysics to ask whether there is, or is not, a first mover. In fact, Reid claims, these sciences can prove the existence of God from the self-evident claims (a) that every event has a cause and (b) that an effect which manifests intelligence, wisdom and goodness must be due to an efficient cause which is itself intelligent, wise and good. We cannot, of course, be sure to what extent God has delegated matters to "the ministry of subordinate efficient causes" but there is no reason to follow those who attribute active power to matter.

Elsewhere Reid marks the difference between causes as he understands them and causes as understood in natural science by making a distinction between efficient and physical causes.(11) But his use of the latter term can be confusing. He takes it to refer to the laws of nature governing a particular effect, whereas we might naturally take it to refer to the prior events which are linked by a causal law with the effect.

In **IP** VI, vi, Reid places the proposition "whatever begins to exist must have a cause which produced it" among the first principles of necessary truths. Its denial would, he claims, put an end "to all philosophy, to all religion, to all reasoning that would carry us beyond the objects of sense, and to all prudence in the conduct of life". Although this principle cannot be proved by reasoning, Reid believes that we all consent to it and presuppose it in the conduct of our everyday lives.(12)

From our point of view the most surprising thing about these passages is Reid's assumption that what he calls an efficient cause is always necessary. This, on his theory, implies that every event must ultimately be traceable back to an agent with will and understanding:

> I think the only distinct and true meaning of this
> maxim is, that there must be something that had
> power to produce the event, and did produce it. We
> are early conscious of some power in ourselves to
> produce some events; and our nature leads us to

think that every event is produced by a power similar to that which we find in ourselves — that is, by will and exertion.(13)

Why should Reid take this view? In the letter just cited he supports his position by pointing out that a child is apt to ascribe agency even to inanimate objects, for example to a weight which falls and hurts it. Language, Reid claims, is "formed upon these early sentiments" and so we use the word 'cause' (misleadingly) of things which we know to be inanimate and passive. Presumably what Reid means here is that the childish instinct which attributes agency to inanimate things reflects a genuine principle of common sense which leads us to trace everything which happens back to some intelligent agent. We go wrong simply in talking as though the inanimate object is itself that agent. But a critic could turn this argument against Reid. If, as Reid concedes, our natural instincts can err in attributing agency to inanimate matter, could they not also err in supposing that all events can be traced back to an agent cause? To defend himself against this objection Reid would need to produce some argument to show that reflective common sense really does require us to believe that there is an efficient cause (in his sense) for everything that happens. But there is nothing in the passage to suggest what this argument might be.

Much the same could be said of the passage in IP VI, vi, where Reid claims that all men, both in speculation and in practice, assume that every event has a cause. He himself, as we have seen, allows that natural philosophers concern themselves with physical rather than efficient causes. The same goes for the practical affairs of everyday life. Here what matters is the capacity to predict and control what happens, and for this one needs to know, not the efficient causes of natural events but the laws which govern their operation. So the conduct of everyday life does not in fact presuppose the belief that there is an efficient cause for everything that happens. If ordinary men think and talk as though this is the case that too could be a relic of primitive animism. A critic could thus accept Reid's argument as showing that common sense requires us to believe that every event has a cause, in some sense of that word, while denying that the ultimate cause must always be an agent.

At this point it may be helpful to summarize the problem

with which we are confronted. Reid maintains both that
inanimate objects cannot, strictly speaking, be active, and
that everything which happens stems from an agent cause. He
realises that these claims conflict, to some extent, with
ordinary ways of talking and therefore treats ordinary
language as, in these respects, misleading. His view must
therefore be that reflective common sense shows that we
cannot avoid accepting the principles in question. But the
passages we have looked at – those in which he discusses the
matter most explicitly – give very little indication of why
he should think this.

I want to suggest that we may find an answer to this
puzzle by following up the suggestion in **IP** VI, vi that the
denial that everything which begins to exist must have a
cause would (inter alia) "put an end to all religion".
Elsewhere Reid puts the point more explicitly: "it is upon
this principle that we ground the rational belief of a
deity".(14) We have seen above how, in writing to Kames,
Reid claimed to derive a proof of the existence of God from
the principles (a) that every event must have an efficient
cause and (b) that effects which manifest intelligence,
wisdom and goodness must have an intelligent, wise and good
cause. In **IP** VI, vi these points are developed at greater
length and are used as the basis for a brief defence of
traditional natural theology. Since God is an agent these
contexts clearly require a principle of efficient causality.
It would not suffice for Reid's purposes to show merely that
every event has what he would call a physical cause.

In these passages and in others like them, Reid has in
mind a form of cosmological argument which was part of the
stock-in-trade of eighteenth-century natural theologians,
particularly those under the influence of Samuel Clarke.(15)
As presented by Clarke this argument starts from the premise
that "whatever exists has a cause, a reason or ground for its
existence".(16) This cause must lie either in the necessity
of its own nature or in the will of some previously existing
being. But the supposition that one dependent being has
succeeded another from infinity is absurd. Therefore there
must be a first cause. Clarke later argues that this first
cause must be a free agent:

> If the supreme cause be not a free and voluntary
> agent; then in every effect ... there must have been
> a progression of causes in infinitum, without any
> original cause at all. For if there be no liberty

anywhere, then there is no agent, no cause, mover, principle or beginning of motion anywhere.(17)

Thus his arguments for the existence of God and for free will are founded on the claim that causality presupposes agency. No explanation in terms of what Reid would call 'physical causes' can ultimately suffice because that would involve the absurdity of an infinite regress.

Clarke's argument, which Reid explicitly endorses, would provide a direct answer to one of our problems, for it purports to show that the principle that every event has a cause commits one to postulating an agent cause for all that happens.(18) To reach this conclusion it assumes that agent explanations, unlike explanations in terms of physical causes, are complete in the sense that the choices of a free agent do not need to be explained in terms of any prior cause. Clarke himself brings this point out when he rejects the argument that volitions must have causes which, in turn, result from previous causes ad infinitum. This, he claims, confuses 'moral motives' and 'physical efficients', i.e. he suggests that to explain a choice in terms of motives is not to cite a previously existing cause and does not therefore involve a regress.(19) Reid is operating within the same framework and it is for this reason, I would suggest, that he takes the principle of causality to imply that there is an efficient cause for everything that happens.

Analogous considerations would explain why Reid holds that the only active power of which we can form any conception must be exercised by beings with will and understanding. Action implies the beginning of motion. We may be able to imagine a purely inanimate being starting into motion without a cause but such an event would be unintelligible in the sense that it could have no explanation. If, on the other hand, a being with will and understanding initiates a motion a satisfactory mode of explanation is available – we can refer to motives. Thus the reason why Reid thinks that we cannot conceive of such material beings as exercising active power is not that such a supposition involves a logical contradiction or that we cannot imagine a purely material being starting spontaneously into motion. The point is rather that we can only make sense of a beginning of motion in the case of a being which acts for a motive.

To explain Reid's arguments in this way does not, of

course, imply that they are sound.  To establish them we
would have to show both that an infinite regress of causes is
absurd and  that agent  explanations  are uniquely  complete.
This in turn  requires that  the distinction between  motives
and causes be  upheld.  The eighteenth century  philosophers
certainly appreciated the  importance  of this  supposed
distinction (it is,  for  example,  the  key  issue  in  the
Price-Priestley debate on liberty and necessity).  I suspect
that  Reid  came  closer  than  any  of  them  to  giving  a
satisfactory account cf it.  But that is another story.

NOTES

(1)  Madden (1982, pp. 313–341).

(2)  **IP** VI, ii (Works, pp. 421–6); VI, iv (Works, pp. 437–9).

(3)  **AP** I, ii (Works, pp. 515–7); IV, iii (Works, pp. 605–6).

(4)  Yolton (1984).

(5)  **AP** I, v (Works, pp. 522–3); cf. Locke (1975, pp. 233–6).

(6)  **AP** I, i (Works, p. 513).

(7)  **AP** I, i (Works, p. 514); I, iv (Works, pp. 521–2); I, v (Works, p. 523).

(8)  **AP** I, vi (Works, p. 527).

(9)  **I** II, ix (Works, p. 113).

(10) **Corr** (Works, pp. 56–60).

(11) **Corr** (Works, pp. 66, 67 & 83–84).

(12) **IP** VI, vi (Works, pp. 455–7); **AP** I, ii (Works, p. 516); I, vi (Works, p. 521); I, v (Works, p. 524); IV, ii (Works, p. 603); IV, iii (Works, p. 608); **Corr** (Works, pp. 75, 82 & 84).

(13) **Corr** (Works, p. 75).  Cf., e.g., **Corr** (Works, pp. 82, 84); **AP** I, v (Works, p. 524); IV, ii (Works, p. 603).

(14) **AP** IV, ii (Works, p. 603).

(15) E.g. **IP** VI, iii (Works, p. 430); **AP** I, v (Works, p. 523); IV, iii (Works, p. 608).

(16) Clarke (1738, II, p. 524).

(17) Clarke (1738, II, pp. 551–2).

(18) **AP**, IV, viii (Works, pp. 623–4).

(19) Clarke (1738, II, p. 552).

John J. Haldane

# REID, SCHOLASTICISM AND CURRENT PHILOSOPHY OF MIND

## I

Let <u>ontological realism</u> be the thesis that there is a pre-existing structured world independent of consciousness. Relative to this idea, epistemological realism may be introduced as the doctrine that in thought we are capable of direct awareness of the world and of knowledge of its structure.

Realism of the first sort has less often been challenged than has that of the second. Certain ancient varieties of scepticism apart, the notions that truth is relative and, more radically, that reality is mind-dependent date from the modern period;(1) and though they are once again in fashion they have never received more than strictly limited support. Epistemological realism, by contrast, has been subject to attack throughout the entire history of philosophy. Indeed, in various periods it has only been held by a minority of writers. In what follows I am concerned with the issue between this sort of realism and its principal rival, viz: <u>epistemological representationalism</u>, as that has arisen in the past and arises again today. More precisely, my interests are in the view of cognition advanced by Thomas Reid, in its resemblance to an earlier and still largely unexamined epistemological tradition, and in the powerful philosophical arguments these provide against theses now widely held among cognitive psychologists and philosophers of mind.

## II

To begin with then, consider the following quotations from sources medieval, modern and contemporary, which illustrate the two main alternative theories of thought and cognition

1. Some have held that our cognitive faculties know only what is experienced within them, for example, that the senses perceive only the impressions made on the organs. According to this opinion the intellect thinks only of what is experienced within it, i.e. the species [ideas] received in

*M. Dalgarno and E. Matthews (eds.), The Philosophy of Thomas Reid, 285–304.*
© *1989 by Kluwer Academic Publishers.*

it.  Thus again according to this opinion, these species  are
what is thought of [quod intelligitur].

   The opinion, however, is obviously false ... because  the
things of  which we  think  are the  same as  the objects  of
science ...  we must  say, therefore, that  species stand  in
relation to  the intellect  as  that by  which the  intellect
thinks or has understanding [quo intelligit intellectus].

                                                     Aquinas(2)


2.  The merit of what you are pleased to call my  philosophy,
lies, I  think, chiefly,  in  having called  in question  the
common theory  of ideas,  or images  of things  in the  mind,
being the  only  objects  of  thought; a  theory founded  on
natural prejudices,  and  so universally  received as  to  be
interwoven with the structure of the language.

                                                        Reid(3)


3.  To think (e.g.) that Marvin is melancholy is to represent
Marvin in a certain  way; viz., as  being melancholy ...  But
surely we cannot represent Marvin as melancholy except as  we
are in some or other relation to a representation of Marvin.

                                                       Fodor(4)


4.  Believing — if we can make determinate sense of it — must
be construed as a relation ... there are two possibilities as
regards the  relata of  believing and  other  propositional
attitudes: either  they  are  things  which are  contents  —
propositions in  one sense  or another — or else  they  are
things which have content ... we are to construe believing as
a relation, not to contents  but to ... inner formulae in  an
inner code.

                                                     Schiffer(5)


The  essential  character  of  representationalism  remains
implicit in these passages but is easily extracted from them.
It is the view that  the immediate objects of cognitive  acts
or states  are  internal entities:  species,  ideas,  images,
sentential formulae and the such  like, which may or may  not
stand in  some further  referential relation  to objects  and
features in  the world;  and that  it is  the former,  inner,
relational  attitudes  which  constitute  the  essential

'object–directed', or intentional character of cognitive states. The opposing realism adverted to by Aquinas in the passage quoted above and argued for there and elsewhere,(6) and which is here laid claim to by Reid, has it that in thought and in perception the cognitive subject can (though may not always) engage directly with reality.

Epistemological realism is currently under attack from those, like Fodor and Schiffer, who suppose that the very notion of contentful psychological states can only be made sense of by positing systems of mental representation. Although it is not possible on this occasion to examine in any full, or even wholly adequate, fashion the various considerations that have been offered in support of this claim, it may yet be useful to show how arguments advanced by Reid and his scholastic predecessors can be employed to effect in undermining the new representational theory of mind.(7) In so doing I also wish to demonstrate something of the surprising extent to which the philosophical cognitive psychology which Reid develops in IP resembles that proposed by Aquinas five hundred years earlier and adopted by his successors, and to suggest that this resemblance may not be accidental.

### III

Like most British philosophers of the period Reid follows Locke's example in declaring his opposition to the doctrines and traditions of the medieval schoolmen and makes the familiar charges against them. He writes, for example: of "the fruitless questions agitated";(8) of the introduction of a multitude of distinctions to no good effect which only create confusion – "Let scholastic sophisters entangle themselves in their own cobwebs";(9) and makes the accusation of being "fruitful of words but barren of works".(10) In relation to the issue of cognition he simply includes them among those who subscribe to some or other version of the theory of ideas.(11) Here, as elsewhere, however, Reid's interpretation of other philosophers is cursory and inaccurate, and it is unfortunate that he should be so dismissive of a tradition that is avowedly realist in its epistemology – especially so since he employs both arguments and (perhaps more surprisingly) vocabulary associated with it in his sustained attack upon philosophical scepticism. In several places he even acknowledges the scholastic origins of some of the terms of his own preferred account. For example, he writes:

To perceive an object is  one thing, to act upon  it
is another; nor is the  last at all included in  the
first ... Logicians [i.e.  schoolmen, cf. **IP**, IV,  i
(Works, p. 363)] distinguish two kinds of  operation
of mind: the first  kind produces no effect  without
the mind; the  last  does.   The  first  they  call
immanent acts,     the     second  transitive.     All
intellectual operations belong  to the first  class;
they   produce   no   effect   upon   any   external
object.(12)

The full explanation of why it is that Reid is hostile to the
schoolmen, including them  within the wholesale  condemnation
of previous philosophers  as advocates of  the way of  ideas,
and yet  draws from  this anti-representationalist  tradition
resources for the formation of his own version of realism, is
doubtless complex but the following three factors are  likely
to feature in  it.   Firstly, Reid is  able to introduce  and
develop his views more dramatically by contrasting them  with
what   he   describes   as   an   unbroken   tradition   of
representationalism.   He writes:

All philosophers, from Plato  to Mr. Hume, agree  in
this, That  we  do  not  perceive  external  objects
immediately,  and  that  the  immediate  object   of
perception  must  be  some  image  present  to   the
mind.(13)

The striking  image of  unbroken ranks  of thinkers  marching
resolutely onwards guided by a single erroneous conception of
the nature of cognition provides a backdrop against which his
own  efforts  at  reformation  appear  more  impressive   by
comparison, but  this image  quickly disintegrates once  one
looks at the work of philosophers of the middle ages.

Secondly,  and  more  creditably  to Reid,  some  late,
neo-Thomist scholastics certainly do subscribe to a theory of
ideas as  cognitive intermediaries,  and he  knew, and  makes
mention of  their work  in the  course of  his attacks  on
epistemological orthodoxy. Gassendi, for example, writes  as
follows:

[an ideas's] objective reality can only be  the
representation of or likeness  to me which the  idea
carries, or  indeed only  that proportion in  the
disposition of  its parts  in virtue of which  they
recall me.(14)

Thirdly, certain aspects of the realist theories developed in the middle ages lend themselves, at least on a superficial reading, to a representationalist (mis)interpretation. In the present context the most significant of these is the claim made several times by Aquinas and often repeated by those familiar with his philosophy (including Arnauld), viz: that ideas may be objects of thought. Given a strongly held conviction that most philosophical errors are the products of a faulty theory of knowledge, and an evangelical attitude to the task of promoting realism, any suggestion whatsoever to the effect that the mind may be directed upon its own contents looks threatening, and it is therefore easy to dismiss as inadequate any theory which implies or countenances this.

Nonetheless, such a claim is compatible with a version of realism close to Reid's own, such as that developed by Aquinas and expounded later by Arnauld. According to this latter, while the first act of the intellect is engagement with the world as brought under concepts, its second act is one of reflection upon the former and its intelligible content — reflection which, as Aquinas and Reid both recognise, is involved in concept formation.(15) In **IP** II Reid quotes Arnauld's rejection of representationalism and his identification of the having of ideas with thinking of extra-mental reality but then goes on to accuse him of yielding to the ancient orthodoxy in its Cartesian manifestation:

> He labours to reconcile these expressions to his own definition of ideas,by observing, that every perception and every thought is necessarily conscious of itself, and reflects upon itself; and that, by this consciousness and reflection, it is its own immediate object. Whence he infers, that the idea — that is, the perception — is the immediate object of perception.(16)

Here, however, Reid has simply misunderstood Arnauld's claim. For it is not that the reflexivity of consciousness entails that the only objects of thought are mental contents, but rather that in addition to thinking of things one may also attend to thoughts themselves. Arnauld is quite explicit in stating his view:

> all perception is essentially representative of something ... and is for that reason called an idea

...[but] it can only be as essentially reflecting
upon itself that its immediate objects can be called
this idea ... Thus there is no need for recourse to
representative    beings    distinct    from    our
perceptions.(17)

And in claiming this he is doing no more than <u>restating</u> the
orthodox Thomist position, as is clear from the same article
of the <u>Summa Theologiae</u> from which I quoted earlier where
Aquinas writes as follows:

However, since the intellect reflects upon itself,
by such reflection it understands both its own
understanding and the species by which it
understands. Thus species are secondarily that
which is understood [i.e., thought of], first is the
reality of which the species is a likeness
[<u>similitudo</u>].

Ironically, in correcting what he takes to be Arnauld's error
Reid proceeds to affirm the very same thesis as the
scholastics:

It is true, that consciousness always goes along
with perception; but they are different operations
of the mind, and they have their different objects.
Consciousness is not perception, nor is the object
of consciousness the object of perception.(18)

Given the reference to an author whose avowed realism is
apparent in his writings, it is surprising that Reid should
have failed to notice the true character of Arnauld's
epistemology. Some commentators, both among his
contemporaries and more recently, have accused Reid of wilful
misrepresentation and plagiarism in connection with the
anti-idealist theories of Arnauld and Buffier.(19) This
particular charge is unjust for he indicates that he finds
merit in their writings and credits both with recognizing the
sceptical implications of Cartesian epistemology and with
challenging its representationalist presuppositions.(20) At
the same time, however, it is clear that Reid prides himself
on what he suggests is the complete originality of his own
views. I have offered some (admittedly not very strong)
reasons as to why such a belief might seem justified but also
claimed that it is false. Moreover, Reid need not have
sought far to find an unequivocal statement of the earlier
realist tradition.

Throughout the periods of scholasticism but particularly in the Fifteenth and Sixteenth Centuries Scotland produced philosophers of international standing. Chief among those of the later period was John Major or Mair (Scotus). Major began his academic life as a regent lecturing in philosophy and theology at Glasgow from 1518 to 1523 (where he subsequently became Principal of the University) and later taught the same subjects at St. Andrews between 1531 and 1550 (during which period he was appointed Provost of St. Salvator's College). He was an important figure in Scottish intellectual history as well as in European late-scholastic philosophy and was known of by Reid who also had access to his writings.(21) It is of considerable interest therefore to find in Major's works the following remarks about the nature of cognition.

> A mental term is a concept of the mind, or an impression naturally signifying, and it is sometimes called an act of the understanding, a notion of a thing, a lively apprehension, an imitation, an image, a similitude, a cognition.(22)

And in relation to thought in the absence of its object — what the medievals termed 'abstract cognition' — he writes

> I say that the abstract idea [notitiam abstractivam] which I have of the pinnacle of St. Genevieve has the pinnacle itself as its immediate object [immediate terminatur].(23)

Now compare the first of these quotations with the following ones drawn from Reid

> All men mean by [the word 'notion'], the conception, the apprehension, or thought which we have of any object of thought. A notion, therefore, is an act of the mind conceiving or thinking of some object.(24)

and earlier he writes:

> It is now proper to observe, that there are different orders of natural signs ... [One] class comprehends those which, though we never before had any notion or conception of the thing signified, do suggest it, or conjure it up, as it were, by a natural kind of magic and at once give us a

conception.(25)

Next compare the second of Major's observations with the
following remark offered by Reid in which, like Major before
him, he makes the anti-representationalist position clear by
use of an example of thought 'at a distance' from its object:

> I can likewise conceive an individual object that
> really exists, such as St. Paul's Church in London.
> I have an idea of it ... the immediate object of
> this conception is four hundred miles distant.(26)

The similarities between Reid's 'new found' realism and
long-established scholastic orthodoxy are striking and again
raise the question of how he could have remained (or, indeed,
whether he was) ignorant of the true character of this
tradition. For all its interest, however, it is not possible
to pursue the purely historical issue further here. Clearly,
though, more needs to be said about the structure of
scholastic epistemology and its relationship to the position
adopted by Reid in Intellectual Powers. At this point,
however, it is appropriate to move from the past into the
present so as to consider a currently influential theory of
the nature of intentionality and mental reference.

IV

Realism being the most natural and attractive account of the
cognitive connections between mind and world it is surprising
that anyone should ever favour representationalism.
Moreover, the arguments of Wittgenstein, Ryle and Austin
against Cartesianism, the theory of ideas and sense-data,
were generally supposed to have removed whatever temptations
there might have been to locate the intellectual subject
within an inner realm insulated from immediate contact with
the world – engaging only with internal objects and
inferring, or otherwise supposing, external causes. Someone
raised in the tradition of these philosophers might
reasonably observe of current philosophy of mind: 'it is as
if they had never written – every achievement seems to have
been forgotten'.

The explanation of the revival of what Fodor calls the
'Representational Theory of Mind' is, very roughly, as
follows. Wittgensteinean-cum-Rylean philosophical psychology
is, or seems to be, a (refined) variety of logical
behaviourism. Folk psychology meanwhile often explains

behaviour by reference to logically prior, operative, cognitive and conative attitudes which the former view construes as dispositions to react in certain ways. This latter suggestion invites several objections but for present purposes it will be sufficient to mention the following. The programme of providing corresponding behavioural–disposition predicates in place of psychological ones shows no sign of even getting under way – a failure explained by the simple but crucially important fact that the individuation of the relevant behavioural types is psychologistic. There is no coherent way of distinguishing patterns of action in terms that can be made sense of in the explanation of what an individual is about other than by reference to the types of psychological attitudes such behaviour expresses. Purposeful behaviour is engaged in for reasons, on the basis of beliefs and desires, so that reference to the former presupposes effective mental states. Furthermore, these states are productive of action in virtue of their interactions one with another and often through practical reasoning. Some psychological elements are best explained in dispositional terms, e.g., standing beliefs and desires, but the behaviour in which such states issue depends upon other episodic mental features. Accordingly, occurrent thoughts, endowed with semantically related contents, cannot be eliminated.

What is called for therefore is an account of mind that recognizes the reality and causal role of mental states. Type identity theories meet this condition but are inadequate for familiar 'variable realizability' reasons. The need, then, is for some account which achieves the following:

(i)    Permits abstraction from particular physiology.

(ii)   Connects psychological states to a) sensation, b) behaviour, and c) one another.

(iii)  Allows the various subject/world transactions to correspond systematically to the informational content of 'internal' states.

Where this has been taken to lead is to a theory that conjoins functionalism with what by itself it fails to provide: an account of content – usually derived from the model of information computation favoured by A(rtificial) I(ntelligence) research. Thus, to instantiate (occurrently) a particular psychological attitude, to believe that p, or to conceive of a, say, is on this account to be in a certain functional state involving a relation with some internal item possessed of information in virtue of its syntactical properties. Such, in general, and in rough, is the argument for the new versions of what is, in essence, an old theory of mind.

Further specification is in order since questions remain to be answered about the character of the system of mental attitudes: what gives them their content? how do they interact? what is their relation to the external world? and so on. As in earlier days these questions are taken to be answered by the proposal that mental activity consists in the manipulation of words (and images). Independent arguments are available to support this representationalist hypothesis. Psychological attitude reports are relational in form and often propositional (or pictorial) in content. They involve individuating and characterizing components; feature attitude–types, e.g., believing, desiring, hoping etc.; and are expressable by oratio obliqua constructions. Moreover they have satisfaction conditions, exhibit logical and semantic relations and in general give good reasons for concluding that what are being reported are quasi–linguistic states.

Finally, there is the consideration that communication involves the employment of artificial signs – marks and sounds that are themselves 'dead' but which in use 'have life breathed into them'. Wittgenstein asks: how is this possible?(27) and the present theory answers that they are animated by having bestowed upon them the intentional content of the representational states which they express. Furthermore, it takes this solution to provide additional support for the claim that in thought the mind (or some sub–personal component) is directed upon internal objects, viz: tokens, inner language Mentalese (and again, pictorial images).

This conclusion immediately prompts a range of objections to the theory's coherence and to its idealist implications. At the same time, however, the line of argument that yields it commands serious attention. For its premises are individually plausible and it does at least proceed in the direction of a solution to the problem of the relationship between mind and world. The appropriate response therefore is to identify the truths it approaches, refute its errors, and then accommodate the former within an alternative account of cognition. The completion of that project cannot be achieved here but it can be begun, and with the assistance of Reid and Aquinas an outline of its general structure may be sketched.(28)

V

The suggestion that words are artificial signs of things and have meaning in virtue of association with intrinsically intentional natural signs in the mind is as old as Aristotle(29) and is the central assumption of scholastic epistemology and semantics. Since the most complex system of instrumental signs is linguistic it is tempting to suppose that what underlies it is also linguistic – hence the language of thought hypothesis. But while the dependency thesis is compelling and is endorsed by Reid,(30) the further conclusion is absurd for a reason which he makes clear in another (earlier) context. He writes:

> Let us suppose that ideas represent things as signs, just as words and writing are known to stand for all things. Allow then that the mind is provided with ideas, not like a camera obscura with pictured images but in the manner of a book written and gone to press, informing us of many external, past and future things. Even this will not solve the problem however, for who will interpret the book for us now? If you show it to an uneducated man who has never heard of letters he doesn't even know that they are signs much less what they signify. If you address someone in a language unknown to them your words may mean something to you but to him they are meaningless. Signs without an interpretation signify nothing.(31)

If thoughts bestow significance upon speech acts they cannot themselves be regarded literally as words, or else a regress ensures with content being accounted for at each stage by reference to a prior meaning-investing element of the same sort as that whose meaning was taken to be extrinsic and derived. There is reason to posit natural signs given that conventional representations are not intrinsically contentful; but there is equally good reason to suppose that however the former signify it is not after the manner of words or pictures. Certainly it is intelligible and even appropriate to describe thought in these terms given its role in the explanation of both language and pictorial representation, but such descriptions can only be analogical.

Aquinas observes this fact when discussing the nature of conceptual thought:

> That which is conceived by the intellect is called an interior word, for it is the interior word that is signified by the spoken word, for the exterior word does not signify the intellect itself, nor the intelligible form, nor the act of thinking itself, but the concept of the intellect, by means of which it signifies the thing: as when I say 'man', or 'man is an animal'.(32)

Likewise, Reid notes a parallel point in connection with imagination, remarking upon the naturalness of analogical descriptions of mental acts but warning against the serious errors that result from then proceeding to regard them as literally true (in this case: concluding that imagining involves images):

> Of all the analogies between the operations of body and those of the mind, there is none so strong and so obvious to all mankind as that which there is between painting, or other plastic arts, and the power of conceiving objects in the mind ... In vain should we attempt to avoid this analogical language, for we have no other language upon the subject; yet it is dangerous, and apt to mislead.(33)

The passage quoted from Aquinas is also of interest in connection with the previously discussed issue of a possible historical influence of scholasticism on Reid, for it makes implicit reference to two important elements of the Thomist theory which feature prominently in Reid's discussions of Conception, Abstraction and Judgment.(34)

The first of these is the distinction between simple and complex (i.e. propositional) thoughts; acts which Aquinas terms 'thinking of simples' or 'simple apprehension' (intelligentia indivisibilium), and 'compounding and dividing concepts' (compositio et divisio) respectively; and which, as the quotation observes, are manifest in different kinds of utterances. Reid similarly insists upon the fact, and importance, of such a distinction between mental operations, and also characterizes it by reference to the types of grammatical constructions involved in the expression of these acts:

the words conceive, imagine, apprehend, have two
meanings and are used to express two operations of
the mind, which ought never to be confounded.
Sometimes they express simple apprehension, which
implies no judgment at all; sometimes they express
judgment or opinion ... The ambiguity is indeed
remedied, in a great measure, by their construction.
When they are used to express simple apprehension,
they are followed by a noun in the accusative case,
which signifies the object conceived; but, when they
are used to express opinion or judgment, they are
commonly followed by a verb, in the infinitive mood.
'I conceive an Egyptian pyramid'. This implies no
judgment. 'I conceive the Egyptian pyramids to be
the most ancient monuments of human art'. This
implies judgment. When the words are used in the
last sense, the thing conceived must be a
proposition.(35)

The second common element in Thomist and Reidean
epistemologies indirectly adverted to in the quotation from
Aquinas is their shared belief that certain psychological
items naturally signify features of the world and that these
are the foundation of cognition – whether in thought or
through language. As was seen, Reid recognizes that basic
mental phenomena cannot be such as logically to require an
interpretation by their possessor, and so is moved to reject
theories which regard such phenomena as being akin to
pictures or words. In the Philosophical Orations III from
which the earlier quotation was drawn Reid's argument is an
essentially negative one. Indeed, he might be read as
arguing against the very coherence of the notion of
intrinsically significant signs, i.e. ones the semantic value
of which is in-built and which therefore require no
interpretation or assignment of significance, as do pictorial
and linguistic representations. However, it is clear that
his objection is not to the claim that certain mental
phenomena are 'about', or intentionally directed upon,
aspects of the world but rather to particular philosophical
accounts of how this is possible.

Furthermore, by the time he came to publish I, and later
IP, Reid was explicit in espousing the view that cognition
involves states of the person which are natural signs of
extra-mental features and which directly suggest these
features to their owner. This view was cited earlier at the
point where I suggested a parallel between claims made by

Reid, and others advanced by the most distinguished of his
scholastic predecessors at Glasgow, John Major.(36) In the
section of the Inquiry devoted to natural signs, Reid
distinguishes three classes of these:

> [First] those whose connection with the thing
> signified is established by nature, but discovered
> only by experience [e.g., smoke and fire]...[second
> those] wherein the connection...is not only
> established by nature, but discovered to us by a
> natural principle, without reasoning or experience
> [e.g. expressive behaviour and psychological
> states]...[and third, those] which, though we never
> before had any notion or conception of the thing
> signified, do suggest it, or conjure it up [e.g.,
> sensations and qualities of objects].(37)

Both the two-fold division of signs into those whose
significance is inductively inferred (class one) and those
for which no interpretation is required but are directly
significant for the subject (classes two and three), and the
examples given throughout Reid's writings, are familiar
features of scholastic treatises on semantics and
semiotics.(38)   Where Reid differs from his realist
predecessors, however, is in his failure to offer any account
of how it is possible for there to be signs of the latter
sort. Indeed, he several times confesses to having little
understanding of the character of 'natural language' (i.e.
non-conventional significance) and does no more than to
indicate the direction of innate endowment as its source,
suggesting that it may be part of "the original constitution
of our minds". For example, he writes:

> [In perception] there is something which may be
> called the sign, and something which is signified to
> us ... by that sign ... Thus, when I grasp an ivory
> ball in my hand, I have a certain sensation of
> touch. Although this ...[has] no similitude to
> anything material, yet, by the laws of my
> constitution, it is immediately followed by the
> conception and belief that there is in my hand a
> hard smooth body of a spherical figure.(39)

In contrast to Reid's disavowal of any attempt to give an
account of natural cognitive significance, Aquinas tackles
directly the issues of mental content and intentional
reference, recognising them to be the central elements of

realist epistemology. The conclusion at which he arrives is
that thoughts have significance by expressing concepts which
are mental counterparts of forms existing in nature.

Thus, when he speaks of species in the mind as images,
similitudes, likenesses and imitations of aspects of reality
the relation he is concerned with is one of formal or
qualitative identity, and not some kind of pictorial
resemblance. He writes as follows:

> When our intellect conceives the character of a
> thing existing outside the mind, there occurs a
> certain communication of the thing, inasmuch as our
> intellect receives, in a certain mode [i.e. in esse
> intentionale] the form of it.(40)

> Hence the intelligible species is a similitude of
> the very essence of the thing, and it is in a
> certain way the very character and nature of the
> thing according to intelligible existence, and not
> according to natural existence as it is in
> things.(41)

> Thus it is by means of a likeness of a visible thing
> that the faculty of sight operates, and similarly
> the likeness of an object of thought is operative in
> intellectual activity.(42)

Aquinas prefaces the last of these passages with the
observation that mental acts are immanent, i.e., unlike
transitive actions, they have no effects beyond themselves.
The medieval origins of this distinction were mentioned
earlier in connection with Reid's use of scholastic
terminology in the presentation of his arguments on behalf of
realism. What should be noted now is that this particular
distinction can again be employed in the service of the same
cause: as providing a reply to the kind of argument for
representationalism advanced by Fodor in the short passage
quoted in section II (and offered by others in the same
tradition). For the expression 'to represent' suffers
process/product ambiguity, and one may well represent Marvin
without there being an entity – a representation – distinct
from this activity and standing as a tertium quid between
one's thought and Marvin. There is, in other words, a
coherent notion of mental representation, as an intentional
cognitive activity, which is compatible with direct realism.
It is the notion characterized by Aquinas and Reid as 'the

immanent processes of conception and judgment'.

This proposal in turn suggests a response to the further representationalist claim that the intentionality of thought requires the introduction of internal relata (ideas) to fill the gaps in cases where nothing in reality corresponds to the indicated object — a claim strengthened by the further consideration that intentional objects may be general or indeterminate. Reid subscribes to an objectual view of intentionality in order to maintain realism and insists that thought can be of the non-existent, the general, and the indeterminate. Yet he rejects the claim that the problem cases necessitate the provision of mental objects.(43) Unfortunately no positive account of the matter is given, but, as before, if we turn to Aquinas a solution is forthcoming. According to this, intentionality is taken to be the property of having mental direction — of aiming (intentio) this way or that. Of course there need be nothing standing at the point indicated though the state has an intentional content, i.e., a conceptual character provided by the species that inform it. This is the sense in which thoughts are always about something. They always involve general features structuring consciousness and thereby directing it. On such a view the only substantial objects of thought are real things, and on occasions the conceptual content of mental acts themselves — be these latter simple or complex.(44)

## VI

In section III, I defended Reid against accusations of deliberately misrepresenting and plagiarizing writers of his own day. Notwithstanding that I have argued that there are striking similarities between his views and opinions held by philosophers of the middle ages, it is not my purpose to substitute in place of the former accusations similar charges in respect of his relationship to his scholastic predecessors. Nor do I wish to suggest that he has nothing to add to their earlier attempts to understand the intellect and its operations. Rather the position seems to be that Reid saw clearly in Seventeenth Century representationalism a flawed and ultimately disastrous philosophy of mind and epistemology.(45) He then set out to refute its presuppositions, and to put in its stead a version of naturalistic psychology which views the intellectual subject as embedded in the world and understands thought as arising from a person's transactions with his environment. The mind is not a storehouse of words or pictures but a set of capacities for abstracting concepts from experience and exercising them through the formation of intentional states whose content is manifest in the use of signs.(46)

This said, the theory bears a remarkable resemblance to that of St. Thomas and later scholastics: and from the language, structure and content of Reid's arguments it is impossible to resist the conclusion that, notwithstanding his criticisms of it, he was influenced by the philosophy of the schools. This is not, however, a matter of his simply resurrecting the skeleton of the older realism and dressing it in a style suited to the times. More likely it is a case of someone's trying to build a secure framework amidst what he believes to be the debris of past failures and who, to his surprise, finds that pieces from an earlier construction suit his purpose very well. Were he not so set in the belief that all before him had gone wrong such a person might wonder if the suitability of these components was not suggestive, and perhaps even speculate whether they might have been designed to fit a structure just like his own. That Reid fails to do this is not, I think, evidence of a lack of modesty but rather is testimony to his enthusiasm to be about the task of rebuilding epistemological realism. Current cognitive psychology and philosophy of mind are such that this task may again be necessary. What the history of philosophy shows is that anyone wishing to embark upon it would do well to consult the work of Reid and of his scholastic predecessors.

NOTES

(1)  This claim is made notwithstanding the attempt by
Berkeley to argue that neither Plato nor Aristotle admit the
existence of things other than ideas.  For this somewhat
unpromising interpretation of the ancients see Berkeley in
Luce and Jessop (1911, pp. 317–21).

(2)  Summa Theologiae, Ia, q85, a2.

(3)  **Corr** (Works, p. 88).

(4)  Fodor (1981, p. 225).

(5)  Schiffer (1981, p. 94).

(6)  See, for example, Summa Contra Gentiles, I, c53; and De
Potentia, q7, a9.

(7)  This title is one happily embraced in Fodor (1981, p.
26).

(8)  **IP** IV, III (Works, P. 376).

(9)  **I** I, VIII (Works, p. 104).

(10) **IP** II, viii (Works, p. 268).

(11) Cf., **IP** I, i (Works, p. 226); II, vii (Works, p. 263);
IV, ii (Works, pp. 368ff).

(12) **IP** II, xiv (Works, p. 301).

(13) **IP** II, vii (Works, p. 263) – emphasis mine.

(14) Haldane and Ross (1967, p. 161).

(15) Cf. Summa Theologiae Ia, a85, a2 with **IP** I, ii (Works,
p. 232); also Summa Contra Gentiles IV, c11: "some sciences
are about things and others are about understood intentions"
(i.e. concepts), with **IP** VI, i (Works, p. 414) where Reid
writes: "There are notions or ideas that ought to be referred
to the faculty of judgment as their source ... to those ...
capable of reflecting upon its operations they are obvious
and familiar".  A proper understanding of this reflective

activity provides a reply to the famous anti–abstractionist argument in Geach (1971) and to the claim therein that Aquinas is not an abstractionist. I discuss these issues in Haldane (1984).

(16) **IP** II, xiii (Works, p. 297).

(17) Emphasis mine. Cited from Des Vraies et des Fausses Idees in McRae (1965, p. 181).

(18) **IP** II, xiii (Works, p. 297).

(19) See Kemp Smith (1902, p. 117); and from Reid's own period, the oft referred to comments by the unnamed translator of the 1790 edition of Buffier's Traite des Premieres Verites.

(20) Cf., **IP** II, xiii (Works, p. 296); VI, viii (Works, p. 468); and **AL** VI, ii (Works, p. 713).

(21) For bibliographical information see Durkan (1950). I am grateful to the librarians of the Universities of Aberdeen and Glasgow for confirming that volumes of Major's writings were in their libraries when Reid was teaching in these institutions.

(22) Cited from Liber Terminorum, I in Broadie (1983, p. 235).

(23) In primu Sententiarum, 3, q2. Cited by Hamilton in his notes to his edition of Reid (Works, p. 815).

(24) **IP** II, xi (Works, p. 289).

(25) **I** V, iii (Works, pp. 121–2).

(26) **IP** IV, iii (Works, p. 374).

(27) Wittgenstein (1976, p. 432).

(28) The philosophical issues are further explored, with some references to the views of Aquinas and Reid, in Haldane (1987).

(29) De Interpretatione, 16a, 2–6.

(30) Cf. **IP** I, v (Works, p. 238); IV, i (Works, p. 361); V,

ii (Works, p. 391); and **AL** I, iv (Works, p. 685).

(31) Philosophical Orations III; translated from Humphries (1
. 35).

(32) De Potentia, I, q9, a5.

(33) **IP** IV, i (Works, p. 362).

(34) **IP**, IV–VI.

(35) **IP** I, i (Works, p. 223).

(36) Since writing this  I have had  the opportunity to  read
Broadie (1986)  in which  he explores  parallels between  the
work of Major (and his circle) and the realism of Reid.

(37) I V, iii (Works, pp. 121–2).

(38) For something  of  the history  of these  subjects,  see
Deely (1982).

(39) **IP** II, xxi (Works,  p. 332).   Cf. I IV, ii (Works,  pp.
117–9); **IP** II, xx (Works, pp. 326–330); and VI, v  (Works, p.
450).

(40) De Potentia, q2, a1.

(41) Quodlibetum, VIII, q2, a2.

(42) Summa Theologiae, Ia, q85, a2.

(43) Cf. **IP** I, i (Works, p. 224); II, xx (Works, p. 327); IV,
ii (Works, pp. 369 and 373–4); V, iii (Works, pp. 394–5); and
V, vi (Works, p. 408).  For some useful discussion of Reid's
position on these issues see Prior (1971), ch.8).

(44) Summa Theologiae, Ia, IIae, q90, a1.

(45) **Corr** (Works, pp. 88  and 91); and  **IP** II, x (Works,  pp.
281–2).

(46) **IP** I, i (Works,  p. 221); III,  vii (Works, pp. 355  and
359).

SECTION 4 – AESTHETICS, MORAL AND POLITICAL PHILOSOPHY

Peter Kivy

## SEEING (AND SO FORTH) IS BELIEVING (AMONG OTHER THINGS); ON THE SIGNIFICANCE OF REID IN THE HISTORY OF AESTHETICS

I

Although it may seem self-serving to say so, I think it altogether appropriate that a discussion of Thomas Reid's significance in the history of aesthetics be included in a conference commemorating the bicentenary of the Essays on the Intellectual Powers of Man. Because Reid, I shall argue, represents a very important 'first' in the history of aesthetics; and it is in the Essays on the Intellectual Powers that that 'first' is first achieved.

Philosophers since Plato have talked about art (or some of the arts) with their philosophical hats on. But no philosopher of the first rank made the philosophy of art a substantial part of his system, with the possible exception of Plato (if Plato can be thought to have had the concept of art at all), until Reid: more specifically, until Reid included, as the final essay of the Essays on the Intellectual Powers, an essay 'Of Taste'.

In modern times, Leibniz and Descartes wrote, here and there, about art; but neither made art a central or systematic concern. If Hume can correctly be described as having a system, the philosophy of art was not a substantial part of it, although Hume wrote small works on aesthetics, and philosophical remarks on art are scattered throughout the Treatise, both Enquiries, and the essays. Francis Hutcheson wrote a treatise devoted exclusively to the subject: perhaps the first. But Hutcheson, as good as he was, was not a philosopher of the first rank. Nor was Alexander Baumgarten, although he was a systematic philosopher and wrote an extended treatise on aesthetics as part of that system. Berkeley, a philosopher of the first rank, made some very perceptive remarks on beauty in Alciphron. But even if Berkeley could correctly be described as having a system, which he cannot, these remarks could not be seen as constituting a part of it.

The fact is, I believe, that the first philosopher of the

307

*M. Dalgarno and E. Matthews (eds.), The Philosophy of Thomas Reid, 307–328.*
*© 1989 by Kluwer Academic Publishers.*

first rank to make the philosophy of art a part of a
philosophical system, or, if you prefer, a part of an
extended chain of philosophical reasoning, is Thomas Reid;
and that is my theme.

But I would hardly have agreed to speak here if all I had
to commemorate was the fact that Reid did something first. I
doubt if I would feel inclined to memorialize the first
anti-Semite, or the first person to fly across the Atlantic
ocean upside down. For a first, clearly, to be a memorable
first, it must be something worthwhile. Reid might well have
been the first philosopher of rank to include aesthetics in
his system, but have had, in the event, nothing of
philosophical interest to say about it. Such, however, is not
the case. What Reid said was original, and valuable,
amounting to something like the culmination of a major trend
in Enlightenment philosophy of art.

But I think something further must be the case for me to
feel it appropriate to commemorate Reid's accomplishment in
the philosophy of art both for its priority and its
importance. I see no reason for calling attention to the fact
that Reid was the first philosopher of rank to make
aesthetics part of an extended philosophical system, even if
it was a valuable piece of work, if its being a part of the
system had nothing to do with its content and value. Why
bother to mention the former at all, except perhaps in
passing? Why not just commemorate the fact that Reid said
something of value for the history of aesthetics and talk
about that? The reason I wish to talk about, and commemorate,
both must be, of course, because I think there is an
important philosophical connection between them: that, in
other words, the inclusion of aesthetics in his philosophical
system had the result of making it the valuable contribution
that it turned out to be. To be more specific, philosophical
insights that Reid had in the philosophy of perception
spilled over into the essay 'Of Taste', broadening and
deepening it.

My theme, then, is more than just that Reid was the first
philosopher of the first rank to include aesthetics in his
system. It is also that that was in part what made it
valuable and original. But before I can make this out, some
extended preliminary considerations must be put forward, with
regard to Reid's most important predecessors in the
philosophy of art, Francis Hutcheson and David Hume. For
Reid's accomplishment is the final fruition of their work,

and not possible without it. It is not some product of solitary genius: that was not the stuff of which Reid's intellect was made.

## II

I begin with a distinction of very recent vintage, which I hope will help to illuminate what I take to be the general evolution of theories of aesthetic perception in Britain, starting with Hutcheson and culminating, so I shall argue, in Reid. In a paper called 'Analysing Seeing', Frank Sibley wrote, a few years ago:

> Certain accounts of perception, particularly some recent ones, may be seen by an admitted simplification as developing or defending one or other of two opposing positions....
>
> These opposing accounts both concern not what is seen but seeing itself....The accounts may conveniently, if not very accurately, be labelled respectively "epistemic" and "non-epistemic". The former attempts to analyse seeing (or perception generally) in terms of belief (or knowledge) or the acquisition of beliefs. According to it, an analysis of seeing things or events necessarily involves reference to believing-that, or to seeing-that, which in turn is analysed, partially at least, in terms of believing-that. It is not held, generally, that seeing-that can occur without seeing things or events; but it is held that the former notion is the fundamental one.
>
> The opposing account holds that there is some basic seeing (or perceiving) that is "non-epistemic", i.e. does not necessarily involve acquisition of beliefs (or knowledge) and can be adequately analysed without reference to the concept of belief at all.(1)

Without imagining that this distinction between epistemic and non-epistemic perception can be applied with anything but an approximate fit to the theories I will be discussing here, it nevertheless serves to mark out an important respect in which Francis Hutcheson's view of how beauty is perceived, at least as presented in the first edition of the Inquiry Concerning Beauty, differed from the view of Reid, as formulated in the

Essays on the Intellectual Powers; and it serves also to mark
out the steps that intervened. In effect, my thesis is that a
gradual evolution can be discerned, from the basically
non-epistemic theory of Hutcheson, to the unqualifiedly
epistemic theory of Reid, with Hume as the intermediary.
And, I shall argue, it was Reid's systematic treatment of
perception in general that enabled him to make
philosophically explicit and unequivocal what, even in the
most mature reflections of Hume, remained for the most part
unspoken and to be inferred. In that sense, Reid put the
capstone on eighteenth-century British aesthetic theory, at
least in so far as it was a theory of perception.

## III

Hutcheson's view, at least in 1725, as I see it, was
something like this. Beauty, as he put it, "is taken for the
idea raised in us, and a sense of beauty for our power of
receiving this idea".(2)   The idea of beauty, which he
sometimes characterized as something like the Lockean idea of
a secondary quality, and sometimes as a pleasure, was caused
to be aroused, he thought, by a quality of objects that he
called uniformity amidst variety. And he made it unmistakably
clear, at least in his earliest and most influential
statement of the view, that the connection between the
quality and the idea is completely untainted by knowledge or
belief; that is to say, the idea of beauty is caused to arise
without the observer either having to know or to believe that
the object being perceived possesses the quality or that such
a quality has any relation to beauty, or even that such a
quality exists. As Hutcheson expressed this crucial point:

> But in all these instances of beauty let it be
> observed that the pleasure is communicated to those
> who never reflected on this general foundation, and
> that all here alleged is this, that the pleasant
> sensation arises only from objects in which there is
> uniformity amidst variety. We may have the sensation
> without knowing what is the occasion of it, as a
> man's taste may suggest ideas of sweets, acids,
> bitters, though he may be ignorant of the forms of
> the small bodies, or their motions, which excite
> these perceptions in him.(3)

In this sense, then, Hutcheson's theory of the perception of
beauty is a non-epistemic one. The quality in objects that

causes the idea is in his view analogous to the micro-structure of matter — "the forms of the small bodies, or their motions" — that cause, without, of course, our necessarily knowing of or believing in their existence and causal efficacy, such sensations as those of the sweet, the sour, and the bitter.

What must first strike us about this representation of the matter, and, indeed, must even have struck Hutcheson in later years, is how counter-intuitive the non-epistemic aspect really is. It certainly does not sound wildly implausible to claim that the perception of the beautiful is at least in part the experience of the pleasurable, and that uniformity amidst variety is at least one of the qualities in objects giving rise to that kind of pleasure. But what we take to be happening is that we become aware of the quality and enjoy our experience of it. We take the object to have this or that relation of parts, and find enjoyment in it. This is even more apparent when the object is not some simple kind of thing, like a coloured pebble, or geometrical figure, but a poem, or a painting, or a musical composition. The perception of beauty, we are forced to believe, is deeply epistemic, at least where the objects of perception are works of art, or things of comparable complexity.

I have said that Hutcheson himself must later have perceived this defect in his theory, and have emphasized that what I am giving here is to be taken only as a reading of the first edition of the Inquiry Concerning Beauty, because there is evidence, in his later works, and even, to a very small degree, in later editions of the Inquiry, of a shift towards a more plausible epistemic view. I wish I had time to go into this matter more deeply here; but we have other fish to fry. Yet I cannot leave it completely unexplored, for it is germane to my thesis.

In a recent article on Hutcheson's theory of aesthetic perception, distinguished both for its thoroughness and its acuity, Emily Michael has given an analysis at variance, in certain crucial respects, with the one I have given above, and from ones I have given elsewhere.(4)   For present purposes, it is important to note only that her account implies, although she does not herself draw the inference explicitly, an epistemic construal of Hutcheson's theory. Thus she writes in one place:

Hutcheson repeatedly tells us that the particular

> regularity which excites a sensible idea of beauty
> in our minds is an apprehension of uniformity;
> aesthetic pleasure is perceived upon finding
> uniformity among sensible qualities that were
> previously received and compared.(5)

I take it that 'apprehend' and 'find' must be understood here
epistemically: that is to say, to apprehend or to find
uniformity amidst variety in something is to come to know, or
at least come to believe that the uniformity amidst variety,
under some relevant description or other, is there. And so,
on Michael's interpretation, the uniformity amidst variety
does not cause aesthetic pleasure in us the way light of a
certain wave-length, reflected off an object with a
particular micro-structure, causes the sensation of redness,
but more like the way my perceiving that you are angry at me
might cause me to be afraid. It is, indeed, a much more
sensible view of the matter. But is it Hutcheson's view, as
expressed in the first edition of the first Inquiry?

My answer must be 'no'. There is no way that that work
can be interpreted epistemically; and, indeed, I do not find
a single passage in it that suggests anything but a
non-epistemic account of the perception of beauty. And this
claim is fully supported by the fact that all of the passages
Michael adduces, suggesting to me an epistemic position, are
from Hutcheson's later works, beginning with the Essay on the
Nature and Conduct of the Passions and Affections of 1728.

There are two ways one can treat a philosopher's texts:
as all of a piece, expressing one integrated point of view;
or as evincing some sort of intellectual development. Michael
has treated Hutcheson's philosophical works in the former
way; I believe they must be treated in the latter, for I can
see no way of bringing the early Inquiry Concerning Beauty
into conformity with the later works on the question of
whether the perception of beauty is epistemic or
non-epistemic: the Inquiry Concerning Beauty clearly presents
us with a non-epistemic theory, while the later works (quite
sensibly) seem to be moving towards an epistemic one. This
neither surprises nor disappoints me. For as I read the
history of aesthetics in eighteenth-century Britain, the
direction of thought was obviously from the non-epistemic to
the epistemic, on quite reasonable grounds; and Hutcheson,
who was a reasonable man, must no doubt have come to see the
problem with the non-epistemic view, both in his
self-critical moments, as well as under the critical

influence of Balguy, Price, Berkeley, and Hume. I cannot go into this evolution of Hutcheson's own thought fully here.(6) But I must go on to say something about Hume, who, I believe, brought matters to the point where Reid could put the very important finishing touches on the developing epistemic theory of aesthetic perception.(7)

IV

I shall distinguish three stages in the evolution of Hume's theory of aesthetic perception, each a step away from the non-epistemic theory of Hutcheson's Inquiry Concerning Beauty. They are: Book III of the Treatise (1740); the Inquiry Concerning the Principles of Morals (1752); and 'Of the Standard of Taste' (1757).

We can, at a certain level of abstraction, characterize Hume's view of the perception of beauty, in the Treatise, as Hutcheson's pretty much all over again. Hutcheson said that the word beauty is taken for the idea raised in us; Hume would have said that the word beauty is taken for the sentiment raised in us. Hutcheson said that this idea was caused to be raised in us by a specific quality in objects, known to him; Hume said that this sentiment was caused to be raised in us by a particular quality in objects known to him.

But as soon as we compare the quality Hutcheson thought arouses the idea of beauty with the one that Hume thought arouses the sentiment, we see directly that their theories, for all of their surface similarity, are already diverging. Hutcheson's quality is uniformity amidst variety, which looks, on first reflection, as if it might plausibly "cause" the idea of beauty to be aroused, in the sense in which a certain wavelength of light, reflected off the surface of an object with a particular micro-structure, causes me to have the sensation of redness. At least before we think carefully about it, a non-epistemic account seems possible with this kind of quality as the cause of the idea. Hume, however, thinks the quality which causes the sentiment is utility: the use which an object might have, and the sympathetic identification one might have with the pleasure its usefulness would bring to the person who possessed it. And it is impossible to think, even in the most unreflective moment, that such a quality could arouse the appropriate sentiment in us the way poison ivy makes us itch. We must perceive that an object has a certain utility before we can be pleased by it. Nor does Hume leave this inference for us to draw; he makes it quite explicit himself, where he says, for example:

> A fertile soil, and a happy climate, delight us by a
> reflexion on the happiness they wou'd afford the
> inhabitants...; [or, again, in] Most kinds of
> beauty...tho' our first object [of perception] be
> some senseless inanimate piece of matter, 'tis
> seldom we rest here, and carry not our view to its
> influence on sensible and rational creatures.(8)

Can there be any real doubt that "reflexion" and "carry...our
view to" are epistemic: that they imply we must come to know
or believe something is useful, and what its use is, before
that supposed use can give rise to the sentiment of beauty?
In spite, then, of his general agreement with Hutcheson, Hume
is already committed, in the Treatise, to an epistemic theory
of how we perceive the beautiful.

What is noticeably lacking in Book III of the Treatise is
any discussion at all of works of the fine arts, the more
surprising in Hume than in Hutcheson, where such discussion
is hardly extensive, although not totally lacking, because
works of art provide a fertile field for an epistemic account
of aesthetic perception, while being recalcitrant to a
non-epistemic one. This obviously became apparent to Hume
later on, for in the second Enquiry we begin to get examples
drawn from the fine arts, rather than from nature or human
artefacts, to illustrate the perception of the beautiful. And
it is of particular significance for my argument that what
Hume is at pains to emphasize, when he talks about art in the
Enquiry Concerning the Principles of Morals, is the role of
reason in perceiving it. Thus he writes in one place:

> Some species of beauty, especially the natural
> kinds, on their first appearance, command our
> affection and approbation; and where they fail of
> this effect, it is impossible for any reasoning to
> redress their influence, or adapt them better to our
> taste and sentiment. But in many orders of beauty,
> particularly those of the finer arts, it is
> requisite to employ much reasoning, in order to feel
> the proper sentiment; and a false relish may
> frequently be corrected by arguments and
> reflection.(9)

Hume maintained, in the Treatise, as well as in the second
Enquiry, a distinction between beauty that speaks immediately

to the sense, for no apparent reason, and beauty which, as he says in the passage just quoted, requires "much reasoning" for its perception.(10) The 'immediate' beauty may well be a lingering vestige of Hutcheson's influence: a similar distinction still survives in Reid. But it is the epistemic perception of the beautiful that becomes the centre of philosophical interest for Hume; and that, it seems to me, more than anything else, sets the stage for Reid's attempt to make the perception of the beautiful (and the sublime) part of a general theory of perception explicitly epistemic in character.

Hume tells us in the second Enquiry, as we have just seen, that "much reasoning" is requisite for the perception of beauty in "the finer arts". What do we reason about? We must turn to Hume's dissertation, 'Of the Standard of Taste', to get at the few hints of an answer that, alas, are all Hume left us.

What we are calling the 'epistemic' perception of beauty Hume maintained in the Treatise to be the arousing of a sentiment upon the apprehension of utility. It should come as no surprise, then, that in 'Of the Standard of Taste' Hume at least suggested that it is functional properties of works of art that we must apprehend in the perception of artistic beauty, and about which we acquire knowledge or belief. These functional properties are of two kinds: the parts of a work of art having specific functions within the work, that contribute to its overall effect; and the overall effect itself, that the artwork is intended to achieve – that is to say, its overall function. So, for example, the parts of a tragedy have their individual functions within the work, all contributing to the function of the work as a whole, which, let us say, for the sake of argument, is the arousal and catharsis of pity and fear. As Hume sketchily expresses the view in one place:

> In all the nobler productions of genius, there is a
> mutual relation and correspondence of parts; nor can
> either the beauties or blemishes be perceived by him
> whose thought is not capacious enough to comprehend
> all those parts, and compare them with each other,
> in order to perceive the consistence and uniformity
> of the whole. Every work of art also has a certain
> end or purpose for which it is calculated; and is to
> be deemed more or less perfect, as it is more or
> less fitted to attain this end.(11)

If there were any lingering doubts that Hume, in spite of his
choice of utility as the operative quality in the perception
of beauty, was giving, in the Treatise, an epistemic account
of aesthetic perception, such passages as this one in 'Of the
Standard of Taste' can leave no similar doubt at all about
the latter work. It is thought, Hume makes unmistakably
clear, that must deliver itself of conclusions about the
functions of art works and their parts before the proper
sentiment of beauty (or its opposite) can be expected to
arise.

If I am right, then, in my reading of the general drift
in theories of aesthetic perception in eighteenth-century
Britain, away from non-epistemic, causal theories like
Hutcheson's, towards a more plausibly epistemic theory like
Hume's, in 'Of the Standard of Taste', it seems natural to
expect Reid should eventually see the theory of aesthetic
perception as just another part of the general theory of
perception that he was developing, since that theory was to
be so distinctively epistemic itself. That, in any case, is
how I see the course of events; and it is now time to play
the last, climactic scene.

V

Reid's account of perception was already fully formed, in its
main outlines, in the Inquiry into the Human Mind, of 1764.
But there is no hint in that work of an attempt to make
aesthetic perception a part of the system. There are,
indeed, some scattered remarks on the fine arts; they are,
however, brief and disconnected, nor do they touch upon any
of the main points of what was later to be Reid's theory of
taste, except in the most perfunctory manner.(12)   If Reid
saw, at that time, any systematic connction between beauty,
sublimity, and any of the qualities of the external world
that a philosophy of perception must deal with, it was a well
kept secret.

In what comes down to us in a manuscript dated 1774 as
Lectures on the Fine Arts, there is a reasonably complete, if
rather sketchy, version of Reid's aesthetic theory.   And
there is, too, just the beginnings of the idea that this
aesthetic theory is not an appendage to Reid's philosophy,
but an integral part of it, at least in so far as that
philosophy is a philosophy of perception. I am thinking here
primarily of the place in the Lectures where Reid says that

> there is a judgment implied in every one of our
> perceptions. It is the same with regard to our
> taste....(13)

Granted, it is only the merest of suggestions; but it is the
linchpin connecting aesthetic perception with perception tout
court that both are to be understood epistemically; and
Reid's way of expressing that idea is always by saying that
in perception, be it the seeing of a red flag, or a beautiful
painting, there is judgment that something is the case. In
the Lectures, however, we merely have this vague suggestion;
in the Essays on the Intellectual Powers we have the fait
accompli. So let me turn, finally to the object of our
celebrations.

It would be an act of sheer folly for me to lecture this
learned company on Reid's philosophy of perception; and I am
much too old a dog to commit it. But never mind; it isn't
necessary anyway. What we need for present purposes is only
the general form; and that, I think, we can all agree on,
without getting into the niceties of interpretation at the
cutting edge of research.

The general shape of Reid's account of perception, as you
all know, is something like this. Let us say that I am
looking at a letter box: the American kind. In that case, the
following things are true of this simple case of perception,
on Reid's view.

(1)  I am having, among other sensations, a sensation of
blueness. This sensation is conceived of by Reid not as an
object but, rather, as an act or event. I am sensing
'bluely'; and, because the sensation is identical with the
act of sensing, the being of a sensation is the sensing of
it; the sensation is just identical with the sensing. You
can't have a smile without a smiling.

(2)  The sensation is a natural sign of a quality in the
object which it signifies. There are three kinds of natural
signs, according to Reid. There are learned natural signs,
as, for example, where clouds are a sign of rain, or smoke of
fire. There is the unlearned emotive language of mankind,
which also serves for Reid as the basis for what we would
call the 'expressive' properties of works of art, as where
facial expressions are signs of emotions felt. And, finally,
there are the unlearned signs that, by the constitution of
our nature, are signs to us of the existence of physical

objects and their qualities, existing independently of us. As Reid says:

> A third class of natural signs comprehends those which, though we never before had any notion or conception of the thing signified, do suggest it, or conjure it up, as it were, by a natural kind of magic, and at once give us a conception and create a belief of it...
>
> I think it is evident, that we cannot, by reasoning from our sensations, collect the existence of bodies at all, far less any of their qualities....It appears as evident that this connection between our sensations and the conception and belief of external existences cannot be produced by habit, experience, education, or any principle of human nature that hath been admitted by philosophers. At the same time, it is a fact that such sensations are invariably connected with the conception and belief of external existences. Hence, by all rules of just reasoning, we must conclude, that this connection is the effect of our constitution, and ought to be considered as an original principle of human nature, till we find some more general principle into which it may be resolved.(14)

The blue sensation, then, by an "original principle of human nature", functions as an unlearned, natural sign of the blue quality in the post box, conveying to us "the conception and belief" of its external existence.

(3) The act of perception, or perceptual event, in which I perceive the blue colour of the post box is a complex process in which I have a sensation, and in which that sensation, as sign, produces in me the conception of and belief in the external quality of blueness. It is because every perception contains, as a constituent part, the forming of some concept and belief of the kind described above that we can properly call Reid's general account of perception an epistemic one, although, of course, it differs in crucial respects from twentieth-century versions of the doctrine.

The general outline of this account, as I have said before, was already in place in Reid's Inquiry; indeed, the long passage that I just quoted comes from that work. But it was only after that that Reid came to realize, apparently, the possibility of including aesthetic perception, along with taste, touch, smell, hearing, and sight, as another special case. In the <u>Essays on the Intellectual Powers</u>, the account of the two aesthetic qualities universally recognized by eighteenth-century British writers — that is, beauty and sublimity (or grandeur, as Reid prefers) — are treated, as far as they allow, in exactly the same way as other perceptual qualities of the external world. Let us see how, for the quality of beauty, Reid does this, with direct reference to the three 'truths' about perception enumerated and explicated above.

The general shape of Reid's account of the perception of the beautiful goes something like this. Let us say that I am listening to a beautiful tune (or air, as Reid would say). In that case, on Reid's view, the following things are true of this simple case of aesthetic perception.

(1a) I am having, among other sensations, a sensation of beauty, whose main distinguishing feature is its pleasureableness. Reid calls it sometimes an "agreeable emotion." I need say no more about this except to add that, presumably, Reid would analyse the sensation of beauty, like other sensations, adverbially: that is to say, as an act or event.

(2a) The sensation of beauty is a natural sign of a quality — Reid calls it an "excellence" — in the object, which it signifies. Reid says:

> The sense of beauty may be analysed in a manner very similar to the sense of sweetness. It is an agreeable feeling or emotion, accompanied with an opinion or judgment of some excellence in the object, which is fitted by Nature to produce that feeling.(15)

The sensation of beauty, then, like all other sensations (of a veridical kind), by "an original principle of human nature", functions as a sign of a quality of beauty in the tune, conveying to us "the conception and belief" of its external existence.

(3a) The act of perception, or perceptual event, in which I perceive the beauty of the tune, is a complex process in which I have a sensation, and in which that sensation, as sign, produces in me the conception of, and belief in, the external quality of beauty. It is because every perception of beauty contains, as a constituent part, the forming of some concept and belief of the kind described above that we can properly call Reid's account of the perception of the beautiful an epistemic one.

I need only add here that Reid's account of our perception of sublimity or grandeur follows exactly similar lines. There is sensation, concept, judgment – the lot. What differentiates the two is the quality of the felt sensations, and the nature of the external features of the world that they signify. But the general outline is the same. So with regard both to the perception of the sublime and of the beautiful, in other words, with regard to aesthetic perception across the board(16), we can say that Reid finally made philosophically explicit what had been lurking in the background since Hume's Treatise and (I suspect) Hutcheson's own second thoughts about his position in the first Inquiry: namely, that aesthetic perception must, at least in the interesting and sophisticated cases, be through and through epistemic and concept-laden.

We cannot, however, let the matter drop with that rather optimistic conclusion. For when it came to working out the details of his aesthetic theory, which, so far, we have presented only in its broadest outlines, Reid did not always go in the right direction. Sometimes there is real insight into the way his epistemic theory must work in order to be an appreciable improvement over Hutcheson's non-epistemic account, whereas sometimes he seems to leave himself open to the same kinds of difficulties, epistemic theory notwithstanding. I shall conclude by making a preliminary exploration of these vagaries, although I do not have the time here and now to do the thorough job I would like to do, and which Reid's theory requires.

## VI

To illustrate that Reid's position on aesthetic perception, epistemic though it is, can fall prey to some of the same objections one might raise against Hutcheson, let me revert, for a moment, to a passage previously quoted, rather unfavourable in this regard. Reid, you will recall, compares the perception of beauty to the perception of secondary qualities like tastes of the palate. The sense of beauty, he says, may be analysed in a manner very similar to the sense of sweetness. But if we take this literally, it does very little good for Reid to add the characteristic epistemic rider that "It is an agreeable feeling or emotion, accompanied with an opinion or judgment of some excellence in the object, which is fitted by Nature to produce that feeling." For what we need is not merely the assurance that having the idea of beauty (as Hutcheson calls it) brings along with it the conviction or belief that something out there, a je ne sais quoi, is the cause, and is really beautiful. Where the knowing or believing, the conceptualizing, must come in is temporally, or at least epistemically, prior to the act of sensation. I must first come to believe or know some things about what I am looking at or listening to before the enjoyable sensation or emotion can arise, and the knowing or believing must have something to do with its arising. If uniformity amidst variety is the operative quality, then I must perceive that relation of parts in the object, at least under some relevant description or other, in order to aesthetically appreciate or enjoy it – which is, of course, what Reid's sensation or emotion of beauty comes down to. It is there, not in some conviction temporally or epistemically subsequent to the sensation, that the epistemic component must lie, if Reid's theory is to be an improvement, in this respect, over Hutcheson's.

But perhaps we have taken Reid's analogy between beauty and sweetness too literally. In a more favourable passage, Reid gives us pretty much what we have just been demanding of an epistemic account. He writes:

Beauty or deformity in an object, results from its nature or structure. To perceive the beauty, therefore, we must perceive the nature or structure from which it results.(17)

Assume again that the "nature or structure" alluded to is Hutcheson's uniformity amidst variety. If that is the case, then Reid is saying just what we thought was appropriate to say in the circumstances and what Hutcheson certainly was not saying: that prior to our having the sensation of beauty – at least in the epistemic sense of 'prior', if not in the temporal sense as well – we must perceive that the object before us has uniformity amidst variety (or whatever the aesthetically operative 'nature or structure' might be). That is the cash value of saying that "To perceive beauty, therefore, we must perceive the nature or structure from which it results". And it is in that prior perception of the nature or structure from which beauty results that we must

locate the epistemic moment of the perception of beauty, or
at least the most important part of it. Without that we have
made only nominal progress away from Hutcheson, and towards a
truly epistemic account of aesthetic perception.

What is somewhat perplexing about this insightful passage
is that, immediately after the insight occurs, Reid seems to
back off from it, as if he does not thoroughly understand
what he has just said, and, quite perversely, attributes the
discovery of the view to Hutcheson who, if I am right, held a
view quite inconsistent with it. Having stated that we must
perceive that 'nature or structure' of an object responsible
for its beauty prior to perceiving the beauty itself, Reid
adds:

> On this account, Dr. Hutcheson called the senses of
> beauty and harmony reflex or secondary senses;
> because the beauty cannot be perceived unless the
> object be perceived by some other power of the
> mind.(18)

It should be noted straightaway that Hutcheson only started
to use the terms 'reflex' and 'secondary' with regard to the
sense of beauty in his later works, where he was already
himself turning away from the non-epistemic position
expressed in the first edition of the first Inquiry; neither
term ever occurs in the first edition of that work, so far as
I can remember. Nevertheless, Hutcheson certainly thought,
right from the beginning, that you must first perceive an
object (and that means, I presume, perceive it under some
description or other, take it to be some kind of thing)
before you can perceive its beauty. But if it appears that
Reid is equating that modest claim with the one he has just
made, he is either paying Hutcheson a compliment he does not
deserve, or misunderstanding his own position in an
unfavourable way. Perhaps it is a little bit of both: new
ideas, after all, are born with difficulty; and it is
comforting both to put at least some of the blame for them on
someone else, as well as to make them seem more like the old
and familiar than they really are. In any event, all that
Hutcheson was saying is that in order to perceive the beauty
of an object, one must first perceive it as an object under
some description; and he was expressly denying that one need
perceive it under the description 'varied and yet unified'
for the idea of beauty to be aroused. Whereas Reid was saying
quite expressly that one must perceive an object under just
that description which includes mention of the 'nature or

structure' responsible for the object's beauty in order to perceive that beauty; in order, that is to say, to feel the sensation of the beautiful. It is not a restatement of Hutcheson's view but an insightful departure from it in the direction of a more plausibly epistemic account of the perception of the beautiful.

The important, and disturbing, question, however, is whether the view I have attributed to Reid here is really consistent with his theory of aesthetic perception when given out as a special case of the general theory; for the former places the epistemic part, the knowing or believing, prior to the act of sensation, whereas the latter places it as subsequent, or at least as simultaneous. Let me conclude by worrying this question just a bit.

There are at least two ways to go here in arguing for the consistency of Reid's position. The first would be to see the claim that we must perceive the nature or structure of an object before perceiving its beauty as being independent of the claim that in every perception of beauty there is knowledge or belief conveyed by sensation. On this interpretation, what happens in the perception of beauty is something like this. I perceive the nature or structure of an object that is responsible for its beauty: (say) uniformity amidst variety. In perceiving that nature or structure, I feel the pleasurable sensation of the beautiful; and that sensation leads me to knowledge of or belief in some excellence in the object.

But what is the 'excellence'? It cannot be the nature or structure, the uniformity amidst variety, for I have already perceived that, and formed a belief in its existence. It must be some other excellence, perhaps the excellence of which uniformity amidst variety is the sign, namely, the designing mind. For, on Reid's view, material things cannot be truly beautiful, but only beautiful as reflections of the mental, which itself is the only thing beautiful in the literal sense. Thus, "if we consider...", Reid says,

> ...the beauty of form or figure in inanimate objects, this, according to Dr. Hutcheson, results from regularity, mixed with variety. Here, it ought to be observed, that regularity, in all cases, expresses design and art: for nothing regular was ever the work of chance; and where regularity is joined with variety, it expresses design more

strongly.(19)

This interpretation works well enough, I suppose; but I can't work up much enthusiasm for it. For it seems to me that Reid's really important contribution to the subject is <u>both</u> his recognition that aesthetic perception is through <u>and</u> through epistemic, <u>and</u> his recognition that such qualities as <u>uniformity amidst variety</u> do not function as causal properties, in Hutcheson's way, but as properties recognized and enjoyed: in other words, perceived epistemically. And if all of Reid's crowing about the role of knowledge and belief in the perception of the beautiful is not in reference to knowledge and belief in these qualities, his theory loses some of its claim to insight and originality. I would prefer an interpretation that can give me a more original and insightful Reid; and I think there is one.

Reid distinguishes between two ways in which beauty is perceived: "the first we may call instinctive", he says, "the other rational". Instinctively, "Some objects strike us at once, and appear beautiful at first sight, without any reflection, without our being able to say why we call them beautiful, or being able to specify any perfection which justifies our judgment..." But there are "judgments of beauty that may be called rational, being grounded on some agreeable quality of the object which is distinctively conceived, and may be specified".(20) And it is important to note, Reid adds, apropos of this distinction, that instinctive and rational perceptions of beauty usually interpenetrate one another, so that in any given case both are operative and difficult to disentangle:

> Although the instinctive and the rational sense of beauty may be perfectly distinguished in speculation, yet, in passing judgment upon particular objects, they are often so mixed and confounded, that it is difficult to assign to each its own province. Nay, it may often happen, that a judgment of the beauty of an object, which was at first merely instinctive, shall afterwards become rational, when we discover some latent perfection of which that beauty in the object is a sign.(21)

If I understand Reid correctly on this point, something like the following kind of thing is often taking place when an adult human being perceives a beautiful object. At first, it strikes him, he knows not why, as beautiful, which is to say, he finds himself sensed to beautifully; and this sensing, as a sign, leads him to the belief in some excellence in the object as its cause. (This is the instinctual part of the process.) But his interaction with the object will not cease here: rather, he will begin immediately to perceive that nature or structure, <u>uniformity amidst variety</u>, let us say, that does in fact constitute the excellence in the object responsible for its beauty. And in perceiving it, he will begin to enjoy its presence, to savour it, so to speak; in other words, he will be further sensed to beautifully. This is the beginning of the rational part of the process. Just the beginning, however; for there is no reason to think that further sensing will not lead to further or renewed conviction in the excellence inhering in the object; nor reason to think that this further or renewed sensing will not lead to further discoveries about the nature or structure of the object's aesthetic features. The perception of the beauty will thus tend to widen and prolong itself, with pleasurable emotion and epistemic perception of the nature or structure of the object mutually interacting one with the other, the richness and duration of the process, of course, determined by the complexity of the object of perception, and the ability of the perceiver to respond to it.

Of this process of perception, I can say that it is through and through epistemic in just the way that I would like to. The nature or structure of the object is what I must perceive, epistemically, prior to my pleasurable emotion or sensation of the beautiful. But the sensation or emotion nevertheless <u>is</u> the sign of just that nature or structure, because after the emotion is felt it drives me to return to the object to further perceive, epistemically, its nature or structure. Therefore, it is perfectly compatible with Reid's doctrine, on this interpretation, to understand his insistent claims regarding the omnipresence of knowledge or belief in the perception of beauty to be claims to the effect that it is the nature or structure of the object which these beliefs are about. It is only in the instinctive perception of the beautiful that this interaction of emotion with object with emotion again is lacking. But that need not bother us much: for instinctive perception of the beautiful, when it occurs in the complete absence of the rational perception of beauty, occurs, for all intents and purposes, only, as Reid puts it, "in brute animals, and in children before the use of reason..."(22) Wherever it occurs in interesting cases, it occurs along with rational perception; and in such cases, there is all the room required for epistemic perception to play its vital part.

This interpretation of Reid has the advantage of representing his doctrine in the very best light possible. Indeed, when I reflect on my own experience of the beautiful, and other aesthetic qualities, it seems to me that what Reid has said, on this interpretation, is not only interesting, but very largely true. I wish I had time to pursue that thought further. But I fear I have tried your patience too much already. Reid enthusiasts though you all are, you may by now have learned more about this particular aspect of Reid's philosophy than you wanted to know. I only hope that you have not learned <u>less</u>.

NOTES

(1) F.N. Sibley, 'Analysing Seeing,' in Sibley (ed.) (1971), p. 81.

(2) Hutcheson (1973), p. 34 (I, ix).

(3) *Ibid.*, p. 47 (II, xiv).

(4) Principally in my book (1976); and my recent article (1984), p. 247.

(5) Michael (1984), p. 247.

(6) I am not the first to see an evolution in Hutcheson's views on various topics. See for example, Scott (1900).

(7) I have spelled out Hume's views in this regard more fully than I have time to do here in my (1984), pp. 198–208.

(8) Hume (1978), pp. 585 (III, iii, 1), and 363 (II, ii, 5).

(9) Hume (1975), p. 173 (I).

(10) See Hume (1978), p. 617 (III, iii, 5).

(11) David Hume, 'Of the Standard of Taste', in Hume (1963), pp. 245–246.

(12) For the curious, these remarks are to be found in the following places: I, IV, ii, (Works, p. 117); V, iii, (Works, pp. 121–122); VI, viii (Works, p. 147); VI, xxii (Works, p. 190).

(13) Reid (1973), p. 37.

(14) I, V, iii (Works, p. 122).

(15) IP, VIII, iv (Works, p. 499).

(16) Reid did recognize, too, the category of "novelty" in works of art and other aesthetic objects, as had others before him. But it did not interest him, nor play much of a role in his position on aesthetic perception, just because it was a relative notion. What is new to one man, may not be so to another; what is new this moment,

may be familiar to the same person some time hence, **IP**, VIII, ii (Works, pp. 493–494). Not being a 'property', it was not subject to Reid's 'critique' of taste, and was thus dismissed as "but a slight impression upon a truly correct taste".

(17) **IP**, VIII, i (Works, p. 492).

(18) Ibid.

(19) **IP**, VIII, iv (Works, p. 505).

(20) **IP**, VIII, iv (Works, pp. 500–1).

(21) **IP**, VIII, iv (Works, p. 501).

(22) **IP**, VIII, iv (Works, p. 500).

Henning Jensen

# REID VERSUS HUME: A DILEMMA IN THE THEORY OF MORAL WORTH

> In short, it may be established as an
> undoubted maxim, that no action can be
> virtuous, or morally good, unless there be
> in human nature some motive to produce it,
> distinct from the sense of its morality.(1)

This single statement from Hume's Treatise goes very far towards locating the main issues which divide Hume and Reid in their moral theories. Reid is certainly correct in observing that many of Hume's reasonings on the subject of morals are founded on the above maxim. It is central to Hume's theory of moral worth, to his explanation of how moral judgments are practical, and to his arguments to show that justice is not a natural but an artificial virtue. But this maxim which Hume holds to be undoubted, Reid pronounces "undoubtedly false" and goes on to give it his strongest censure. Identifying it as a doctrine maintained only by Epicureans, he says it "savours of the very dregs of that sect". He continues:

> It agrees well with the principles of those who
> maintained, that virtue is an empty name, and that
> it is entitled to no regard but in as far as it
> ministers to pleasure or profit.(2)

The arguments presented by Hume and Reid respectively for and against the above maxim may be viewed as disclosing the existence of a dilemma which tends to continue to underlie our thinking about moral worth. In what follows I want to show how this dilemma emerges from their arguments in the conviction that doing so will contribute significantly to our understanding of their moral theories and will prepare the way for suggestions as to how the dilemma may be resolved.
The first horn of the dilemma which we shall disclose is that which adopts the maxim of Hume's under consideration. The framework in which this maxim appears and the consequences of its adoption may be outlined as follows. Hume takes over a framework which was largely supplied by Francis Hutcheson. As in Hutcheson's case, when Hume's moral sense theory is conjoined with his theory of motivation the results are

*M. Dalgarno and E. Matthews (eds.), The Philosophy of Thomas Reid, 329–340.*
*© 1989 by Kluwer Academic Publishers.*

conceptually catastrophic.(3)  These undesirable results  may
be viewed as being  generated by Hume's  combining a view  of
moral judgment as the  disinterested approval of a  spectator
with a strong insistence  that morality is practical in  that
it influences actions and  affections.  Problems appear  when
it comes to explaining how morality is practical – how  moral
judgments and  moral  sentiments  influence action.       If
benevolence or  some other  natural motive  such as  parental
affection is the motive  to virtuous or morally good  actions
which are  approved by  a disinterested  spectator, then  the
moral sentiment  is  in danger  of  being superfluous  as  an
action guide.  The consequence is that Hume gives an  account
according to which conscientious  action or action  motivated
by a sense of duty is either wholly impossible or  is given a
very implausible  explanation.   That the sense  of duty  can
never be  a motive  to virtuous  or morally  good actions  is
really the thrust of an argument of which Hume's maxim is one
of the  premises.    This  argument, although not  rendered
explicit  by  Hume, emerges  quite  unmistakably from   his
materials and may be restated as follows: What we.ought to do
is to perform  virtuous actions  – actions giving  rise to  a
sentiment of disinterested  approval.  But  no action can  be
virtuous, or morally  good, unless there  be in human  nature
some motive to  produce it,  distinct from the  sense of  its
morality.  The motives which  are distinct from the sense  of
the morality of  actions and  which are in  fact approved  as
virtuous are such natural motives as benevolence and parental
affection.   Therefore, what  we ought  to do  is to  perform
actions from  motives,  distinct  from  the  sense of  their
morality, such  as benevolence  and parental  affection.   It
follows, similarly, that any action performed simply out of a
sense of its morality  cannot be virtuous and, hence,  cannot
be our duty.(4)

     If we suppose that the  above is an accurate account  of
Hume's doctrine, what are we  to make of his contention  that
it is no  objection to  this doctrine to  maintain that  "the
sense of morality or duty  may produce an action without  any
other motive"?(5)  H.A.  Prichard  is convinced  that in  so
contending Hume has  simply abandoned his  view that we  only
think an act to be a duty if it would  be virtuous.(6)  But I
believe that Prichard is mistaken and that Hume's account may
be saved from inconsistency.  Hume says:

     When any virtuous motive or principle is common  in
     human nature, a person, who feels his heart  devoid
     of that motive, may  hate himself on that  account,

and may perform the action without the motive, from
a certain sense of duty, in order to acquire by
practice, that virtuous principle, or at least, to
disguise to himself, as much as possible, his want
of it.(7)

An outline showing that the above is consistent with the rest
of Hume's doctrine might proceed as follows. Whereas actions
from motives such as benevolence and parental affection give
rise to our disinterested sentiment of approval, this
approval, which is a kind of pleasure, may in turn give rise
to a desire for such approval and for the performance of
those virtuous actions which are approved. Such a desire is
the motive when we act from a sense of duty or morality. The
sense of duty is thus derivative from or parasitic upon our
having the full-blooded motivation, such as benevolence, for
acting virtuously. Actions motivated solely by the sense of
duty could have no virtue or moral worth in themselves, but
would have moral worth only in serving as the required means
to promoting, facilitating, and acquiring virtuous
principles. Without any relationship to the motives,
distinct from a sense of duty, which produce moral actions,
acting from the sense of duty would degenerate into hypocrisy
and observance of the outwardly respectable.

Hence Hume is saved from inconsistency. There is
nothing inconsistent in maintaining that our duty is to do
virtuous actions, i.e. actions from motives such as
benevolence which are distinct from duty, and in maintaining,
at the same time, that acting out of a sense of duty or
regard for virtue may be required as a means to the end of
doing virtuous actions. However, although saved from
inconsistency, Hume is now seen to be defending a very
curious and questionable account of the sense of duty and of
the practical, action-guiding character of moral judgments.
On his view, actions motivated solely by a sense of duty can
never be virtuous or have moral worth if considered simply in
themselves and not as means to the performance of virtuous
actions. And the practical, action-guiding character of
moral judgments and moral sentiments consists solely in their
giving rise to a regard for virtue, that is, to a desire for
acting from an approved motive. As regards the sense of
duty, Hume's account runs against our ordinary convictions
that actions done from a sense of duty have a moral worth
which is not simply derivative from and parasitic upon our
performing virtuous actions from a certain motive such as
benevolence. As regards the action-guiding character of

moral judgments, Hume's answer to the question 'What ought I
to do?' instructs me to do the action which, if and when I do
it, I will be doing from a certain motive. Concerning this
rather mind-bending view, W.K. Frankena remarks that "one can
hardly go about looking to see what motive he will be acting
from, if he does a certain action, as a way of determining
what to do".(8)

In overview, therefore, we see in the foregoing account
the implausible and paradoxical conclusions which follow from
arguments which include Hume's maxim as a key premise and
which have led us to describe the adoption of this maxim as
one horn of a dilemma. The limitations of our topic prevent
detailed reference to Hume's theory of justice. However, it
is important to note, as Reid argues, that this maxim also
underlies Hume's argument to show that justice is not a
natural but an artificial virtue. According to Hume, since
the motive for performing just acts must be distinct from a
sense of their morality and since no natural motive exists
for performing just acts, justice is an artificial virtue and
just acts are approved because they involve certain
conventions invented by men for their own well-being.

The second horn of the dilemma which we are disclosing
is that advocated by Reid, which consists in the denial of
Hume's maxim concerning the motivation which, according to
Hume, must be antecedent to a regard for virtue. We shall
proceed by considering the following: (i) Reid's arguments
directed specifically against Hume's maxim; (ii) the wider
framework of Reid's theory within which his denial of Hume's
maxim appears; (iii) the consequences of his rejection of
Hume's maxim.

In the arguments which he directs specifically against
Hume's maxim, Reid is mainly concerned with an attempt to
refute and provide counter-examples to a more general thesis
about the nature of moral judgment which, he believes,
underlies Hume's maxim. Reid ascribes to Hume the following
view:

> When we judge an action to be good or bad, it must
> have been so in its own nature antecedent to that
> judgment, otherwise the judgment is erroneous. If,
> therefore, the action be good in its nature, the
> judgment of the agent cannot make it bad, nor can
> his judgment make it good if, in its nature, it be
> bad. For this would be to ascribe to our judgment

> a strange magical power to transform the nature of
> things, and to say, that my judging a thing to be
> what it is not, makes it really to be what I
> erroneously judge it to be.(9)

In arguing against Hume, Reid begins by claiming that the
above thesis about moral judgment renders absurd some of the
indisputable principles of morals and common sense. For an
example of such a principle, he turns to scripture, quoting
from Paul: "Let every man be persuaded in his own mind. He
that doubteth is condemned if he eat, because he eateth not
of faith; for whatsoever is not of faith is sin;" – "To him
that esteemeth any thing to be unclean, it is unclean". Reid
interprets this passage as placing the sum of virtue in
"living in all good conscience", in acting so "that our
hearts condemn us not".(10) In support of such common sense
principles and against Hume's thesis concerning moral
judgment, Reid turns to consider the role of beliefs and
intentions in our moral judgments. He maintains that to be
called 'benevolent' an act must be done from a belief that it
tends to promote the good of our neighbour. Also, "nothing
is more evident", he maintains, "than that a man who tells
the truth, believing it to be a lie, is guilty of
falsehood".(11) Yet, he argues, Hume's thesis about moral
judgment would view such a role of beliefs and intentions as
absurd. Just as one cannot be benevolent without intending
the good of others or malicious without intending hurt, so,
Reid concludes, one cannot be virtuous without intending
virtue.

According to Reid, the fallacies which attend Hume's
arguments concerning moral judgment may be revealed by
drawing a clear distinction between two meanings of the term
'moral goodness'. The first ascribes moral goodness to an
agent on account of an action he has done. Reid adds that
although we call it a good action, "the goodness is properly
in the man, and is only by a figure ascribed to the action".
The second meaning is involved in our ascribing moral
goodness to actions "considered abstractly, without any
relation to the agent". An action which is morally good in
the latter sense is "an action which ought to be done by
those who have the power and opportunity, and the capacity of
perceiving their obligation to do it".(12) According to
Reid, this distinction between two meanings of 'moral
goodness' will now enable us to refute Hume's maxim and the
thesis about moral judgment which underlies it. Using this
distinction, Reid argues that although it is true that no

belief or judgment can alter the character of what is morally good in the abstract sense, the kind of moral goodness ascribed to agents depends very much upon the intentions and opinions of the agent.

Unfortunately, the above arguments against Hume are undercut disastrously by Reid's failure to recognize that the way in which beliefs and intentions function in judgments about the moral goodness of agents and their actions is not really inconsistent with the thesis about moral judgments against which Reid has been arguing and which he ascribes to Hume. Reid's error is a familiar one and arises out of confused thinking about the fact that an agent, as he deliberates and acts, is necessarily incapable of distinguishing between the moral goodness of his act in the subjective sense relating to himself as an agent and the moral goodness of his act in the objective sense which, as Reid says, belongs to actions considered abstractly without relation to agents. Such a distinction may be made by critics or observers, but not by the agent himself while he deliberates and acts. This will be evident as soon as one realizes that an agent cannot distinguish between his deliberating whether an action is morally good and his deliberating whether his belief that it is morally good is justified. As Leon Pearl has observed, "a person is not given different instructions when he is told to do what is morally right from being told to do what he believes to be morally right".(13)

It is a mistake, however, to conclude from the foregoing that believing that something is morally good makes it so. It is true that one of the conditions for the moral goodness of an act in the subjective sense is that an agent must have a certain belief about the moral goodness of the act in question. However, to maintain that an act is morally good in the subjective sense is not to maintain simply that the agent believes that this act is morally good in this same subjective sense. This would indeed be to violate the thesis ascribed to Hume about moral judgment by claiming that belief that something is so makes it so. Instead, to maintain that an action is morally good in the subjective sense is to maintain that the agent believes, after careful reflection on the available evidence, that this action is morally good in the objective sense or, in Reid's terms, the sense considered in abstraction from the agent. Hence, there is no sense in which the belief that an act is morally good makes it, in the same sense, morally good.

We may therefore conclude that the thesis concerning moral judgment which Reid ascribes to Hume is preserved. Furthermore, Reid believes that Hume's maxim concerning moral motivation rests upon the thesis about moral judgment. Hence, in failing to prove that there are moral judgments which are incompatible with the thesis about moral judgment, Reid has also failed to do what he set out to do, namely, to disprove Hume's maxim about moral motivation.

Although his arguments directed specifically against Hume's maxim have thus proved to be invalid, we may still look to Reid's theory of moral worth for the elaboration of a position which, even if not always directed specifically against Hume's maxim, concerns the implications of its denial. As a background for examining Reid's theory of moral worth, we should note briefly that he is an intuitionist in the sense that he believes we have intuitive or immediate knowledge of basic moral concepts and of the truth of basic moral principles. Two claims are central to his theory of moral worth. First, he claims that an appeal to our moral consciousness will reveal the presence of an underivative notion or conception of duty which, he says, "is too simple to admit of a logical definition".(14) Second, he claims that this appeal will also reveal the presence of one motive which, contrary to Hume's maxim about motivation, is not antecedent to morality and which is always present whenever actions are morally good. This motive is of course a regard for duty.

Several questions are now suggested by the fact that single actions may often be said to have a number of what C.D. Broad calls 'motive-components', using the term 'motive-component' to refer to any belief about an action which attracts one towards doing it.(15) One such question concerns whether dutiful actions may be overdetermined by being performed from the motive of duty together with some other motive, whether moral or non-moral. On this score, Reid maintains explicitly that, although a sense of duty may be the sole motive for an action, it may also concur with other motives or oppose them. If overdetermination is therefore possible, a further question arises concerning the respective weights to be given to motive-components. Reid's view is that moral goodness is greater in proportion as an act is done from the motive of duty and that it is greatest when it is motivated solely by duty and when, as he adds, "all other motives distinct from this are on the other side".(16) Because of the foregoing claim, we might expect

Reid to deny moral worth – as Kant does – to actions which are not performed from the predominant motive of duty. However, the position which Reid actually defends is that such primary virtues as love of God, love of neighbour, gratitude and justice are all, he says, "necessarily accompanied by the conviction of their being morally good".(17) We are left with the interesting possibility, which Reid does not discuss, that some actions which are performed for some predominant motive such as love of neighbour are morally good, provided the sense of duty is at least minimally a motive–component. It may be that Reid simply assumed that the motive of duty must always be predominant in dutiful action. However, since the possibility that it need not be is closer to our common sense judgments, it is exasperating that he did not discuss it.

In pressing for an overview, we may note that Reid's Essays on the Active Powers of the Human Mind appeared in 1788 three years after the publication in 1785 of Kant's Foundations of the Metaphysic of Morals. It is remarkable, therefore, that Reid, independently of Kant, presented what is perhaps the clearest and most sustained defence in modern philosophy of what Richard Henson, writing about one of two views of moral worth which he attributes to Kant, refers to as the 'battle–citation' view of moral worth.(18) On this view of moral worth, according to Henson, to attribute moral worth to a person is to say, in effect, that he has won a moral victory in untoward circumstances and against odds. In Reid's terms, such a person has acted from duty and all other motives were on the other side. This view no doubt has remoter origins in the Stoics in whom, as Reid says, "regard to the honestum swallowed up every other principle of action". It is of course most famous for the role it plays in Kant's moral theory. It is evident that Reid's version of the 'battle–citation' view of moral worth emerges as the result of his denial of Hume's maxim about moral motivation, of his subsequent emphasis on the sense of duty as the sole moral motive, and of his claim that the moral worth of overdetermined dutiful actions is in direct proportion to the weight given to the motive of duty.

Apart from its appearance in Reid, this 'battle–citation' view has been subjected to exhaustive criticism. On the positive side, it is generally agreed that there does appear to be a kind of moral assessment in which the moral worth of an action is increased by its being performed in untoward circumstances. But there is more to be

said on the  negative side.   The most formidable  objections
against it have become rather standard.   First, right actions
performed out  of  motives such  as  love or  compassion  are
normally ·judged  morally  preferable  to  the  same  actions
performed solely from  the sense of  duty.   Thus,  similarly,
recipients of help  prefer to  receive benefits from  someone
motivated by friendship, love, or gratitude rather than  from
someone motivated solely by duty.   A devout Christian such as
Reid is faced with an embarrassing consequence.  Although  he
claims that the  virtue of love  of neighbour is  necessarily
accompanied by  a regard  for  virtue, his  'battle–citation'
view commits  him to  holding that the  greatest moral  worth
resides in  actions in  which  the motive  of duty  has  most
weight and in which other motives, such as the love  extolled
by Christianity, have the least or,  ideally, none at all.   A
second  main  objection  is  that,  according  to  the
'battle–citation' view, whereas saints may have no  conflicts
to overcome,  here on  earth the greatest moral worth  would
have to be attributed  to the person,  who, in a state  which
must border on  the psychotic,  suffers unceasingly from  the
agonies of temptation to do wrong, but who always manages  to
act from  a sense  of  duty.   Worse still,  this view  might
suggest  that  since  greatness in  moral  worth is  surely
desirable, one  should  suppress,  as far  as  possible,  any
non–moral motives which cooperate with the sense of duty.  As
Richard Henson  observes, on  the  'battle–citation' view  of
moral worth, "it would in a way be better if  a person's acts
never had it,  because it would  be better not  to be in  the
sort of situation in which it is possible".(19)

     Reid's theory  includes  nothing that  would  meet  the
foregoing objections.   Thus, in the  light of our  arguments
that his  'battle–citation' view has  consequences which  are
extremely  puzzling  and which  go  against our  ordinary
judgments, we  can  only .conclude  that  Reid's  persistent
defence  of  this  view  represents  a  departure  from  his
characteristic commitment to common sense.

     This paper  has  been devoted  to  the disclosure  of  a
dilemma which  emerges from  the moral theories of Hume  and
Reid.   In brief outline,  the dilemma is as follows.   Hume's
defence of his maxim  concerning moral motivation is  crucial
to arguments leading him to a position according to which the
moral sentiment  is  in danger  of  being superfluous  as  an
action guide  and motivation  by a  sense of  duty is  either
wholly impossible  or given a  very implausible  explanation.
On the  other hand,  Reid's denial  of Hume's  maxim and  his

subsequent emphasis on the sense of duty as the sole moral motive are crucial to arguments leading him to defend a 'battle-citation' view of moral worth which is subject to formidable objections and is repugnant to common sense.

Recognition of the origins and nature of the above dilemma may itself be helpful in formulating a more acceptable theory of moral worth. The limitations of this paper suggest the folly of proposing summary solutions to issues requiring careful and painstaking formulation. With this disclaimer, the following comments are merely an invitation to such further thoughtfulness concerning the problem of moral worth.

One general comment suggested by an overview of the dilemma under consideration is that in their preoccupation with identifying predominant moral motives or, in some cases, a sole moral motive, moral philosophers have tended to neglect the possibility that many or even all moral actions might be overdetermined.

However, the most obvious and perhaps most usual way of challenging the above dilemma is to maintain that there are two different kinds of intrinsic goodness of agents and actions. The one is present when agents and actions are motivated by a sense of duty; the other is present when agents and actions are motivated by certain desires such as love or parental concern. Some, like Prichard, have recommended that the species of goodness involving the sense of duty be called 'moral' and that the other, involving intrinsically good desires, be called 'virtuous' but 'non-moral'. However, this restricted use of the term 'moral' has the unwelcome consequence that the value of morality is at stake when we prefer the ministrations of grandmothers who are spontaneously kind to those of unfeeling uncles acting solely from duty.

In addressing these problems, Sidgwick recognizes a certain "natural incompatibility" between those acts which are done from calculation and without natural warmth and those which spring from spontaneous warmth and kindliness. However, he maintains that, when confronted by such conflicts of dutiful calculation and spontaneous fervour, "Common Sense is somewhat puzzled which to prefer; and takes refuge in an ideal that transcends this incompatibility and embraces the two".(20) I leave to the reader the question whether the latter ideal, which embraces such disparate forms of moral

assessment, should be   viewed as a   well-earned refuge to   be
taken in   reward for   honest   toil or   whether it   should   be
viewed   as   an   escape   from   our   duties   to   seek   further
resolution of these vexing problems.

## NOTES

(1)  Hume (1958, p. 479).

(2)  **AP**, V, vi (Works, p. 667).

(3)  Cf. Jensen (1971).

(4)  Hume (1958), Book III, Part II, Section I, passim.

(5)  Hume (1958, p. 479).

(6)  H.A. Prichard (1949, p. 157).

(7)  Hume (1958, p. 479).

(8)  Goodpaster (1976, p. 158).

(9)  **AP**, V, iv (Works, p. 648).

(10) Ibid. (Works, p. 647).

(11) Ibid. (Works, p. 648).

(12) Ibid. (Works, p. 649).

(13) Pearl (1971, p. 416).

(14) **AP**, III, III, v (Works, p. 587).

(15) Broad (1952, p. 256).

(16) **AP**, V, iv (Works, p. 650).

(17) Ibid. (Works, p. 647).

(18) Henson (1979, p. 42).

(19) Ibid., p. 50.

(20) Sidgwick (1872, p. 213).

Peter J. Diamond

## REID AND ACTIVE VIRTUE

> To be drawn by study away from active life is
> contrary to moral duty. For the whole glory of
> virtue is in activity; activity, however, may often
> be interrupted, and many opportunities for
> returning to study are opened. Besides, the
> working of the mind, which is never at rest, can
> keep us busy in the pursuit of knowledge even
> without conscious effort on our part. Moreover,
> all our thought and mental activity will be devoted
> either to planning for things that are morally
> right and that conduce to a good and happy life, or
> to the pursuits of science and learning.(1)

It is far from apparent that Reid was much interested in the
contemporary Scottish problem of teaching men to live
virtuously in a modern commercial society. For his published
writings are almost all devoted to investigating the powers
and faculties of the human mind. Reid himself, in old age,
believed that his philosophy had merit insofar as it
questioned the theory of ideas, which he took to be the basis
for Hume's system of principles describing the mind's
operations.(2) I wish to suggest, however, that Reid's
preoccupation with the theory of ideas was part of his larger
concern with depicting a science of human nature, a project
which, he believed, would teach men the compass of human
power and enable them to "make great improvement, in
acquiring the treasures of useful knowledge, the habits of
skill in arts, the habits of wisdom, prudence, self-command,
and every other virtue".(3) The outlines of that science are
evident in his Glasgow lectures, although its traces may be
discerned in his Essays on the Intellectual Powers of Man and
his Essays on the Active Powers of the Human Mind.

I shall sketch the lineaments of Reid's science of human
nature by comparing it with Hume's 'science of man'. I shall
argue, first, that such a comparison suggests that Reid
cannot profitably be regarded as merely Hume's antagonist:
while he rejected Hume's commitment to the pursuit of virtue.
Second, that Reid differed from Hume because he believed that
a science of human nature ought to contribute directly and

341

*M. Dalgarno and E. Matthews (eds.), The Philosophy of Thomas Reid, 341–354.*
*© 1989 by Kluwer Academic Publishers.*

substantively, not just instrumentally (as Hume implied), to human improvement. Third, that Hume may consequently be regarded as a philosopher of civic virtue, but Reid's effort should be depicted in terms of his commitment to 'active virtue'.

Most scholars do not take Reid's modest avowal concerning the merits of his philosophy seriously, and rightly so. But his remarks do provide a clue to his intentions. For Reid was convinced that the deep-going scepticism arising from Hume's exposition of the ideal theory threatened the first principles of pneumatology, thereby jeopardizing the systematic study of human nature. Now Reid's objections must be understood in terms of his attempt to place philosophy on a law-governed (scientific) footing. He believed that progress in knowledge depends on reasoning from first principles. Although he did not join Turnbull in maintaining that general laws would guarantee certain knowledge – Hume, to Reid's satisfaction, had put an end to that belief – Reid did hold that if philosophy was subjected to the discipline of methodological first principles it would furnish a grammar by which to understand the 'languages of things themselves' as they appear to the human mind. This was the message of Reid's first two Philosophical Orations. 'Laws of practising philosophy' would, in Reid's estimation, provide criteria whereby true and legitimate works of philosophy could be distinguished from spurious ones and philosophy's status as a progressive science be made secure.(4) Flushed with confidence over Newton's methodological success in natural science, Reid was certain that philosophy could analogously progress toward a rule-governed condition, thereby facilitating moral and civic progress. Thus Reid proposed, in the second of his Philosophical Orations, that "experiments of the arts should be gathered and arranged in order, not only so that individual arts can be more readily perfected..., but also, and this is much more important, so that the streams of all experimenters can flow together from all directions into the sea of philosophy and render the philosopher more equipped both for tracing out the causes of things and discovering inventions useful to the human race".(5) The proper ordering he envisioned among the sciences began with the delineation of procedural rules – Reid's own regulae philosophandi – and moved on to pneumatology, ethics and then politics, the sequence of his Glasgow lectures.(6) That Reid devoted the bulk of his published and unpublished writing to studying the powers and faculties of the human mind is best understood in

light of his belief that, compared to the exact sciences,
pneumatology was yet in its infancy. By 1759, the date of
his third Philosophical Oration, Reid had decided that the
theory of ideas was the principal engine of Hume's scepticism
and had to be refuted and replaced by first principles
arrived at through introspection before pneumatology could be
of use to the improvement of reasoning.

   In spite of Reid's opposition to Hume's ideal theory,
which may be regarded (as I shall argue below) as a
disagreement over the means to human improvement, Reid
nevertheless shared Hume's belief that the purpose of
philosophy or of the science of man must be the pursuit of
virtue.(7) Hume, it is often remarked,(8) forswore the
comprehensive, systematic science of the Treatise upon its
lacklustre public reception in favour of the polite essay.
As an essayist, Hume preached as well as practised the civic
responsibility of belles lettres, discussing the moral
make-up of his readership and the manner and propriety of
enlightening them. When one recalls the terrifying
scepticism towards which the reader of Book I of the Treatise
was relentlessly led, the role Hume occupied in subsequent
essays was one of exquisite delicacy. The shift was dramatic
and not without irony. For, as Hume maintained in Book III
of the Treatise, the pursuit of virtue depends on men
recognizing that their self-interest recommends society.
"'Tis certain", he explained, "that no affection of the human
mind has both a sufficient force, and a proper direction to
counter-balance the love of gain, and render men fit members
of society, by making them abstain from the possessions of
others. Benevolence to strangers is too weak for this
purpose; and as to the other passions, they rather inflame
this avidity, when we observe that the larger our possessions
are, the more ability we have of gratifying all our
appetites".(9)

   Hume realized that, at its best, philosophy could
exercise a positive though highly limited role in the
reformation of character by teaching men to consult their
experience in everyday life. He saw himself as "a kind of
resident or ambassadour from the dominions of learning to
those of conversation" whose duties were two-fold. By
maintaining the learned world's ties to the commerce of
sensible conversation Hume hoped to rescue philosophy from
her unintelligible style and chimerical conclusions; by
providing such "topics of conversation fit for the
entertainment of rational creatures" as "history, poetry,

politics, and the more obvious principles, at least, of
philosophy", Hume wished to improve men's and women's
sensibilities for the tender and agreeable passions and
thereby defeat "the enemies of beauty and reason, people of
dull heads and cold hearts".(10) But the chief benefit of
philosophy "arises in an indirect manner, and proceeds more
from its secret insensible influence, than from its immediate
application".(11) Philosophers can offer no guidance on the
ends of life.

Although Reid attended carefully to the moral philosophy
of Hume's Treatise and of the subsequent essays, he remained
captivated by the stunning logic and sceptical conclusions of
Book I of the Treatise; he failed entirely to appreciate that
Hume in his later writings had granted the philosopher a new
and positive role in cultivating virtue. Yet, despite Reid's
misunderstanding, their disagreement was real and
far-reaching; but it concerned, largely, the means of
improvement. Reid wrote for the same highly literate
audience that cultivated the polite arts and sciences and he
believed, with Hume, that the truly virtuous life is lived by
cives whose private moral culture is reflected in the public
character of a nation. But he did not adopt the Addisonian
language of civic virtue which Phillipson has taught us to
associate with Hume.(12) There are important differences in
emphasis in their approaches to virtue which stem from Reid's
account of man's social acts of mind and which, at bottom,
reflect the Aberdeen and Glasgow contexts of his thought.
For Addison's language was more suited to the cultural life
of metropolitan Edinburgh than to the considerably more
closely-knit and clerically-dominated worlds of Aberdeen or
Glasgow.(13) Reid was by no means uncomfortable with the
Addisonian emphasis upon cultivating private virtue through
belles lettres and the cultural institutions of the
metropolis; these vehicles of improvement were also adopted
by the staunchly academic yet still-impoverished clerisy of
Aberdeen and the somewhat dour elite of Glasgow. But Reid's
vision of human improvement was framed in the distinctive
academic worlds of Aberdeen and (to a lesser extent) Glasgow,
and was in part to be effected through the scientific
education of young minds. Reid's thoughts on cultivating
civic virtue were not expressed in polite essays, but were
embedded in his pneumatological writings and were composed
for boys attending his lectures.

In contrast to Hume, who believed that civic virtue
depends upon the creation and nurturing of social intercourse

as a means of harnessing an individual's 'interest', Reid
assumed that man enjoys a natural (rather than 'artificial',
in Hume's sense) devotion to virtue, which proceeds directly
from his constitution.   He rejected Hume's attempt to
predicate "the first formation of society" on "a regard to
interest" by enunciating a non-reductive account of the
mind's active powers.   His theory effectively restored the
classical antithesis between reason and the passions and
denied the efficacy of a social theory based on
counter-vailing passions.(14)

    Reid intended that philosophy exercise a dual role
defined by the nature of man's intellectual and active
powers.   First, he believed that philosophy contributed
substantively to human improvement by informing men of the
nature and limits of their powers.   His essentially
Ciceronian commitment to such improvement was based on the
assumption that man is by nature active, that he possesses "a
power over the determinations of his own will", and that the
virtuous life is to be lived in accordance with the rational
determinations of his conscience. By providing men with a
"just knowledge" of these of his active powers, a task for
which pneumatology is eminently suited, Reid's philosopher is
obliged to explain "the powers, the faculties, the Operations
and the Nature of Minds as far as he can discover them by
reason and reflection".(15)

    Reid maintained that the principles of the human mind
thereby determined ought to underlie the sciences of ethics
and politics.(16)  Such powers, he observed, "are undoubtedly
given us by Nature for the discovery of truth and our
improvement in real knowledge ... Errors in judgment are not
the natural issue of our Reasoning powers, just as distempers
in the body are not the natural issue of its Texture".   They
are the result of prejudices and natural tendencies which
Bacon, in Novum Organum, and Locke, in Of the Conduct of the
Understanding, had warned against. Relying on Bacon, Reid in
his Glasgow lectures carefully recapitulated and extended the
former's account of the four 'Idols'.   Reid believed that
pointing out such defects is "the means of restoring the
rational powers to their natural Exercise".(17)   Here is
surely the most rationalist aspect of his thought.   Where
Bacon confined his doctrine to the world of learning,
believing it necessary "in moral and civil government ... to
set affection against affection and to master one by
another",(18) Reid regarded such "Idols of the Tribe" as
"party passion, vanity and the desire of victory" as defects

of the rational powers which are reparable through proper education.

Second, the thrust of Reid's Ciceronian approach is unceasingly didactic: among the fine arts he considered eloquence by far the most important, because it gives man a "noble and extensive command" over the minds of his fellow men. The calculus of improvement was for Reid straightforward: without society there can be no language, and men, consequently, would never learn to reason. "The tender charities of Husband and Wife, of Parents and Children, of Brothers and Sisters and near relations are as so many adamantine Chains that bind men in Society; and Society produces the gradual improvement and advancement of the human faculties".(19) Where Hume's civic morality depended on the capacity of the polite arts to leaven the passions, Reid believed that the cultivation of the specifically civic virtues depends on training the rational powers of the mind.(20)

There is considerable lack of agreement among scholars whether the moral, political and economic discourse among Scottish thinkers of the eighteenth century is primarily concerned with 'the practice of citizenship as an active virtue', and thus an extension or a replacement of what has come to be termed 'the civic humanist paradigm', or whether it is an attempt 'to establish the principles of human nature', and consequently a development of Continental civil jurisprudence.(21) Although I cannot here provide a full account of the appearance of both 'languages' in Reid's considerations on the science of man.(22) I shall suggest that Reid employed a discernibly civic idiom in his Glasgow lectures on politics and in certain of his Literary Society essays, but that his intention (unlike Hume's) in devising a science of human nature cannot be explained in terms of the civic humanist paradigm. Reid often pointed out that politics ("like most other branches of knowledge that relate to practice") may be treated as an art or as a science. He recognized the idiom of civic virtue to be particularly suited to describing the art of politics, in which men and states are understood in terms of their past. But the idiom disappeared when Reid considered politics as a science whose principles are "borrowed" from those of pneumatology, and it vanished entirely when he treated the subject of morals. I have accordingly sought to associate Reid's science with the cultivation of 'active virtue', thereby ridding it of the exclusively civic connotations which accompany Hume's thought.

It is not difficult to identify elements of the classical republican or Commonwealth ideology articulated, in Aberdeen, by Viscount Molesworth's followers, Fordyce and Turnbull. For Reid's lectures and essays on political matters, in their reliance upon and reaction to Hume's science, reflect a pattern of thought that was influenced by the civic writings of Machiavelli, Harrington and Montesquieu. The civic humanist paradigm requires that the human personality be regarded (in Pocock's words) as "that of a zoon politikon and fully expressed only in the practice of citizenship".(23) The paradigmatic form of political association is the classical republic, wherein the legislative, executive and judicial powers are balanced so as to ensure the preservation of public virtue. The paradigm also recognizes that citizenship may be threatened by the disintegration or corruption of the republic by the loss of its institutional balance: private, material interests, it was feared, would dissolve the moral commitment of citizens to participate.(24) Corruption might be forestalled by subordinating private concerns to the public good; Hume in particular believed that corruption could be prevented once citizens realized that their self-interest recommends public-spiritedness.

We know that Reid believed that preservation of the British constitution

> Has a tendency to a corruption of morals...[which] grows from the influence and the example of a Court, the manner in which elections and nominations to office are carried on, the number of oaths, the profanation of the sacrament in being made a qualification to a place, the abuse of liberty of speech and of the press, its degeneration into a spirit of licentiousness, the contempt of religion and of the clergy, the numbers that live a city life, the increase of trade which makes everything be bought or sold.(25)

Of course, Reid did not develop what Pocock has described as "the anti-Christian possibilities latent in the civic ideal"; indeed, Reid believed that an autonomous though disciplined clergy would help moderate the passions of an undisciplined citizenry. He apparently considered the question of whether "a proper church discipline" or the clergy itself might

supply the function of the censorial power in ancient
republics, but we do not know if Reid had a specific answer.
He recognized that the system of patronage obtaining in the
churches of Scotland and England had a tendency to corrupt
the morals of the clergy, "which must be followed by a
corruption among the people". In general terms, Reid was
predisposed to follow the strongly didactic approach of his
Aberdeen predecessors. He believed that ministers of
religion as well as magistrates could help promote and
preserve virtue in a state by educating its citizenry through
example.(26)

In questions concerning the art of politics, Reid
relied, largely, upon Montesquieu. Reid explained that as an
art, politics addresses, by means of historical inquiry, the
problem of "modelling and governing a state so as to answer
the end intended by it. The business of the politician", he
added, "is either to frame a model of government for a larger
or lesser political society. Or to preserve, repair, alter
or amend a government already formed".(27) Now, Reid was
always careful to point out that political reasoning
considers not what men may do, or what they ought to do, "but
what it may be expected they will do in the present weak and
corrupted state of human nature".(28) For Reid, the language
of classical republicanism was mostly an appropriate means of
depicting man as a zoon politikon in particular circumstances
– especially in his weak and corrupt state. He reckoned, in
the first of his Philosophical Orations, that among modern
philosophers, Machiavelli, Harrington and Hume had made
"strong progress" in political reasoning by not confusing
morals with politics (Reid chided Francis Hutcheson for
failing to heed the difference) and by relying upon "the
experience of past ages" and "the fate of the governments of
both ancient and modern peoples". Reid maintained that only
Montesquieu had outstripped them by setting forth "most
lucidly the causes, principles, and effects of laws, morals
and politics, from the first beginnings of human nature".(29)
He, too, wisely upheld the distinction between morals and
politics, thereby advancing the study of those arts by
stripping them of irrelevancies. The artistry of Reid's
predecessors consisted of attending historically to the
behaviour of men and states and of considering "the general
tenor of conduct common to [the] whole species" united in
political society.(30) They had not made politics a science,
but they had, to Reid's satisfaction, displayed a commitment
to an inductive search for political principles.

It is important to recognize that Reid understood  civic
discourse as situation-specific and that politics, as the art
of modelling  or  governing  a  state so  as  to  answer  its
intended end, reflects the historical contingency of  events.
Thus, he realized that  the British constitution – which  "is
more admirably  fitted  for  preserving the  liberty  of  the
Subject than  any form  of government that  ever existed,  or
even any model that ever was proposed, even Oceana itself"  –
"is the work of time and of accidents".(30)  Reid was acutely
aware, throughout  his lectures,  that the  poliical art  was
bound  in  time.   "If  the  Oceana  of  Mr.  Harrington  is
considered <u>in itself only</u>," he averred,

> Or  if  it  were  once  established  in  a   nation
> sufficiently enlightened, ... I  conceive it to  be
> the best  model of republican  government that  has
> ever been proposed. [Harrington] ... has united in
> one uniform and consistent  system the best  things
> in all  the ancient  republics as well  as that  of
> Venice.  I confess I think it difficult to conceive
> how any of  it could be  better contrived, <u>for  the
> time in which he lived.</u>(32)

Reid's  carefully  modulated  praise  was  meant  to  counter
Montesquieu's criticism  that  Harrington  had  erected  an
imaginary government  in  sight of  one possessing  the
sought-after  qualities.   He  argued,  much  as  Hume   had
done,(33)  that  Harrington's  agrarian  law  would  not  be
adequate security against an undue accumulation of wealth  in
the  hands of  one  or  a  few.   He  also  doubted  whether
Harrington's  model  offered  sufficient  provision  for
preserving that degree of  morals and public virtue which  is
necessary in a commonwealth.(34)   Reid observed a number  of
factors  which  differentiated  Harrington's  time  from  the
present:  the  improvement  in  such  arts  as  farming   and
manufacturing, the pursuit of  trade "carried to the  highest
pitch", the creation of  a monied interest distinct from  the
landed and  trading  interests, and  the invention  of  paper
credit; all led to the spread of luxury and to the corruption
of  public   morals.(35)   What  Machiavelli,   Harrington,
Montesquieu and  Hume  had  not  provided was  a  science  of
politics whose first principles were "borrowed" from those of
pneumatology.  Reid did not doubt that men could be  rendered
virtuous through good  laws, but he  was convinced that  such
laws would have to  be informed ultimately by the  scientific
understanding of the powers and operations of the human mind.

Reid did not (in his extant manuscripts) further discuss the properties of an art, perhaps because the distinction between an art and a science was well known to contemporary auditors.(36) It is important that although Reid envisioned a reciprocal relationship between an art and a science – an art may inform a science, which may improve the practice of an art – he also imagined a continuum along which an art might progress, by means of the inductive method, toward scientific status.(37)

The unmistakable implication of Reid's discussion of politics was that contemporary reasoning remained non-scientific because it was based on an imperfect grasp of the principles of human nature. Reid's meta-philosophical writings confirm the impression.(38) As pneumatology matures, yielding principles by which the nature and extent of human power will be more fully understood, political inquiry will, pari passu, "form much more certain conclusions with regard to the conduct of a body of men united in political society".(39)

Reid wrote little and published nothing about the nature of political science; his published works indicate that he believed his energies were best spent studying pneumatology and morals. But this should not be allowed to obscure the fact that Reid's conception of political science and its possibilities as an improvement-oriented discipline were dramatically out of keeping with contemporary, civic, approaches. For the political norms of civic humanist thought, as Pocock has explained, reflected a conception of political personality "which did not admit of change and so could only expect decay". Reid's view of human improvement presupposed both the fluidity of man's nature and the possibility that the science of politics, as part of the science of man, would effect change. Hume's civic approach, on the other hand, was grounded in the political maxim "that every man must be supposed a knave" until he becomes virtuous through enlightened self-interest.(40)

Thus, Reid's science of politics ultimately rejects the civic paradigm by denying that man is an entirely self-interested being and by asserting that in contriving a system of government, Hume's beliefs to the contrary notwithstanding, man ought to be reckoned a being capable, not of moral perfection, but of considerable improvement through the proper training of his 'social intellectual' powers. Although Reid believed that political science should

not consider questions concerning how men ought to act, he
did presume that the pneumatological grounding of such a
science would ensure that it be devoted to human improvement.
We must recognize, Reid pointed out, that man's 'social
intellectual' powers of mind dispose him towards what appears
to be his duty, and not just towards his own interest.
Purely civic discourse failed to inform the science of
politics adequately by neglecting those principles of human
action which tend to moral rather than merely civic virtue.
Where the art of politics could be expressed in a civic
idiom, for it concerns the modelling and governing of a state
according to a particular, historically-circumscribed end,
the science of politics must reflect an awareness that human
behaviour is not necessarily static. As a subset of the
science of man, Reid's political science seeks to transcend
the historical circumstances of man's moral corruption by
embodying first principles which reflect a progressive,
improvement-oriented view of human nature.

NOTES

(1)  Cicero (1913, p. 21).

(2)  Corr, Letter to James Gregory (Works, p. 88).

(3)  **AP**, I, vii (Works, p. 530).

(4)  Reid (1977, p. 946).

(5)  Reid (1977, p. 949).

(6)  Hume, at the beginning of his (1978), declared that his
"logic" would serve as the foundation for his science of man
and comprise two related but independent principles: the
first he described as the first principle of his new science,
what Reid termed the theory of ideas, the second, the
association of ideas.  Reid (Works, p. 102), regarded these
principles as nothing less than an attempt – a perverse
attempt to be sure – to devise "a complete system of the
sciences, upon a foundation entirely new, to wit, that of
human nature".

(7)  I shall follow eighteenth–century usage in interchanging
'philosophy' and 'science'.

(8)  Cf. Phillipson (1979, pp. 140–61).

(9)  Hume (1978, p. 492).

(10) Hume (1963, p. 570; Cf. pp. 3–7).

(11) Hume (1963, pp. 172–3).

(12) See Phillipson (1979).

(13) Although Glasgow was a city of merchants and
manufacturers, during Reid's tenure university life was
dominated by the Church.  Forty–eight percent of the
matriculated students of Glasgow University during the period
1765–74 entered the ministry, whereas just over twelve
percent turned to industry and commerce.  See Matthew (1966,
p. 85).

(14) See Hirschmann (1977, pp. 24–6; 31–42).

(15) AUL MSS 2131/4/II/1 and 2131/7/V/4.

(16) Ibid. I assume that pneumatology, ethics and politics together constitute Reid's science of human nature. However, Reid did not (I think) explicitly make this claim. But Reid's manuscripts suggest that he would not in principle have disagreed with this description.

(17) See AUL MS 2131/4/II/14. The reader is confronted, in Reid's manuscripts especially, with a panoply of the mind's powers, i.e. active, rational, social, social intellectual, which, in certain cases, overlap. Their variety reflects Reid's determination to counteract the "disposition in human nature to reduce things to as few principles as possible" (I, VII (Works, p. 206)). On the Baconian character of Reid's thought see AUL MS 2131/4/I/31.

(18) Quoted in Hirschmann (1977, P. 22).

(19) AUL MS 2131/4/I/31.

(20) See AP, III, II, viii (Works, pp. 577–8).

(21) See Pocock (1983, PP. 235; 246).

(22) Diamond (1985).

(23) Pocock (1983, p. 235).

(24) Robertson (1983, p. 138).

(25) AUL MS 2131/4/III/2.

(26) AUL MS 2131/4/III/9.

(27) AUL MSS 2131/4/III/3 AND 2131/4/III/1.

(28) AUL MS 3061/6.

(29) Reid (1977, pp. 937–8).

(30) AUL MS 2131/4/III/3.

(31) AUL MS 2131/4/III/8.

(32) AUL MS 2131/4/III/6, emphasis added.

(33) See Hume (1963, pp. 501–2).

(34) AUL MS 2131/4/III/6.

(35) See AUL MSS 2131/4/III/10 and 2131/4/III/17.

(36) For example, Dr. Johnson defined 'art' as skill, "the result of habit regulated by <u>rules</u>; as opposed to <u>science</u> which is determined by laws". Reid's usage (as well as Johnson's) conforms to the Aristotelian notion of <u>praxis</u>, and th refers to an activity which has as its object the good that is aimed at by action. Harrington also believed that the 'frame of government' depends upon art. See Harrington (1977, pp. 802-3).

(37) This is apparent in Reid (1977, pp. 934; 942; 949-56) where, despite the fact that he sometimes uses 'art' and 'science' interchangeably, he explained that "arts do not owe their origin to the laws governing them, but, on the contrary, laws arise from the progress and advanced state of the art itself".

(38) See Reid (1977, p. 955).

(39) AUL MS 2131/4/III/3.

(40) Cf. Hume (1963, pp. 40-47).

Kenneth Mackinnon

## THOMAS REID ON JUSTICE : A RIGHTS-BASED THEORY

Reid's account of justice follows the familiar pattern of ad
hominem arguments against Hume blended with an exposition of
an alternative theory.   The reasons for Hume's treatment  of
justice  as  an  artificial  virtue  are  well-known.    For
Hume,being just means to accord  to each what is his due,   as
of right,   under  the established  rules  of property.    Put
crudely, the  virtue  of  justice  lies  in  its  utility  in
maintaining property  as  a  bulwark  of stable  society;   its
artificiality  lies  in  its  dependence  on  the  man-made
conventions which  create property  rights.   Because of  the
attention it gives to property rights, Hume's theory has been
classified as rights-based in  contrast to theories based  on
need or  some sort  of  merit or  desert.(1)   However it  is
better to regard it  as a goal-based rule-utilitarian  theory
and to take  Reid's theory  as an example  of a  rights-based
one.(2)   Hume's goal  is  the  stability  of  property  and
society.   Individual rights are thus incidental to that goal.

In criticizing Hume's theory of justice, Reid argues that
its utility  is  insufficient  to distinguish  justice  from
natural virtues  such  as benevolence,  since they  too  have
utility.(3)  However, Hume's case  is that the sole merit  of
an artificial  virtue  is  its utility.   Reid  then adopts  a
different line  of attack: in  practice,he says,  individuals
rarely contemplate the  benefit to the  common good of  their
just acts  and thus  this cannot  be the sole  motive to  act
justly.  But this  again is to  misunderstand Hume who  would
readily concede  that just  acts are  done for  a variety  of
reasons, sometimes out of habit  or a sense of duty.   Hume's
aim is  to justify  justice  in those  instances where  these
contingent reasons  are all absent.  Reid in turn doubts  that
this can be  done in  terms of  public  utility and cites  the
case of "the sensible knave"  who acts unjustly on the  basis
that his few acts of injustice will not destroy the fabric of
property rules and  of society.(4)   Hume admits  that it  is
difficult to convince such a person that he ought not  to act
in such a way except  by appealing to the knave's  "antipathy
to  treachery and  roguery",  his  "inward  peace  of  mind,

M. Dalgarno and E. Matthews (eds.), The Philosophy of Thomas Reid, 355–367.
© 1989 by Kluwer Academic Publishers.

consciousness of integrity [and] satisfactory review of [his] own conduct".(5)    But this    concession by Hume    is a    hollow victory for Reid, since it is a concession Hume need not have made.

Having failed   to   identify   serious   inconsistencies   in Hume's account   of   utility   as   the   key   to   justice,   Reid realises   that   it   is   the   narrowness   of   Hume's   entire conception of justice which   jars against man's common   sense notion of justice:

> He seems,   I   know   not   why, to   have   taken   up   a
> confined notion of justice,   and to have   restricted
> it   to   a   regard   to   property   and   fidelity   in
> contracts.(6)

Reid's way   forward   is   to   provide   a   better,   alternative account of justice   through an examination   of a wider,   more generally accepted notion of justice.

## Justice and Rights

As in other areas of his philosophy, the key to Reid's theory of justice is the involvement of judgment over and above   any feelings or sensations.   He asserts that justice is   natural and relies   on   the   common   sense   method   of   appealing   to experience to back up this claim.   He points to   the everyday reactions of gratitude   and resentment produced   respectively by favours and injuries   done.   Everyone, including Hume,   he says, allows   that   these are   natural   to man.     Yet   these notions are inseparable from that of justice:

> The conception   of a   favour   in every   man come   to
> years of   understanding, implies   the conception   of
> things not due, and   consequently the conception   of
> things that are due... The conception of things   due
> and not due   must therefore be   found in every   mind
> which has any   rational conception   of a favour,   or
> any rational   sentiment   of gratitude...   An   injury
> implies more than   being hurt...   There must be   the
> will and intention of the agent to do the hurt...   An
> injury....implies in it the notion of injustice.(7)

Reid earlier distinguishes between the notion of duty and the sense of duty   and the   same is being   done with   justice.(8) The notion of an injury, of an intended hurt contrary to what is judged due carries along with it the sense of justice:

The very conception of justice implies its
obligation. The morality of justice is included in
the very idea of it: nor is it possible that the
conception of justice can enter into the human mind,
without carrying along with it the conception of
duty and moral obligation. Its obligation,
therefore, is inseparable from its nature, and is
not derived solely from its utility, either to
ourselves or to society.(9)

Our sense of the duty or obligation to abstain from injury is
part of the application of the notion of injury to specific
cases or types of case. Thus Reid rejects Hume's accusation
that, while an individual may be motivated to act justly
because to do so is a duty, this reasoning is circular.(10)
That the individual ought to do x, a just act, is not simply
because it ought to be done but because the moral faculty
judges in a motivating way that it is owed, as of right, to
another. It is the right of the other which triggers this
set of judgments.

Not surprisingly, then, Reid finds that the most
effective way of handling the various instances of the duty
of 'abstaining from all injury' is in terms of rights:(11)

The direct intention of Morals is to teach the duty
of men: that of Natural Jurisprudence to teach the
rights of men.(12)

Although describing rights and duties as correlative, he
sees certain advantages in regarding injustice as the
violation of rights and justice as yielding to every man
what is his right,(13) including the fact that people
pay more attention to rights and that it emphasizes the
strong obligation of justice.(14) As individuals are
most aware of their rights when these rights are
violated, Reid first identifies the "various ways in
which a man may be injured":

A man may be injured, first, in his person, by
wounding, maiming, or killing him; secondly, in
his family, by robbing him of his children, or
any way injuring those he is bound to protect;
thirdly, in his liberty, by confinement;
fourthly, in his reputation; fifthly, in his
goods, or property; and, lastly in the
violation of contracts or engagements made with

him. This enumeration, whether complete or
not, is sufficient for the present purpose.(15)

Elsewhere he does indeed add to the list:

> [Justice] implys that we invade no Mans
> property nor violate his Right. That we do not
> injure him in his person in his family, in his
> good name or in his friends. That we pay our
> just Debts, make Reparation to the best of our
> Power for any damage we have done or offence we
> have given to others. That we fullfill our
> contracts and be faithfull to our promises.
> That we use no fraudulent dealing nor take
> advantage of the weakness Ignorance or
> Necessity of those with whom we deal.(16)

Thus Reid is able to identify rights or interests to be
protected. He claims that man has innate natural rights
to life, family, liberty and reputation (and might
include rights to friends and at least some forms of
reparation, from his fuller list). These, in contrast
to property and contractual rights, are "founded upon
the constitution of man, and antecedent to all deeds and
conventions of society",(17) whereas the others are
acquired rights, which depend on some act or deed by
which they are acquired.

Without at this stage going into a full discussion
of these six rights, it is clear that Reid's list of
rights departs significantly from Hume's property-right
conception of justice. Firstly, Reid extends justice
beyond a concern for property rights. Secondly, the
rights he sets out (including, he claims, property
rights, as will be seen) and, consequently justice, are
pre-legal and can exist before or outside political
society. Justice, that is, means to accord to each man
his natural rights. It is indeed, to answer Hume's
original question, a natural, rather than an artificial
virtue, though admittedly a complex one involving
judgment as well as sentiment.

> When a man's natural rights are violated, he
> perceives intuitively, and he feels that he is
> injured. The feeling of his heart arises from
> the judgement of his understanding; for if he
> did not believe that the hurt was intended, and

unjustly intended, he would not have that
feeling... The natural principle of resentment
is roused... These sentiments spring up in the
mind of man as naturally as his body grows to
its proper stature.(18)

There are here in Reid marked similarities with the view
of Adam Smith:

Justice is violated whenever one is deprived of
what he had a right to and could justly demand
from others, or rather, when we do him any
injury or hurt without a cause.(19)

However for Smith rights, identified by the spectator
device, are inter-subjective and to that extent
conventional – an instance of what Reid considers to be
the mistake of taking the shadow for the substance of
what existed objectively in nature.(20) While thus
describing rights as existing in nature, as natural
rights, Reid would nevertheless agree entirely with
Hume:

Nothing can be more unphilosophical than those
systems, which assert, that virtue is the same
with what is natural, and vice with what is
unnatural.(21)

Reid is making no such equation. These rights are not
to be respected because they are natural but because
such respect is self-evidently due to them.

Reid is confident that he has produced an
alternative to Hume's theory of justice, which at a
general level is defensible, and to reinforce his view,
he makes a familiar common sense appeal to common
language and learned opinion:

Justice, in common language, and in all the
writers on jurisprudence I am acquainted with,
comprehends the four branches above
mentioned.(22)

He then leaves the topics of life, liberty, family and
reputation, but prudently decides to examine further the
branch of justice central to Hume's case, property
rights.

## Justice and Property

Reid opens his discussion of property by admitting:

> The right of property is not innate, but acquired.
> It is not grounded upon the constitution of man; but
> upon his actions.(23)

However, it can be acquired, initially through occupation and
through labour, in a state of nature, prior to political
convention, and it is natural in another sense in that it
flows from the exercise of man's (natural) right of liberty:

> Every man, as a reasonable creature, has a right to
> gratify his natural and innocent desires, without
> hurt to others. No desire is more natural, or more
> reasonable, than that of supplying his wants. When
> this is done without hurt to any man, to hinder or
> frustrate his innocent labour, is an unjust
> violation of his natural liberty.(24)

But suddenly Reid announces that there are two kinds of
property:

> The first is what must presently be consumed to
> sustain life; the second, which is more permanent,
> is what may be laid up and stored for the supply of
> future wants.(25)

Although it is not immediately apparent, this distinction has
far-reaching consequences. It transpires that these two
kinds of property correspond to two slightly different
rights: a right to the 'necessities of life' (deriving not
from the right of liberty, but from the right to life itself)
on the one hand; and a right to permanent property or
'riches' (which is derived from the right to liberty) on the
other. Reid's claim is:

> Some kind, or some degree, of property must exist
> wherever men exist, and that the right to such
> property is the necessary consequence of the natural
> right of men to life and liberty.(26)

But what he has not explained is why this should involve a
natural right to private property. A right to life's
necessities might be satisfied by public provision, while a
right of liberty to labour does not entail a right "to the

fruit of that labour".(26)    Indeed Reid denies, without
disproving, Hume's view that the connection between a man and
the fruits of his labour is merely one of psychological
association of ideas. He writes that:

> Property is no Physical Quality in the thing nor any
> association between it and the Proprietor in the
> imagination but a relation between the thing and the
> Actions of the Proprietor and of other more
> agents.(27)

But if so, it is hard to see why an internal mental desire
should be sufficient to found property, unless there were an
agreement to that effect.

Reid's case may be stronger where there has been actual
occupation without injury to another's interests. Would it
not indeed be unjust and injurious to dispossess such an
occupier?  This Reid can translate into a natural right of
property. He holds that everything was originally held in "a
negative community of goods" as if God were holding a feast
to which everyone may help themselves so long as no harm is
done to others:

> This is occupation.   If any man should pretend to
> take from me what I have thus helped myself to he
> injures me and is guilty of a trespass against me,
> against the Master of the feast and against the
> company. This is the invasion of my property.(28)

There are, however, limitations to this right to property and
on occasion Reid lists more than a dozen,(29) but the most
dramatic is perhaps the most fundamental:

> What was said above, of the natural right every man
> has to acquire permanent property, and to dispose of
> it, must be understood with this condition, that no
> other man be thereby deprived of the necessary means
> of life.   The right of an innocent man to the
> necessaries of life, is, in its nature, superior to
> that which the rich man has to his riches, even
> though they be honestly acquired.   The use of
> riches, or permanent property, is to supply future
> and casual wants, which ought to yield to present
> and certain necessity.

As, in a family, justice requires that those who are

> unable to labour, and those who, by sickness, are
> disabled should have their necessities supplied out
> of the common stock, so, in the great family of God,
> of which all mankind are the children, justice, I
> think, as well as charity, requires that the
> necessities of those who, by the providence of God,
> are disabled from supplying themselves, should be
> supplied from what might otherwise be stored for
> future wants.(30)

This is a very radical stance for Reid to adopt. Despite his
belief that God and nature gave man the wisdom to store up
goods for future use, Reid views the right to these goods,
the right to permanent private property, as conditional: it
cannot be exercised until every right to necessities is
satisfied. These rights of the needy constitute a prior
claim in justice. It is not simply that they create an
exception to the property-right, far less that their
satisfaction is a mere claim upon charity. The right to
necessities is part of the right to life, more important than
the right to liberty upon which the right to permanent
property or riches is based. That Reid is prepared to
organize rights into a hierarchy in this way reveals the
natural law ideology which lies behind his theory of justice:
the common good is the supreme value in social life and it
would be a mistake to isolate Reid's 'rights talk' from
that.(31)

Additionally the passage quoted indicates that justice
may require positive action from others (which contrasts with
Adam Smith's view that as long as an action does nothing to
actively cause injury it is just), since the right to
necessities appears to be a claim-right that others supply
these necessities for those who cannot fend for themselves.
If this muddies the division between justice and charity, it
is because Reid sees these as a continuum:

> It is hardly possible to fix the precise limit
> between justice and humanity...they run into each
> other.(32)

This Hume (and Smith) would consider as a great weakness in
Reid's system insofar as it undermines the certainty of
property.

However Reid's is not the totally egalitarian type of
scheme which is the real target of Hume's criticism.(33)

THOMAS REID ON JUSTICE

Certainly it creates what might be described as a welfare
safety-net, but once everyone's necessities are provided, it
permits great inequalities in the distribution of riches.
There is thus plenty of scope for incentives for industry.
Some of the uncertainty over exactly when the demands of
justice upon the individual property-owner are satisfied
would be alleviated by the intervention of a rule-governed
tax system. Reid freely admits that (human) law and
convention will quite properly regulate and amend natural
rights, particularly property. So the right to property
which begins to emerge is the right not to be injured in
whatever one owns, shares, etc. innocently and legitimately
under the laws in force at the time within the limitations
imposed by natural law or the common good. And, where it can
be done innocently – without infringing anyone's natural or
conventional rights – the most obvious natural means of
acquisition is by occupation.

Only in such a context can sense be made of an otherwise
startling comment in Reid's unpublished notes. on Hume's
theory of justice:

> If the virtue of justice is conceived to extend no
> farther than to the regulation of property I should
> agree with Mr Hume that justice might be resolved
> into utility and derived its merit from its
> utility.(34)

Of course, Reid does not accept that justice extends only to
property, far less that it extends no farther than the
regulation of property. What he is prepared to concede is
that once the natural (or abstract) right to property is
granted to be one of the areas of justice, the detailed rules
governing that right in a particular society will be chosen
so as to best suit that society – they are not universal.
Similar reasoning applies to the regulation of contracts and
promises: breaking contracts is universally unjust, but what
counts as a contract will vary from one society to another.
Within limits, in civil society natural rights are regulated
by considerations of utility. Relying on this Reid does
towards the end of his life propose, on grounds of utility,
the abolition of private property and its replacement by
common ownership.(35) But while private property remains,
each has a duty in justice to respect it, a duty which is
essentially natural.

**Law and Justice**

Reid conceives of law as merely regulating existing natural
rights of justice "as the price of that protection and
security which he [the citizen] receives from civil
society".(36) Hume on the other hand maintains that justice
is the product of law or conventional rules of property.
Reid relies on arguments from common sense and common
language to show that there is a pre-legal notion of justice.
While he cannot prove Hume wrong if Hume refuses to accept
that one's duty is itself a sufficient motive for action, he
can point out that Hume's account is not consistent with the
popular conception of justice. He takes up some of Hume's
hypothetical cases to demonstrate that, instead of proving
Hume's point, they merely emphasize the strangeness of Hume's
concept of justice. For example, where there is famine or a
siege, Hume says, the rules of justice or property are
suspended so that food is distributed to the starving: but it
seems peculiar to Reid that such a distribution is considered
by Hume to be not just, since Reid believes that justice is
not "suspended" in such a situation but rather that it is
justice which demands such a redistribution so as to protect
and preserve people's right to life.(37) In other less
unusual situations, Hume's position seems odd:

> As all works of men are imperfect,human laws may be
> unjust; which could never be, if justice had its
> origin from law, as the author [Hume] seems here to
> insinuate.(38)

Reid is quite correct here: far from being the product of
law, justice stands against law, as a yardstick for assessing
law's moral worth for the use both of lawmakers and their
critics. It must be possible to criticize laws in terms of
their justness or unjustness, even if one wishes, as Reid
does, to argue that on occasion a point of justice might have
to be sacrificed to utility. Any incursion upon justice,
upon man's rights, by the lawmaker has to be positively
justified.

However Reid does seem slightly uneasy about the
relationship between justice in relation to natural rights
and the law. Given that he otherwise is consistent in his
use of the term 'justice', as respecting the rights of man,
it is surprising to find him employing it rather differently:

> Justice requires that a member of a state should
> submit to the laws of the state, when they require
> nothing unjust or impious...For all these particular

> laws and statutes derive their whole obligation and
> force from a general rule of justice antecedent to
> them — to wit, That subjects ought to obey the laws
> of their country.(39)

Reid does not explain in what sense 'justice' is being used
here. Perhaps he is relying on a social contract which
justice requires the citizen to adhere to. Alternatively, it
may be that natural rights can only be fully protected in
civil society and for that reason the citizen has a duty in
justice to maintain the laws of that civil society. If
either of these is the correct explanation, then the first
sentence quoted is at least compatible with his general
theory. In contrast the second sentence yields too much:
justice could only obligate the citizen to obey just laws,
though either utility or the common good might sanction an
unjust law. A suspicion persists that Reid leaves the
citizen without guidance in the face of an unjust law simply
because Reid himself is undecided about the detailed
inter-relationship of natural rights, law and justice.

On the other hand, Reid's purpose is more limited. On
the central issue of whether justice is artificial or natural
Reid is clear. He has shown, in terms of common sense and
common language, that it makes sense to talk of justice as
natural — more sense than Hume's unduly narrow approach
makes. While it is open to a critic to reject Reid's common
sense methods and to criticize particular claims which he
makes, Reid has at least pointed out a route by which the
natural lawyer can counter Hume's attack on the natural law
tradition.

NOTES

(1)   Cf., e.g., Miller (1976).

(2)   For these terms see Dworkin (1977, pp. 171–3).

(3)   **AP**, V, v (<u>Works</u>, pp. 652–3).

(4)   **AP**, V, v (<u>Works</u>, pp. 653–5).

(5)   Hume (1975, p. 283).

(6)   **AP**, V, v (<u>Works</u>, p. 657).

(7)   **AP**, V, v (<u>Works</u>, p. 655).

(8)   **AP**, III, Pt. III, v & vi (<u>Works</u>, pp. 586–92).

(9)   **AP**, V, v (<u>Works</u>, p. 655).

(10) Hume (1978), p. 478.

(11) AUL MS 2131/8/IV/3.

(12) **AP**, V, iii (<u>Works</u>, p. 643).

(13) **AP**, V, v (<u>Works</u>, p. 656).

(14) **AP**, V, v (<u>Works</u>, p. 644).

(15) **AP**, V, v (<u>Works</u>, p. 656).

(16) AUL MS 2131/8/IV/3 (Spelling and punctuation follows the manuscript).

(17) **AP**, V, v (<u>Works</u>, p. 657).

(18) **AP**, V, v (<u>Works</u>, p. 656).

(19) Smith (1978, p. 9); Cf., Smith (1976). Reid's Aberdeen Philosophical Society Paper on Justice was delivered in 1758, prior to the publication of Smith's ideas.

(20) Cf., **AP**, III, Pt. II, II (<u>Works</u>, p. 557).

(21) Hume (18978), p. 475.

(22) **AP**, V, V (<u>Works</u>, p. 657).

(23) **AP**, V, v (<u>Works</u>, p. 657).

(24) **AP**, V, v (<u>Works</u>, p. 658).   Reid's right to liberty is clearly then not simply a freedom from confinement as implied on p. 656; it is a freedom to act in gratifying desires, a positive rather than a negative liberty.   But, as Reid acknowledges, the right to gratify desires is restricted not simply by what would hurt others but also by the duties of an individual to God and to self.

(25) **AP**, V, v (<u>Works</u>, p. 658).

(26) **AP**, V, v (<u>Works</u>, p. 658).

(27) AUL MS 2131/7/VII/1c.

(28) AUL MS 2131/7/VII/1c.

(29) AUL MS 2131/7/VII/II.

(30) **AP**, V, v (<u>Works</u>, p. 659).

(31) See AUL MS 2131/7/VII/II.   For an application of Hohfeld's 'Rights' terminology to Reid's work, see Dalgarno (1984) and (1985).

(32) **AP**, V, iii (<u>Works</u>, p. 645).

(33) Hume (1975), p. 194.

(34) AUL MS 2131/7/III/Ib.

(35) AUL MS 3061/6.

(36) **AP**, V, V (<u>Works</u>, p. 659).

(37) **AP**, V, v (<u>Works</u>, pp. 659–60).   Cf. Hume (1975), p. 186.

(38) **AP**, V, v (<u>Works</u>, p. 662).

(39) **AP**, V, v (<u>Works</u>, p. 662).

Melvin T. Dalgarno

## TAKING UPON ONESELF A CHARACTER : REID ON POLITICAL OBLIGATION

The contract theory of political obligation which Reid espouses in an unpublished manuscript (Aberdeen University Library MS 2131/2/II/10) is of considerable interest for the use made of the idea of taking upon oneself a character or office to which rights and duties attach. But before turning to this, it may help to place Reid's contract theory of political obligation in context if we consider it in relation to three developments of historical and intellectual significance for eighteenth-century contractarian thought. In more or less chronological order, these are the double contract theory of Pufendorf, the Whig Ideology with Hume's response to it, and the publication of Rousseau's Discourse on the Origin of Inequality.

### Contracts of Society and Government

It is widely accepted that a high water mark in the development of social contract theory came with Pufendorf's version of the theory in his De Jure Naturae et Gentium (1672).(1) Especially on the Continent, Pufendorf's theory of two contracts with an intervening decree loomed large for a century or more in the works of writers on politics and society.(2) To follow Pufendorf was to distinguish a first contract among individuals to form a society. This contract of society was followed by the decretum which laid down the form of government which that society was to have. The second contract, the contract of government, was then required for the actual institution of a government taking that form. The sovereign-to-be is bound 'to the care of the common security and safety', and the rest to render obedience: such a pactum subjectionis was required over and above the pactum unionis and the intervening decretum to produce a 'finished state'.(3)

In Scotland, Carmichael produced in 1718 an edition of Pufendorf's De Officio Hominis et Civis for the use of his students at Glasgow. He wished to defend the duo pacta et unum decretum theory in its entirety against the growing revisionist tendency to jettison the first of the contracts.

369

*M. Dalgarno and E. Matthews (eds.), The Philosophy of Thomas Reid, 369–385.*
*© 1989 by Kluwer Academic Publishers.*

His successor at Glasgow, Francis Hutcheson, continued to uphold the same doctrine.(4)  Reid includes a marginal note in his Glasgow lectures on jurisprudence to direct him to explain to his class the distinction "between Society & Political Union" which instances the survival, if only by mention, of Pufendorf's doctrine.(5)

## Whig Ideology

Although contract theory in Scottish philosophy can be seen in the earlier part of the eighteenth century as following the Continental trend with the reception by Carmichael and Hutcheson of Pufendorf's doctrine,(6) it became increasingly preoccupied with what may be a peculiarly British high water mark in contract theory: the original contract of the apologists of the 1688 revolution.(7) Hume's essay of 1748 Of the Original Contract manifests this preoccupation and acted to increase it.

Hume's remark about the 'refined and philosophical' system of the original contract being a "little unshapely" in its workmanship, would certainly strike a cord with the student of Pufendorf so far as Hume's presentation of the system was concerned. There is no clear cut distinction between the contract of society and the contract of government. Hume presents the Whig Ideology as appealing to a somewhat jumbled mix of the two. If anything, Hume's essay may be somewhat reactionary in that while he utterly rejects the full-blooded contract of government, he goes against the developing trend of being sceptical about the contract of society:

> When we consider how nearly equal all men are in
> their bodily force, and even in their mental powers
> and faculties, till cultivated by education, we
> must necessarily allow, that nothing but their own
> consent could at first associate them together, and
> subject them to any authority. The people, if we
> trace government to its first origin in the woods
> and deserts, are the source of all power and
> jurisdiction... The conditions upon which they were
> willing to submit, were either expressed, or were
> so clear and obvious, that it might well be
> esteemed superfluous to express them. If this,
> then, be meant by the original contract, it cannot
> be denied, that all government is, at first,
> founded on a contract, and that the most ancient

rude combinations of mankind were formed chiefly by
that principle.(8)

What Hume disputes is the continued and present relevance to
practical politics of the thesis he allows. In particular,
he denies the theory of political obligation the Whig
Ideology attempts to rest upon it. That present political
orders rest upon a contract of government is a claim which
does not correspond to facts. To regard 'the establishment
at the Revolution' of 1688 as a standard showing other states
to be monstrous and irregular is preposterous. That
Revolution concerned only the succession in <u>part</u> of the
government which was changed by a majority vote on the part
of seven hundred. These facts do not confirm a contract of
government where that means government as a whole.

With his essay <u>Of the Original Contract</u>, Hume, as so
often elsewhere in his writings, provides Reid with a
determinate target at which to aim. Reid shows no sympathy
for what Hume might have professed as the aim of the essay:
encouraging a moderate scepticism which pointed to a
resolving <u>via media</u> between the extremes of the Whig and Tory
ideologies. It is the practical and political tendency of
Hume's essay with which Reid is sharply impatient:

> The sentiments which Mr Hume has on many occasions
> expressed of the claims of the house of Stuart
> [Stewart ], & of the Conduct of those who opposed
> their pretensions; make it less surprising' that he
> should oppose a principle upon which those who
> brought about the revolution justified that
> Conduct. If the Lords & Commons who found the
> throne to be vacant upon this ground among others
> that King James had broke the Original Contract
> between King and People acted upon chimerical
> principles they are not to be justified and we
> ought either to condemn the Revolution altogether
> or justify it upon different Principles. But if on
> the other hand this Notion of a Contract between
> King and People has a Meaning, & a meaning
> consistent with the Principles of Justice and
> Equity why should it be traduced as chimerical &
> Visionary by those who have no intention to throw a
> Reproach upon the Revolution.(9)

For Reid, Hume's essay is mischievous in that there does not
lie behind it any practical intention to promote a reversal

of the 1688 settlement. His counter, as we shall see, is to defend a version of the contract of government theory.

## The Natural State of Man

The publication in 1755 of Rousseau's Discourse on the Origin of Inequality quickly attracted notice in Scotland. Within a year, Adam Smith had reviewed it in the then short-lived Edinburgh Review. The Minutes of the first meeting of the Aberdeen Philosophical Society record, 12 January 1758, Mr Trail intimating his intention to make the subject of his discourse in April "An Abstract of a Discourse of Mr Rousseau on the Source of Inequality among Mankind; with some observations upon it".

A profound and enduring effect on Scottish philosophy of Rousseau's discourse was to provoke a sharpening of principles of method for the study of society. Hume, in endorsing the thesis that the first origins of society lay in contract, argued that "we trace it plainly in the nature of man, and in the equality, or something approaching equality, which we find in all the individuals of that species".(10) But developed with the extravagance of a Rousseau and underpinning a discourse of considerable length, this method of attempting a speculative reconstruction of a pre-historical past, cried out for the thorough and systematic criticism it was to receive at the hands of Adam Ferguson in his History of Civil Society (1767).

Ferguson's concern was to expose the gross irrationality of the principle enunciated by Rousseau in his Preface:

> It is by no means a light undertaking to distinguish properly between what is original and what is artificial in the actual nature of man, or to form a true idea of a state which no longer exists, perhaps never did exist, and possibly never will exist; and of which it is, nevertheless, necessary to have true ideas, in order to form a proper judgment of our present state.(11)

This is to ground conclusions about the present condition of human beings in society on premises which are unknown, unknowable, and anyhow irrelevant as relative to conditions in a pre-historical past. Sound thinking requires one to argue from the known: from data established by observation or attested records. This was the methodological principle

Ferguson systematically developed and which clearly associates his work with the Common Sense philosophy upheld by Reid. In refusing to speculate beyond and behind the data of observation and history, in dismissing theories which rested on such speculations, Ferguson was applying in social philosophy the lesson about hypotheses Reid had taken from Bacon and Newton as "the very key to natural philosophy, and the touchstone by which everything that is legitimate and solid in that science, is to be distinguished from what is spurious and hollow".(12)

There is an argument in a short one-page manuscript of Reid's entitled "What is the Natural State of Man" which confirms the extent to which his thinking is in line with Ferguson's:

> It is the nature of Gold to be Malleable fusible Soluble in A. Regia. But if it were asked whether Gold were in its Natural State when it is fluid or when hardned' by cold I suspect this Question has hardly any meaning. For the fluid State is as natural to it in a certain degree of heat as the hard State is in another.(13)

On this line, our knowledge of the nature of man is to be based on studying human behaviour in the full variety of situations where it can be observed or where it is reliably recorded. Such data is available for how human beings have lived in groups and companies in various situations, but not for any pre-social condition of human beings.(14)

The argument of MS 2131/3/III/6 reappears in Reid's Active Powers where he objects to Hume's suggestion in the Treatise that 'in his rude and more natural condition, if you are pleased to call such a condition natural' a man would find it completely unintelligible to be told that a regard for justice, a sense of duty and obligation, gave him a reason or motive to return a loan. In a very Fergusonian passage, Reid insists that it is in the nature of the individual, as well as of society, to be progressive:

> If one should say that the state of infancy is a more natural state than that of manhood or of old age, I am apt to think this would be words without any meaning. In like manner, in human society, there is a natural progress from rudeness to civilization, from ignorance to knowledge. What

> period of this progress shall we call man's natural
> state?   To  me they  appear all  equally  natural.
> Every state of society is equally natural,  wherein
> men have access to exert their natural powers about
> their proper objects, and  to improve those  powers
> by the means which their situation affords.(15)

Thus, the infant or the individual whose circumscribed mental
powers have not  allowed the  development of the  conceptions
required to  act from  the rational principle  of regard  for
duty,  may  well  find  the  answer envisaged  by  Hume
unintelligible.   But this  proves nothing  to Hume's  point.
Reid's argument is that such  a person could not properly  be
described as  performing that  social operation of the  mind
known as accepting a loan.  To take something into your hands
is one thing; but to  accept something on a knowingly  shared
understanding that it  is to be  returned, is something  very
different.   Reid insists that it is contradictory to  suppose
an individual capable of the latter operation of the mind but
lacking  a  conception  of  the  obligation  to  repay.
Accordingly, he complains that it would have been proper  for
Hume "to  have given,  at least,  a single  instance of  some
tribe of the human race that was to be found  in this natural
state".(16)

Even where  Reid talks  of the  state of  nature, as  in
Essay V, ch.iv of the Active Powers, it is clear that he does
not understand  a pre-social  condition of  individuals.   He
envisages the position of families  who are not subject to  a
common superior.

In a very late work, his Glasgow Literary Society  paper
of 1794 "Some  Thoughts on  the  Utopian System"  (AUL  MS
3061/6), Reid  talks  of  man  as  nature  has  formed him,
declaring the  subject of  his discourse  to be  'the Man  of
Nature, the Subject of  Speculative Politicks'.  But this  is
no sudden conversion to Rousseau. So far as that discourse is
concerned, the Man  of Nature  is simply the  being with  the
capacities and  potentialities,  intellectual  and  active
powers, Reid had made the subject of his published works:

> a Being  who brings  into  the World  with him  the
> Seeds of  Reason  and Conscience,  along  with  the
> various Appetites  and  Passions, by  which  he  is
> often misled  into Error,  and  seduced into  wrong
> Conduct by Temptations that  arise from within,  or
> from external  circumstances:  At  the  same  time

> capable of a high Degree of Improvement in
> Knowledge & Virtue, by right Education and good
> Government; and on the other hand, of great
> Degeneracy, to Barbarity & even to Brutality, by
> the Want or the Corruption of these Means. This is
> the Man of Nature.

This is the species whose history is currently being acted
out: the being who is to be found in a state of his nature,
as Ferguson·puts it, here, now and all around us.(17)   We do
not encounter any hypothetical construction of that nature in
a pre-social condition.   Indeed, by affirming the family to
be the one 'Government that can be said to be purely the
Institution of Nature', the discourse confirms the argument
that Reid did not look to contract or artifice for the
origins of social union.

## MS 2131/1/II/10

The fullest treatment of the contractarian theory of
political obligation by Reid is in this eight page
manuscript.   It is without heading and opens with the
cancelled sentence "The word Contract is like many others
taken sometimes in a larger sometimes in a More restrained
Sense".  While the manuscript is not a fragment, it concludes
somewhat abruptly.   The ideas in the concluding paragraphs
are presented in short, jerky fashion compared with the
developed, polished manner of exposition which marks the
earlier portion.  It seems to be brought to a somewhat tired
or hurried end with the concluding 10 lines of text
sandwiched in the middle third of the page, with note
headings lined off above.  Then follows a couple of notes of
topics.  But these are topics treated in the text rather than
items still to be treated. After these come further notes
headed 'Remarks on D. Humes' Essay on the Original Contract'.
A further note about Hume is inserted up and down the right
hand margin.

The manuscript is undated.  References to Hume's 'Of the
Original Contract' place it after 1748 when that essay was
added to the enlarged third edition of the Essays.    The
remark about the sentiments Mr Hume has on many occasions
expressed of the claims of the house of Stuart, suggests it
would not have been written before 1756 when Hume published
the second volume of his History of the Stuarts.    The
manuscript has much more the appearance of an occasional
paper or related draft than lecture material.    But the

internal evidence which points to a date not earlier than
1756 would be consistent with its being intended either for
the Aberdeen Philosophical Society or the Glasgow Literary
Society. The records of the former suggest no convenient
hook on which to hang it, while the Glasgow records offer a
possible hook by noting a discourse given by Reid, 1 April
1767: 'Whether the Supposition of a tacit Contract at the
beginning of Societies is well-founded'.

**Taking on a Character**

Reid begins MS 2121/2/II/10 by enlarging on the idea of how
the consent essential to contract can be expressed by
explicit words in writing or speech, by other signs
artificial or natural, or even by silence. He then proceeds
to give examples of transactions where the terms of the
contract are understood by the parties though not expressly
stated:

> Thus I send for a Taylor' [;] I desire him to make
> me a suit of Cloaths' of superfine Cloath of such
> a Colour; he takes my Measure makes a bow and walks
> off, under the same obligation as if by [a deed
> upon<sup>c</sup>] <sup>s</sup>an Indenture<sup>s</sup> stamped paper we had been
> mutually bound to each other, he to chuse' the
> cloath according to his best skill[,] to cut it
> according to the fashion and the rules of his Art
> [,] to fit it to my size and shape [,] to furnish
> and make it up workmanlike & to charge a reasonable
> price, & I on the other hand to take it off his
> hand(s) & to pay him for it. This is all implyed'
> in the order I gave him though not a tittle of it
> be expressed.

This is followed by the example of the farmer who borrows an
ox from a neighbour for a week. Here the consent of the
owner would be presumed for the ox being used moderately for
standard farming purposes, though such restrictions on use
were not expressly stated.

But a third example leads Reid from the idea of tacit
obligations being understood by the parties, to the idea of
obligations attaching to a position. His example is that of
applying to 'a man who professes the healing Art', who
prescribes on hearing my symptoms. Reid insists that so far
as the physician is concerned, it is not merely his duty to
prescribe faithfully and honestly because he took the

Hippocratic oath: "his taking upon him the Character virtually & implicitly binds him to this without Oath or Promise". He argues that oaths one is required to swear in taking up office, binding oneself faithfully to discharge the duties of that office, are merely intended to strengthen an obligation already contracted.

An apparent difficulty for this last claim is the fact that taking such an oath often counts formally as taking up office. Thus, in a temporal sense, the obligations are undertaken with the taking of the oath and not before. But the point essential to Reid's argument stands. The performance of any act, be it standing on one's hands, which counts as formally taking up office, would have the effect of bringing one under the obligations of the office. It is the act under the description of taking up office, and not essentially as swearing an oath, which brings the agent under the obligations in question. This makes Reid's claim about already contracted valid from the logical standpoint. And it will also hold in the temporal sense whenever there is a gap between actually taking on an office and some formal investiture ceremony. Elizabeth II took up office immediately upon the death of her father and prior to the Coronation ceremony. But there seems to be some determination in the United States to avoid such gaps. Thus President Reagan had to be sworn into office for his second term immediately his first term was up. The determination to avoid a lacuna amused some of us on this side of the Atlantic. Allowing Sundays to be inappropriate for public inauguration ceremonies, why not put the business off until Monday. This was, of course, what was done, but not without the precaution of a private swearing in of the President on the Sunday. Reid's considerable influence in the United States does not appear to have extended to giving the American people confidence that they could impeach a President for actions he took in that capacity on a Sunday if he were not sworn in until the Monday.

Reid does not move from the example of the physician to the case of the ruler, before making it clear that he is advancing a perfectly general thesis:

> He who claims the character of a Man binds himself
> to the duty of a Man, he who enlists in the Army
> binds himself to the duty of a Soldier, & he who[s]
> takes the office of a General binds himself to do[s]
> the [office[c]] duty of a General. It is so in every

office in Society from the lowest to the highest.

This idea of duties attached to social roles, which one tends
to associate with F.H. Bradley's "My Station and its Duties"
in Ethical Studies, is clearly consonant with Reid's repeated
insistence in his moral philosophy that knowledge of our duty
is given level to the apprehension of all men, and that this
apprehension develops as our understanding does. It is part
of acquiring the conception of a soldier to grasp the
incidents of that role in terms of its duties. In this way,
social morality is a constitutive part of perfectly ordinary,
everyday conceptions.

For Reid, two clearly distinct questions arise: one
concerns the content or nature of the rights or obligations
which attach to a particular character or office; the second
is how these become the rights or duties of a particular
person. His line with regard to the second is firmly
voluntaristic. In turning to the case of a King, Reid
insists "I onely' beg this as a postulation that no man is
under a Necessity of being a King, that he takes this
Character upon himself voluntarily and may lay it down when
he will". Thus, taking upon oneself a character or office is
a voluntary act implying, tacitly, the contract to do the
duty of it.

An obvious line of objection is that not all characters
are voluntarily undertaken. While a man may choose to do
something which results in his becoming father of a son, the
son does not choose to be born. While Elizabeth II may have
elected to be Queen, I did not choose to be born her subject.
Reid's example of the person who claims the character of a
man, suggests how he might respond. Hobbes did not choose to
be born of the male gender, but he could choose whether or
not to present himself to the world as having the courage
conventionally associated with that gender. By declaring
himself born a twin with fear, he appears to have elected to
crave the allowance in the matter of conscription which he
describes in Leviathan:

> There is allowance to be made for natural
> timorousness, not only to women...but also to men
> of feminine courage... But he that enrolleth
> himself a soldier, or taketh imprest money, taketh
> away the excuse of a timorous nature, and is
> obliged not only to go to the battle, but also not
> to run from it, without his captain's leave.(18)

Reid could take this sort of line with the offspring who renounces being a son to his father. Others may condemn that renunciation as unwarranted and immoral, but there are cases where there would be widespread sympathy with such behaviour. Everything is what it is: to renounce a character is one thing; to pretend but fall short of it is another.

Failure to renounce a character which others attribute to you, could count as the voluntary sign that you take that character upon yourself. The person who is branded a rogue and a cheat, may accept that the cap fits and be prepared to wear it. But surely it will not do to hold that this rogue may thereafter live down, one might say rather than up, to the obligations attaching to this character.

One response might be to insist on a distinction which is familiar in Reid's thinking between essential duties coeval with human nature, and adventitious duties. Thus the rogue who takes on this character may have the obligation to reform and make reparation as an essential duty of humanity, although he has no self-imposed obligation to this effect.

Another response might be to question the assumption that the obligations attaching to the character of a rogue do not extend to reform and reparation. But this view seems warranted only if the character in question is specified as that of a rogue who wishes to remain within the so-called moral community. But can an individual renounce that character in favour of the character of a rogue outside the moral community? If an individual could be the latter, it does not seem that this could be the effect of renouncing the former character. As Rousseau points out, this sort of renunciation is a moral act presupposing moral agency.(19) To be capable of bringing of the act requires the moral agency one is attempting to deny. One takes upon oneself the character of moral agent in the purported renunciation. This second line of argument is not unlike the first in suggesting the idea of some fundamental or architectonic character which is objective. One either has the conceptions required for a sense of obligation sufficient to be morally responsible for one's actions, or one has not. This points to moral agency as a non-voluntary, inalienable character, with obligations incident to it which are essential.

Such issues arise for Reid in the context of the following claim:

> I know onely' one way in which a Sovereign can
> plead freedom from this Contract, & that is if he
> has taken a protestation at his entring' upon this
> Office that in his administration he is to have no
> Regard to Justice or Mercy any farther than he
> finds them answer his own Ends.

Rehoboam, son of Solomon, and Richard II of England are
examples cited by Reid of rulers who made such profession.
However tyrannical the government of either might be, neither
could be charged, according to Reid, with breaking the
contract. But to say that these men have no contractual duty
to regard justice, is not to say they have no duty whatever
to regard justice. Reid can be allowed to mean strictly what
he says in affirming the former; but he has clearly moved
from a doctrine of tacit contract where an act of voluntlary
will, taking up office, implies the contract to do the duties
of that office, to a doctrine of contract which allows
voluntary will to determine the content or even existence of
these duties.

It is the first of these doctrines which allows Reid to
maintain:

> It is of no Consequence in the present Question in
> what way he acquires his Kingly Authority whether
> by Conquest, or hereditary Succession or Election,
> whether by force or fraud or fair Means, whether
> his people obey him willingly & freely or through
> Necessity; still this Relation implys' in the very
> nature of it an obligation to those prestations
> towards his people which belong to the kingly
> office.

If the status is acquired by force or fraud, but the duties
attach, independently, to the status itself, this is
compatible with holding that the usurper has undertaken these
duties whether he likes it or not. The content of the duties
and their attachment to the office are quite independent of
his will. But if Reid is to allow Rehoboam and Richard II,
by explicit protestation, to escape these obligations arising
from their taking office, it is hard to see why the usurper
should not do so by implied protestation. Taking the office
by acts of force and fraud may spell out very clearly the
character of the intended rule.

There is evidence here of tension between on the one

hand Reid's voluntarism and desire to shore up the contract of government theory under attack from Hume, and his natural jurisprudence line on the other. His Jurisprudence lectures are unequivocal in holding that the "End of Government ought to be the good and happiness at the Governed".(20) The benefit and need of government can be established. Thus, the duties of ruler and ruled can be arrived at as what is necessary for the end, given the nature of the majority of individuals and the situation in which they find themselves. The incidents of each status are worked out so as to interlock in facilitating the ultimate end. Such definition is independent of contract. Following this line, Reid will allow that subjects can be shown to have a duty to pay taxes which they have not consented to by direct vote or by the votes of their representatives. The appeal to contract on this doctrine is restricted to locating the voluntary acts whereby the person or persons who rule took on that status, and whereby others took on the status of subjects.

With regard to the tacit contract of the King to do the duty of a King, Reid is confident that this accords with the real facts of political life. He instances James I of England telling his Parliament in 1609 "That the King binds himself by a double Oath, to the Observation of the fundamental laws of his kingdom: Tacitly by being a King and so bound to protect the People & the laws, & expressly by his oath at his Coronation". But Reid does not shy away at the prospect of finding the tacit contract of the subject. He explains there is variety in that character. The subject who is a Privy Counsellor has more extensive obligations than "someone who barely acquiesces in the Government submitting to the laws and paying his taxes". But the behaviour of the latter amounts to presenting himself as a subject.

It could be asked why Reid insists on talking of implied or tacit <u>contract</u> in this context. In terms of the distinction between covenant which is a unilateral binding undertaking on a single party, and contract which is a bilateral undertaking, should he not rather talk of the tacit covenant of the ruler and the tacit covenant of the ruled. How are these linked into contract? The natural jurisprudence story does not appear to provide an answer. To find facts for the interpretation of these voluntary acts as linked into contract, Reid may need to point to a shared understanding between ruler and ruled about the significance of their acts, each of which is a tacit covenant. This directs him to finding a contract between ruler and ruled within which the tacit covenants fit.

But there is another reason for Reid being pushed towards a kind of double contract doctrine. The question of how a subject ought to behave, is not the same question as how a subject has actually undertaken to behave. To establish that he ought to undertake an obligation is not to prove that he has actually undertaken it. Reid's natural jurisprudence deduction of the duties attaching to the status needs to be supplemented by his story about actually taking that status upon oneself. But while this is necessary, it is not sufficient. Kingly office can exist as an abstraction in the mind of the speculative thinker on politics. But an actual person in an actual ·society cannot enter into an actual office of that description unless that position has actually evolved along with a public, shared conception of it. Otherwise it is simply not there to be entered into by any act voluntary or otherwise.

MS/2131/1/II/10 shows Reid attempting to utilise the idea of an original contract to deal with this problem:

> If it should be asked when this Contract was made, the Answer was obvious, The Political Contract which constitutes a State was made when the State began to exist, & continues untill' the State be dissolved, & this Contract may continue firm under various Revolutions & Forms of Government[.]

> The contract between a Particular King or civil Magistrate & his People began when he began to be King or Magistrate & continues while he exercises that office. When he violates the essential Obligations of a King which he came under by taking that Office he breaks the Contract.

This has to be read together with the earlier passages in the MS where Reid discusses the evolution of the earliest Kingly government taking place 'in the Simple and primitive Periods of Society'. There it was understood that the leader in an emergency situation was to be obeyed and supported so far as he led for the good of those he was to lead. Both leader and led shared this understanding. As the office and conceptions of it changed from that of temporary warlord to that of permanent king, into particular forms like that of Absolute Monarchy to Monarchy as simply a branch of the legislative power, the essentials of the original understanding were unchanged so far as two related ideas were concerned: that government was to be in the interests of the governed and that obedience was due to government which fulfilled the essential duties of that office. This for Reid was the preponderating fact in history over the bulk of the globe and a fact evidencing conclusions endorsed as normatively justified byjurisprudential moral thinking.

Mrs Thatcher has three times taken office as Prime Minister. Clearly, she has not shared the conception of that office which had become current in the decade or so prior to her first taking office. It may be doubted whether she thought much about Bradley's notorious warning that to wish to be better than the world, to live to a higher morality than is conventionally given, is already to be on the threshold of immorality. But she appears to have believed that the established view was a misconception of the office and that anyhow public opinion was changing. It was no longer generally thought incident to the office of Prime Minister to have the duty of seeking the middle way of consensual politics. But even if such changes in the ongoing contract have been taking place, they would be peripheral for Reid, to the essential terms of the contract as it originally was and as it presently continues. Mrs Thatcher is Prime Minister of a Government which has a duty to govern Britain in the interests of the people of Britain. This duty is incumbent on her in taking the office. She has this as a self-imposed obligation; it is not just a matter of what any decent, upright person ought to do.

MS/2131/1/II/10 contains a kind of double contract doctrine: the doctrine of the original standing contract, and the doctrine of how by tacit covenant one takes upon oneself the duties of an office which have evolved through the operation of the standing contract.

## NOTES

(1)   Cf. Gough (1936, p. 118).

(2)   A list of principal 'adherents of Pufendorf's trichotomy' i iven by Bernard Freyd in Gierke (1939, pp. 104 & 128-9).

(3)   Pufendorf (1934, p. 975).

(4)   See Hutcheson (1755, p. 227).

(5)   AUL MS 2131/8/IV/9.

(6)   The contract theory has its own particular seventeenth-century pedigree in Scotland where it is deeply enmeshed in the theology of covenant.   See, for example, Torrance (1981, pp. 225-243).

(7)   In so far as the Whig Ideology has roots in Locke's Second Treatise which is influenced by Pufendorf, there is an inner connection to be traced.

(8)   Hume (1963, p. 454).

(9)   MS 2131/2/II/10.  The notations explained below are used in this and subsequent quotations from Reid's manuscripts. They are designed by the General Editor of the Reid Publication Series.

$[^c]$   a cancellation or stroke out which is decipherable
$^s/_s^s$   as spelled in the original text
            a word or phrase superscribed above  the regular
            line of text
[.]   punctuation supplied
( )   the letter within parenthesis has been omitted

(10)  Hume (1963, p. 454).

(11)  Rousseau (1973, p. 39).

(12)  Corr, letter to Lord Kames (Works, p. 56).

(13)  MS 2131/3/III/6.

(14)  "In the most savage state that was ever known of the human race, men have always lived in societies greater or

less" (**AP**, V, vi, <u>Works</u>, p. 666).

(15) **AP**, V, vi (<u>Works</u>, p. 668).

(16) <u>Ibid</u>.

(17) Towards the conclusion of MS 3061/6, Reid gives a Fergusonian warning against undue confidence in conclusions deduced from over general knowledge of human nature: "We often see, not onely' Individuals, but great Bodies of Men act a part very different from [what ] that which by the common principles of human Nature we would have expected".

(18) Hobbes (1968, p. 270).

(19) Rousseau (1973, p. 170).

(20) MS 2131/4/III/9.

# SECTION 5 – HISTORICAL CONTEXT AND INFLUENCES

Charles Stewart-Robertson

THOMAS REID AND PNEUMATOLOGY: THE TEXT OF THE OLD, THE
TRADITION OF THE NEW

In perpetually disavowing his ancestry, the eighteenth-
century Pneumatologist both frees himself and sows the  seeds
of confusion in those who would come to know the science.  In
view of the weighty baggage of Aberdeen debate from the 1750s
which he  had scarcely  unpacked when,  in 1764,  he took  up
residence in Glasgow,  Thomas Reid  is surprisingly quick  to
strike the bell of  liberty.  Yet even  as he does so, he  is
seeking out the well tried  and the familiar.  From the  very
beginning, he  prepared his  students for the  prospect of  a
session or  two  of dusted-off  reflections of  a  distinctly
Aberdonian cast.(1)  An  admitted 'stranger' to Adam  Smith's
'System'; a professed borrower of 'light from every  quarter'
(if only it be 'sound & Solid'); and at root a most agreeable
mind, ready to 'change' its 'opinions' or even its  'Methods'
upon advantage – the Pneumatologist appears to make easy  the
uneasiness of  his  station ("I  cannot but be  filled  with
confusion",  he  confesses  readily)  by  simply  letting  his
script settle where it will.

A year after his Glasgow debut, Reid is still reiterating
the basic tenets of his  science, as first pronounced in  the
'Abstract of some  Statutes and Orders  of King's College  in
Old Aberdeen', in 1753.(2)  The impression he would leave  is
that of a free thinker – one who would, in  his words, 'Judge
for himself'(3) – and yet also that of an apologist  for that
already ageing order which saw the philosophy of mind rearing
such seemingly disparate offspring as rhetoric and politicks,
oeconomicks and natural religion.  How long could he  sustain
the  balance  between  bold  invention  and  clutching
traditionalism,  without  arousing  nervous  suspicion  that
perhaps there was neither direction in nor foundation to this
alleged science to nurture all sciences?

Clearly the  foundation was  not  lacking.  It was  very
deeply set and  well piled with  texts and abstracts,  theses
and inquiries.  Moreover,  it housed "some [eminent]  writers
in Pneumatology [who] have  disputed [sic] the Authority  of
the  Senses, of the Memory, & of every human  Faculty",(4) as

389

M. Dalgarno and E. Matthews (eds.), The Philosophy of Thomas Reid, 389–411.
© 1989 by Kluwer Academic Publishers.

well as one whose 'wisdom' in the 'workmanship' of the mind is 'infinitely superior to that of Man'.(5) The well illuminated and the darkly sceptical thus alternately raised or lowered the ceiling of eighteenth-century perspective on the mind. Reid was surely sensible to erect his Pneumatological house in Glasgow on the Corinthian pillars of Hutcheson and Smith, and equally shrewd to build distance between himself and the 'two great Ornaments' of the University.(6) "It shall be my endeavour ... to follow them", he pledges, "tho at a great distance".

But how great a distance could the Scottish Pneumatologist reasonably put between himself and the tradition to which, in this instance, he had not once, but twice fallen heir? There had been shoes to fill earlier at Aberdeen, if not immediately awesome in stature, then at least more remotely of considerable influence.(7) What Turnbull had once been to his various successors in Aberdeen, Hutcheson and Smith were now to Reid, and in two-fold measure. The distance, however, and thus the extent to which tradition literally weighed (from the Latin, pensare, thence 'pensive') on Reid's thinking after 1764, was greater still than the shaping powers of these truly 'eminent' inquirers.

Perhaps a useful as well as fitting starting-point would be the figure of William Law. He was Professor of Moral Philosophy at Edinburgh from 1708 to 1729, and a critical Scottish disseminator of the views of the anti-Cartesian Dutch philosopher, Gerardi de Vries.(8) Gaining the distance here is properly a measure of the gradual separation of ontology or metaphysics from the science of mind. In Law's Annotationes on de Vries (undoubtedly the latter's De natura dei et humanae mentis ... and de catholicis rerum attributis ejusdem ...), the commentaries on Metaphysics and Pneumatology (Annotationes in Metaphysicae et Pneumatologicae) are wedded in presupposition. The Cartesian ambivalence between the very being or reality of mind and its nature and relations still dogs the critic's heels. Hence, a proportionately large amount of space and attention is paid to questions of the mind's finitude and thereby imperfection, on the one hand, and to questions of its problematic relation, as an incorporeal substance, to the body qua res extensa, on the other. Foremost too among the topics considered, and the resulting Theses Metaphysicae et Pneumatologicae for student defence, are epistemological concerns respecting both deum and mentem as well as queries touching on the relation between pneumatologia as the study *de natura dei et humanae mentis* and moral philosophy (specifically, as Turnbull later put it, of the principles of 'the rights and duties of mankind'). Not surprisingly, overshadowing the whole lay the avowed importance of revealed religion (*religio revelata*) to every inquiry and of individual faith in a divine mind – '*Deus optimus maximus*'.(9)

In the midst of this complex interplay of seventeenth-century preoccupations, Pneumatology is fairly bound: on the one side by repeated reminders of the human mind's essential inferiority (or incapacity), and on the other by elaborate demonstrations of the divine existence (or attacks on the feasibility of such 'demonstrations'). It does emerge fully as *scientia contemplativa spiritus*, but its treatment of the various 'modes' (or powers) of mind, both active and passive, as well as its analysis of the three 'species' of mental 'apprehension' – namely, sense, imagination, and recollection – are cursory and restricted. But again it is the sheer 'wonder' of the mind's union with the body ('*Ut mirandum animae & corporis unionem aliquo modo explicent*') which predominates even under this head.(10)

As the 'science of Spirits' Pneumatology did, of course, originate in, and would thereby lend itself to, such governing concerns. Bacon had subsumed it as an 'Appendage both to Inspired & Natural Theology',(11) and that coupling with Natural Theology – whether under or beside is a matter of historical shading – lasted well through the next century. The entry in *l'Encyclopedie* under 'ESPRIT' – to which d'Alembert's account of 'PNEUMATIQUE' refers, for further explication – allies '*la science des esprits et des substances spirituelles*' quite pointedly with *les philosophes chretiens*. It is they who give recognition to three sorts of spirits, namely, *Dieu*, *les anges*, *et l'esprit humain*. (For his part, d'Alembert is quite frankly interested more in the widely accepted use of *pneumatique* to signify the science of air and its properties, and can scarce conceal a note of derision in respect of its other meaning.(12)) Close ties of this sort are not readily broken, however, and it is over the half century between William Law at Edinburgh and, for example, John Craigie at St. Leonard's College, St. Andrews (1691–1747),(13) Francis Hutcheson at Glasgow (1730–1746) or William Cleghorn at Edinburgh (1745–1754) that the breaking-up of traditional forms occurs. A gradual separation, it was also fraught with anxieties over the respective entitlements, custodial rights, and future relations of the once compatible partners.

Francis Hutcheson's Synopsis Metaphysicae of 1744
(subtitled Ontologiam et Pneumatologiam complectens) might at
first glance appear not to have advanced the cause of
Pneumatology to any significant degree. As de Spiritus
scientia or the science de Mente Humana it still constitutes
only the second part (pars secunda) of Metaphysics, although
from the outset Hutcheson is at pains to demonstrate that the
method under which this is so, and which considers first the
question of being and the common attributes of things,
secondly the doctrine of divine and human minds (doctrinam
... de Deo et Mente Humana), and lastly physics or scientia
de corpore, is of 'more recent' origin (recentioribus
quibusdam arrisit alia methodus). That the science of the
thinking substance (substantia cogitans) must await a lengthy
preamble through the axioms, properties, praecipuae (or
'principle things'), and categories of being, does not,
however, forestall Hutcheson's considerably amplified
treatment of the powers of the mind (de animae viribus).
Significantly too, Hutcheson's sequence is not bullied about
by an obsessive concern to accommodate and define the
relation between mind and body. The reining in of this
Cartesian preoccupation is, of course, commensurate with the
growth of a distinctively Scottish philosophy of man and his
social frame.

Even a lesser figure such as William Cleghorn, Pringle's
sometime deputy, then himself Professor of Moral Philosophy
at Edinburgh, can be said to have assisted this philosophy in
taking giant strides away from Cartesianism – strides which,
as we shall eventually see, still appear through the lens of
time to have been inadequate to Reid. Cleghorn and his
contemporaries found themselves in the thick of a
jurisdictional battle which, like wars between nations,
conceded as much as it took away certain rights to inquiry
and instruction. If one may transpose somewhat Reid's own
words (or rather those of Emmerich de Vattel on whom he
chiefly relies) on the subject of 'Solemn War' between two
parties, "each while it defend[ed] its own Right against its
Enemy [found that it had] to treat that Enemy not as one who
had laid aside all regard to Right but as one who injures
them from prejudice and false Opinions of his Right".(14)
The parties here in dispute – as listed under their
philosophical as well as their institutional names – were
Pneumatics, Ethics or Moral Philosophy, and Logic. The hard
lesson to be learned by the (probably) unsuspecting prelector

like Cleghorn was that the boundaries holding among all three were neither set in stone by ancient title nor (as one might expect) amenable to easy adjustment or redefinition. With or without Town Council's Acts, such as that passed in Edinburgh in 1708 (by which Colin Drummond assumed the rights to Logic and Metaphysics, while William Law gained possession of Moral Philosophy),(15) the situation was fluid and sometimes volatile. The net result of this was that, at one and the same time, the prelector ascending to his Chair was relatively free to redraw the map of his constituency as he saw fit (that is, according to his own 'prejudice') and yet he was circumscribed on all sides by rival claims which arose from a 'false (or perhaps even true) Opinion' of the same right. In short, the state of nature in Philosophy was gloriously, if always ironically, Hobbesian!

Determined to set things right, Cleghorn complained that no 'system' had hitherto 'sufficiently' answered the purpose of representing '[the Doctrine of Spirits] under a Clear and Distinct conection [sic] with the Doctrine of morals, to which it is designed to pave the way'.(16) Paving the way is not to be construed, however, as an invitation to connect what must clearly be distinguished; for Pneumatics is 'the knowledge of the parts or Systems of minds taken separately', while Ethics (or 'morals') constitutes 'the knowledge of these parts [taken] conectedly and of the Actions that arise from the[ir] regular and well adjusted cooperations'. Those Pneumatic 'parts' seemed to fascinate Cleghorn. 'Strictly speaking', he maintained to his students, they ought to recognise one 'species' as being 'prerequisite to the knowledge of Ethic' and another as 'previous to the knowledge and practice of Logick'. Let there be no confusion. Logic and Ethic both treat of the nature of mind − hence Pneumatics makes smooth the passage to both − but Logic has the 'intermediate end' of Truth, while Ethic has for its 'absolute end' the mind's relation to the 'good'. Of this conception in distinction were born 'Ethical Pneumatic', as Cleghorn named it, and its less happily baptized mate, 'Logick Pneumatic'. Clumsy in name only, this latter species was to be entrusted with the high responsibility of the order and determination of faculties, as well as with the 'habits' requisite to the mind's 'attainment of Truth'.(17) The hero of this science is the true 'Spectator' − the Smithsonian variety notwithstanding; his Ethical fellow having the 'Character of an actor in the great Theatre of the universe and ... a Real part in its composition'. Mental order and social order: these were the original children of Scottish

Pneumatology, and their descendants would number among their
respective champions the likes of George Jardine and Adam
Ferguson.

As much as they are wont to play together, children like
also to go their separate ways. 'Ethical Pneumatic' and
'Logick Pneumatic' were no different. While still in their
infancy, and well before Jardine would raise the latter to an
unprecedented stature of integration and accomplishment or
Ferguson would lift the former to a vision of creative action
and 'human ingenuity' virtually unknown since the
Renaissance,(18) the Pneumatic offspring sported in different
corners, for example, of Dodsley's The Preceptor, first
published in 1748. William Duncan, like Reid a product of
the regency of Marischal College (1733–37), exhibited
youthful pride in establishing the new and proper terrain of
'The Elements of Logick'. It is 'by Culture', he wrote

> and a due Application of the Powers of our Minds,
> that we increase their Capacity, and carry human
> Reason to Perfection. Where this Method is
> followed, Knowledge and Strength of Understanding
> never fail to ensue; where it is neglected, we
> remain ignorant of our own Worth: and those latent
> Qualities of the Soul, by which she is fitted to
> survey this vast fabrick of the World, to scan the
> Heavens, and search into the Causes of Things, lie
> buried in Darkness and Obscurity. No Part of
> Knowledge therefore yields a fairer Prospect of
> Improvement, than that which takes account of the
> Understanding, examines its Powers and Faculties,
> and shews the Ways by which it comes to attain its
> various Notions of things. This is properly the
> Design of Logick, which may be justly stiled the
> History of the human Mind ... It is thus that we are
> let into the natural Frame and Contexture of our own
> Minds ... .(19)

'Frame and Contexture', however, were not quite the same
thing as its 'Constituent Principles', and it took David
Fordyce, a near contemporary of Reid at Marischal College(20)
(he took his MA Degree in 1728, having read Philosophy under
Daniel Garden), in his small corner, to sort this out.

Drawing from various sources, not the least of whom were
Bacon and Hutcheson, Fordyce put little store by Ethick's
indebtedness to its Pneumatic parent. Indeed, if one looks

behind his contribution to The Preceptor, to an earlier
(1743) lecture at Marischal College (where he was Professor
of Moral Philosophy from 1742 until his tragic death in
1751), he confines 'Pneumatics or Pneumatology' to a
consideration of 'the nature & properties of thinking Beings
or Spirits', and is careful to comprehend under its head
'Natural Theology'.(21)    Ethics, on the other hand, very
distinctly 'Enquiries into the active & moral parts of mans
constitution, & thence deduces the Rule of Life & Conduct, &
explains the several Offices or Duties to which he is obliged
by the Laws of Nature'. Its ally, moreover, is 'the science
of Politics'. A dual parentage is thus manifest here, with
the active side of man's nature linked genetically with
Cicero's de Officiis, thence with the more recent titles of
Pufendorf, de Officio Hominis et Civis (1673) or Heineccius,
A Methodical System of Universal Law, as so translated by
Turnbull in 1741.(22) The intellectual side would be left to
trace its own family history.

Nevertheless, of the urgent need for that active
component to be distinguished from Logick, as the refiner of
the instruments of mind, Fordyce was quite certain. Moral
Philosophy, he asserts, enquires

> not how Man might have been, but how he is
> constituted; not into what Principles, or
> Dispositions his Actions may be artfully resolved,
> but from what Principles and Dispositions they
> actually flow; not what he may by Education, Habit
> or foreign Influence, come to be, or do, but what by
> his Nature, or Original Constituent Principles he is
> formed to be and do.(23)

When, by the end of the century, the lines of demarcation had
blurred and the tone had softened under the shadow of a
different sense of urgency, that 'might have been' in respect
of human nature would become a 'may yet be'. Once again,
Reid would prove to be a seminal figure in this metamorphosis
of attitudes towards human nature.(24)    It was really
Jardine, however, and to a lesser extent Dugald Stewart, who
attended the consummation.

By the end of the century husbandry, and no longer
reasoning, was the new rule of Mind.(25) Dugald Stewart
certainly felt the shifting of ground, although in the form
of his Edinburgh successor, Thomas Brown, he had some
misgivings about the direction which a 'concentrated inner

reflection' would take.      Sometimes Brown harvested more
deeply than he had sown.      (Husbandry, or the Culture of  the
Mind,   likewise  called  for  'precision  in language',  and
'loose' talk  was rampant(26)).   Nevertheless,  in spite  of
these reservations, Pneumatology was on  the threshold of  a
new era into which,  however boldly it  might step, it  would
still enter  as  a fledgling  species, susceptible  to  fresh
assaults now from  different quarters  (the Jeffrey stand  in
the Edinburgh Review; phrenologists such as George and Andrew
Combe; and eventually the real 'trojan horse' in the Scottish
camp, James Frederick Ferrier).   One might almost say that it
had attained its 'capital' moment, were this assessment to be
understood within  the  context  of Jardine's  own  revised
affirmation of its status and of the dependency of all  other
inquiries upon it.

At the  outset  of  his career  at  Glasgow,(27)  Jardine
strode the Logick platform  in fairly traditional dress,  one
which  Fordyce  or  Duncan  would  readily  have  recognised.
Philosophy, declares the early Jardine (within earshot of the
late-practising Reid)  encompasses "all   the   liberal ...  or
Intellectual habits"; yet  it  is  "sometimes and more  justly
defined to be that knowledge of divine and human things which
we attain by means of our reasoning powers".(28)  By at least
1790, and perhaps as early  as 1783, he is edging towards   a
revised structure of 'Logick Pneumatic' (in Cleghorn's phrase
still), whose fully developed form will not appear until  the
1797 Synopsis of  the Lectures on  Logic and Belles  Lettres.
Significantly, an extant  set  of  dictates from that  earlier
date reflects  both  past  and  emerging  prejudices;  it  is
headed,   'A   Student's   lecture  notes   on   Logic   and
Psychology'.(29)  Jardine's fourfold division  in the  later
Synopsis has reached only three stages – namely, descriptions
of the 'Powers of the Intellect', the 'powers of Taste',  and
the  'Powers  of  Communication'  and  their  means  of
improvement(30) – and, like Drummond and others at  the
beginning of the century, his 'Logick' still includes a  (now
condensed) treatment of Metaphysics with its dual branches of
Ontology and, not unexpectedly,  Pneumatology. What is  most
striking perhaps is the  sheer propinquity of Reid (the  Reid
almost certainly now of an Intellectual Powers frame of
mind), in Jardine's depiction of Pneumatology. There is more
than  a  hint  here  of  a  science  in  the  throes  of
reconstruction,  one  which is  undergoing  an  extensive
refurbishing according to 'modern' tastes and attitudes.

Taking one step back into the tradition, Jardine  defines

Pneumatology as "the Doctrine of spirits. As the Divine and Human mind". Two steps forward, however, he qualifies his definition: "with the Moderns a spirit is that being which is endowed with Intelligence and Will". Then a final step backward: "We must consider the human mind before the Divine mind, because the one gives light to the other".(31) The very sway of this movement of the Scottish mind is suggestive; not so much of uncertainty or a wavering of position, as of a gentle easing from one rhythm of thought to another. Again, for all his faltering steps in the first years of the Glasgow professorship (the demonstration of which would require a separate exegesis), Reid was almost singularly responsible for striking new and, for many decades to follow, determinative ground.

The recent author of the Inquiry had left behind him in Aberdeen Gerard and Beattie, David Skene and George Campbell, among others. The last-named had, of course, since 1759 held the office of Principal of Marischal College, and would a dozen years later (in 1771) become that College's Professor of Divinity. Even in that latter capacity, he would prevail upon his students of 'systematic theology and pulpit eloquence' to regard 'not merely as important' but as 'necessary' preparations for their studies a reading of 'moral philosophy, pneumatology [and] natural theology' as well as of Latin and history 'both ancient and modern'.(32) Although never himself a lecturer in Moral Philosophy or Pneumatology, Campbell had clearly stimulated Reid's thinking in numerous areas of these subjects. Reid's notes, for example, on 'An Argument to prove that the Identity of a person does not consist in Consciousness against Mr Locke by Mr[r] G Campbel [sic]' (from perhaps 1758) will eventually appear in the Intellectual Powers as the case of the 'brave officer' who, as a boy, was found guilty of 'breaking an orchard'.(33) No doubt much to his regret, he would have to miss Campbell's query for 22 January, 1765, 'Whether the manner of living of parents affects the genius or intellectual abilities of the children?'; for the subject was very dear to Reid's own concern for the 'Oeconomicks of the family'.(34) It is perhaps treacherous, and certainly curious, to remark that looking back on this period, at least one writer (Robert Hall of Leicester) judged Campbell to have been 'superior' to both Reid and Stewart. ("He could have done all that Reid or Stewart has accomplished, and neither of them could have written his Preliminary Dissertations to his work on the Gospels.")(35)

More immediately still, Reid would miss Dr David Skene
whose 'Discourse on the different branches of Philosophy
particularly the Philosophy of the Mind' – read before the
Philosophical Society at Aberdeen, in 1758(36) – is one of
the finest statements of what Jardine had called the position
of the 'Moderns'. The hands of Bacon, thence Turnbull,(37)
are manifestly at work in shaping the 'two branches of
knowledge", namely, the natural and the mental, into a
condition of 'progress' in which the former 'has got greatly
the Start' over the latter. Moreover, they give form to the
new 'Metaphysical or abstract Philosophy of the mind' (as
Skene puts it) whose natural complement is no less than the
'Philosophy of life and manners, or the knowledge of Men".
(Bacon had ordained the title 'Human Philosophy' –
Philosophia Humanitatis – to encompass both the Doctrina
circa corpus hominis and the Doctrina circa animam hominis.)
Reid could not himself have fashioned a more precise
statement of this 'metaphysic', wearing now the dress of
'Pneumatology', than that cut out by Skene. The business of
such philosophy, writes the Aberdeen doctor, is:

> to take a general survey of the human Mind in all
> its constituent Powers, to furnish out an exact
> delineation of its structure[,] to enquire into its
> primary and fundamental faculties, to observe their
> connexions and dependence upon each other, to mark
> their various combinations and the qualitys [sic]
> resulting from them, to fix their Limits and assign
> their different functions – It examines the whole
> stock of our Perceptions – enquiries into the nature
> of every particular Idea, traces it to its origin in
> the mind and assigns the sense of which it is the
> Creature, whether of one or more[;] in a word it
> considers the principles of connexion and endeavours
> to explain all the various relations, divisions and
> Compositions of which our ideas are capable. – Here
> is an extensive field of knowledge and almost
> inexhaustible fund of enquiry ... The only solid
> foundation upon which this Philosophy can seat is a
> thorough acquaintance, with the primary original
> powers of the mind.(38)

In Skene too, brought forward again from Bacon through the
traditio, was that characteristically 'modern' division of
the faculties of the mind into those respecting man as a
'rational' and those affecting him as 'a social active
being'.(39) Skene's analysis would long be remembered, but

now through the intellectual loyalty of his friend, Thomas Reid.

A different sort of loyalty had bound Alexander Gerard to the 'Genius of Lord Bacon's Philosophy', and filled the lecture-halls of Marischal College not only with new fervour, but also with a new 'Logic'. This last, now a 'genuine', field of knowledge, was to be the omega of the sciences, held in abeyance until the final hour, in order to conduct a 'critical review' of all the others. (Hegelian Reason was scarcely as tightly reined in as Gerard's Logic, although the latter would be no match for the reputed 'cunning' of the former!).(40) Strictly speaking, under the Baconian model, it was to be Logic which 'discoursed of the Understanding and Reason' (Logica de intellectu et ratione), while Ethics treated of the voluntary, appetitive, and affective aspects of the mind (ethica de voluntate, appetitu, et affectibus disserit).(41) From that position, the province of Logic would encompass those faculties of the mind which are responsible for the originating and ordering of our ideas, as well as for the regrouping and recollecting of them through imagination and memory. For this function, as Duncan had earlier noted, a veritable 'History of the Mind' is requisite, not to mention both preliminary and detailed sketches of its topography. Pneumatology, Gerard seemed to say in his lectures, precisely fits that bill; for its mission is nothing less than the 'Natural history of Spirits'.(42) Mindful still perhaps of his mentor's injunction in the Advancement of Learning, Gerard no doubt realised that an abstract 'doctrine of Signs' and communication (as Locke had designated Logic) was simply no match - in the theatre of young minds - for "knowledges that are drenched in flesh and blood, civil history, morality, policy, about the which men's affections, praises, fortunes do turn and are conversant".(43) Was it just possible to 'drench' the tales of understanding in 'flesh and blood'?

Gerard excepted, James Beattie was perhaps Bacon's most ardent disciple - at least in that generation prior to the rediscovery of Lord Verulam, in the late 1790s, by Lord Webb Seymour and Thomas Brown and, later still, Macvey Napier and others,(44) - and he was undoubtedly the most likely candidate to become the Homer of Scottish Philosophy. The Odyssey of human knowledge would yet have its drenching, as History took the lead part in that Baconian quartet of both abstract (Mathematics and Philosophy) and creative (Poetry) subjects.(45) The Baconian influence seems stronger still,

when Beattie sub—divides Pneumatology, as the 'speculative'
side of the 'Philosophy of Spirits', into Ethics and Logic:
the former to treat of the 'Improvement of our Moral
Faculties', and the latter to regard the 'Improvement of our
rational Faculties'.(46)   He is meticulous, moreover, in
following Bacon's definition of the science of Logic, as that
which 'explains whatever relates to the inventing, Judging[,]
retaining[,] and communicating [of] Truth'.(47)   Although
Reid eventually devised a new accommodation for the
improvement of the rational faculties – specifically, under
the roof of his private '12 O'clock' prelections on the
'Culture of the Mind', – these lectures, like his earlier
efforts at King's College, are replete with concerns very
similar to those voiced by Beattie under 'Logic' or the 'Art
of Judging'.(48)   Concurrent with these concerns of
Reasoning, however, is a drenching of a different sort.

The field of blood is now less Homeric; less steeped in
the flesh of history or the dreadful wrath of Achilles.
Ironically, it is also less Baconian, although the spirit
moving philosophical thought remains, in its fashion,
faithful to Lord Verulam.   Pneumatology cannot simply be
Logic and Ethics, as Bacon imagined, for these are spineless
without the peculiar laws, structures, or even 'field'
discoveries which only an independent science of mind can
effect.   In the order of knowledge, the science of the
constituent powers and principles of the mind had long been
granted primacy of the realm. The rule of understanding, as
Locke had taught, meant knowing precisely what might, or
might not, be lying in wait as well as what might, or might
not, be taken in.   In this kingdom of beginnings, the
sciences of attention and retention were all: l'etat c'est
nous, they seemed to say.   It is not surprising, therefore,
that Beattie and his fellows should come to recognise the
utter dependency of all sciences, and especially Ethics and
Logic, on that science which had as its object 'the
operations of our own minds'.   "The Science of Human Nature
is of Great consequence", declared a very Humean Beattie,
relatively early in his Marischal professorship.   "Moral
Philosophy[,] Logic[,] and Criticism depend altogether upon
it for it is the Human Mind That Judges of all human
Sciences".(49)   The question which a new generation –
including here an aging Reid – had to face was whether
'Pneumatology' had outlived its usefulness to fulfil such an
onerous mandate.

If Logic could no longer simply play speculativa to

Ethic's practica, if in truth they were to be governed by a
'modern' head of state, to what part might each be assigned?
Logic, with its high point in Rhetoric, must attain new
heights of communication for civilized men; as for Ethics,
the final end of which was civic order under Virtue (and, for
Reid, under Piety as well), it must provide the sympathetic
grounds for such communion. (Even those who criticized
Smith's doctrine would be touched by it!) These goals of
Rhetoric and social order would indeed meet, but only when
the mind, being first properly examined, could then be
cultivated precisely to be itself. The reflective operation
and self-realization of mind would thus become the backbone
of social harmony and integration. Was it any wonder that a
Hamilton-based Brown and that later generation of thinkers
should turn inwards with a vengeance?

"Of Pneumatology I do not know any compleat system",
Beattie apparently complained, at about the same time that
Reid was turning over the reins in Glasgow to Archibald
Arthur. Although Beattie would recommend Reid's analysis of
the senses in the Inquiry, he could find nothing that did not
contain 'a great deal of inaccuracy' in respect of 'a theory
of the human mind', and saw only a modicum of 'advantage' in
Descartes, Hutcheson and Watts on the passions.(50) Not half
a dozen years earlier, Reid is known himself to have lamented
the relative 'infancy' of Pneumatology, and to have argued in
his classes that as Natural Philosophy '150 years ago' was in
a labyrinthian state, so now (in 1755-76) is Pneumatology.
Nevertheless, he could voice the hope that "Pneumatology in
some future period, will more receive the face of a science
than at present it has".(51) Ironically perhaps, and at
Reid's own hands within a decade, that would be so, but only
at the cost of the leopard changing its spots.

More sadly, Reid's endeavours on behalf of Pneumatology,
and its handmaidens Logic and Ethics, would earn him
something of a reputation for obfuscation. Not that he was
alone in this: Professors Clow and Jardine would own their
share of the guilt too, although only the latter receives
specific mention, along with Reid. In a letter addressed to
Beattie and dated 8th December, 1778, a tutor to a 'young
Gentleman' of Glasgow and an enthusiastic admirer of the
Doctor's Essay on Truth, contrasts the 'Plan of teaching' at
Glasgow with that obviously more familiar to him at Aberdeen.
Aside from remarking on Reid's 'unmusical' language and
'ungainly' manner, Beattie's correspondent (one 'Alex.
Peters' by name) recounts the unsteady history of Glasgow's

Logic and Pneumatology since 1727 (the year of the 'Royal Visitation').(52) What is particularly striking in this account is the author's suggestion that numerous liberties have regularly been taken by the Logic and Pneumatology professors with the stipulated requirements for their respective courses. "The Gentlemen", he notes, "take the Liberty of deviating from this Plan, as they see occasion". Hence Dr Reid, who ought strictly to have turned his attention to Ethics and 'that part of Pneumatology which treats De Deo', is found to be dealing primarily with 'the powers of the understanding' and, only secondarily, with Natural Theology and subsequently Ethics. 'Mr Jarden [sic]' for his part, likewise first 'explains the powers of the human Mind', before turning to their means of improvement and the cause of communication.(53) It is small wonder that, to the spectator's eye at least, Logic and Pneumatology should be seen to 'interfere with one another'. While one had to applaud the sense of freedom, one might also feel compelled to lament the anarchy which ensues. Reid was similarly bitten late in life.

The view presented here was, of course, merely an impression, and an outsider's at that. Neither is it wholly accurate or fair, especially to Reid who undoubtedly gave more than his due to the subject de Deo, and plotted the course of Ethics with a careful and deliberate eye. Nevertheless, if one bears in mind that Reid taught his own version of 'Logic' at Glasgow, as earlier he had at King's College, albeit latterly under the title of 'Lectures on the Culture of the Mind', Beattie's correspondent is perhaps not entirely wrong in his intimation that 'Scottish metaphysicians' – as another generation would scornfully call them – were beginning to play fast and loose with their sacred or at least statutory responsibilities to sound learning and social cultivation.

But just how did Reid regard these responsibilities, and in what manner did he eventually discharge them? Was it indeed the case that when he came to read the text of Pneumatology in 1764, fresh on the heels of his Glasgow appointment, he set about to read the old text in the light of new understanding – an understanding which, in time, bore witness to the fulfilment of the old canons in a freer and more attentive science of the human (if not quite the divine) mind or spirit? Did he perhaps sense that the days of Pneumatology were numbered; that their final hour was nearer at hand than ever the loyal Hutchesonians could have

admitted?   Might he   have   taken a   special satisfaction   in
having the   first pull   of the rope   of Pneumatology's   death
knell?

   The time   was never   more auspicious.   The the   Inquiry,
newly published, had been the ideal baptism for his work;   it
gave him a   proper sense of   where and how   to begin, and   he
would openly profess it.(54)   The spectre of the last   great
Hutchesonian, Adam Smith, had moreover kindly stepped   aside,
and Reid would   exorcize it   in a singular   gesture of   first
left, then right knee-bending homage (he tries, then   deletes
'so worthy and so able a Professor', and finally settles   for
'the learned and ingenious Gentleman').(55)   And lastly, his
twelve-year apprenticeship in the tradition at Aberdeen –   of
which his   four   Orationes give   a   fair, if   rather   sparse,
indication,(56)   –   and his   vigorous involvement   in   the
curriculum debates of   the 1750's, provided   him with all   of
the self-confidence   which he   might   need.   In short,   Reid
arrived   in   Glasgow   well   steeped   in   a   pneumatological
tradition of which   Duncan and   Fordyce, Gerard and   Beattie,
were heirs fully recognised or apparent.   He had come   not to
destroy, but again to save Pneumatology from 'some [eminent]
writers'   in   the field   who   disputed 'the   authority of   the
senses, of memory, &   of every human   faculty ... '.(57)   He
who could quote St Matthew beside Juvenal,(58) and who   would
invoke 'the voice of Reason and Common Sense' to advocate the
'establishing some   publick form   of   Religion by   Law' in   a
nation, and   that with   'proper Articles   of Belief',(59)   he
would surely have approved the analogy.

NOTES

(1) AUL MS 2131/4/II/9 (f. 4). "In the mean time", affirms Reid with just a hint of apology, "I must [probably] for this Session [at least] at least proceed in my Prelections in that Method & and with those Materials which my own Thoughts & Studies and my former Experience in this Profession have suggested". The hesitancy over 'at least' – first taking it away, then restoring it – is perhaps indicative of Reid's state of mind in October, 1764, as he looks apprehensively ahead and wistfully behind.

(2) The 'Abstract' had ranked the sciences dependent upon Pneumatology in the following order: "... the <u>Sciences depending on the Philosophy of the Mind</u>, are understood to be Logic, Rhetoric, the Laws of Nature and Nations [i.e. Jurisprudence], Politicks, Oeconomicks, the fine Arts and natural Religion" (Item V, p. 19). In AUL MS 4/II/1 (d. 'Nov[r] 5 1765'), Reid condenses the list slightly (omitting, most noticeably, natural Religion) to this form: "For the first principles of almost all the Sciences, particularly of Logic and Retorick [sic] and of all fine Arts as well as of morals & politicks are to be found in the Science of Human Nature" (f. 12). I shall have occasion later to compare this list with that found in MS 4/II/11 (D. 1764);see also MSS 4/I/29 (f. 1), 8/I/1 (f. 1; nd.) and 4/II/2 (f. 24 ns.; d. 1769).

(3) AUL MS 4/II/18 (f. 76; this MS constitutes the continuation of 4/II/1); cf. MS 7/V/4 (F. 16): '... I shall not confine my self by any Text Book'; also again MS 4/II/9 (F. 10).

(4) AUL MS 4/II/2 (f. 44).

(5) AUL MS 4/II/2 (f. 25 ns.).

(6) AUL MS 4/II/9 (f. 4). Although the words are lined out, it is not obvious that the cancellation, whether for stylistic or other ends, was made prior to the maiden delivery of Reid's inaugural lecture at Glasgow. Some at least of the cancellations were almost certainly made later, as Reid adapted this opening address for possibly perennial purposes.

(7) Andrew Rait (1734–51) had preceded Reid in his Regency

at King's College.

(8) Gerardi de Vries' Exercitationes rationales de Deo
(1695) was among those books sorted for identification – and
no doubt on many occasions perused – during Reid's brief
tenure as librarian of Marischal College, Aberdeen.   Reid's
signature appeared with that of  John Skene at the bottom  of
each page  of the  Catalogue.   See Catalogue of  the  Books
belonging to the Library  at [Marischal College], AUL MS   72.
Less  immediately, although  well  within  the  realms   of
probability, Reid is quite  likely to have learned  something
of de Vries' De natura dei et humanae mentis  determinationes
pneumatologicae (3rd ed.; Ultrajecti, 1690) and De catholicis
rerum  attributis  determinationes  ontologicae.  . In   usum
collegiorum (5th  ed.;  Edinburgh 1712  and  1718),  although
perhaps only secondhand, from  George Turnbull's lectures  on
pneumatology at Marischal College.  (They are so referred  to
in the Preface to Turnbull (1740, p. xii): "this enquiry", he
writes,  is  'the  substance  of  several  pneumatological
discourses, (as they are called in the school language)  read
above a dozen years ago  to students of Moral Philosophy,  by
way of preparative to a course of lectures, on the rights and
duties of  mankind  ...').   Turnbull, who  graduated  from
Edinburgh in  1721,  would  in  turn have  very  likely  been
exposed to  William  Law's Annotationes  which,  fortunately,
have survived in  a  fairly legible form.   See Edinburgh
University Library MS DC.  7.  79.   It is  known that  John
Stevenson, the  Professor  of  Logic  (1730–75) at  Edinburgh,
also favoured  de Vries'  De catholicis (also  referred  to
simply as  the  Ontologia) in his  instruction.   See Grant
(1884, vol. II,  pp. 328–9); also McCosh (1875, pp.  107–8).
Hamilton mentions, but only in passing, the controversy which
raged between 'the Cartesian Roell' (author of Dissertationes
Philosophicae) and the 'anti–Cartesian De Vries'. His  main
concern, however, was to  castigate Brown  for the  latter's
reading of  the Cartesian form  of representationalism (Reid
only 'lightly bear[s] the reproach of 'exactly reversing' the
notorious doctrine  of Descartes').   See Mansel  and  Veitch
(1877, vol. II, pp. 49–50).

(9)  Law's Annotationes, EUL MS DC. 7. 79 (ff. 93–96).

(10) See Law's Annotationes, Sections II and III (ff.  96–154
et seq.).

(11) Cf. Advancement of Learning,  Bk. II (1871 ed., vol.  I,
26–27); de Augmentis, Lib. III, cap. ii & iii (1871 ed., vol.

II, 331–332).

(12) '... la science des proprietes de l'air, & les lois que
suit ce fluide dans sa condensation, sa rarefaction, sa
gravitation, &c.    Voyez AIR.' l'Encyclopedie, tome XII
(Paris, 1757), 805 b. Cf. Reid's own use of 'Pneumaticks' in
this sense in his Aberdeen lectures on Natural Philosophy, as
outlined summarily in his 'Scheme of a Course of Philosophy'
dated (1752), AUL MS 2131/8/V/1 (f. 2).  See also a student's
notes on the lectures on Natural Philosophy, from a later
date (1757–58), AUL MS K. 160 (p. 10).

(13) Vide 'Dictates of John Craigie,' St. Andrews University
Library, MS 168.    Scholastic terminology – substantia,
accidentia, immutabilis, de Essentia et Existentia, &c. –
abounds throughout, although the 'speculative' concerns of
Metaphysica, pneumatica, physica, Geometria, &c. are more
than balanced by the 'practical' ones of logica, Ethica,
politica, &c., the latter particularly showing distinct signs
of the influence of seventeenth–century Jurisprudential
writers on natural and positve law.

(14) Vide AUL MS 8/IV/8 (f. 2).  Reid's perusal of Emmerich
de Vattel's The Law of Nations (first published a Londres in
1758, with an anonymous translation of the French text
published in 1760) is dated quite specificially as 'Sept
1766.' His 'Extracts' from the same work became thereafter
an integral part of his Jurisprudence lectures on the law of
nations.  See further AUL MSS 2131/3/II/5 and 4/III/23c.

(15) See Grant (1884, vol. I, pp. 261 ff.).  The Professor of
Pneumatology and Moral Philosophy (properly titled) was 'to
be apparently the apex of the whole teaching establishment.'

(16) Cleghorn's dictates appear in two sets from marginally
different periods of his Edinburgh lectureship (1745–54); the
earlier, belonging to one 'William Dalgleish – Linlithgow',
is dated 1746–47; the later probably 'Anno Domi: 1752',
although other dates appear therein. See EUL MS DC. 3.3, and
St. Andrews University Library, MS 1951.  The words quoted
are from the latter.

(17) St. AUL MS 1951, numbered pages 12–19.

(18) "Man is formed for an artist", declared Ferguson, "and
he must be allowed, even when he mistakes the purpose of his
work, to practise his calling in order to find out for

himself what it is  best for him  to perform" (Principles of
Moral and Political Science I,  p. 299).  The object of  art,
according to  Ferguson,  was· "to exercise  the  faculty  and
accomplish the  ends of  human ingenuity" (ibid.,  290).   By
thus  exercising  his  ingenuity  on  the  situations  which
everywhere confront  him, man  effects  a transformation  not
only of this or that  situation, but of himself.  This  last,
as Pico della Mirandola  ever reminds us, is the  Renaissance
vision of man; sc. of man the self-creator and transformer of
his very existence.

(19) 'The Element  of  Logick,'  in The  Preceptor,  3rd  ed.
(London, 1758),  vol. II,  2.   Just four  years later  (i.e.
1752), the  new Regent  of King's College,  Thomas Reid,  was
using a  similar  phrase  in  his  'Scheme  of  a  Course  of
Philosophy' (AUL MS 2131/8/V/1): 'Next to the History of  the
Human Mind and its Operations & Powers ...'

(20) Reid had written to  a London acquaintance in  [1737-8?]
to provide  David  Fordyce with  a formal  introduction;  see
Birkwood Collection, Letters,  E.1.1.  Significantly,  Duncan
himself joined the pilgrimage of Scottish youths to London in
1739.   (Reid, of  course, had  made the  same journey  three
years earlier, in 1736.)

(21) AUL MS M184;  entitled 'A brief  Account of the  Nature$_t$
Progress and Origin  of Philosophy delivered  by the late  M$^t$
David Fordyce  P.P.  Marish.  Col: Ab.$^{dn}$ to  his  Scholars,
before they  begun [sic]  their Philosophical  course.   Anno
1743/4.'  Sect.  37.   In  The Preceptor,  vol. II,   242,
Pneumatology is rather lost  among Ontology and  Metaphysics,
or,  more  generally,  'PHILOSOPHY'  as  the  'Knowledge  of
whatever exists' or the 'Science of Things Human and  Divine'
(these phrases being themselves culled from Bacon).

(22) Robert  Dodsley  had  arranged  for  a  quite  separate
treatment of the 'Principles  of Society' and the 'Origin  of
Government' in Part  XI of The  Preceptor, entitled 'On  Laws
and Government.'

(23) 'The Elements  of Moral Philosophy,'  in The  Preceptor,
vol. II, 243.

(24) Indeed, the credit  may rather  go to the  Philosophical
Society in Aberdeen which sponsored critical thinking on such
topics as 'Whether Mankind  with regard to Morals always  was
and is the same[?]'  Vide Philosophical Society Minutes  (or

'Questions Proposed [1] in the Philosophical Society in Aberdeen'), AUL MS 539[1], No. 25 (12 June, 1759). Reid's own answer was resoundingly negative; he had already thrown in his lot with the new enterprise of _georgica animi_, so dear particularly to the Aberdeen circle, and therefore would never discourage 'the Noblest Efforts of human Power' to 'make men better.'

(25) See J C Stewart-Robertson (1987).

(26) See Dugald Stewart (1829, Vol. VI, pp. 430-1). Brown had found the 'circumstances attending [his] situation' to be 'most unpleasant' indeed; still he forged ahead. Stewart took his revenge in a poorly concealed 'Note' in the third volume of his _Elements of the Philosophy of the Human Mind_ (1827 ed.), in which he found Brown to be guilty of gross impatience in his 'science of mind'. When he 'not to the end of his own sounding-line', smarted Stewart changing our metaphor slightly, Brown thought 'he had reached the bottom of the ocean'. Cf. Brown's testimony in a letter to William Erskine, in Welsh (1925, p. 195). No doubt, Reid would have felt the same way about _his_ eventual successor at Glasgow, the 'Sensationalist' James Mylne (1797-1839).

(27) Jardine was appointed assistant to James Clow (1752-77) as Professor of Logic in 1774, and continued lecturing as sole professor from 1787, opposite Mylne, until 1824. An abridged set of his dictates, by one David Reide, survive from the year 1777.

(28) AUL MS 2344 (f. 2).

(29) Glasgow University Library, MS Gen. 166 (italics mine). The date appearing at the end of a section entitled 'Appendix to Logic' is '10th Jan - 1783.'

(30) Jardine's (new) 'Second Division' in the _Synopsis_ is seemingly an expanded sub-division of his earlier first head. It reads: "The art of improving those faculties of the mind, by which a knowledge of the causes, and properties, relations of things is acquired. - Illustrated by the history of Logic, and an explanation of the principal rules of that art" (p. 6). The 'history' of the 'progress' of this science has not significantly altered from Duncan's text, as noted _supra_, and retains all of its Baconian flavour.

(31) GUL MS Gen. 166 (ff. 112-13).

(32) Vide 'Theological Lectures on systematic theology and pulpit eloquence. Introductory discourses. 1782–83'. 4 vols. AUL MS M. 191–201; vol. I, M. 191, Lect. i, 3–4.

(33) Reid's notes appear on f. 3 on AUL MS 6/III/5, above an entry in a different script dated 'Dec 1 1758.' In IP, III, vi (Works, p. 351), Reid uses the more familiar phrase, 'for robbing an orchard'; whether his own or Campbell's, the word 'breaking' here has the sense of 'violating' or 'removing a part from' the orchard. Compare also Reid's notes on Campbell's Question to the Philosophical Society in Aberdeen (No. 23), 'The Nature of Contrariety' (originally, 'Whether Matter has a Separate and permanent Existence'), in AUL MS 4/I/22. The question is listed among the signed 'Questions Proposed in the Philosophical Society in Aberdeen' (AUL MS 539 1) for 30 May, 1759.

(34) See Query No. 72 of the Philosophical Society, the final paragraphs (only) of which may be found in AUL MS 3107/3/10. Cf. also Alexander Gerard's Query (No. 76) for 13 August, 1765.

(35) See the papers for the family of Alexander Leslie, AUL MS 2814/6/45.

(36) The full date and title are given in AUL MS 3107/I/4 as: 15 November, 1758, 'Reflections on the different Branches of Philosophy particularly the Study of Nature & Philosophy of the Mind.' The text appears in AUL MS 37 and MS 475. I am indebted to Kathleen Holcomb's meticulous and higher useful cross-indexing of the Thomas Gordon and Philosophical Society Papers for the 'Early Discourses of the Philosophical Society of Aberdeen' (forthcoming).

(37) See Advancement of Learning (1871 ed.), vol. I, Bk. ii, 26–27; also de Augmentis (1871 ed.), vol. II, Lib. II, 'Ratio,' 312–13. Turnbull was eager to applaud the Baconian perspective on the 'training up' of young minds. See, for example, Turnbull (1742 vol. II, p. 126), wherein he describes the natural order of the mind's curiosity as proceeding directly from 'What is it?' to 'What is it for?'

(38) AUL MS 27, f. nd. 124.

(39) Advancement of Learning, vol. I, Bk. ii, 45. Bacon describes the one as 'respecting [man's] understanding and reason, and the other his will, appetite, and affection;

whereof the former produceth direction or decree, the latter action or execution.'

(40) See Gerard (1755, pp. 20–33).

(41) de Augmentis, Lib V, i, 354; cf. Lib IV, iii, 352a.

(42) AUL MS M. 205.2 (1758), 25v. Gerard experiments with various divisions – including that recommended in Locke (1975, pp. 720–1), viz. 'Physica, Practica, and Logic, or the doctrine of signs') – before he settles upon his tripartite scheme, of Pneumatology, Ethics, and Logic.

(43) Advancement of Learning, vol. I, Bk. II, 46a.

(44) See J C Robertson (1976, pp. 37–49).

(45) Cf. Advancement of Learning, Bk. II, where Mathematics is strictly subsumed under Natural Philosophy. A plethora of sets of students' notes, ranging from the 1762–63 period to that of 1780–84, attests to Beattie's long–standing fidelity to the four–fold schema although one, perhaps better advised, omits Mathematics from the list. Compare AUL MS 555 [c. 1762–63–1772–73); MS M. 185 [d. 1779–80]; and MS 186 [d. 1784]; also MS M. 185.3 (d. 1766); EUL DC. 5 116–117 [c. 1762]; and GUL MS Hamilton 55 [d. 1767]. See also the published version of Beattie (1790, pp. ix ff.), Intro., ix. et seq..

(46) EUL, DC. 5. 116–117. These are the notes of a William Henderson (1758–62); see Album Studiosorum Marischal College), AUL MS M. 3, 1762.

(47) Cf. AUL MS 555, EUL MS DC. 5. 116–117, and GUL MS Hamilton 55.

(48) These included the demonstration of common sense as the 'ultimate standard of truth'; the respective evidences of 'mathematics' and of 'sense'; an examination of forms of reasoning of a 'probable or experimental' nature; and, in general, the 'kinds of evidence' commensurate with all the 'different Sciences'. GUL MS Hamilton 55 ('Logic' or 'The Art of Judging'). Compare, for example, AUL MSS 2131/4/I/19 (on probable reasoning); 4/I/21, 4/II/12 and 14, 6/I/22 and 6/III/4 (on judgment); 6/III/3 (on kinds of evidence); and 4/II/12 and 14 (on types of reasoning – syllogistic, probable & demonstrative). Some indication of Reid's earlier work on

Logic, while he was still a Regent at King's College, may be found in John Cmapbell's anthology of 'Observations on Logic: by Several Professors' – dated 1775, but including compendia of lectures on logic delivered much earlier by Watson at St. Andrews, Stevenson at Edinburgh, and Reid at Aberdeen; EUL MS DK. 3.2. It was Watson who in fact taught Campbell, in 1765–66.

(50) AUL MS M. 185; notes by A Martin, dated <u>circa</u> 1779–80 or 1782.

(51) These remarks are gleaned from the excellent set of notes by Robert Jack, taken during the 1775-6 session. See in particular Lecture VIII, for 31 October, 1775; GUL MS Gen. 116–18.

(52) Peters incorrectly puts the date at 1721; see AUL MS 30 c. 322. Jardine (1825, pp. 17–24) had occasion to tell his own version of that history.

(53) In Jardine's class too, he observed, 'Hutcheson's Compend is used, which contains a great deal of the Scholastic Jargon'.

(54) Cf. AUL MSS. 2131/4/II/12 (f. 1), which is boldly explicit ('This Lecture was read from the Enquiry'), and 4/II/8 ('Lect 2'), whose Axioms, Definitions, and Propositions concerning the 'Powers of Simple Perception' are simply condensed from the elaborations in the <u>Inquiry</u>.

(55) AUL MS 4/II/9–19 (f. 3).

(56) See O. Cf. also AUL MS 8/V/1.

(57) AUL MS 4/II/2 (ff. 44–45).

(58) AUL MS 8/IV/1 (f. 5); the quotations are, respectively, from St Matthew 26:39 and 6:31–33, and from Satire, X, 11. 346–62.

(59) AUL MS 8/IV/9 (f. 8).

Kathleen Holcomb

# REID IN THE PHILOSOPHICAL SOCIETY

Dugald Stewart hints that without the encouragement of his friends in the Aberdeen Philosophical Society, Reid would have been too diffident to publish the Inquiry:

> The plan appears to have been conceived, and the subject deeply meditated, by the author long before; but it is doubtful whether his modesty would have ever permitted him to present to the world the fruits of his solitary studies, without the encouragement which he received from the general acquiescence of his associates in the most important conclusions to which he had been led.(1)

Perhaps Stewart overestimates Reid's modesty. Certainly Reid perceived very early that the Society could serve such a function. He was ready to benefit from the criticism of the others and to use their insights to strengthen his own positions. He profited from debate which indicated that his approaches were too simple. Reid appears to have exploited fully the possibilities of the Society.

Let me review the history of the Philosophical Society. It was founded in January of 1758 by Thomas Reid, George Campbell, David Skene, John Gregory, John Stewart, and Robert Trail. Very shortly afterwards, Thomas Gordon, Alexander Gerard, John Farquhar and John Ross were invited to become members, and later James Beattie, William Ogilvie, James Dunbar, George Skene and William Trail became members. Each member read a major Discourse each year, of about 30 minutes in length. Each member was expected to contribute Questions for debate and to lead the debate on his Question and to abstract what was said. Discourses and abstracts of Questions were to be copied into the Society's books, but these have not survived intact.

However, the list of Questions, part of the Minute Book of the Society, has always been available for study. Although the Discourses have been elusive, Campbell, Gregory,

413

*M. Dalgarno and E. Matthews (eds.), The Philosophy of Thomas Reid, 413–420.*
© *1989 by Kluwer Academic Publishers.*

Reid and Gerard (and later Beattie and Dunbar) published work
which derived from their Discourses, and scholars have always
assumed that the published material was representative of its
origin. In addition, Skene kept copies of his own Discourses
and of some Questions. Reid kept copies of some Questions,
though not of the Discourses which became the Inquiry.

Moreover, recently recovered manuscripts have provided a
clearer picture of what actually went on in the meetings of
the society. Thomas Gordon became Secretary in 1761. He
made copies of most of the Discourses read between 1758 and
1761, a total of 21 including some he was not present to
hear. In addition, when the books were broken down in 1773,
he acquired his own Discourses and Questions as well as a few
fragments belonging to other members. This material, along
with Reid's and Skene's manuscripts, makes possible a better
understanding of the activity of the Society, especially the
interaction among its members.

The meetings were designed to encourage active exchange
of ideas. The members expected their Discourses to be
criticized by their colleagues. Elaborate provision is made
in the Rules for substantive criticism; Gordon refers to such
an exchange in his second discourse on Memory, and some
members record similar interchanges regarding debate on
Questions. Members also kept notes of discourses they
admired. For example, Skene has notes of Campbell's second
Discourse, on Wit, Humour and Ridicule,(2) and remarks that
he has re-read them and still finds them valuable.(3) One of
Reid's Glasgow lectures on rhetoric is partly derived from
this same Discourse.(4) But the Gordon papers are remarkable
because of the magnitude of his effort — they are copies
Gordon made of others' Discourses, not pages taken from the
society's books and not rough drafts in the handwriting of
the others. Although his set is by no means complete, it
appears that Gordon had begun a systematic effort to keep an
inclusive record. Gordon's papers include all but one of
Reid's Discourses.

Members offered their Discourses with varying
expectations. Although Campbell did publish his Discourses
as The Philosophy of Rhetoric, the published version did not
appear until 1776, eighteen years after its first appearance
before the Society. Campbell was a theologian, not a
rhetorician. Gregory's A Comparative View of the State and
Faculties of Man with those of the Animal World appeared in
1765, bearing obvious marks of its origin as Discourses,

which were removed in the second edition (1766). Only Discourse I depends on Gregory's professional training as a physician. Gerard's Essay on Genius eventually saw publication in 1774; Gerard used the opportunity offered by the Society first to test his university lectures on Pneumatology and, in subsequent years, to refine the lectures. Thus, in the early years, only Reid used the Society both to test ideas for relatively quick publication and to develop work relevant to his profession.

Moreover, Reid's interaction with his colleagues is quite evident. Apart from the rhetoric material he borrowed from Campbell, three important instances are (1) in a Question for which Reid's prepared remarks were inadequate, as debate apparently showed him; (2) in the extensive revision and rearrangement of the first Discourse, which became, in part, Chapter 6 of the Inquiry; and (3) in a reconsideration of the value of genius.

I shall discuss these three instances in turn.

I

The first instance of Reid's changing material after the Society had considered it is the debate over Question 44. The Question was originally proposed by Reid: "Whether moral character consists in affections wherein the will is not concerned or in fixed habitual & constant purposes".(5) Though the Minutes are unusually sketchy on this debate, the sequence can be derived from the papers that remain.

The Question is first mentioned on April 15, 1761. No subsequent debate is recorded, but on October 7 Reid presented his abstract. It was not read immediately, as Reid mentioned he had noted what was to be said on only one side of the question, so George Campbell and David Skene were charged with writing a supplementary abstract.(6) Presumably, they were the members most active on the other side. However, Skene was absent during most of the spring and summer; only at the previous meeting, September 8, were both present. Both abstracts were read at the November 10 meeting, and "the meeting entered upon some further consideration of both the abstracts". Although Skene was not present at that meeting, the abstract appears among his papers, so in this reconstruction he will be assumed to be Reid's opponent.

Because Reid had proposed the Question, he was

responsible for leading the discussion on it. He brought to
the April 15 meeting a brief paper, neatly written,
considering a position so obvious he felt no need to do more
than to state it. Moral character consists in fixed purposes
that influence the conduct. However, debate on the subject
was apparently lengthy or heated, with legitimate points to
be made on the other side. The abstract Reid brought to the
October 7 meeting is eight times as long, with numerous cases
adduced as support for fixed purposes and will as the springs
of moral character. In that abstract, Reid presents a
carefully worked out position for his side of the debate.

That abstract, perhaps with the original paper, was given
to Skene and Campbell; Skene refers to the abstract
frequently and uses examples from the first paper. The reply
considers the Question by showing that cases Reid used in
support of fixed purposes of the will could be interpreted as
relevantly as support for affections and dispositions. In
fact, Skene uses Reid's points and cases to argue that will
is not a faculty of the mind at all.

When the meeting considered both abstracts, it apparently
considered Reid's position preferable to the Skene-Campbell
position, for Reid's abstract was ordered to be recorded.
Reid did not use this material in the Inquiry. However, it
has an important function in the Essays on the Active Powers.

## II

The Inquiry is substantially represented in Gordon's papers.
However, it was not read to the Society in the order in which
it was arranged in 1764. When it was published, the order in
which the senses are considered was changed, and the chapter
on sight was greatly modified. Reid read his Discourses in
the following order: sight, smell and taste, hearing, touch,
and seeing. The order in the Inquiry is Smelling, Taste,
Hearing, Touch, Seeing. Gordon recorded all but the second
Discourse on seeing.

In the first Discourse, Reid explains why he is beginning
with sight: "The perceptions we have by the external senses
seem to be the first, the simplest, & the most distinct
operations of the mind, & therefore proper to be first
considered in an analysis of it. I shall therefore at this
time make some observations on the perceptions we have by
sight".(7) However, by the time Reid read his next
Discourse, he had apparently decided that to begin with sight

was a mistake: "The order  in which the sensations are to  be
considered, is  by giving  precedence, not to  the noblest  &
most useful, but to  the simplest &  those whose objects  are
least in danger of being mistaken for other things — & may be
as follows Smelling, tasting,  hearing, Touch, & last of  all
Sight".(8)  This is the  order which appears in the  Inquiry.
The revision of the order allows Reid to prepare his reader's
mind for the discussion  of the really difficult problems  of
perception.   In a  philosophical climate  dominated by  what
Reid called the ideal philosophy, it would be easy to  attack
a common-sense claim that colour is a quality of bodies,  not
a sensation in the mind.  It would be much  harder to contend
that the odour is not somehow in the rose.

     Reid revised each  Discourse before  including it in  the
Inquiry. The significant revisions, though, are those made on
the first Discourse, which  became the  Introduction of  the
Inquiry and parts of Chapter 6, 'Seeing'.  Reid did more than
simply transpose the seeing observations to his last chapter:
he revised it extensively.  The major source of new  material
is his  optics  lecture  series  for his  course  in  Natural
Philosophy.(9)  The material on the Idomenians, the  geometry
of visibles, is  much expanded.  The revisions  in all  this
material will require careful study.

                              III

Because of Reid's revisions,  Gordon's notes of Reid's  first
Discourse correspond only sketchily  to the opening  sections
of the  Introduction in  the  Inquiry.(10)   Besides  minor
revisions, two important additions to the Discourse  material
appear in  the  published version;  one  on the  language  of
philosophers and  one on  the  possibility of  success in  an
analysis of human faculties,  a possibility which depends  on
caution and humility: "It is genius, and not the want  of it,
that adulterates  philosophy,  and fills  it with  error  and
false theory.   A  creative imagination  disdains  the  mean
offices of digging for a foundation, of removing rubbish, and
carrying materials".(11)   This attack on  genius, which  is
prominently featured in the Inquiry, has no equivalent in the
first Discourse.  Where did it come  from, and why did  Reid
think it necessary to introduce it?

     Reid read  his Discourse  on 14  June 1758.   Later  that
year, Alexander  Gerard began his  series of  Discourses  on
Genius.   On 28  August 1759,  John Gregory  read his  second
Discourse; here  Genius comes  under mild  attack as  Gregory

weighs the apparent advantages of a superior degree of genius
and finds their claims to be overrated:

> A superior degree of  genius & understanding is  not
> found to  qualify  a man  either  for being  a  more
> useful member  of society  or for  being happier  in
> himself. . . . But  it ever has been the  misfortune
> of Philosophical  genius to grasp  at objects  which
> Providence has placed beyond its reach, & to run  up
> to general  principles & the  building of  systems
> without that  previous large  collection and  proper
> arrangement of  facts which  alone can  give them  a
> solid foundation.(12)

Gregory recommends  the  study  of  Sir Francis  Bacon  as  a
corrective.  In a  Discourse read a  few weeks later,  Gerard
made  ambitious  claims  for  Genius.(13)   Gerard,  though
recognizing occasional  excesses,  demonstrated that  genius
tests the activities  of a  vigorous imagination against  the
comprehensive design  it has  formed.  Were  this truly  the
case, the strictures noted by Gregory should be  invalidated.
But when Gregory  revised his  Discourse for publication,  he
strengthened and expanded his warning, in phrases which  echo
those Reid had used in the Inquiry:

> Genius is naturally impatient of restraint, keen and
> impetuous in its pursuits; it delights therefore  in
> building with  materials  which  the  Mind  contains
> within itself, or such as the Imagination can create
> at pleasure.  But  the materials, requisite for  the
> improvement of any useful  Art or Science, must  all
> be collected from without, by such slow and  patient
> observation, as little suits the vivacity of Genius,
> and generally requires more bodily activity than  is
> usually found among Philosophers.(14)

It is reasonable to speculate that Reid and Gregory are  both
responding to a  danger perceived in  Gerard's system.  Reid
would have  found  Gregory's position more  acceptable,  and
might even  have been  alarmed by Gerard's  enthusiasm.  The
increasing  energy  in  the  attacks  on  genius  (Gregory's
Discourse, Reid's  Inquiry,  and Gregory  (1765))  occurs,  I
believe, in  reaction  to Gerard's  novelties  (Fabian calls
Gerard's work pioneering).(15)   Both Reid and Gregory were
admirers of  Bacon's  slow  inductive method,  a  method not
requiring genius, perhaps even intolerant of it.  They would
not be inclined  to endorse Gerard's  notion of the  sweeping

power of this faculty. Reid's ingenuous question at the  end of the Introduction does  not appear in the Discourse:  "have not men of genius in former ages often made their  own dreams to pass for her [Philosophy's] oracles?".

Philosophy's oracles, at least  in Aberdeen, were not  to be dreams. The  tests of rigorous  inquiry to be applied  by the Society were designed to obviate that danger.  Whether or not he designed those tests, Reid certainly profited by them. And though many have pointed to the Question list as proof of the Society's wide-ranging interests,  the fact is that  even the  Questions  are  far  more  narrowly  directed  towards philosophical matters  than  those offered  by  the  Literary Society of Glasgow, to say  nothing of the Select Society  of Edinburgh.  The Rules  establish the purpose of the  Aberdeen group as the exploration of philosophical matters and outline the  framework  within  which  they  can  be  discussed.(16) Professor W.L. Davidson,  in his  unpublished paper  on  the history of the Society, speculates that Reid formulated  this objective himself.(17)

In addition,  there  is  some evidence  that  a  member's inaugural lecture  should address  the  problem of  correctly understanding the  human  mind.  Of  nine  such  Discourses identifiable in the Gordon MSS or elsewhere, five  explicitly mention the problem;  a sixth, Campbell's which was read  as its first  Discourse,  would have  been composed before  the Society was formally constituted.  But when the Philosophy of Rhetoric was  published,  familiar  phrases  about  the  mind appear in the  Preface (vii).  Of the  remaining three,  one (Gordon's, on Memory) fits the category but does not use  the language;  two (Trail's,  on Rousseau, and Ross's,  on  a scientific question)  have not  been found;  but only  Ross's might not address the problem of correctly understanding  the human mind.  Gordon has fragmentary notes of John  Farquhar's inaugural Discourse,  "On the  nature and  operations of  the imagination, in  which Mr.  Humes theory of  this faculty  is particularly  considered".  It  offers  a  hint  about  the purposes of the group which has not hitherto been  available: "Difficulty of attaining a true  Philosophy of the mind –  to remove these  one principal  design of the  society –  hopes success will be considerable as the design is useful".(18)

I think we can concede that success was considerable.

## NOTES

(1) Dugald Stewart in Reid <u>Works</u>, p. 7.

(2) AUL MS 475, pp. 310–4.

(3) MS 475, No. 1.

(4) Cf. MS 2131/8/I/5.

(5) MS 145 f. 18r.

(6) MS 539 (Minute for October 7).

(7) MS 3107/1/1 p. 19 (14 June, 1758).

(8) MS 3107/1/3 p. 58 (14 March, 1759).

(9) MS K. 160.

(10) MS 3107/1/1 p. 19 (14 June, 1758).

(11) I I, ii (<u>Works</u>, p. 99).

(12) MS 3107/1/4 pp. 2–3.

(13) MS 3107/1/3 (13 November, 1759).

(14) Gregory (1765, p. 44).

(15) Fabian (1973, p. 135).

(16) Cf. especially Rule 17 (MS 539, p. 4).

(17) MS U. 568/6/1 pp. 27–28.

(18) MS 3107/1/3 p. 35.

Jack Fruchtman, Jr.


## COMMON SENSE AND THE ASSOCIATION OF IDEAS; THE REID-PRIESTLEY CONTROVERSY


Joseph Priestley's 1774 attack on the Scottish commonsense school of philosophy was so vehement in tone he later regretted it. In his Memoirs some years later, Priestley noted that his earlier work, written principally against Thomas Reid but also against James Oswald and James Beattie, was written "in a manner I do not entirely approve [of]".(1) He had called Reid's philosophy 'an ingenious piece of sophistry' and an 'incoherent scheme'.(2) While he later felt sorry for using such language, he still hoped that "upon the whole", his tract had been "of service to the cause of free inquiry and truth".(3) Writing some years afterward, Alexander Chalmers remarked that "the flippant and sarcastic style he [Priestley] assumed on this occasion was disapproved of even by his own friends".(4) The nature and cause of Priestley's extreme reaction is the subject of the present essay. Not only were the divergent philosophical views of these two intellectual giants averse to one another, but the epistemological foundations of their thought, especially Priestley's in regard to his political views, greatly contrasted as well.

## Reid's Epistemological Conservatism

According to Reid (as well as Beattie and Oswald), man came to know things not through the unconscious, materialistic process of association, as Priestley thought, but through an immediate perception of the train of ideas. Common sense, Reid wrote in his Essay on the Intellectual Powers of the Mind was a 'gift of Heaven' the 'first born of reason'.(5) To Priestley, such ideas were not only wrongheaded and misplaced. They also presented the foundations for political conservatism, because they suggested that whatever one perceived was in fact the way things ought to be. Priestley thought this approach to understanding downgraded the importance and centrality of God in political and moral affairs. As a consequence, he thought that the proponents of common sense had provided a dangerous intellectual means to destroy the idea of God's moral purposes to give man the

M. Dalgarno and E. Matthews (eds.), The Philosophy of Thomas Reid, 421–431.
© 1989 by Kluwer Academic Publishers.

capacity to use his reason for progressive, even radical, causes.

First, Reid's common sense. Writing of Hume's scepticism, Reid had said that his reaction to the Treatise on Human Nature had made him feel that he had been

> only in an enchanted castle, imposed upon by spectres and apparitions. I blush inwardly [he continued] to think how I have been deluded; I am ashamed of my frame, and can hardly forbear expostulating with my destiny ... I see myself, and the whole frame of nature, shrink into fleeting ideas, which, like Epicurus' atoms, dance about in emptiness.(6)

Our only hope of attaining knowledge was through common sense, for the mind alone allowed man to perceive and understand his life experiences.

Priestley agreed with Reid that Hume's scepticism negated all means for man to understand or to know anything with certainty. But whereas Priestley opted for association, Reid denied that the mind operated by purely empirical and mechanical means. The true processes were "common sense, and are practised every day in common life".(7) Reid thus sought to investigate the anatomy of the mind to demonstrate common sense, just as "all that we know of the body, is owing to anatomical dissection and observation".(8) His goal was to consider human thought, opinion, and perception and to trace to them the general laws and first principles of the power in the mind that led to the immediate discernment of all phenomena in life.

Priestley therefore objected when Reid made a statement such as the following: "I am resolved to take my own existence, and the existence of other things upon trust".(9) Reid could believe that snow was cold and honey sweet because these things were spontaneously and immediately knowable by common sense. Priestley, however, could not. For him, what Reid and the others argued was tantamount to saying that what we perceive, we know to be a true and faithful representation of reality, as it is and as it ought to be, and no farther.

Reid went on. Every operation of the human senses, he said, implied judgment and belief, and not mere apprehension.

> Thus, when I feel the pain of the gout in my toe, I
> have not only a notion of pain, but a belief of its
> existence, and a belief of some disorder in my toe
> which occasions it.

Mind and the senses, reflection and sensation, were not to be
regarded as two separate operations which had to be bridged
by intellectual manoeuvrings. Judgments and beliefs were not
produced by the association, connection or comparison of
ideas, but were "included in the very nature of sensation".
Reid concretized this with the following illustration:

> When I perceive a tree before me, my faculty of
> seeing gives me not only a notion or simple
> apprehension of the tree, but a belief of its
> existence ... and this judgment or belief is not got
> by comparing ideas, it is included in the very
> nature of the perception'.(10)

These judgments were

> the inspiration of the Almighty.... They serve to
> direct us in the common affairs of life.... They are
> a part of our constitution, and all the discoveries
> of our reason are grounded upon them. They make up
> what is called the common sense of mankind.... The
> strength of them is good sense.(11)

The external world was immediately perceivable and
believable. Men could make immediate, reasoned, and moral
judgments about their perceptions. Indeed, Priestley
thought, men would perforce accept what they perceived as
political and moral givens. His critique of Reid's
epistemological conservatism was concerned only with Reid's
Inquiry into the Human Mind. He never commented on his two
later works. Even so, in the twenty years separating the
Inquiry from the Essay on the Intellectual Powers, Reid seems
to have maintained a consistent idea of common sense.(12)   In
the later work, he said that it was that faculty

> which is necessary to our being subjects of law and
> government, capable of managing our own affairs, and
> answerable for our conduct towards others; this is
> called common sense, because it is common to all men
> with whom we can transact business, or call to
> account for their conduct.(13)

## Priestley's Epistemological Radicalism

Priestley's view of knowledge as a progressive force for radical change in society and politics stood, he thought, in striking contrast to Reid's conservative common sense. Priestley had derived his epistemological ideas principally from David Hartley. Hartley's scheme attracted Priestley because it demonstrated to him precisely how man achieved human progress. Through his physical being, Hartley had said, man's mind first acquired ideas, enhancing the understanding. This unity of man's physical and intellectual attributes, this materialism, furnished a vehicle for Priestley to demonstrate the unity of man and God in the realm of material particularity. For Priestley, it was only through the association of ideas that man's knowledge increased. And as his knowledge increased, he would acquire ideas for progressive political purposes. Even more important, man could easily understand that this progress was to fulfill God's plan in history. Thus, for Priestley, an irrefutable bond linked progress in the material world to man's consciousness of God's plan and his knowledge of the world.

For Hartley and later for Priestley as well, man acquired moral judgment, not by some ethereal process like intuition or common sense, but by the very same process by which he learned anything: by associating pleasurable sensations with certain objects.(14) While man could certainly associate pleasure with the wrong object, Hartley believed that a benevolent Deity ruled mankind. He thus avoided the idea that man might associate pleasure with the wrong, perhaps evil, object. God was a central factor in assuring the rightful functioning of the entire system. Priestley clearly acknowledged this place of God in one's understanding in his Introductory Essays to Hartley's Theory of the Human Mind, published in 1772:

> who can help admiring the admirable simplicity in nature, and the wisdom of the great Author of it, in this provision for the growth of all our passion, and propensities, just as they are wanted, and in the degree in which they are wanted through life.(15)

Attracted to the associationist principle by its overall comprehensiveness of ideas, mind, body, and God, Priestley held that it was the vehicle necessary for men to arrive at the truths of the order of nature.

The association of ideas was a process that was always taking place. For Priestley, its best use was when men resided in a political community where free inquiry and free expression were the ruling political principles. Men in such a community could understnad both the truths of nature and God's purposes: God had given to man the means to bind the progress of his mind to the progress of society in general, thus hastening man's trek on the path to the millennium. In his Introductory Essays, Priestley alluded to this when he wrote that association

> tends in a very eminent degree, to enlarge the comprehension of the mind, to give a man a kind of superiority to the world and to himself, so as to advance him in the scale of being, and consequently to lay a foundation for equable and permanent happiness.(16)

This expansion of the human consciousness was how man achieved happiness in political society. He noted in his Essay on the First Principles of Government (1768) that the single standard of good government was whether it had attended to the happiness of its citizenry.(17) The achievement of happiness was the first principle of good government: it was a prerequisite for progress to take place in society, and progress for Priestley was directly linked to man's advancing intellectual capabilities.

The incident that may have specifically sparked Priestley's attack on Reid, Beattie, and Oswald was the failure of the Feathers Tavern Petition in 1772.(18) The year before, a group of radical Dissenters and liberal churchmen had drafted this document in an effort to relieve them from having to subscribe to the Thirty-Nine Articles of Faith of the Church of England. Led principally by Theophilus Lindsey and Archdeacon Francis Blackburne, the group also included such well-known figures as Christopher Wyvill, John Jebb, and Richard Price. The Petition itself declared

> the belief of the petitioners in a natural right to the free exercise of their judgement in matters of religion: a natural right upon which the Reformation was founded and incompatible with the existence of the Thirty-Nine Articles as a subscriptive creed.(19)

Such a creed made Priestley, Price, Lindsey, and the other

Dissenters feel that they were barely tolerated in a world dominated by the Established Church.

The Crown and Parliament opposed the measure. Lord North stated, for example, that "every person is allowed to go to Heaven his own way. The only restraint laid upon us is that we create no public disturbance". Hence, the measure was unnecessary and even redundant. Burke continued the argument:

> I would have [he thundered] a system of religious
> laws that would remain fixed and permanent, like our
> civil constitution, and that would preserve the body
> ecclesiastical from tyranny and despotism, as much
> at least as our code of common and statute law does
> the people in general: for I am convinced that the
> liberty of conscience, contended for by the
> petitioners, would be the forerunner of religious
> slavery.(20)

The Commons defeated the measure by 217 to 77. While Priestley blamed the establishment, he saved his greatest attack for the common-sense philosophers. James Beattie had spent part of the summer and autumn of 1771 in London where he enjoyed a spectacular reception. His Essay on Truth by then was well known, even to the King who told him he greatly admired it. Indeed, later Beattie was to be awarded an honorary doctorate from Oxford and an annual pension of two hundred pounds from George III himself. While in London, he met the likes of Lord Mansfield, Dr. Johnson, and Edmund Burke, among others. One year later in September of 1772, Archbishop York suggested to him that he certainly ought to consider a ministry (though Beattie was not ordained) in the Church of England: "as far as I can judge", said York, "the ministry in the church of England would be the profession the most agreeable to your qualification and inclination".(21)

For Priestley, it all fitted neatly together: common sense provided a retrogressive epistemology which inexorably led to the acceptance of the status quo, no matter how immoral or ungodly that status quo might be. In the Examination, for example, Priestley noted that politicians:

> may venture once more to thunder out upon us their
> exploded doctrines of passive obedience and
> non-resistance. For having now nothing to fear from
> the powers of reason, and being encouraged by the
> example of grave divines and metaphysicians, they

may venture to assert their favourite maxims with the greatest confidence; appealing at once to this ultimate tribunal of common sense, and giving out their mandates as the decisions of this new tribunal.(22)

Priestley thus focused his assault on Thomas Reid and the common sense school from the perspective of associationism. Unlike Locke, Priestley did not think of the associative principle in purely mechanical terms where ideas were connected by their contiguous relationships only. Man, said Priestley, was an ingenious creature who possessed the power to make linkages between ideas and thus acquire knowledge. Unconscious though this process was, man became aware of the process and used it for progressive purposes (like seeing the inutility of the Test and Corporation Acts). For Priestley, common sense contained a fundamental error: people like Reid had contrived to meld together the operations of sensation and reflection to argue favourably for man's innate ability to make immediate judgments at the very moment of perception. This meant that Reid could affirm whatever he perceived as a true reflection of reality and thus accept it.

In fact, said Priestley, there was no unity of perception with judgment and belief. If such a unity existed, the associative principle would have been obviated. Without the association of ideas, the progress of human knowledge would cease, and with this cessation, progress and positive change in society would be lost. The demise of the principle of association meant for Priestley no less than the ruination of all progress in the world. Moreover, it meant the befuddlement of God's plan in history. And this in turn meant that without progress in the mind, the millennium would be precluded. When viewed in these terms, the association of ideas philosophy had world-historical dimensions for Priestley.(23)

In undermining the principles of common sense, Priestley wanted to show that man could progress toward a perfect society. Cause and effect, the processes of time, and the nature of matter were all involved in a movement forward that reached to a providential Deity. These phenomena were not relegated to the faculty of common sense, because they were never immediately discernable at the moment of sensation. Indeed, there was, for Priestley, no direct connection between sensation and reflection. On the contrary, man's ideas were the basis of societal progress. Hence, man could only arrive at these ideas because sensation and reflection were separate. We turn our perceptions into action only <u>after</u> reflection. We have choices to make, and as we make these choices, progress can result.

Common sense, on the other hand, he said was only 'instinct'. This was the proper term for the power of the mind when one artificially linked sensation with reflection. For Priestley, through association, man could actually know more than what merely appeared to exist, even when he was not consciously trying to make associations:

> nature has sufficiently provided for that in the simple power of association, whereby one idea or motion introduces another associated idea or motion mechanically, and without the exertion of any voluntary power in us.(24)

Reid, meanwhile, had condemned human progress by confining understanding to instinct. Belief and judgment were not immediately apprehendable or merely instinctive. Instinctual characteristics may be subjective. No one knew for certain what was in the mind of another person. What Priestley perceived as cold snow might not have been Reid's judgment of either snow or coldness. Progress in man's understanding by means of the principles of common sense was, then, always uncertain. When common sense, like that of Thomas Reid, sought to make propositions into axioms based on 'some unaccountable, instinctive persuasion', the effort was unfounded, because it depended 'upon the arbitrary constitution of our nature'.(25) In short, it was subjective and dependent on one's narrow vision of the world.

For Priestley, association was an intellectual power that helped man develop in a progressive manner. The course of human events showed, he wrote in his <u>Lectures on History and General Policy</u>, that human progress occurred when human knowledge advanced. In fact, men today were currently happier than their forebears, and they enjoyed greater individual security and political liberty than at any other time in history. Men could see how the power of the mind favourably affected the growth of human society.

> We can see the strength of [the mind's] powers, the connexion of its principles, and the variety to which individuals of the species are subject, together with many other particulars, equally

curious and useful.(26)

Political changes were absolutely imperative as man's mind
progressed through time according to God's unfolding plan.
Positive changes, however, could only occur through the
association of ideas, and by no other means: certainly never
by the retrogressive epistemology offered by the proponents
of common sense.

NOTES

(1) Joseph Priestley, The Memoirs of Dr. Joseph Priestley L.L.D., F.R.S., To the Year 1795 Written by Himself (London, 1806–7), in Rutt, ed. (1816–31, Vol. I, Pt. 1, p. 202).

(2) Priestley, An Examination of Dr. Reid's 'Inquiry into the Human Mind on the Principles of Common Sense'; Dr. Beattie's 'Essay on the Nature and Immutability of Truth'; and Dr. Oswald's 'Appeal to Common Sense in Behalf of Religion' (London, 1774), in Rutt (1816–31, III, pp. 4, 8).

(3) Priestley, Memoirs, in Rutt (1816–31, I, 1, p. 202).

(4) Chalmers, ed., 'The Life of Dr. James Beattie', in (1810, Vol. XVIII, p. 520n.

(5) **IP**, VI,ii (Works, pp. 422, 425).

(6) I, I, vi (Works, p. 103).

(7) I, I, i (Works, p. 97).

(8) Ibid., (Works, p. 98).

(9) Reid noted the following of how common sense worked, even among the labouring poor: "the day labourer toils at his work, in the belief that he shall receive his wages at night; and if he had not this belief, he would not toil". (**I**, Dedication, Works, p. 95).

(10) **I**, VII (Works, p. 209).

(11) Ibid.

(12) Wood does, however, see changes. Cf. Wood, (1985, pp. 29–45).

(13) **IP**, VI, ii (Works, p. 422).

(14) Kallich (1970); Willey, (1961, pp. 136–43).

(15) Priestley, Hartley's Theory of the Human Mind, on the Principle of the Association of Ideas with Essays Relating to the Subject of It in Rutt (1816–31, III, p. 188).

(16) Ibid., pp. 184–85.

(17) Priestley, An Essay on the First Principles of Government, and on the Nature of Civil, Political, and Religious Liberty in Rutt (1816–31, XXII, p. 13).

(18) This is suggested in Wood, 'Thomas Reid's Critique of Joseph Priestley'.  Wood kindly allowed me to read this as-yet unpublished manuscript.

(19) Lincoln, (1971, p. 203).

(20) Both quoted in Lincoln, pp. 207–08.

(21) Sir William Forbes, (1807, Vol. I, pp. 268–346) and Chalmers, (1810, XVIII, pp. 521–22). For York's letter, see Forbes (Op.cit.), I, pp. 308–10.

(22) Priestley, Examination, in Rutt (1816–31, III, p. 102).

(23) For Priestley's millennialism, see Fruchtman, Jr., (1983).

(24) Priestley, Examination, in Rutt (1816–31, III, p. 50).

(25) Ibid., pp. 70–71.

(26) Priestley, Lectures on History and General Policy, in Rutt (1816–31, XXIV, p. 428).

Paul Wood

## REID ON HYPOTHESES AND THE ETHER; A REASSESSMENT

In recent years historians of science have come to see that Thomas Reid's Essays on the Intellectual Powers of Man had a profound impact on the development of British methodological thought in the late-eighteenth and early-nineteenth centuries. Larry Laudan has argued that Reid was "the first major British philosopher to take Newton's opinions on induction, causality, and hypotheses seriously"; and that Reid was thereby instrumental in changing the character of British methodological discourse in the Enlightenment.(1) Geoffrey Cantor has examined in detail the influence of Reid's critique of ether theories and hypotheses in the Essays on leading protagonists in the nineteenth-century debates surrounding the wave theory of light,(2) and Richard Olson has traced the origins of the scientific style of British physics in the Victorian period to the writings of Reid and other Common Sense philosophers.(3) As well as delineating Reid's influence, Laudan, Cantor, and Olson have attempted to identify the problems to which he addressed himself in articulating his methodology, and they have analysed with some care the internal structure of his methodological views. Thanks to the work of these historians, therefore, we have a fairly comprehensive picture of Reid's methodology and its fortunes in the nineteenth century.

Certain aspects of this picture are, however, highly problematic. Perhaps the most questionable feature is the lack of any temporal dimension in the current interpretation of Reid's methodological ideas. Because Cantor, Olson, and to a lesser extent Laudan are interested in Reid's influence, they have not dealt with the chronological development of the various facets of Reid's methodology. Moreover, it would have been difficult for them to do so since they have confined themselves to the exegesis of Reid's printed works and have not explored systematically the manuscript materials available. Drawing on these archival sources and on the published texts, my main aim in this paper is to reconstruct the evolution of Reid's attitudes towards hypotheses and the ether. In doing so, I hope to show that David Hartley was not the catalyst for Reid's attack on the hypothetical method as

433

*M. Dalgarno and E. Matthews (eds.), The Philosophy of Thomas Reid, 433–446.*
*© 1989 by Kluwer Academic Publishers.*

Laudan has claimed,(4) and that Reid's attitudes towards hypotheses and ether theories were more complex than has been realized hitherto.

Unfortunately the early development of Reid's methodology is difficult to document because of the lack of evidence. Initially, Reid's methodological outlook was probably shaped by his teacher at Marischal College Aberdeen, George Turnbull. Like many of his contemporaries Turnbull was an ardent admirer of Newton, and as early as 1723 he argued in print that Newton's twin methods of analysis and synthesis ought to be used in the moral sciences.(5) Furthermore, Turnbull echoed Newton's anti-hypotheticalism, writing in his Principles of Moral Philosophy that hypotheses were not "to be any further admitted [in natural or moral philosophy], than as questions, about the truth or reality of which it is worth while to enquire".(6) It is likely that Reid would also have read first-hand Newton's and Cotes's polemics against hypotheses in the course of his studies, and thus it would seem that the origins of his view of the hypothetical method lay in the prelections of Turnbull and the texts of Newton and Cotes. Reid may well have been influenced by other writers such as Henry Pemberton at this stage in his career, but none of the surviving manuscripts from the period $\underline{c}$. 1730 to 1751 shed any light on the question.(7)

In the years following his appointment as Regent at King's College Aberdeen in 1751, however, we are able to chart more accurately the evolution of his methodological ideas. In his natural philosophy prelections, Reid cautioned his students about the use of hypotheses, and he cited Fermat's and Leibniz's derivation of the sine-law in optics "to show that the most ingenious men when they trust to Hypothesis ... have only the chance of going wrong in a more ingenious way".(8) It would also seem that after the curriculum reforms of 1753 Reid warned against hypotheses in the introductory lectures to his pneumatology course, for in a fairly detailed course outline he included the heading 'The Danger & Mischief of Hypotheses'.(9) Within the specific context of the philosophy of mind, the primary target for Reid's strictures on hypotheses was, as is well known, the theory of ideas. Although the texts of Reid's pneumatology lectures at King's College have apparently not survived, his Philosophical Orations delivered in 1759 and 1762 give us some idea of the criticisms of that theory which Reid probably made in his prelections.(10)

In the two orations which he devoted to the science of the mind, Reid levelled various objections at the theory of ideas, the most pertinent for the purposes of this paper being that ideas could not actually explain the phenomena of perception and memory, and that the proponents of the theory had failed to prove that ideas actually existed. Reid dismissed the notion of ideas as being either symbols or images on the grounds that there cannot be images, strictly speaking, of tastes, sounds, and smells; that it was difficult to see how images of extended things could be 'painted' on to immaterial and unextended minds; and that it was unclear how we could ever learn to interpret our ideas as being symbols or representations of external objects. As for the existence of ideas, Reid asserted that there was no evidence, anatomical or otherwise, which demonstrated that ideas did in fact exist. Rather, the belief in the existence of ideas had, according to Reid, been sustained by a spurious analogy between the motions of bodies and the actions of the mind.(11) Implicit in these objections are the two criteria for true causes which Reid later formulated explicitly, namely that the posited cause be sufficient to explain the relevant phenomena and that it be shown to exist. Significantly, Reid did not, however, appeal to Newton's First Rule of Philosophizing in making these objections and we shall see that it would seem that his distinctive vera causa interpretation of the First Rule only emerged in the mid-1760s.(12)

During the 1750s, if not before, Reid was interested in the physiology as well as the philosophy of perception. His concern with this branch of physiology partly grew out of his critical review of the evidence adduced in support of the theory of ideas, but he also chose to lecture on other aspects of human physiology in his natural history course at King's. In his prelections his avowed aim was to demonstrate that 'The Origin of Motion in the human Body ... is not Mechanical'(13), and to achieve this end he drew heavily on the work of Robert Whytt. Whytt was a staunch opponent of mechanistic and materialistic theories of man, and he was one of the first British physiologists in the eighteenth century to reject the standard causal mechanisms of ethers and animal spirits, and to question whether the phenomena of the human body were explicable in terms of the attractive and repulsive forces active in the animate realm of nature. In doing so, Whytt emulated Newton's cautious inductivism, anti-hypotheticalism, and avoidance of undue speculation about efficient causes, and he eschewed the reductionist style of physiological theorizing prevalent in Britain during the first half of the eighteenth century.(14)    Reid was deeply influenced by Whytt's approach to the study of the animal economy and there is little doubt that Whytt's critique of the major physiological theories then current reinforced Reid's opposition to the use of hypotheses and shaped his understanding of the science of physiology.

In his natural history lectures, Reid also dealt with the sensitive subject of the generation of animals. Although the text of his prelections on generation have not survived, we know from manuscripts dating from the 1730s and from his Glasgow period that Reid was convinced that the formation and growth of an embryo could not be explained in purely material terms. For metaphysical reasons, Reid subscribed to a variant of the doctrine of preformation, arguing that the development of an embryo was essentially an 'unfolding' of an 'organized atom' which had originally been created by God.(15) Consequently, when Reid first encountered the initial volumes of Buffon's monumental Histoire Naturelle in the 1750s, he was not disposed to accept the epigenetic explanation of reproduction outlined therein, not least because Buffon's theory seemed to rest on a suspiciously heterodox view of the powers of matter. Moreover, the theory of the earth which Buffon advanced in the Histoire probably struck Reid as being highly subversive as well, since inter alia Buffon denied the validity of invoking the Noachian deluge to account for geological phenomena and insisted that events in the past ought to be explained in terms of causes operating in the present. Given that Buffon was apparently one of the targets of Reid's later attack on the conjectural nature of '[a]ll our curious theories of the formation of the earth, [and] of the generation of animals', it is likely that Reid's engagement with the Histoire Naturelle in the 1750s provided a further stimulus for his critique of hypotheses.(16)

All of these motifs from the 1750s were developed in the most systematic statement of Reid's methodology dating from the King's College years, his Inquiry into the Human Mind, On the Principles of Common Sense. Four points regarding the Inquiry need to be made here. First,most of Reid's major criticisms of the theory of ideas were variations on Newtonian themes.  For example, Reid capitalized on Newton's Fourth Rule of Philosophizing when he argued that the hypothesis of ideas had led its proponents to deny two cardinal facts about human nature: (i) that our conceptions of extension and the other primary qualities of bodies are

different in kind from our sensations, and (ii) that all of
mankind have an unshakeable belief in the reality of an
external material world. Echoing the rhetoric of the Fourth
Rule, Reid observed:

> These facts are phenomena of human nature, from
> which we may justly argue against any hypothesis,
> however generally received. But to argue from an
> hypothesis against facts, is contrary to the rules
> of true philosophy.(17)

In this as well as in other instances Reid thus mobilized the
methodological resources of the Newtonian corpus in his
attack on the theory of ideas.(18)

Secondly, Reid's general remarks on the hypothetical
method in the introduction to the Inquiry display his
indebtedness to Bacon. Playing on Bacon's
theologically-charged distinction between the anticipation
and the interpretation of nature, Reid underlined the
disparity between the products of man's finite intellect and
those of the infinitely-wise Creator. For Reid, our
conjectures cannot begin to capture the complexities of the
creation since they inevitably reflect the limitations of our
reason and imagination. To anticipate nature by relying
on hypotheses was, he maintained, to set up human reason as a
false measure of the wisdom and power of God. Consequently,
true knowledge could only be obtained by interpreting
nature,that is, by piously studying God's works utilizing the
empirical methods of observation and experiment. Reid's use
of this distinction should serve to remind us that he paid
more than simple 'lip-service' to Bacon's ideas, and it also
suggests that he was profoundly influenced by the
intrinsically religious character of Bacon's empiricism.(19)

Thirdly, in the chapter 'Of Seeing' Reid dismisses what
he takes to be the standard physiological explanations of
perception associated with the theory of ideas, and it is
significant that his comments foreshadow his later polemic
against David Hartley. Having reviewed the various hypotheses
which had been put forward to explain how images of external
objects are conveyed from the retina to the mind, Reid asked:

> how can the images of sound, taste, smell, colour,
> figure, and all sensible qualities, be made out of
> the vibrations of musical chords, or the undulations
> of animal spirits, or of aether? We ought not to

suppose means inadequate to the end.(20)

Reid returned to this point in the Essays, where he argued that the permutations of Hartley's vibrations and vibratiuncles were insufficient to explain the variety of our sensations, and he again questioned whether 'the emotions of animal spirits, [or] the vibrations of the elastic chords, or of elastic aether, or of the infinitesimal particles of the nerves' could actually produce images resembling the qualities of material bodies.(21) We see, therefore, that there was a continuity in Reid's approach to the physiology of perception and to medullary ethers, a continuity underlined by the fact that in the Essays his analysis of Hartley occurred in a chapter surveying the theories of Descartes, Briggs, and Newton, which he had already discussed some twenty years before in the Inquiry. The terms of Reid's methodological assault on Hartley were thus predetermined by his earlier campaign against the theory of ideas launched during his years at King's College.

Finally, Reid's attitude towards hypotheses was in the end somewhat ambivalent, for he did allow that they have a legitimate, if circumscribed, role to play in philosophy.(22) Citing the precedent of the Queries appended to Newton's Opticks, Reid held that conjectures and hypotheses should be identified as such, that they should be clearly distinguished from conclusions inductively inferred, and that they should be used primarily to suggest further empirical research. His own hypothesis concerning squinting included in the Inquiry designedly satisfied these criteria, and his manuscripts from the 1750s provide us with another example of Reid following these guidelines when tentatively accepting an hypothesis. Prior to 1756, Reid familiarized himself with Benjamin Franklin's theory of electricity, and when he came to discuss the operation of Franklin's electrical fluid, he formulated a series of 'Conjectures concerning Electricity to be confirmed or refuted by future Experiments'.(23) We see, then, that Reid's anti-hypotheticalism was qualified by his recognition of a limited heuristic function for hypotheses, and that in practice he adopted conjectures subject to the criteria he specified in the Inquiry.(24)

Reid's provisional acceptance of Franklin's theory also shows that he did not entirely eschew speculations involving unobservable causal mechanisms. Although some commentators have claimed that Reid stipulated that only observable entities should be involved in scientific theories, Laudan is

closer to the mark when he suggests that Reid was willing to
appeal to "observable or (at least) instrumentally detectable
entities and properties".(25)    Thus Reid accepted the view
that light was particulate in nature even though the
constituent particles of light were far too minute to be
directly perceived, because the empirical evidence available
supported this conclusion.(26)    Moreover, in the Inquiry he
spoke of 'effluvia of vast subtilty' made up of 'volatile
particles [which] probably repel each other' when explaining
the physical causes of smelling. Perhaps the most likely
source for this effluvial theory was Stephen Hale's Vegetable
Staticks (1727), wherein Hales endeavoured to prove
experimentally:

> that there is diffused thro' all natural, mutually
> attracting bodies, a large proportion of particles,
> which ... are capable of being thrown off from dense
> bodies by heat or fermentation into a vigorously
> elastick and permanently repelling state.(27)

Prompted by the researches of Lavoisier and other French
chemists, Reid later entertained the idea that heat is a
subtle fluid consisting of mutually-repellent particles.(28)
These examples therefore illustrate that Reid was prepared to
adopt theories which postulated unobservable entities
provided there was sufficient indirect evidence to attest to
their existence.

Indeed, it would seem that Reid's primary worry
concerning ethers and subtle fluids was not the question of
the type of evidence adduced to demonstrate their existence,
but was rather their status as efficient causes. Put simply,
as a theist Reid did not want any of the links broken in the
causal chain leading from the phenomena of nature to God. If
ethers were seen as possessing some form of intrinsic active
power, then heterodox conclusions, such as that nature was
self-sustaining or that life was simply a manifestation of
the activity of an all-pervasive ether, would follow.(29)
Consequently, Reid insisted that ethers were not to be
regarded as being efficient causes. Writing to Lord Kames in
December 1780, Reid argued that the "natural philosopher may
search after the cause of a law of nature; but this means no
more than searching for a more general law, which includes
that particular law, and perhaps many others under it". He
continued:

This was all that Newton aimed at by his ether. He

thought it possible, that, if there was such an
ether, the gravitation of bodies, the reflection and
refraction of the rays of light, and many other laws
of nature, might be the necessary consequences of
the elasticity and repelling force of the ether.
But, supposing this ether to exist, its elasticity
and repelling force must be considered as a law of
nature; and the efficient cause of this elasticity
would still have been latent.(30)

According to Reid it was left to the metaphysicians to
speculate on efficient causes, and Reid's metaphysics were
such that he held that it was an axiom of common sense that
matter is passive and he attributed all activity in nature to
immaterial causes.(31)    Thus it is arguable that Reid's
attitude towards ethers and subtle fluids was largely
conditioned by his opposition to materialism, and that his
concerns were mainly metaphysical rather than epistemological
in character.

Following the publication of the Inquiry, Reid moved to
Glasgow and in his lectures from this period his distinctive
explication of Newton's First Rule of Philosophizing appears
for the first time. Notes dating from 1765 show that when
Reid enumerated the competing physiological theories of
perception in his prelections, he rejected them on the
grounds that:

When Men pretend to account for any of the
Operations of Nature & to assign the Cause of them,
the Cause assigned ought to have these two Qualities
other ways [sic] it is good for Nothing. First it
ought to be true & not a meer Fiction or Bare
Conjecture without Proof. Secondly it ought to be
sufficient to produce the Effect assigned to it.(32)

Later, in 1768–69, Reid revised his lectures, and he
sharpened his formulation of the vera causa principle,
explicitly presenting it as an elaboration of Newton's First
Rule. Reid explained the Rule thus:

This is a  Golden Rule in Philosophy, by which we
may always distinguish what is sound and solid ...
from what is hollow and vain. If a Philosopher
therefore pretends to tell us the Cause of any
Natural Effect, whether relating to Matter or to
Mind; Let us first consider whether there is

> sufficient Evidence that the Cause he assigns really
> exists. If we find sufficient Evidence of its
> Existence we are next to consider, whether the
> Effect it is brought to explain, necessarily follow
> from it. If the Cause he assigns has these two
> properties it is to be admitted as the true Cause;
> Otherwise it is not.(33)

By 1769, therefore, Reid had evolved the interpretation of
Newton's First Rule which he subsequently published in the
Essays. That this interpretation was formulated in the late
1760s is highly significant, for it would seem that it was
only in 1774 that he confronted David Hartley's defence of
the hypothetical method and an etherial physiology.(34)
Consequently, Hartly was apparently not the catalyst for
Reid's anti-hypotheticalism, even though sections of the
Essays give this impression. The evidence reviewed above
demonstrates that Reid developed his views on hypotheses in
the context of his response to the theory of ideas, to the
heterodox speculations of Buffon, and to contemporary
physiological theories. While Reid's attack on hypotheses in
the Essays may have focused on Hartley, the Englishman
seemingly contributed nothing to the genesis of Reid's
critique of conjectures and hypotheses.

In the decade following 1774 Reid became increasingly
preoccupied with Joseph Priestley's materialism,
necessitarianism, and the Dissenter's use of Hartley's ideas.
Prior to his retirement from teaching in 1780, Reid began to
censure Hartley's physiological ether in his lectures, and
his remarks served as the basis for what he later published
in the Essays. During the 1780s Reid delivered a series of
discourses before the Glasgow Literary Society on Priestley's
matter-theory which included a lengthy discussion of Newton's
Rules of Philosophizing designed to controvert Priestley's
claim that:

> if we suffer ourselves to be guided in our inquiries
> by the universally acknowledged rules of
> philosophizing we shall find ourselves entirely
> unauthorized to admit any thing in man besides the
> body which is the object of our senses.(35)

The work of Hartley and Priestley thus elicited significant
restatements of Reid's methodology, but it should be
emphasized that in his writings from this period Reid merely
elaborated on the position he had developed in the 1750s and

1760s.

    To conclude, we may summarize the evolution of Reid's
views on hypotheses and the ether as follows. In the years
1722 to 1751 it would seem that Reid assimilated the
teachings of his regent at Marischal College George Turnbull
as well as the methodological message of the Newtonian
corpus. Stimulated by his teaching responsibilities at King's
College, Reid then articulated his Baconian critique of the
use of hypotheses in general, and formulated his specific
criticisms of the theory of ideas and of physiological
theories of perception. After moving to Glasgow in 1764 Reid
appears to have arrived at his highly influential
interpretation of Newton's First Rule of Philosophizing in
the course of revising his pneumatology lectures, and by 1770
his anti-hypotheticalist position was clearly defined. The
1770s and 1780s saw him attacking new targets (namely Hartley
and Priestley), but his comments were variations on previous
themes.

    We have also seen that Reid's attitudes towards
hypotheses were somewhat ambivalent, and that he recognized
that hypotheses did have a limited role to play in the growth
of science. Reid himself adopted a number of hypotheses
during his long career, and he endeavoured to pattern his
practice in this regard on his precepts. Finally, I have
argued that Reid did not object to ethers or subtle fluids on
the grounds that they were unobservable entities. His demand
that the existence of theoretical entities be proven was not
equivalent to a requirement that they be directly
perceivable. The evidence suggests that Reid was instead
worried by the heterodox implications of treating ethers or
subtle fluids as efficient causes. Thus it was the threat of
materialism rather than a rigid empiricist epistemology which
motivated his assault on assorted ethers and hypotheses.

## Acknowledgements

The author wishes to thank: the Archivist and Keeper of Manuscripts of Aberdeen University Library, Mr. Colin McLaren, and the Keeper of Special Collections of Glasgow University Library for permission to quote from manuscripts in their care; and the Social Sciences and Humanities Research Council of Canada for financial support in the form of a Post-Doctoral Research Fellowship and for a travel grant which enabled him to attend the Reid Bicentennial Conference.

## NOTES

(1)  Laudan (1970, p. 106).

(2)  Cantor (1971, pp. 69–89; Cantor (1975, pp. 109–32).

(3)  Olson (1975).

(4)  Laudan (1981, p. 171).

(5)  Turnbull (1726).

(6)  Turnbull (1976, I, 20); compare Cotes's preface to Sir Isaac Newton (1968, I, [iii]). Turnbull's Principles were probably based, at least in part, on his Aberdeen lectures.

(7)  An undated reading note on Pemberton survives among Reid's papers; see AUL, 2131/3/I/20.

(8)  AUL MS K.160, p. 263. Reid also quoted Newton's Fourth Rule of Philosophizing (which also deals with hypotheses) in the introductory lecture to his natural philosophy course; see ibid., p. 8.

(9)  AUL MS 2131/8/V/1, Fol. 2r.

(10) In his orations for 1753 and 1756 Reid discussed the question of method in philosophy, and his own third law of philosophizing ruled out the use of hypotheses; see Humphries (ed.) (1937, pp. 23–24).

(11) Humphries (1937, pp. 34–38).

(12) Reid's criticism of the theory of ideas parallels Cotes's attack on the Cartesian theory of vortices; see Newton (1968, I, xv–xviii).

(13) AUL MS 2131/7/II/17, fol. 1r; see also 2131/8/V/1. fol. 1v.

(14) Whytt (1768, pp. v–vi, 2, 6, 31, 98, 110, 142–43, 145, 147–48, 152–53, 171–72). On anti–reductionism in mid–eighteenth–century British physiology see Schofield (1970, ch. IX), and Brown (1974, pp. 179–216).

(15) For the most succinct statement of Reid's views on generation see Reid to Lord Kames, [c.1775], in Works, pp. 53–54; a draft of this letter is to be found in AUL MS 2131/2/III/3. On the development of Reid's ideas concerning generation see Wood, 'Thomas Reid, Natural Philosopher: A Study of Science and Philosophy in the Scottish Enlightenment' (unpublished Ph.D. dissertation, University of Leeds, 1984, ch. V, sect. i).

(16) I, I, i (Works, p. 97); see also Duncan (ed.) (1981), pp. 106–7. I have discussed Reid's response to Buffon in more detail in Wood (1987).

(17) I, V, viii (Works, p. 132).

(18) See also I, V, vii, (Works, p. 128).

(19) I, I, i (Works, p. 97); compare here Reid's 'A Brief Account of Aristotle's Logic. With Remarks.', in Kames (1774, II, p. 237). Laudan views Reid's use of Bacon as being largely rhetorical; see Laudan (1970, pp. 121–22). Yet in his Glasgow lectures on the 'Culture of the Mind' Reid discussed in some detail the specifics of Bacon's inductive method as outlined in the Novum Organum; see AUL MS 2131/4/II/14, fol. 5r.

(20) I, VI, xix, (Works, p. 179).

(21) IP, II, iii, (Works, pp. 249–252), II, iv (Works, pp. 256–7).

(22) Laudan notes this ambivalence; see Laudan (1970, pp. 116–17).

(23) AUL MS 2131/6/V/11, fol. 1v; the final section of the

manuscript dates from 1756. In the 1750s Reid considered Whytt's theory of irritability to be 'the most probable Hypothesis yet advanced' to explain involuntary motion, and adopted it accordingly. He did not, however, discuss Whytt's 'hypothesis' in the highly formalized way that he did Franklin's. See AUL MS 2131/7/II/2. Guided primarily by metaphysical considerations, Reid also developed his theory of 'organized atoms' as a working hypothesis; for details see the references cited above in note 15.

(24) Reid also stressed the heuristic function of hypotheses in one of his letters to Kames; Reid to Lord Kames, 16 December 1780, in Works, pp. 56–57.

(25) Laudan (1970, p. 112).

(26) AUL MS K.160, p.13; AUL MS 21316V23; I, VI, i (Works, pp. 132–133).

(27) I, II, i (Works, pp. 104–5); Hales, (1969), pp. xxvii. Hales derived his theory from Query 31 of Newton's Opticks and Freind's Chymical Lectures (London, 1712).

(28) See especially AUL MS 2131/2/I/4. It should be noted that in his lectures in the 1770s Reid mentioned Newton's etherial explanation of gravity and suggested that electrical phenomena were the result of the activity of an ether; see GUL MS Gen. 116, p. 112 (original pagination).

(29) The use made of ethers by Hume and Cullen could certainly be perceived as being heterodox in intent; see Christie, 'Ether and the Science of Chemistry: 1740–1790', in Cantor and Hodge (1981, pp. 87–88, 93–94).

(30) Reid to Lord Kames, 16 December 1780, in Works pp. 57–58.

(31) AUL MS K.160, p. 10.

(32) AUL MS 2131/4/II/1, p. 20 (original pagination).

(33) AUL MS 2131/4/II/2, insert, p. 5.

(34) The first mention of Hartley which I have found in Reid's manuscripts occurs in reading notes dated 19 June 1774; see AUL MS 2131/3/I/25, fols. 1v–2v. I have developed this argument further in Wood (1985, pp. 29–45).

(35) Rutt (ed.) (1816–31, III, p. 202). On Reid's response to
Priestley see Wood, 'Thomas Reid, Natural Philosopher',
chapt. V, sect. iii.

David F. Channell


## THE ROLE OF THOMAS REID'S PHILOSOPHY IN SCIENCE AND TECHNOLOGY; THE CASE OF W.J.M. RANKINE


> The faculties of our minds are the tools and
> engines we must use in every disquisition; and the
> better we understand their nature and force, the
> more successfully we shall be able to apply
> them.(1)


Thomas Reid's technological metaphor assumes that the application of the faculties of the mind to practical purposes is dependent upon a knowledge of the scientific laws which govern the mind just as the practical application of tools and machines requires a knowledge of the laws of natural science. Today, although some people might question Reid's assumption that the faculties of the mind can be scientifically explained, almost no one would question that modern technology is basically applied science. It is a significant characteristic of the modern world that science and technology are not separate modes of knowledge but have become a single hyphenated concept. Therefore many people might not appreciate the importance of Reid's assumption that the application of tools and machines to practical purposes requires a knowledge of scientific principles. But, when Reid published his remark in 1785, the idea that science should be applied to technology was a very new, and not yet widely accepted, idea. James Watt had applied the notion of latent heat to his analysis of the steam engine but little else was known about the science of thermodynamics. Although Newton had discovered the laws of mechanics, the laws had little influence on the design of structures or machines. Reid's technological metaphor not only provided a model for the scientific study of the mind, but it also provided a model for the application of science to technology.

One of the most significant problems that faced nineteenth-century engineers was the relationship between science and technology.(2) Although new technological developments were becoming more and more dependent upon science, especially in such areas as the strength of

447

*M. Dalgarno and E. Matthews (eds.), The Philosophy of Thomas Reid, 447–455.*
© *1989 by Kluwer Academic Publishers.*

materials, the expansive use of steam, and naval
architecture, the laws of natural science never seemed quite
to fit the phenomena of the real world. Engineers needed a
model for a new body of knowledge – an engineering science –
that would provide the missing connections between the laws
of natural science and the real structures, engines, and
ships that they had to design.

Although both the French and the Germans contributed a
great deal to the development of engineering science, one of
the most influential figures in the creation and
institutionalization of the field was the Scottish Professor
of Engineering, William John Macquorn Rankine (1820–1872).
He was both a scientist and engineer, and he spent the
greater part of his professional life trying to establish a
connection between science and technology.(3) Through his
position as Regius Professor of Civil Engineering and
Mechanics at Glasgow University (1855–1872) and his
production of a series of works that became the standard
textbooks for university-trained engineers throughout the
second half of the nineteenth century and well into the
twentieth century, Rankine became one of the leading figures
in engineering science, influencing the development of the
field in Europe, America and Japan.

Rankine had a background in both science and technology.
By the time he was appointed to his position at Glasgow
University, he had received formal training in natural
philosophy under James David Forbes at the University of
Edinburgh and practical training in the engineering
profession both as a pupil of Sir John MacNeill and as an
established engineer in Glasgow and Edinburgh. Rankine had
particularly distinguished himself in the world of science
through his development of the laws of heat and light. This
work brought him honours from the Royal Societies of London
and Edinburgh and established him as one of the founders of
the new science of thermodynamics.

When Rankine became Regius Professor in 1855, he
realized that he could not teach pure science since that
would duplicate courses already being taught in natural
philosophy and chemistry. Further, pure practice could not
successfully compete with the established apprenticeship
system. He would need a model or framework in which science
and technology could be combined into an engineering science.
My argument is that Rankine derived the framework he needed
from the Common Sense philosophy of Thomas Reid and Dugald

Stewart, and that the concept of engineering science has its roots in Scottish thought and culture.

During Rankine's two years as a student at the University of Edinburgh, he spent a great deal of his leisure time reading philosophy – especially those philosophers associated with Common Sense.(4) He was most likely first introduced to Reid's philosophy through the writings of Dugald Stewart. His interest in Common Sense philosophy would have been reinforced in the natural philosophy courses taught by J.D. Forbes, who, as a student, won a prize for a paper 'On the Inductive Philosophy of Bacon'.(5) Forbes saw a close connection between moral and natural philosophy.(6) As a student in Forbes' advanced natural philosophy class, Rankine won a gold prize for his essay 'Methods of Physical Investigation'.(7) Although Rankine's student essay is lost, his later engineering science reflected a continued interest in the issues addressed by Common Sense philosophy.

The Common Sense philosophy of Reid and Stewart provided Rankine with two important elements he needed to create engineering science. First, the philosophy of Common Sense helped Rankine bridge the gap between science and technology. Even in Rankine's time, most engineers throughout the world were suspicious of science. For them, science was purely theoretical and abstract and therefore distinct from the practical problems of engineering. But a central tenet of Common Sense philosophy drawn from Francis Bacon was that knowledge did not exist for its own sake but should be applied to some practical problem. Reid insisted that it was "evidently the intention of our Maker, that man should be an active and not merely a speculative being". He claimed that knowledge "derives its value from this, that it enlarges our power, and directs us in the application of it".(8) Dugald Stewart repeated this claim by Reid in noting that "the more knowledge ... we acquire, the better can we accommodate our plans to the established order of things".(9) And Forbes argued: "Knowledge is good because it leads directly to useful results".(10)

In his first lecture to his engineering class at Glasgow, Rankine observed that progress in both science and engineering had been hindered by what he called "the fallacy of a double system of natural laws"; that is, the belief that theoretical, geometrical rational laws which had been discovered by contemplation were separate and distinct from practical, mechanical, empirical laws which had been

discovered by experience.(11) Although natural philosophers
in the sixteenth and seventeenth centuries had overthrown
this fallacy, Rankine argued that the "discrepancy between
theory and practice, which in sound physical and mechanical
science is a delusion, has a real existence in the minds of
men; and that fallacy, though rejected by their judgments,
continues to exert an influence over their acts".(12)
According to Rankine, the separation of theory from practice
had its most detrimental effect on engineering since "a large
number of persons, possessed of an inventive turn of mind and
of considerable skill in the manual operations of practical
mechanics, are destitute of that knowledge of scientific
principles which is requisite to prevent their being misled
by their own ingenuity".(13) Rankine believed that it was
the role of engineering science, as it would be taught in
universities such as Glasgow's, to apply "scientific
principles to practical purposes" which would bring about
"harmony of theory and practice".(14) Rankine's view that
scientific principles were an essential part of engineering
was an important element in the transition of technology from
traditional craft to modern engineering and it reflected the
emphasis Common Sense philosophers had placed on the
application of knowledge to practical purposes.

Common Sense philosophy not only helped Rankine
transcend the old distinctions between theory and practice in
order to create engineering science, but also provided him
with the conceptual framework he needed to re-cast scientific
theories into a form that could be used in engineering.
Although theory and practice depended on the same first
principles, their modes of instruction might differ since
practice would call "into operation a mental faculty distinct
from those which are exercised by theoretical science".(15)
Here Rankine seems to parallel Reid's argument that the
powers of the mind could be divided into the intellectual
powers of understanding and the active powers of will.(16)

For Rankine, the difference in the modes of instruction
in science and practice seems to centre on the use of
hypotheses. During the nineteenth century, the role of
hypotheses in scientific theories was the subject of much
debate. Although Reid had argued strongly against the use of
hypotheses, Stewart was willing to allow them a role in
scientific theories.(17) For example, Stewart explained
that: "although a knowledge of facts must be prior to the
formulation of a legitimate theory; yet a hypothetical theory
is generally the best guide to the knowledge of connected and

useful facts".(18)     Most   of   Rankine's   work   in   science,
especially his studies  of the  laws of heat  and light,  was
based  on  a  new  theory  of  matter  which  he  termed  the
hypothesis of  molecular  vortices.(19)   According  to  this
hypothesis, the  atoms  of  matter  consisted  of  a  nucleus
enveloped by an elastic atmosphere.  By postulating that heat
was the vis viva  of the revolutions  of the atmospheres  and
that light was transmitted by the oscillations of the nuclei,
Rankine had  a  powerful model  for solving  such  scientific
problems as double  refraction, the  specific heat of  gases,
and the relationship between heat and work.  He realized that
hypotheses could  "never  attain the  certainty  of  observed
fact", but, like Stewart, he believed they could be a  "means
of advancing physical science".(20)

    Although Rankine's scientific research was based on  the
molecular vortex, the hypothesis played no direct role in his
technological works.   For example,  in the engineering  work
most closely associated with his scientific research, Rankine
states   that   "it   is   possible  to  express  the  laws  of
thermodynamics in the form of independent principles, deduced
by  induction  from  facts  of  observation  and  experiment,
without  reference  to  any  hypothesis  as  to  the   occult
operations with which the sensible phenomena may be conceived
to be connected; and that course will be followed in the body
of  the  present  treatise".(21)    Here Rankine  appears to  be
returning to Reid's argument that "what can fairly be deduced
from facts duly observed or sufficiently attested, is genuine
and pure".(22)

    Rankine    seems    to    have    realized    that    his
scientific-hypothetical theories could not simply be  applied
to  engineering  problems  that  required  a  more  inductive
approach.  The relationship between a hypothetical theory and
an inductive theory was most explicitly explained by  Rankine
in  his  essay  'Outlines  of  the  Science  of  Energetics',
published in the same year, 1855, he became Regius  Professor
at Glasgow.(23)   Although  many scholars  have treated  this
essay  as  a  major   contribution  to  the  creation  of   a
positivistic theory  of thermodynamics,(24) I  would like  to
argue  that  it  provides  the  key  to  understanding   the
relationship between Rankine's  science and  technology  and
that it is the  basis of his  engineering science.  As  such,
the essay shows how the  Common Sense philosophy of Reid  and
Stewart  provided  a  conceptual  framework  for  modern
engineering.

According to Rankine's essay, the development of a physical theory takes place in two stages: first, through either observation or experimentation, relationships between phenomena come to be expressed as formal laws; second, the formal laws of an entire class of phenomena are reduced to a science.(25) This can be compared to Reid's description of human knowledge as "like the steps of a ladder. The first step consists of particular truths, discovered by observation or experiment: the second collects these into more general truths".(26) This still leaves open the question of Reid's 'blind step' of how the laws are reduced to a science. Rankine argued that two methods could be used. The first of these was the hypothetical method, where conjectures not apparent to the senses are used to deduce laws based on modifications of some previously known laws. Hypothetical theories could reduce the laws of complicated phenomena to a 'few simple principles',(27) but there were also disadvantages. Rankine argued that the success of such hypotheses led to a tendency "to explain away, or set aside, facts inconsistent with these hypotheses, which facts, rightly appreciated, would have formed the basis of true theories".(28) It is just such 'inconsistent facts' that are most important to a practical theory of technology.

But there was a second way to formulate a physical theory. Rather than supposing "physical phenomena to be constituted, in an occult way" of mechanical processes, the abstractive method assigned a name or symbol to the properties which a group of phenomena had in common, "as perceived by the senses".(29) Through a process of induction from the observed facts, a series of more and more general laws could be generated. The abstractive method would not eliminate the need for hypotheses since Rankine believed that "a hypothetical theory is necessary, as a preliminary step, to reduce the expression of the phenomena to simplicity and order, before it is possible to make any progress in framing an abstractive theory".(30)

Therefore Rankine's essay reflected both Stewart's argument for the use of hypotheses and Reid's support of a purely inductive method. Stewart had argued that hypotheses were "the first rudiments or anticipations of Principles".(31) But, according to Stewart, the principles that are anticipated by hypotheses cannot be considered as the truth until they are empirically tested and made part of the kind of inductive theory supported by Reid.(32) That is, although hypotheses could be a preliminary step toward a complete theory, one had to return to the principles of Reid in order to re-cast the principles gained from hypotheses into an inductive theory.

I believe Rankine used a similar set of arguments in his essay to create a model for engineering science. This work provides a key to understanding the relationship between science and technology in Rankine's work. I would like to argue that Rankine's engineering science was based on his attempt to re-cast his hypothetical model of science into an abstractive, inductive theory. This argument can be supported by the fact that in his essay on energetics, Rankine used examples drawn from engineering to explain the abstractive method; while he used examples from science to explain the hypothetical method.(33)

Some conclusions can be drawn from this study of Rankine's engineering science. The Common Sense philosophy of Reid and Stewart provided Rankine with the conceptual and methodological frameworks he needed to bring together science and technology into engineering science. Several scholars have studied the relationship between Common Sense philosophy and science, but the emphasis has usually been on the changes brought about by Common Sense on the content and methodology within particular sciences, such as the creation of an experimental tradition within physics or chemistry.(34) But, as study of Rankine has shown, Common Sense philosophy may have played an equally important role in the transformation of science into engineering science. One of the most long-lasting influences of the philosophy of Thomas Reid may be his contribution to the philosophical framework of modern engineering.(35)

## NOTES

(1)  **IP**, Preface (<u>Works</u>, p. 218).

(2)  See Reingold and Mollela (1976).

(3)  For biographical information on Rankine see Channell (1984) and Tait (1881).

(4)  Tait (1881, p. xxi).

(5)  See Olson (1975, pp. 225–6).

(6)  See Davie (1964, pp. 186–7, 197–8).

(7)  Tait (1881, p. xxi).

(8)  **AP**, Preface (<u>Works</u>, p. 511).

(9)  Stewart (1793, p. 3).

(10) Forbes (1849, p. 7).

(11) Rankine (1856, pp. 4–5).

(12) Rankine (1856, pp. 9–10).

(13) Rankine (1856, pp. 13–14).

(14) Rankine (1856, pp. 17–18).

(15) Rankine (1856, p. 20).

(16) **IP**, I, vii (<u>Works</u>, p. 242).

(17) See Olson (1975, pp. 106–111).

(18) See Stewart (1814, vol. 2, p. 332).

(19) 'On the Mechanical Action of Heat Especially in Gases and Vapours', in Rankine (1881).

(20) Rankine (1864, p. 132).

(21) Rankine (1859, p. xviii).

(22) **IP**, I, iii (<u>Works</u>, p. 236).

(23) 'Outlines of the Science of Energetics', in Rankine (1881, pp. 209–28).

(24) E.g., see Olson (1975, pp. 271–87).

(25) 'Outlines of the Science of Energetics', in Rankine (1881, p. 209).

(26) Corr, Letter to Lord Kames (Works, p. 53). Also see Stewart, Philosophy of Mind, II, p. 266.

(27) 'Outlines of the Science of Energetics' in Rankine (1881, p.212).

(28) Ibid.

(29) Op.cit., pp. 210, 213.

(30) Op.cit., p. 213.

(31) Stewart quoting Dr. Gregory (1814, vol. 2, p. 337).

(32) Stewart (1814, vol. 1, pp. 371–3).

(33) 'Outlines of the Science of Energetics' in Rankine (1881, pp. 212, 215, 226).

(34) For example, see Donavan (1982) and Olson (1975).

(35) This study is based on work supported by the U.S. National Science Foundation under Grant No. SES–8015514.

Carolyn E. Channell


GEORGE JARDINE'S COURSE IN LOGIC AND RHETORIC : AN
APPLICATION OF THOMAS REID'S COMMON SENSE PHILOSOPHY


The teaching of English composition to undergraduates in
American universities is receiving much notice lately as
programmes in the humanities attempt to regain some degree of
their former prominence and respect. Overflowing enrolment
at a series of University of Chicago workshops on writing and
higher order reasoning is evidence of faculty members'
recognition that writing is a way of developing reasoning
abilities and values. There is also an acknowledgement that
writing has not, generally, been well taught in American
universities and that many of the methods and goals of
writing teachers have been misguided. Often heard is I.A.
Richards' 1936 description of rhetoric as the "dreariest and
least profitable part of the waste" that is known as Freshman
English.(1) Richards was siding with Whately's view that not
only had rhetoric not progressed through the ages, but it had
actually been perverted during certain periods, among them
the 18th century. It seems that composition teachers today,
seeking the origin of past errors, have also laid a share of
the blame on Common Sense Realism.

Common Sense Realism was popular and influential in
America until the 1850's. As James Berlin points out, it was
"compatible with the American belief in individualism,
equality, and self-government"(2) and, because it recognized
a spiritual and a material reality, was also compatible with
"the materialistic bent of the economic expansion taking
place ... with its emphasis on technology".(3) But Berlin
argues that in spite of 'lip service' to democracy, American
colleges became centres of conservatism and that Common Sense
philosophy provided conceptions of knowledge and language
that served this conservatism well: at least, Americans'
application of this philosophy led to courses in rhetoric and
composition that trained speakers to regard themselves as
authorities speaking on behalf of the status quo, encouraged
the idea that truth was outside the consideration of
rhetoric, and promoted the idea that success in life depended
to a great extent on correct English, the dialect of the

457

*M. Dalgarno and E. Matthews (eds.), The Philosophy of Thomas Reid, 457–465.*
*© 1989 by Kluwer Academic Publishers.*

upper classes and of 'polite letters'.(4)  Pedagogically, the
idea of faculty psychology  led to rote exercises in  grammar
and even spelling.  A theoretical work like George Campbell's
led  to  practice  in  the  application  of  various  general
principles of composition.   There was a decline in  interest
in invention but an increase  in concern for style and  form.
I am  not taking issue with  Berlin on the  question of  how
Americans interpreted  Common Sense  philosophy.    But I  can
show that such a model  was not inevitable from a reading  of
Thomas Reid.  Very different pedagogical applications of  his
philosophy  were  anticipated  by  Reid,  although  their
development was, in fact, largely left to colleagues.

     I refer to George  Jardine's Logic and Rhetoric class  at
Glasgow,  a  course  that   can  be  characterized  as   best
demonstrating  the  pedagogy  of  Common  Sense  philosophy.
Jardine (1742–1827), a student  of Reid's at Glasgow and  his
friend for over twenty  years, revised the curriculum of  the
logic  class  so  that  it  correlated  with  Reid's  views  on
knowledge and  language, taught  the course  along these  new
lines from 1774  until 1824,  and wrote a  book, Outlines  of
Philosophical Education, promoting his pedagogical  views.(5)
So imbued with Reid's ideas  was Jardine, he confessed as  he
wrote  his  Outline  that  it  was  "extremely  difficult  to
distinguish  thoughts  and  sentiments  suggested  by  that
excellent person from those which may have derived from other
sources".(6)    I  would  like  to  point  out  some  of  the
similarities in their views, and, in the process, to  suggest
that  Common  Sense  philosophy  had  many  implications  for
composition studies that must be seen as progressive.

     Jardine's altering  of the  course indicates  significant
borrowings from Reid.   Reflecting Peter Ramus's  designation
of style and delivery as the areas appropriate to  rhetorical
study,  the  traditional syllabus  of the  Scottish course  in
Logic and Rhetoric  included Longinus's  On the Sublime,  but
emphasized  logic,  particularly  Aristotelian  dialectics.
Before Jardine's  appointment  at  Glasgow,  Adam  Smith  had
directed the course to what he thought was a more interesting
and useful plan.  According to Dugald Stewart, this was to be
"an examination  of  the  several ways  of  comunicating  our
thoughts by speech, and  from an attention to the  principles
of those literary compositions which contribute to persuasion
or entertainment".(7)   Thus,  Adam Smith turned the  course
away from scholasticism towards  the relationship of  thought
and language; but he was more interested in the emotional use
of language  than  in  the  intellectual,  in  the  students'

aesthetic sense rather than in their powers of reasoning. While Hugh Blair carried the belletristic approach forward at Edinburgh, Jardine changed the focus of the Glasgow course from rhetoric, or eloquence, to logic, to the intellectual operations as evidenced by language. Jardine's course reflects Reid's traditional definition of logic as concerned with both enquiry and communication.(8) As W.S. Howell explains, "Reid did not envisage the break one day to take place between logical theory and the theory of communication. He thought instead that logic ... would continue to have a voice in literary and rhetorical enterprises".(9) Therefore, a course in logic would include some consideration of persuasion and aesthetics, but for Jardine, a detailed study of eloquence or belles lettres was not at all appropriate for a first philosophy class. Historical, philosophical, scientific – all discourse could serve as evidence, including, especially in fact, essays by the students themselves. While the direction taken by Adam Smith opened up rhetoric to include scholarly discourse, the belletristic movement's overriding concern with style and form makes Jardine's more interdisciplinary approach now seem a wiser plan.

Jardine's teaching method drew up Locke's idea that learning ought to be inductive. Knowledge was based on the natural process of observation and generalization. Reid applied these ideas to his study of the human mind, and Jardine went one· step further and used it as a pedagogical method for the same subject. But Jardine gave a particularly Reidian tone to this inductive study: he made it social, a search for knowledge to be shared by a community. This was his main innovation, and it is an important one in light of Reid's interest in language as a social act and in the social operations of the mind. Although it is true, as George Davie claims, that Jardine was a brave defender of the "pedagogical potentialities of the old system" of general, philosophical education,(10) and of the Scottish tradition of lecturing, he regarded his book as rather revolutionary. First, he explained that the English tutorial model was superior if the ultimate end of university education was seen as the communication of knowledge. But for improvement of the mental powers, which was to him the only correct end of education, the Scottish system was potentially superior.(11) Yet because of its failure to deliver, Jardine in 1772 "vowed revenge against" the current system.(12) The unexploited potential lay in the opportunity to make knowledge operative in the interaction of a community. Knowledge is for Jardine the same as for Reid: it "derives its value from this, that it enlarges our power, and directs us in the application of it".(13) And in Jardine's plan, all systems of education "must give way to that of public, active, virtuous life".(14)

Jardine realized that if the students were to interact as a community in search of knowledge, the discipline necessary for such pursuit must not be imposed from above, that is, from the professor. His system was therefore not authoritarian. The students were to stand as much "in awe of one another as of the professor",(15) and Jardine was to accomplish this by exploiting the natural emotion of emulation. That is, a system of prizes was to operate as motivation in the class, and the students themselves were to decide on the awarding of them. While it is true that Reid classified emulation as a malevolent affection because the desire for superiority among rivals leads to envy, he also said that as a natural element of the human constitution, it was given to us "for good ends" and has, provided it is directed by reason and virtue, "a manifest tendency to improvement".(16) In Jardine's class, the students were responsible for seeing that rewards were fairly dealt out. In this feature of the course, I especially see Jardine as applying a theory of Reid's and decidedly combining knowledge with moral action in a community.

Reid also cautioned that the reasoned use of emulation meant that no one should compete without a decent chance of success. With students of widely varying ages and backgrounds coming into Jardine's class, that meant that the only fair basis for competition would be overall improvement, based on effort in the class as well as on essays read aloud. In addition to the egalitarianism here, it is important to note as well the public and oral treatment of writing, as it contrasts with the emphasis on written discourse taken by the belletristic tradition.

Turning more specifically to the role of language in Jardine's course, we see that although Reid and Jardine saw reality as external to discourse, they were progressive in their recognition of the reciprocal relationship of language and knowledge. It was more a tool than an object of knowledge,but as an object, it was the same for Jardine as for Reid, who recognized that language was central to knowledge. Reid admits this with some reluctance in his discussion of Bacon's Idols: "language ... is an instrument of thought as well as the communication of our thoughts. ...

it happens that no man can pursue a train of thought or
reasoning without the use of language".(17) Jardine made
theories of universal grammar a feature of his course, both
as evidence of first principles of the mind (particularly
important to Reid) and as proof of "the constant relation
between the progress of reason and that of language".(18)
The study of language was not to be

> confined to the mere properties ... of the
> different parts of speech, but [to] extend to the
> connexion which subsists between these external
> signs and the mental operations they denote – to a
> comparison of the matter with the language in which
> it is clothed, and to a consideration of their
> reciprocal influence upon each other – to an
> examination of the principles which, in different
> languages, give occasion to peculiarities in their
> arrangement – and, lastly, to diversity of style,
> as founded upon varieties in the character and
> talents of individuals, or of nations.(19)

The idea was that the search for relationships and
similarities would better reward the students' time and
effort than would minute attention to the particulars of a
single language.

Because language was a social act, it was never to be
considered apart from meaning. Sentences were seen not as
constructions of parts of speech, but rather as units of
meaning which grammarians have broken down into categories
for the purpose of description. In fact, Reid correctly
understood the difficulty of defining the various parts of
speech(20) and reducing language to a series of principles:
the growth of language "is the effect of the united energy of
all who do or ever did use it". The 'artifices' of language
have come from "necessity, convenience, and long practice"
rather than rules.(21) Like Campbell, he saw usage as
determined by practice, but did not suggest, as Campbell did,
that the guides were to be literary.

But language as an object of study was secondary to
language as an instrument of thought. The role of
composition directly opposed the concept of education as
mental discipline through drill and memorization, methods
associated with classical education in philology.
Essay-writing, not examinations, was the appropriate
pedagogical method. As George Davie has pointed out, Jardine

was a proponent of essay–writing as "a leading feature: in
all subjects of the Arts course. Even in physics and
mathematics, essays requiring students to apply philosophical
principles were the "chief means of testing the students'
powers".(22) And Jardine's defence of essay–writing followed
Reid's point that the division of mental operations into
faculties was an artificial one, done for the purpose of
description and analysis.(23) Essay writing, rather than
developing the faculties separately, employed them in
combination.

What strikes composition teachers today as most modern
about Jardine's course, and what has earned him considerable
praise in a recent Modern Language Association
publication,(24) is his attention to the process of writing
rather than its product. To be scientific, teaching needed a
method. He created a developmental sequence of assignments
based on the topics of Reid's Essay on the Intellectual
Powers. With the power of genius or invention (defined
pre–Romantically: the ability to discover new relationships
among objects) as the ultimate goal, the sequence was based
on the premise that the powers of reason and imagination
could be improved, as they have a foundation in the anterior
powers of apprehension and concept formation. These, Reid
argued, it was within the power of all men to improve.(25)
Reid felt that indistinct conceptions were to blame for most
poor and obscure writing; Jardine's class began with
assignments to put into writing the topics of the day's
lecture. Jardine's students were as young as thirteen; his
consideration of their needs and limitations seems very
modern. Those of us teaching eighteen–year–olds today are
considering the implications of research by Lawrence
Kohlberg, William Perry, and others who are extending the
work of Jean Piaget to see how young adults continue to
change their approaches to problems and complexity.

Jardine was highly regarded as a teacher, and his
methods were carried to other universities in Scotland, most
notably by William Spalding at Edinburgh in the 1840's, but
the general, philosophical education and the attendant
attitudes toward composition had disappeared by the end of
the nineteenth century. George Davie explains this
disappearance in terms of the increased Anglicization of the
Scottish universities. I have found no evidence of Jardine's
having had any influence on American composition studies of
the time. I doubt if his method could have achieved
popularity here because although Americans rejected the

English model of education as authoritarian and aristocratic, and seemed to embrace the Scottish concept of the democratic intellect, they would not have wanted to give up a deductive pedagogy. An education that communicates knowledge is easier for those on both sides of the lectern, especially in a composition class, and it best serves the status quo. As an historian of the American university system has argued, Americans really did not want from college a rigorous intellectual experience.(26) They were impatient for the skills and certification to compete in a growing industrial society.

Finally, one wonders how widely accepted was Jardine's definition of the teachers' role. The professor was to be the experimenter and observer whose field of interest was the students themselves. His was the humble role of laying a foundation for others' genius, not of seeking the highest rank in his department.(27) Perhaps this is what makes Jardine's course most in line with Reid's understanding of knowledge: teaching was a moral act because it was an act of generosity.

NOTES

(1)  Richards (1936, p. 3).

(2)  Berlin (1984, p. 37).

(3)  Berlin (1984, p. 9).

(4)  Berlin (1984, p. 56).

(5)  Jardine (1825).  The book was first published in 1818.

(6)  Jardine (1825, p. 152).

(7)  As quoted in Smith (1963, p. xvi).

(8)  **AL**, VI, ii (<u>Works</u>, p. 711).

(9)  Howell (1971, p. 391).

(10) Davie (1964, p. 10).

(11) Jardine (1825, pp. 433–4).

(12) Mure (1894, p. 295).

(13) **AP**, Introduction (<u>Works</u>, p. 511).

(14) Mure (1894, p. 296).

(15) Jardine (1825, p. 396).

(16) **AP**, III, II, v (<u>Works</u>, pp. 566–7).

(17) **IP**, VI, viii (<u>Works</u>, p. 474).

(18) Jardine (1825, p. 84).

(19) Jardine (1825, p. 221).

(20) **AL**, II, v (<u>Works</u>, p. 692).

(21) <u>Corr</u>, Letter to James Gregory (<u>Works</u>, p. 72).

(22) Davie (1964, pp. 16–7).

(23) **IP**, I, vii (<u>Works</u>, p. 242).

(24) Homer (1982).

(25) **IP**, IV, i (<u>Works</u>, p. 366).

(26) Rodolf (1962, p. 63).

(27) Jardine (1825, pp. v–vi).

# BIBLIOGRAPHY

List of works cited in the text and notes (other than the major works of Thomas Reid).

Armstrong, D.M.: 1961, Perception and the Physical World, London, Routledge and Kegan Paul.

: 1968, A Materialist Theory of the Mind, London, Routledge and Kegan Paul.

Austin, J.L.: 1962, Sense and Sensibilia, Oxford, Clarendon Press.

: 1970, Philosophical Papers, Oxford, Oxford University Press.

Barker, S.F. and Beauchamp, T.L. (eds.): 1976, Thomas Reid: Critical Interpretations, Philadelphia, Philosophical Monographs.

Beanblossom, R.E.: 1975, 'In Defence of Thomas Reid's Use of "Suggestion"', Grazer Philosophische Studien, 1.

Beanblossom, R.E. and Lehrer, K. (eds.): 1983, Thomas Reid's Inquiry and Essays, Indianapolis, Hackett Publishing Co. Inc.

Beattie, A.: 1790, Elements of Moral Science, Edinburgh.

Ben-Zeev, A.: 1984, 'The Passivity Assumption in the Sensation-Perception Distinction', British Journal for the Philosophy of Science, 35.

: 1986a, 'Reid's Model of Direct Perception', Studies in History and Philosophy of Science, 17.

: 1986b, 'Making Mental Properties More Natural', The Monist, 69.

: 1988, 'Can Nonpure Perception be Direct?', The Philosophical Quarterly, forthcoming.

Ben-Zeev, A. and Strauss, M.: 1984, 'The Dualistic Approach to Perception', Man and World, 17.

Berkeley, G.: 1911, A. Campbell Fraser (ed.), Selections from Berkeley, Oxford, Clarendon Press.

Berlin, Sir I. and others: 1973, Essays on J.L. Austin, Oxford, Clarendon Press.

Berlin, J.: 1984, Writing Instruction in Nineteenth-Century American Colleges, Carbondale, Ill., Southern Illinois University Press.

Broad, C.D.: 1925, The Mind and its Place in Nature, London, Routledge and Kegan Paul.

        : 1952, Ethics and the History of Philosophy, London, Routledge and Kegan Paul.

Broadie, A.: 1983, Lokert, Late Scholastic Logician, Edinburgh, Edinburgh University Press.

        : 1987, 'Medieval Notions and the Theory of Ideas', Proceedings of the Aristotelian Society, 87.

Brody, B.A.: 1971, 'Reid and Hamilton on Perception', The Monist, 55.

Brown, T.: 1851, Lectures on the Philosophy of the Human Mind, Edinburgh.

Brown, T.M.: 1974, 'From Mechanism to Vitalism in 18th Century English Physiology', Journal of the History of Biology, 7.

Buckland, R.: 1974, 'Eyewitness Testimony', Scientific American, 231, 6.

Cantor, G.N.: 1971, 'Henry Brougham and the Scottish Methodological Tradition', Studies in History and Philosophy of Science, 2.

        : 1975, 'The Reception of the Wave Theory of Light in Britain: A Case Study Illustrating the Role of Methodology in Scientific Debate', Historical Studies in the Physical Sciences, 6.

Cantor, G.N. and Hodge, M.J.S. (eds.): 1981, Conceptions of Ether: Studies in the History of Ether Theories, 1740–1900, Cambridge, Cambridge University Press.

BIBLIOGRAPHY                                                    469

Chalmers, A. (ed.): 1810, The Works of the English Poets from Chaucer to Cowper, London.

Channell, D.: 1984, Scottish Men of Science – William John Macquorn Rankin, FRSE, FRS, Edinburgh, Scotland's Cultural Heritage.

Chappell, V.C. (ed.): 1962, The Philosophy of Mind, Englewood Cliffs, N.J., Prentice-Hall.

Chisholm, R.M.: 1957, Perceiving, Ithaca, New York, Cornell University Press.

Cicero, M.T.: 1913, W. Miller (transl.), De Officiis, Cambridge, Mass., Harvard University Press.

Clarke, S.: 1738, A Demonstration of the Being and Attributes of God, in Works, Vol. II, London.

Coady, C.A.J.: 1973, 'Testimony and Observation', American Philosophical Quarterly, 10, 2.

: 1975, 'Collingwood and Historical Testimony', Philosophy, 50.

: 1981, 'Mathematical Knowledge and Reliable Authority', Mind, XC.

Cousin, V.: 1857, Philosophie Ecossaise, Paris.

Cross, R.: 1967, Evidence, London, Butterworth.

Cummins, P.D.: 1974, 'Reid's Realism', Journal of the History of Philosophy, 12.

Dalgarno, M.T.: 1984, 'Reid's Natural Jurisprudence – The Language of Rights and Duties', in V. Hope (ed.), Philosophers of the Scottish Enlightenment, Edinburgh, Edinburgh University Press.

: 1985 'Reid and the Rights of Man', in C. Stewart-Robertson and D.H. Jory (eds.), Man and Nature IV, Edmonton, Alberta, Proceedings of the Canadian Society for 18th Century Studies.

Davie, G.E.: 1964, The Democratic Intellect, 2nd edn., Edinburgh, Edinburgh University Press.

Deely, J.: 1982, Introducing Semiotic, Bloomington, Indiana, Indiana University Press.

Descartes, R.: 1965, Adam and Tannery (eds.), Dioptrique, Paris, Vrin.

Diamond, P.J.: 1985, The Ideology of Improvement, unpublished Ph.D. dissertation, Johns Hopkins University.

Dodsley, R.: 1775, The Preceptor, London.

Donavan, A.: 1982, 'William Cullen and the Research Tradition of Eighteenth-Century Chemistry', in R.H. Campbell and A. Skinner (eds.), The Origins and Nature of the Scottish Enlightenment, Edinburgh, Edinburgh University Press.

Ducasse, C.J.: 1951, Nature, Mind and Death, La Salle, Ill., Open Court Publishing Co.

Duggan, T. (ed.): 1970, Reid's Inquiry into the Human Mind, Chicago and London, University of Chicago Press.

Duncan, E.H. (ed.): 1981, Thomas Reid's Lectures on Natural Theology, (1780), Washington, D.C.

Durkan, J.: 1950, 'The School of John Major: Bibliography', Innes Review, 2.

Dworkin, R.: 1977, Taking Rights Seriously, London, Duckworth.

Eggleston, R.: 1978, Evidence, Proof and Probability, London, Weidenfeld and Nicolson.

Engel-Tiercelin, C.: 1982, Intuition et Inference: la critique peircienne de la metaphysique, unpublished doctoral dissertation, University of Paris.

Evans, G.: 1982, The Varieties of Reference, Oxford, Clarendon Press.

Fabian, B.: 1973, 'An Early Theory of Genius: Alexander Gerard's Unpublished Aberdeen Lectures', in R.F. Bissenden (ed.), Studies in the Eighteenth Century, Vol. II, Toronto, University of Toronto Press.

Feibleman, J.K.: 1944, 'Reid and the Origins of Modern Realism', Journal of the History of Ideas, 5.

Fisch, M.: 1954, 'Alexander Bain and the Genealogy of Pragmatism', Journal of the History of Ideas, 15.

Flower, E.: 1980, 'Some Interesting Connections between the Common Sense Realists and the Pragmatists, Especially James', in P. Caws (ed.), Two Centuries of Philosophy in America, Oxford, Blackwell.

Fodor, J.A.: 1981, Philosophical Essays on the Foundations of Cognitive Science, Sussex, Harvester Press.

    : 1983, The Modularity of Mind, Cambridge, Cambridge University Press.

Forbes, J.D.: 1849, The Danger of Superficial Knowledge: An Introductory Lecture to the Course of Natural Philosophy in the University of Edinburgh, London.

Forbes, Sir W.: 1807, An Account of the Life of James Beattie LLD., Edinburgh.

Fruchtman, J.: 1983, 'The Apocalyptic Politics of Richard Price and Joseph Priestley', Philadelphia, Transactions of the American Philosophical Society, 73, 4.

Gazzaniga, M.: 1977, 'On Dividing the Self: Speculations from Brain Research', in Excerpta Medica International Congress Series, No.434: Neurology, Amsterdam–Oxford, Excerpta Medica.

Geach, P.: 1971, Mental Acts, London, Routledge and Kegan Paul.

Gerard, A.: 1755, Plan of Education in the Marischal College and University of Aberdeen, Aberdeen.

Gierke, O.: 1939, The Development of Political Theory, transl. B. Freyd, London, Allen and Unwin.

Goodpaster, K.E. (ed.): 1976, Perspectives on Morality: Essays of William K. Frankena, Notre Dame, University of Notre Dame Press.

Gough, J.W.: 1936, The Social Contract, Oxford, Clarendon
     Press.

Grant, A.: 1884, The Story of Edinburgh University, London.

Grave, S.A.: 1960, The Scottish Philosophy of Common Sense,
     Oxford, Clarendon Press.

Greenberg, A.R.: 1976, 'Sir William Hamilton and the
     Interpretation of Reid's Realism', Modern
     Schoolman, 65.

Gregory, J.: 1765, A Comparative View of the State and
     Faculties of Man with those of the Animal World,
     London.

Griffin-Collard, E.: 1976, 'Les croyances naturelles de Hume
     et les principes de sens commun de Reid', Revue
     Internationale de Philosophie, 30.

     : 1979, 'L'argumentation et le raisonnable dans une
     philosophie de sens commun', Revue Internationale
     de Philosophie, 33.

Hacking, I.: 1975, Why does Language Matter to Philosophy?,
     Cambridge, Cambridge University Press.

Haldane, E.S. and Ross, G.R.T. (eds.): 1967, Philosophical
     Works of Descartes, Vol.2, Cambridge, Cambridge
     University Press.

Haldane, J.J.: 1984, 'Concept Formation and Value Education',
     Educational Philosophy and Theory, 16.

     : 1987, 'Psychoanalysis, Cognitive Psychology and
     Self-Consciousness', in P.J. Clark and C.J.C.
     Wright (eds.), Mind, Psychoanalysis and Science,
     Oxford, Blackwell.

Hales, S.: 1969, Vegetable Staticks, London, Macdonald.

Harrington, J.: 1977, 'Valerius and Publicola', in J.G.A.
     Pocock (ed.), The Political Works of James
     Harrington, Cambridge, Cambridge University Press.

Henson, R.G.: 1979, 'What Kant Might Have Said: Moral Worth
     and the Overdetermination of Dutiful Action',

Philosophical Review, 88.

Herrnestein, R.J. and Boring E.G. (eds.): 1965, A Sourcebook
    in the History of Psychology, Cambridge, Mass.,
    Harvard University Press.

Hirschmann, A.O.: 1977, The Passions and the Interests,
    Princeton, Princeton University Press.

Hobbes, T.: 1968, C.B. Macpherson (ed.), Leviathan, London,
    Penguin Books.

Hont, I. and Ignatieff, M. (eds.): 1983, Wealth and Virtue:
    The Shaping of Political Economy in the Scottish
    Enlightenment, Cambridge, Cambridge University
    Press.

Horner, W.: 1982, 'Rhetoric in the Liberal Arts: Nineteenth
    Century Scottish Universities', in J.J. Murphy
    (ed.), The Rhetorical Tradition and Modern
    Writing, New York, The Modern Languages Association
    of America.

Howell, W.S.: 1971, Eighteenth-Century British Logic and
    Rhetoric, Princeton, Princeton University Press.

Hume, D.: 1957, Charles W. Hendel (ed.): An Enquiry
    concerning the Principles of Morals, Indianapolis
    and New York, Bobbs-Merrill.

    : 1963, Essays Moral, Political and Literary,
    Oxford, Oxford University Press (World's Classics
    Series).

    : 1975, L.A. Selby-Bigge (ed.), Enquiries
    Concerning Human Understanding and Concerning the
    Principles of Morals, 3rd edn., revised with notes
    by P.H. Nidditch, Oxford, Clarendon Press.

    : 1978, L.A. Selby-Bigge (ed.), A Treatise of Human
    Nature, 2nd edn., with text revised by P.H.
    Nidditch, Oxford, Clarendon Press.

Humphries, W.R. (ed.): 1937, The Philosophical Orations of
    Thomas Reid: Delivered at Graduation Ceremonies in
    King's College, Aberdeen, 1753, 1756, 1759, 1762,
    Aberdeen, Aberdeen University Press.

Hurvich, L.M.: 1981, Color Vision, Sunderland, Mass., Sinauer
     Associates.

Hutcheson, F.: 1755, A System of Moral Philosophy, London.

          : 1973, P. Kivy (ed.), An Inquiry concerning
     Beauty, Order, Harmony, Design, The Hague, Martinus
     Nijhoff.

Immerwahr, J.: 1978, 'The Development of Reid's Realism', The
     Monist, 62.

Jackson, F.: 1977, Perception: A Representative Theory,
     Cambridge, Cambridge University Press.

Jardine, G.: 1825, Outlines of Philosophical Education,
     illustrated by the Method of Teaching the Logic
     Class in the University of Glasgow, 2nd edn.,
     Glasgow.

Jensen, H.: 1971, Motivation and the Moral Sense in Frances
     Hutcheson's Ethical Theory, The Hague, Martinus
     Nijhoff.

Kalich, M.: 1970, The Association of Ideas and Critical
     Theory in 18th Century England: A History of a
     Psychological Method in English Criticism, The
     Hague, Martinus Nijhoff.

Kames, Lord: 1774, Sketches of the History of Man (two
     volumes), Edinburgh and London.

          : 1779, Essays on the Principles of Morality and
     Natural Religion, 3rd edn., Edinburgh.

Kant, I.: 1929, Critique of Pure Reason, transl. N.
     Kemp-Smith, London, Macmillan.

Kemp-Smith, N.: 1902, Studies in the Cartesian Philosophy,
     London, Macmillan.

Kivy, P.: 1976, The Seventh Sense: A Study of Francis
     Hutcheson's Aesthetics and its Influence in 18th
     Century Britain, New York, Burt Franklin.

          : 1984, 'Hume's Neighbour's Wife: An Essay on the
     Evolution of Hume's Aesthetics', British Journal of

Aesthetics, XXIV.

Laudan, L.L.: 1970, 'Thomas Reid and the Newtonian Turn of British Methodological Thought', in Butts, R.E. and Davis, W. (eds.), The Methodological Heritage of Newton, Oxford, Blackwell.

Laudan, L.L.: 1981, 'The Medium and its Message', in Cantor, G.N. and Hodge, M.J.S. (eds.), Conceptions of Ether: Studies in the History of Ether Theories 1740–1900, Cambridge University Press.

Lehrer, K.: 1974, Knowledge, Oxford, Oxford University Press.

: 1983, see Beanblossom, R.E. and Lehrer, K., 1983.

Lehrer, K. and Smith: forthcoming, 'Reid on Testimony and Perception', Canadian Journal of Philosophy.

Lincoln, A.: 1971, Some Political and Social Ideas of English Dissent, 1763–1800, New York, Octagon.

Locke, J.: 1975, P.H. Nidditch (ed.), An Essay Concerning Human Understanding, Oxford, Clarendon Press.

Luce and Jessop (eds.): 1949, The Works of George Berkeley, London, Nelson.

McCosh, J.: 1875, The Scottish Philosophy from Hutcheson to Hamilton, New York.

McRae, R.: 1965, '"Idea" as a Philosophical Term in the Seventeenth Century', Journal of the History of Ideas, 26.

Madden, E.: 1982, 'Common Sense and Agency', Review of Metaphysics, 36.

: 1983, 'The Metaphilosophy of Commonsense', American Philosophical Quarterly, 20.

Mansel and Veitch (eds.): 1877, Lectures in Metaphysics and Logic, Edinburgh and London.

Marcil-Lacoste, L.: 1982, Claude Buffier and Thomas Reid, Kingston and Montreal, McGill-Queen's University Press.

Matthew, W.M.: 1966, 'The Origins and Occupations of Glasgow Students, 1740-1839', Past and Present, 33.

Melzack, R.: 1973, The Puzzle of Pain, New York, Basic Books.

Melzack, R. and Wall, P.D.: 1983, The Challenge of Pain, New York, Basic Books.

Michael, E.: 1984, 'Frances Hutcheson on Aesthetic Perception and Aesthetic Pleasure', British Journal of Aesthetics, XXIV.

Miller, D.: 1976, Social Justice, Oxford, Oxford University Press.

Moore, G.E.: 1922, Philosophical Studies, London, Routledge and Kegan Paul.

       : 1959, Philosophical Papers, London, Allen and Unwin.

Mundle, C.W.K.: 1971, Perception: Facts and Theories, Oxford, Oxford University Press.

Mure, Baron: 1894, 'Correspondence of Baron Mure', in Selections from the Family Papers preserved at Caldwell, Vol.2, Glasgow.

Nagel, T.: 1965, 'Physicalism', Philosophical Review, 74.

Newton, Sir I.: 1968, The Mathematical Principles of Natural Philosophy, transl. Andrew Motte, (two volumes), Berkeley, University of California Press.

Oatley, K.: 1978, Perceptions and Representations, London, Methuen.

Olson, R.: 1975, Scottish Philosophy and British Physics, 1750-1880, Princeton, Princeton University Press.

Pastore, N.: 1971, Selective History of Theories of Visual Perception, 1650-1950, New York, Oxford University Press.

Pearl, L.: 1971, 'Objective and Subjective Duty', Mind, LXXX.

Peirce, C.S.: 1931-58, Hartshorne and Weiss (eds.), Collected

Papers of C.S. Peirce, Vols. I-VI; Burks (ed.), Vols. VII-VIII, Cambridge, Mass., Harvard University Press.

Perkins, M.: 1983, Sensing the World, Indianapolis, Hackett Publishing Co.

Phillipson, N.: 1979, 'Hume as Moralist: A Social Historian's Perspective', in S.C. Brown (ed.), Philosophers of the Enlightenment, Sussex, Harvester Press.

Pitcher, G.: 1969, 'Minds and Ideas in Berkeley', American Philosophical Quarterly, 6.

    : 1971, A Theory of Perception, Princeton, Princeton University Press.

Pocock, J.G.A.: 1983, 'Cambridge Paradigms and Scotch Philosophers: a study of the relations between the civic humanist and civil jurisprudential interpretations of eighteenth-century social thought', in I. Hont and M. Ignatieff (eds.) (1983).

Price, H.H.: 1950, Perception, London, Methuen.

Prichard, H.A.: 1949, Moral Obligation, Oxford, Clarendon Press.

Prior, A.: 1971, Objects of Thought, Oxford, Clarendon Press.

Pufendorf, S.: 1934, De Jure Naturae et Gentium, transl. C.H. and W.A. Oldfather, Oxford, Clarendon Press.

Rankine, W.J.M.: 1856, Introductory Lecture on the Harmony of Theory and Practice in Mechanics, London.

    : 1859, Manual of the Steam Engine and other Prime Movers, London.

    : 1864, 'On the Use of Mechanical Hypotheses in Science, Especially in the Theory of Heat', Proceedings of the Royal Society of Glasgow, 5.

    : 1881, W.J. Millar (ed.), Miscellaneous Scientific Papers, London.

Reid, T.:   1941, A.D.  Woozley (ed.), Essays on the
            Intellectual Powers of Man, London, Macmillan.

        : 1977, D.D. Dodd (ed.), Philosophical Orations,
            transl. S.M.L. Darcus, in Philosophical Research
            Archives, 3.

        : n.d. Of Constitution, Aberdeen University Library
            MS. 3061/8.

Reingold, N. and Mollela, A. (eds.): 1976, 'The Interaction
            of Science and Technology in the Industrial Age',
            Technology and Culture, 17 (Special Issue).

Richards, I.A.: 1936, The Philosophy of Rhetoric, New York,
            Oxford University Press.

Robertson, J.: 1983, 'The Scottish Enlightenment at the
            Limits of the Civic Tradition', in I. Hont and M.
            Ignatieff (eds.) (1983).

Rollin, B.E.: 1978, 'Thomas Reid and the Semiotics of
            Perception', The Monist, 61.

Rousseau, J.-J.: 1973, Hall and Brumfitt (eds.), The Social
            Contract and other Discourses, transl. G.H. Cole,
            London, Dent.

Rudolf, F.: 1962, The American College and University: A
            History, New York, Vintage Books.

Russell, B.: 1921, The Analysis of Mind, London, Allen and
            Unwin.

        : 1927, The Analysis of Matter, London, Paul,
            Trench and Trubner.

Rutt, J.T. (ed.): 1816–32, The Theological and Miscellaneous
            Works &c of Joseph Priestley, (26 volumes), London.

Ryle, G.: 1949, The Concept of Mind, London, Hutchinson.

        : 1971, Collected Papers, London, Hutchinson.

Schiffer, S.: 1981, 'Indexicals and the Theory of Reference',
            Synthese, 49.

Schofield, R.E.: 1970, Mechanism and Materialism: British Natural Philosophy in an Age of Reason, Princeton, Princeton University Press.

Schulthess, D.: 1983, Philosophie et sens commun chez Thomas Reid, Berne, P. Lang.

Scott, W.R.: 1900, Frances Hutcheson: His Life, Teaching and Position in the History of Philosophy, Cambridge, Cambridge University Press.

Sibley, F.N. (ed.): 1971, Perception, London, Methuen.

Sidgwick, H.: 1872, The Methods of Ethics, London.

Smith, A.: 1963, J. Lothian (ed.), Lectures on Rhetoric and Belles Lettres, London, Nelson.

: 1976, D.D. Raphael and A.L. Macfie (eds.), The Theory of Moral Sentiments, Oxford, Clarendon Press.

: 1978, R.L. Meek, D.D. Raphael and P.G. Stein (eds.), Lectures on Jurisprudence, Oxford, Clarendon Press.

Sternbach, R.: 1968, Pain: A Psychophysiological Analysis, New York and London, Academic Press.

Stewart, D.: 1793, Outlines of Moral Philosophy: For the Use of Students in the University of Edinburgh, Edinburgh.

: 1816, Elements of the Philosophy of the Human Mind, Boston.

: 1829, Works, Cambridge.

Stewart-Robertson, J.C.: 1976, 'A Bacon-Facing Generation: Scottish Philosophy in the Early Nineteenth Century', Journal of the History of Philosophy, 14.

: 1987, 'The Pneumatics and Georgics of the Scottish Mind', Eighteenth-Century Studies, 20.

Strawson, P.F.: 1966, The Bounds of Sense, London, Methuen.

Stroud, B.: 1968, 'Transcendental Arguments', Journal of
       Philosophy, LXV.

Swartz, R.J. (ed.): 1965, Perceiving, Sensing and Knowing,
       New York, Doubleday.

Tait, P.J.: 1881, 'Biographical Memoir', in W.J. Millar
       (ed.), Miscellaneous Scientific Papers of W.J.M.
       Rankine, Glasgow.

Torrance, J.B.: 1981, 'The Covenant Concept in Scottish
       Theology and Politics and its Legacy', Scottish
       Journal of Theology, 34.

Turbayne, C.M.: 1959, 'Berkeley's Two Concepts of Mind',
       Philosophy and Phenomenological Research, XX.

Turnbull, G.: 1726, De Scientiae Naturalis cum Philosophia
       Morali Conjunctione, Aberdeen.

         : 1740/1976, Principles of Moral Philosophy,
       London.

         : 1742, Observations upon Liberal Education in all
       its Branches, London.

Welsh, D.: 1825, Account of the Life and Writings of Thomas
       Brown, M.D., Edinburgh.

Whewell, W.: 1840, The Philosophy of the Inductive Sciences,
       London.

Wigmore, J.H.: 1940, A Treatise on the Anglo-American System
       of Evidence in Trials at Common Law, Boston.

Willey, B.: 1961, The Eighteenth-Century Background: Studies
       on the Idea of Nature in the Thought of the Period,
       London, Chatto and Windas.

Winch, P.: 1953, 'The Notion of "Suggestion" in Thomas Reid's
       Theory of Perception', Philosophical Quarterly, 3.

Wittgenstein, L.: 1976, Philosophical Investigations, Oxford,
       Blackwell.

Wood, P.: 1987, 'Buffon's Reception in Scotland: the Aberdeen
       Connection', Annals of Science, 44.

Wood, P.B.: 1985, 'Thomas Reid's Critique of Joseph Priestley: Context and Chronology', in Man and Nature, 4, Edmonton, Alberta, Proceedings of the Canadian Society for Eighteenth-Century Studies.

Yolton, J.: 1984, Thinking Matter, Oxford, Oxford University Press.

# INDEX OF NAMES

Addison, J. 344
Alembert, J. d' 391
Aquinas, T. 286, 287, 289, 290, 295, 296, 297, 299, 300, 301
Aristotle 225, 233, 295, 302
Armstrong, D. 38, 41, 46
Arnauld, A. 49, 289, 290
Arthur, A. 401
Augustine 225, 243
Austin, J. L. 41, 226, 292

Bacon, F. 199, 345, 373, 391, 394, 398, 399, 400, 409, 418, 437, 444, 449, 460
Bain, A. 218, 219
Balguy, J. 313
Baumgarten, A. 307
Beanblossom, R. 188
Beattie, J. 397, 399, 400, 403, 410, 413, 421, 425, 426
Bennett, J. 23
Berkeley, G. 11, 14, 15, 18, 20, 23, 27, 30, 55, 76, 122, 126, 130, 131, 145, 150, 184, 218, 225, 233, 234, 249–265, 269, 272, 302, 307, 313
Berlin, J. 457
Blackburne, F. 425
Blair, H. 459
Bradley, F. H. 145, 378, 383
Briggs, W. 438
Broad, C. D. 375
Broadie, A. 304
Brown, T. 18, 25, 395, 396, 399, 401, 405
Buffier, C. 190, 266, 290
Buffon, G. 436, 441, 444
Burke, E. 426

Campbell, G. 397, 411, 413, 414, 415, 416, 419, 458, 461
Campbell, J. 411

Cantor, G. 433
Carmichael, G. 369, 379
Chalmers, A. 421
Chisholm, R. 41
Cicero 345, 346, 395
Clarke, S. 280, 281
Cleghorn, W. 391, 392, 393, 396
Clow, J. 401
Combe, A. 396
Combe, G. 396
Condillac, E. 104
Cousin, V. 187
Craigie, J. 391
Cross, R. 230, 244
Cummins, P. 84, 88

Dalgarno, M. 367
Davidson, W. L. 419
Davie, G. E. 459, 461, 462
Descartes, R. 9, 11, 13, 18, 19, 21, 27, 28, 30, 49, 54, 65, 103, 122, 161, 181, 197, 240, 249, 260, 307, 401, 438
Diderot, D. 26
Dodsley, R. 394, 407
Dretske, F. 41
Drummond, C. 393, 396
Duggan, T. 58, 84, 88, 233
Dunbar, J. 413
Duncan, W. 394, 396, 399, 403

Engel-Tiercelin, C. 223
Erskine, W. 408
Evans, G. 244

Fabian, B. 418
Farquhar, J. 413, 419
Feibleman, H. 218
Ferguson, A. 372, 373, 375, 406, 407
Fermat, P.-S. de 434
Ferrier, J. 396

Fisch, M. 218
Fodor, J. 140, 286, 287, 292, 299
Forbes, J. 448, 449
Fordyce, D. 347, 394, 396, 403
Frankena, W. 332
Franklin, B. 438

Garden, D. 394
Gassendi, P. 288
Gazzaniga, M. 73
Geach, P. 303
Gerard, A. 397, 399, 403, 410, 413, 415, 417, 418
Goldman, A. 41
Gordon, T. 409, 413, 414, 417, 419
Grave, S. 188, 218
Gregory, James 11, 16
Gregory, John 413, 414, 417, 418
Griffin-Collard, E. 218, 223
Gunderson, K. 69

Hacking, I. 9, 32
Hale, S. 439
Hall, R. 397
Hamilton, W. 188, 189, 205, 218, 271, 401, 405
Harrington, J. 347, 348, 349, 354
Hartley, D. 26, 424, 433, 437, 438, 441, 442, 445
Heineccius, J. 395
Helvetius, C.-A. 26
Henson, R. 336, 337
Hobbes, T. 20, 26, 28, 30, 378
Hohfeld, W. 367
Holcomb, K. 409
Howell, W. 459
Hume, D. 9, 11, 12, 15, 16, 18, 20, 22, 23, 24, 27, 29, 30, 31, 55, 65, 66, 76, 122, 126, 129, 130, 131, 145, 150, 152, 159, 160–166, 170, 177, 181, 213, 225, 236, 237, 249, 254–257, 260–261, 270, 288, 307, 308, 310, 314, 315, 316, 320, 329–339, 341–350, 355–365, 369–383, 419, 422

Hutcheson, F. 307–316, 320–324, 329, 348, 370, 390, 392, 394, 401

Immerwahr, J. 79

Jack, R. 411
James, W. 212
Jardine, G. 394, 395, 396, 398, 401, 408, 458, 459, 460, 461, 462, 463
Jebb, J. 425
Jeffrey, F. 396
Johnson, E. 76
Johnson, S. 354, 426

Kames (Henry Home) 12, 250, 252, 267, 273, 277, 439
Kant, I. 9, 10, 15, 26, 31, 32, 159, 160–167, 173–186, 218, 249, 252, 336
Kenyon, J. 187
Kepler, J. 27
Kohlberg, L. 462

La Mettrie, J. 26
Laudan, L. 12, 433, 434, 438
Lavoisier, A. 439
Law, W. 390, 391, 393, 405
Lehrer, K. 145, 148, 188, 193, 195, 200, 202, 233, 244, 245
Leibniz, G. 307, 434
Leslie, A. 409
Lindsey, T. 425
Locke, J. 9, 11, 15, 16, 18, 20, 21, 23, 27, 29, 30, 52, 54, 66, 76, 91, 122, 160, 163, 213, 225, 234, 249, 257, 260, 266, 276, 287, 345, 399, 400, 410, 427, 459
Longinus 458

Machiavelli, N. 347, 348, 349
Madden, E. 145, 275
Major, J. 291, 292, 298
Malebranche. N. 11
Mansfield, Lord 426
McNeill, J. 448

Melzack, R. 72
Michael, E. 311, 312
Mill, J. S. 9
Molesworth, Viscount 347
Montesquieu, C. 347, 348
Moore, G. E. 41, 145, 146–152, 155, 172,
    264, 266
Mylne, J. 408

Napier, M. 399
Newton, I. 12, 13, 29, 276, 342, 373, 433,
    434, 435, 436, 438, 439, 440, 441,
    442, 445, 447
North, Lord 426
Norton, D. 189

Oakley, T. 202
Ogilvie, W. 413
Olson, R. 433
Oswald, J. 421, 425

Pappas, G. 45
Pearl, L. 334
Pearson, K. 212
Peirce, C. 205, 206, 207, 209, 211, 212,
    213, 214, 215, 216, 217, 219, 220,
    221, 222
Pemberton, H. 434, 443
Perkins, M. 45
Perry, W. 462
Phillipson, N. 344
Piaget, J. 462
Pitcher, G. 38, 46
Plato 225, 288, 302, 307
Pocock, J. 347, 350
Price, H. 41
Price, R. 282, 425
Prichard, H. 330, 338
Priestley, J. 18, 20, 26, 282, 421,
    422–428, 441, 442
Pringle, J. 392
Pufendorf, S. 369, 395

Quine, W. 237

Rait, A. 404
Ramus, P. 458
Rankine, W. 448, 449, 450, 451, 452, 453
Reid, T., *passim*
Richards, I. A. 457
Ross, J. 413, 419
Rousseau, J.-J. 199, 369, 372, 374, 379,
    419
Russell, B. 28, 66, 95, 148, 150
Ryle, G. 23, 292

Schiffer, S. 286, 287
Seymour, W. 399
Sibley, F. 309
Sidgwick, H. 338
Sinclair, A. 101
Skene, D. 397, 398, 413, 414, 415, 416
Skene, G. 413, 414
Skene, J. 405
Smart, J. 69
Smith, Adam 359, 362, 366, 372, 389,
    401, 403, 458, 459
Smith, J-C. 193, 195, 200, 202, 233, 244,
    245
Spalding, W. 462
Sternbach, R. 72
Stevenson, J. 405
Stewart, D. 49, 188, 189, 190, 395, 397,
    408, 413, 448, 450, 451, 452, 453, 458
Stewart, J. 11, 25, 413
Strawson, P., 176, 226
Stroud, B. 190

Torrance, J. 384
Trail, R. 413, 419
Trail, W. 413
Turbayne, C. 130
Turnbull, G. 342, 347, 390, 391, 395,
    398, 405, 409, 434, 442

Vattel, E. 392
Vries, G. de 390, 405

Wall, P. 72

Watts, I. 401, 447
Whately, R. 457
Whewell, W. 202
Whytt, R. 435, 436
Wittgenstein, L. 149, 226, 292, 294
Wolffius, C. 9, 26

Wood, P. 430, 431
Woozley, A. 20, 88, 188
Wyvill, C. 425

Yolton, J. 276

Aberdeen Philosophical Society 372, 376, 398, 408, 409, 413–416, 419
abstraction 98, 123, 131, 132, 135, 139, 296, 301, 303, 313
action 18, 19, 140–142, 152, 154, 206, 207, 209–211, 216, 235, 256, 275, 277, 281, 293, 330–333, 335–338, 379, 428
aesthetics 307, 308, 310–313, 316, 320, 323, 459
agency 142, 275–282, 332–334, 338, 356, 379
analytic truth 169
analytical philosophy 11
argument from analogy 130, 251, 255, 256
art 231, 296, 307, 308, 311, 314–317, 323, 327, 344, 346, 348–350, 354, 404, 407, 418

beauty 262, 263, 309–316, 319–325, 344
behaviourism 75, 292
belief 11, 15, 22, 23, 25, 31, 35–47, 51–58, 59, 61, 66–70, 73, 75, 76, 80, 98, 113, 114, 121, 126, 129–131, 139, 140, 142, 143, 145–147, 153, 160–163, 166, 171, 172, 175, 176, 178–181, 185, 193, 194, 196–198, 201, 205–211, 213, 214, 216–220, 222, 225, 230, 233, 236–238, 243, 259, 262, 293, 309, 310, 315, 318–320, 323–325, 333, 334, 422, 423, 427, 428

Cartesian doubt 13, 214
Cartesian dualism 20, 61, 110, 123, 140, 260, 264, 265, 392
causal relationships 15, 70, 82, 84, 85, 86, 92, 110–112, 114, 123, 124, 161–163, 165, 254, 275, 277–282,

433, 435, 438, 439
causal theory of perception 91–99
certainty 11, 146–154, 161, 164, 172, 190, 193, 238, 422
coherentism 193–195, 198–201
common sense 11, 12, 15–19, 22, 31, 55, 105, 109, 110, 112, 115, 127, 128, 131, 143, 145–152, 154, 155, 159, 160, 167–173, 176, 177, 179–182, 186, 188–190, 192, 194, 198, 205, 213, 237, 238, 245, 266, 273, 275, 276, 279, 280, 333, 336–338, 356, 359, 364, 365, 373, 403, 410, 417, 421–424, 426–430, 433, 436, 440, 448–451, 453, 457, 458
conception 14, 18, 22–24, 35–39, 42–46, 70, 76, 80, 82, 85–87, 107, 110, 113, 114, 121–143, 206, 210, 211, 262, 276, 281, 291, 292, 296, 298, 300, 318, 319, 462
conscience 345, 374
consciousness 11, 30, 35, 36, 39, 43–45, 53, 54, 58, 61, 65, 73, 77, 103, 105, 112, 115, 129, 136, 142, 146, 148, 149, 154, 171, 178, 201, 205–207, 210, 212, 215, 219, 250, 255, 260, 261, 278, 285, 289, 290, 300, 335, 397, 425
consistency 149, 177, 194, 199, 235
contractarianism 369, 370, 375, 380–383
corpuscularian philosophy 28
correspondence theory of truth 195, 200

demonstration 154, 170
desire 293, 338, 360, 361, 367
duty 143, 330, 331, 335–338, 341, 351, 355, 356, 357, 363, 365, 367, 369, 373, 374, 376–381, 383, 391, 405

Edinburgh Select Society 419

education 344, 346, 370, 375, 395,
    458–463
egoism 15
empiricism 65, 76, 87, 182, 186, 215,
    237, 249, 437, 442
Enlightenment 308, 433
epistemology 27, 28, 30, 31, 32, 37, 40,
    41, 45, 121, 122, 125, 129, 142, 150,
    151, 159–161, 163, 165, 166, 168,
    172, 174, 179–181, 185, 200, 201,
    223, 225, 234, 236, 239, 241, 285,
    287, 288, 289, 290, 292, 295, 297,
    299–301, 390, 421, 423, 424, 426,
    429, 440, 442
evidence 27, 28, 43, 45, 104, 105, 110,
    112, 121, 122, 129, 130, 142,
    152–155, 170, 171, 177, 237, 238,
    245, 254, 275, 278, 410
external world 11, 14, 22, 25, 35, 36, 37,
    39, 42, 52, 56, 61, 76, 79, 80, 83, 86,
    87, 91–99, 108, 110, 111, 113–115,
    121, 126, 129, 138, 146, 150, 151,
    162, 163, 165, 170, 177, 178, 189,
    212, 213, 250, 252, 254, 257, 261,
    271, 275, 276, 278, 288, 294, 316-319,
    423, 435, 437

fallibilism 152, 193, 216, 223
first principles 12, 13, 104, 105, 121,
    122, 130, 134, 146–152, 154,
    164–168, 170, 171, 175, 177–183,
    186, 191–196, 198–200, 215,
    237–239, 245, 246, 250, 253, 254,
    256, 278, 342, 349, 351, 404, 422,
    450, 461
foundationalism 32, 152, 159, 161,
    163–166, 172, 185, 193, 200
functionalism 293

generalization 131–135, 137–139, 151
Glasgow Literary Society 376, 419, 441
God 15, 94, 111, 112, 132, 168, 169, 179,
    181, 194, 198, 246, 249, 253–256,
    264, 275, 278, 280, 281, 361, 362,

367, 391, 402, 418, 421, 423–425,
    427, 429, 436, 437, 439, 449

hypotheses 433, 434, 436–438, 441–443,
    445, 450–453

idealism 145, 147–149, 155, 159, 160,
    173, 176, 181–186, 214, 294
induction 12, 32, 124, 128–130, 162, 163,
    170, 177, 198, 200, 201, 234, 235,
    240, 245, 254, 258–260, 270, 278,
    298, 348, 350, 418, 433, 435, 438,
    444, 449, 451–453, 459
innate principles 121–124, 127–129, 134,
    143, 179, 206, 232, 233, 236, 298,
    318, 319, 350
intentionality 292, 294, 295, 297–301
intentions 302, 333, 334, 356
intuitionism 335, 424

judgment 14, 23, 24, 37, 42, 51, 68,
    141–143, 152–154, 166, 168, 171,
    189, 195, 196, 208, 211, 213, 215,
    219, 220, 226–229, 231, 232, 241,
    243, 258, 263, 266, 296, 297, 300,
    302, 317, 319, 320, 324, 329–335,
    345, 356–358, 422–424, 427, 428
jurisprudence 346, 357, 359, 370, 381,
    382
justice 143, 208, 329, 332, 336, 355–359,
    361–365, 371, 373, 380

knowledge 10–13, 19, 24, 28, 29, 36, 40,
    57, 65, 97, 104, 105, 107, 111, 125,
    129–135, 143, 146, 147, 159–164,
    166–168, 171–177, 179–183, 185,
    193, 197, 200, 201, 206, 213, 215,
    222, 234–238, 243, 249, 251,
    253–256, 260, 261, 263, 264, 285,
    309, 310, 315, 323–325, 335, 341,
    342, 345, 346, 373, 375, 393, 394,
    398–400, 422, 424, 427, 428, 437,
    447–450, 452, 457–460, 463

law 133, 167, 225, 228–231, 244, 348, 349, 363–365, 403, 407, 423, 426
laws of nature 28, 39, 111, 125, 193, 198, 246, 277–279, 395, 439, 440, 447–449
logic 10, 41, 86, 123, 152, 153, 173, 175, 178–180, 185, 194, 197, 206, 215, 219, 223, 258, 260, 262, 281, 288, 294, 352, 392–396, 399–402, 404, 407, 408, 410, 411, 457–459

materialism 13, 20, 26–28, 123, 124, 421, 424, 435, 440–442
mathematics 29, 137–139, 167, 169, 194, 241, 399, 410, 462
mechanical philosophy 13, 27
memory 16–18, 20, 24, 31, 46, 50, 68, 70, 94, 98, 153, 154, 165, 171, 178, 195, 196, 205, 207, 218, 228, 234, 236, 241, 389, 399, 414, 435
mental acts 24, 36, 38, 39, 50–53, 81, 92, 98, 113, 115, 291, 299, 300, 344
metaphysics 16, 61, 103, 111, 112, 115, 135, 160, 165, 166, 173, 178, 180, 181, 184, 196, 198, 207, 214, 218, 223, 275, 276, 278, 390, 392, 393, 396, 398, 407, 440, 445
mind 10–20, 25, 28, 30, 32, 36, 49–61, 76, 81, 94, 91–99, 103, 104, 106–109, 111, 121–124, 128–131, 135–137, 139, 140, 143, 166, 168, 175, 187, 188, 199, 201, 205, 206, 208–210, 212, 223, 225, 227, 228, 232, 233, 235, 238, 250–254, 257, 259–261, 263, 271, 285, 286, 288–294, 296, 299, 300, 322, 341–343, 345, 349, 351, 357, 389–394, 396–402, 407–409, 416, 417, 419, 422–425, 428, 429, 434–437, 440, 447, 450, 459, 461
mind-body relationship 114
morality 71, 72, 98, 123, 139–142, 169, 186, 208, 313, 329, 330, 332–338, 341, 342, 344–351, 353, 357, 364, 378, 383, 392–395, 399–402, 407,

410, 415, 416, 421, 423, 449, 460
moral sense theory 329
motivation 329–332, 335–338, 355, 373, 460

natural kinds 29, 69, 70, 73
necessitarianism 441

ontology 19, 20, 390, 396, 407
other minds 15, 23, 129–131, 145, 146, 151, 178, 200, 249–251, 253–257, 259, 261, 263, 264, 266, 428

passions 29, 94, 98, 153, 194, 261–264, 317, 319, 321, 325, 343–347, 374, 401, 424
perception 12, 13, 17, 18, 21, 23, 24, 26, 28, 29, 35–47, 49–61, 66–69, 73, 77, 79–87, 91–98, 104, 108, 111, 112, 121, 123, 137, 150, 151, 153, 177, 178, 195, 196, 201, 205, 211–213, 218, 225, 228, 232–236, 239–242, 244–246, 253, 256–259, 262–264, 266, 273, 287, 289, 290, 308–312, 314–323, 325, 327, 398, 411, 416, 417, 421–423, 424, 428, 435, 437, 438, 440, 442
personal identity 146, 165, 178, 397
persons 23, 86, 89
phenomenology 32, 83, 84, 112, 215
philosophy of language 9, 226
philosophy of nature 12, 167, 260, 277, 401, 406, 410, 417, 434, 443, 448, 449
pneumatology 342–346, 349–351, 353, 389–407, 415, 434, 442
politics 342, 344–351, 353, 369, 371, 374, 382, 389, 395, 404, 421, 423–425, 428, 429
political obligation 369, 371, 374–383
pragmatism 11, 205, 211, 212, 213, 218
prima facie credibility theory 41
primary qualities 21, 28, 60, 63, 107, 108, 122–129, 131, 132, 134, 136–139, 142, 233, 436

psychology 26, 32, 36, 41, 42, 121, 122, 160, 161, 166, 168, 172, 173, 176–181, 205, 214, 218, 219, 228, 236–239, 257–260, 285, 287, 292, 293, 297, 300, 301, 361 396, 458

rationalism 249, 345
realism 40, 44, 45, 79, 81, 84, 88, 205, 213, 217, 221, 233, 285, 287–290, 292, 298–301, 304, 457
reason 10, 12, 13, 15, 16, 28, 31, 121, 128, 129, 141, 153, 154, 163, 170, 172, 181, 182, 184, 188–190, 192, 194, 198, 206, 210, 213, 214, 236–238, 240, 245, 270, 344, 345, 374, 394, 399, 403, 409, 421–423, 426, 437, 461, 462
reasoning 12–15, 35, 37, 40, 41, 73, 79, 82, 94, 96, 98, 109, 113, 121, 122, 125, 126, 129, 130, 137, 139, 140, 148–150, 153, 161–164, 167, 168, 170, 171, 177–181, 192, 198, 215, 220, 230, 231, 233, 235–238, 240, 250, 251, 254–256, 258–262, 268, 270, 278, 293, 298, 308, 314, 315, 318, 329, 345, 348, 350, 395, 400, 457, 459, 461
relativism 15
reliabilism 41, 193
representative theory of perception 15, 38, 65–75, 110, 150, 183, 285–290, 292, 294, 299, 300, 405
rights 355, 356, 358–365, 367, 369, 378, 391 405, 425

scepticism 10, 11, 14–16, 22, 31, 55, 121, 122, 131, 143, 145, 147–149, 151, 154, 155, 159, 160, 162–164, 168, 170–177, 181–183, 185, 186, 190, 214, 237, 249, 250, 252, 260, 261, 268, 285, 287, 290, 342, 370, 371, 422
scholasticism 287, 288, 290–292, 295, 296, 298–301, 411, 458
science 10–12, 14, 25, 30, 106, 124, 127, 128, 201, 202, 217, 222, 223, 227, 229, 230, 232, 239, 241, 250, 275, 277, 278, 286, 302, 342–344, 346, 348–354, 373, 389–393, 395, 396, 399–401, 404, 410, 418, 433, 435, 436, 438, 442, 447–453
secondary qualities 14, 21, 28, 60, 63, 107, 108, 124, 126–128, 136, 138, 310, 320
self 23, 31, 145, 212, 251, 266
sensation(s) 19–21, 23, 26, 30, 31, 36, 38, 40, 43–47, 49–63, 65–77, 79–87, 92, 94, 95–98, 104–106, 108, 109, 111, 114, 115, 121–124, 127, 128, 131, 134, 138–140, 142, 189, 206, 213, 222, 232, 233, 250, 252, 253, 259, 262, 264, 293, 298, 310, 312, 313, 317–321, 323, 325, 356, 423, 424, 427, 428, 437, 438
signs 19, 21, 27, 28, 39, 44, 51, 52, 56, 82, 108, 114, 125, 126, 128–131, 140, 207, 212, 213, 215, 223, 232–234, 239, 254, 259, 263, 272, 291, 294, 295, 297, 298, 301, 317–319, 376, 399, 410
solipsism 15
speech-act theory 226
speech acts 226, 227, 295

taste 14, 98, 263, 304, 308, 313–317, 319, 320, 328, 396, 416
technology 447–453, 457
testimony 153, 154, 165, 193, 195, 199, 214, 225, 227–230, 232, 234–246, 252, 264, 273
theory of ideas 9, 10, 14–16, 18–20, 22–26, 29–31, 35, 36, 38, 56, 49–61, 91–99, 103–105, 109, 110, 122, 131, 138, 139, 152, 155, 216, 233, 249, 260, 271, 286–288, 292, 341, 342, 352, 417, 434–438, 441, 442, 444
theory of knowledge – see epistemology
theory of signs 21, 125
transcendental arguments 22, 31, 159,

173, 175, 176, 180–183
truth 27, 29, 37, 103, 112, 133, 151, 152,
    154, 160, 166, 172, 174, 177, 180,
    194, 202, 216, 217, 223, 227, 228,
    235, 254, 285, 345, 393, 400, 401,
    410, 426, 434, 457

universals 24, 43, 134, 138, 223
utilitarianism 355

virtue 329–333, 336–338, 341–349, 351,
    355, 358, 359, 363, 375

will 124, 199, 208, 210, 220, 225, 233,
    239, 275–281, 345, 356, 380, 397,
    409, 450